Additional Praise for *The Skilled Facilitator*

"Practical, credible, insightful, and relevant, the newest edition of *The Skilled Facilitator* is sure to find a special place on your bookshelf. Roger presents the most current practices that are both steeped in theory and immediately applicable."

—**Elaine Biech,** author of *Training and Development for Dummies*,
and editor of *101 Ways to Make Learning Active Beyond the Classroom*

"The third edition of *The Skilled Facilitator* is a winner. The mutual learning approach builds in transparency and integrity in conflict resolution processes, its integration with the team effectiveness model makes this the preferred approach for team interventions. This is the stuff that organizational *TRUST* is built on. It will continue to be my go-to resource in my work as an organizational ombudsman and coach."

—**Thomas P. Zgambo,** former World Bank Group ombudsman
and former President of The Ombudsman Association
(now the International Ombudsman Association)

"Roger Schwarz smartly updates his classic text on facilitation, taking into account contemporary brain research and framing his approach in terms of the proper, 'mutual learning' mindset for working with groups effectively. Schwarz offers a system that will help professionals in the field become trusting, trusted, and—with practice— terrific facilitators."

—**Ed Frauenheim,** Director of Research and Content
at Great Place to Work, and coauthor of *Good Company:
Business Success in the Worthiness Era*

"The expanded, revised edition provides new, innovative approaches and insights not only to professional facilitators but also to those who want to use facilitation skills to be effective leaders, consultants, or coaches. Roger makes facilitation skills and techniques understandable and usable. These skills are particularly important in labor-management relations and other settings in which leaders must generate commitment rather than compliance and where mutual understanding is critical to productive relationships."

—**Robert Tobias,** former president,
National Treasury Employees Union,
and professor of public administration, American University

"In an increasingly demanding business setting, the ability to adapt quickly is critical. Skilled facilitation is a key competence to making change happen. This insightful and practical book offers all those involved with facilitation tools they can use. By using these tools, they will help their organization win in changing markets."

—**Dave Ulrich,** Rensis Likert Professor, Ross School of Business,
University of Michigan, Partner, the RBL Group

"Roger Schwarz's third edition of *The Skilled Facilitator* is a must-read for anyone who is responsible for facilitating team meetings, leading group discussions, or conducting training sessions. His insights and practical tips for managing group process and group dynamics are invaluable. Whether you are new to facilitation or a seasoned pro, Schwarz's techniques, models, and concrete examples will help you get better results with the groups you lead and manage."

—**Karen Lawson,** PhD, president, Lawson Consulting Group, Inc., and author of *The Trainer's Handbook, 4th edition*

"*The Skilled Facilitator* continues to be an outstanding resource for both new and seasoned facilitators, managers, and organizational leaders as well as consultants and coaches. The additions and enhancements in the third edition, particularly the new chapter on facilitating virtual meetings, make this well-written book a must for anyone who works with face to face and/or virtual groups. Roger is an exceptional consultant and inspirational teacher who walks his talk."

—**Nadine Bell,** Certified Professional Facilitator, past Chair of the International Association of Facilitators, inaugural inductee to the International Association of Facilitators Hall of Fame

"Roger's book is still the best text on group facilitation available in English. The third edition continues his thoughtful and completely useful guidance on facilitating group processes and has benefited from the ongoing dialogue he has shaped within the facilitation field. Readers will get the core skills and mindsets necessary for effective group facilitation and perhaps more importantly, will be cautioned against the multitude of missteps that can sabotage the best intentions. His precision with language led to a number of changes in the new edition that clarify and simplify descriptions of the key facilitative rules and the applications of facilitation in coaching, training, and consultation."

—**Douglas Riddle,** PhD, Senior Fellow, Center for Creative Leadership

"At the heart of the Skilled Facilitator approach is the premise that how you think is how you facilitate—or consult, coach, train, or mediate. No matter our profession, Roger's book offers us all practical and useful information for making any human interaction more effective and successful. After reading *The Skilled Facilitator*, I found myself listing all the ways I could immediately use Roger's six-step mutual learning approach, eight behaviors of mutual learning, and especially the content from 'Diagnosing and Intervening on Emotions (the Group's and Yours).' *The Skilled Facilitator* is an outstanding reference book that I will come back to again and again. I am glad I have it on my trainer's bookshelf!"

—**Sharon L. Bowman,** author of *Training from the BACK of the Room* and *The Ten-Minute Trainer!*

The Skilled Facilitator

The Skilled Facilitator

A Comprehensive Resource for Consultants, Facilitators, Coaches, and Trainers

Third Edition

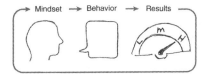

Roger Schwarz

JB JOSSEY-BASS™

A Wiley Brand

Library of Congress Cataloging-in-Publication Data:

Names: Schwarz, Roger M., 1956- author.
Title: The skilled facilitator: a comprehensive resource for consultants, facilitators, managers,
    trainers, and coaches / Roger M. Schwarz.
Description: Third edition. | Hoboken, New Jersey : John Wiley & Sons, Inc., [2017] |
    Includes index.
Identifiers: LCCN 2016029060 (print) | LCCN 2016042887 (ebook) | ISBN 9781119064398 (cloth) |
    ISBN 9781119064411 (pdf) | ISBN 9781119064404 (epub) | ISBN 9781119176572 (obook)
Subjects: LCSH: Communication in management. | Communication in personnel
    management. | Group facilitation. | Teams in the workplace. | Conflict management.
Classification: LCC HD30.3 .S373 2017 (print) | LCC HD30.3 (ebook) | DDC 658.4/5–dc23
LC record available at https://lccn.loc.gov/2016029060

To Kathleen, Noah, and Hannah

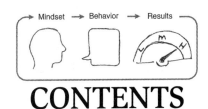

CONTENTS

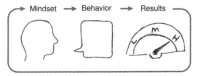

Mindset → Behavior → Results

PREFACE TO THE THIRD EDITION

Since I wrote the first edition of *The Skilled Facilitator* in 1994, it has become a standard reference in the field. Many readers have told me that the book has fundamentally changed how they help the groups they work with. They return to it again and again when faced with challenging or new situations. I am gratified that many people in different roles across many fields have found the book so valuable. I hope you will be among them.

WHAT *THE SKILLED FACILITATOR* IS ABOUT

The Skilled Facilitator is about how you can help groups become more effective, whether you're a consultant, facilitator, coach, trainer, or mediator. When I wrote the first edition, facilitative skills were something you called on a facilitator for. Now these skills are recognized as a core competency for anyone working with groups.

The book describes one approach to facilitation—the Skilled Facilitator approach. It's a relatively comprehensive and integrated approach, so you can learn it and use it as you work with groups. The approach is based on research and theory that I cite throughout the book.

The Skilled Facilitator approach has several key features. It's based on a set of core values and assumptions—what I call mindset—and principles. Whether you're serving as a facilitator, consultant, coach, trainer, or mediator, you can always figure out what to do in a particular situation by turning to the core values, assumptions, and principles to guide your behavior.

The Skilled Facilitator approach integrates theory and practice. Throughout the book, I answer three questions: "What do I do? How do I do it? Why do I do it that way?" By answering the first question, you understand what specific tool, technique, or method to use in any particular situation. This gives you a general idea of how to respond in any situation. By answering the second question, you understand exactly what to say in that situation. Answering these first two questions is necessary, but not sufficient. By answering the third question, you understand the theory and principles that make all the tools, techniques, methods, and your specific behaviors work. When you know the answers to these three questions, you no longer have to use the tools and methods exactly as you learned them—you can modify them and design your own tools and methods to help a group, no matter what situation you're in.

The Skilled Facilitator approach is a systems approach for helping groups. All the parts of the approach fit together and reinforce each other because they are all based on the same set of core values, assumptions, and principles. The logic of the approach is transparent, and you can share it with the groups you're helping. This makes the approach more powerful and practical.

In the Skilled Facilitator approach, the mindset and behaviors that you use to help a group are the same mindset and behaviors that the group can use to improve its effectiveness. There isn't a secret set of principles, techniques, or methods for you and another set for the group. When you act effectively, you're modeling effective behavior for the group. This makes it much easier for you to help the group increase its effectiveness. Recently, I wrote *Smart Leaders, Smarter Teams* for the groups and teams you are helping. The book uses the very same approach (including the same models and behaviors) that I describe here to help teams develop the mindset, skill set, and team design to create better results. If you find *The Skilled Facilitator* useful and want to help teams learn how they can apply it in their leadership roles, *Smart Leaders, Smarter Teams* will show them how.

At the heart of the Skilled Facilitator approach is the premise that how you think is how you facilitate (or consult, coach, train, or mediate). Research shows that in challenging situations almost all of us use a mindset that leads us to behave in ways that reduce our ability to help the groups we're hired to help. The Skilled Facilitator approach teaches you how to rigorously reflect on your own thinking and feeling so that you can more consistently operate from a productive mindset. This will enable you and the groups you help to get three results: better performance, stronger working relationships, and individual well-being.

WHO THIS BOOK IS FOR

Most people who need to use facilitation skills aren't facilitators. If you need facilitation skills to help groups that you're not a member of, I wrote this book for you. *The Skilled Facilitator* will help you work more effectively with groups so that they can better achieve their results. You'll find this book useful if you work in any of these roles:

- You're a **facilitator** who helps work groups: boards, top leadership teams, management teams, work teams, task forces, committees, labor-management groups, interorganizational committees, or community groups. This includes facilitators who specialize in Lean, Six Sigma, or other process improvement approaches.
- You're a **consultant** who works with groups as you provide expertise in any content area, such as strategy, marketing, operations, process improvement, or any other area.
- You're an **organization development consultant** who needs facilitative skills to help groups and organizations manage change.
- You're an **HR consultant** who serves as a business partner to the leadership teams you support and are often involved in difficult conversations regarding employee performance or behavior.
- You're a **coach** working with teams, groups, or individuals.
- You're a **trainer** who facilitates discussion as part of your training.
- You're a **mediator** who wants to develop your facilitative skills or work with groups.
- You're a **faculty member** who, as a practical scholar, teaches courses on groups or teams, facilitation, consultation, coaching, organization development, or conflict management, in the fields of management, health care, engineering, public administration, planning, psychology, social work, education, public health, or in other applied fields.

If you're the leader or member of a team, I've written another book for you: *Smart Leaders, Smarter Teams*. It uses the same approach that I describe in this book, but it's designed for your specific role. If someone has suggested you read *The Skilled Facilitator*, you might find *Smart Leaders, Smarter Teams* a better fit for your needs.

HOW THE BOOK IS ORGANIZED

I have organized *The Skilled Facilitator* into four parts. Here are brief descriptions of the chapters within them.

Part One: The Foundation

In Part One, I lay the foundation for using facilitative skills.

Chapter 1, "The Skilled Facilitator Approach." In this chapter, I give an overview of the Skilled Facilitator approach, including what it will help you accomplish and the questions I answer throughout the book.

Chapter 2, "The Facilitator and Other Facilitative Roles." How do I figure out what role to use when working with a group? What do I do if I need to play more than one role? In this chapter, I describe how you can use the Skilled Facilitator approach in any role you serve: consultant, facilitator, coach, trainer, or mediator. I describe each role, explain when to serve in each one, and discuss how to serve in multiple roles when working with groups.

Chapter 3, "How You Think Is How You Facilitate: How Unilateral Control Undermines Your Ability to Help Groups." The most challenging part of facilitating, consulting, coaching, or training is being able to work from a productive mindset. This chapter describes how almost all of us operate from an unproductive mindset—unilateral control—when we're faced with challenging group situations. I describe how unilateral control leads you to think and behave in ways that reduce your effectiveness and your ability to help groups.

Chapter 4, "Facilitating with the Mutual Learning Approach." The mutual learning approach is the foundation of the Skilled Facilitator approach. In this chapter, I describe how the mutual learning mindset enables you to think and act in ways that help you and the groups you're working with get results that aren't possible with a unilateral control approach. I describe the specific values, assumptions, and behaviors that make up the mutual learning approach.

Chapter 5, "Eight Behaviors for Mutual Learning." This chapter describes the eight behaviors that put the mutual learning mindset into action and how you can use them to increase your effectiveness and to help groups increase their effectiveness. I explain how each behavior contributes to better results and when and how you use each one.

Chapter 6, "Designing and Developing Effective Groups." If you're helping groups get better results, it's important to understand what it takes for groups to get those results. Building on the mutual learning approach, this chapter provides a model of group effectiveness that explains how to design new groups to be effective and how to help existing groups improve their results.

Part Two: Diagnosing and Intervening with Groups

In Part Two, I describe how to observe a group, figure out what is happening that is limiting the group's effectiveness, and intervene to help the group become more effective.

Chapter 7, "Diagnosing and Intervening with Groups." How do I figure out what's happening in a group that's reducing its effectiveness? What do I say to the group when I figure it out? In this chapter, I introduce the mutual learning cycle that you can use to answer these questions and to diagnose and intervene effectively with a group.

Chapter 8, "How to Diagnose Groups." There are so many things to pay attention to in a group; how do I decide what to look for? In this chapter, I show you how to use the mutual learning cycle to look for the important things occurring in a group, figure out what they mean, and decide whether to intervene with the group.

Chapter 9, "How to Intervene with Groups." After I decide to say something to the group, what exactly should I say, who should I say it to, and when should I say it? In this chapter, I show you how to intervene so you can determine if the group is seeing what you're seeing and decide together what, if anything, the group or you should do differently.

Chapter 10, "Diagnosing and Intervening on the Mutual Learning Behaviors." In this chapter, I give verbatim examples of how to intervene when group members are not using each of the eight mutual learning behaviors.

Chapter 11, "Using Mutual Learning to Improve Other Processes and Techniques." This chapter shows you how to use the Skilled Facilitator approach to help a group improve how it uses any process or technique, such as Lean and Six Sigma processes, performance management processes, strategic planning, or problem solving.

Chapter 12, "Diagnosing and Intervening on Emotions—The Group's and Yours." What do I do when people start to get emotional? What do I do when I start to get emotional? In this chapter, I explain how you and the group members generate your emotions, and how you can help group members and yourself express emotion so it makes the conversation and problem solving more productive.

Part Three: Agreeing to Work Together

In Part Three, I describe how to reach an agreement to work with a group; how to decide whether to work with a partner, and if so, how; and how to work internally in your organization.

Chapter 13, "Contracting: Deciding Whether and How to Work with a Group." The agreement you develop with a group about how you will work together creates the foundation for your helping relationship. Poor contracting generates problems throughout the relationship. In this chapter, I describe a detailed five-stage process you can use to ensure that you and the group develop a healthy working relationship that meets both of your needs.

Chapter 14, "Working with a Partner." Working with a partner can be more valuable to a group—if you and your partner can work well together. In this chapter, I describe the potential advantages and disadvantages of working with a partner, how to decide whether to work with a partner, and ways to divide and coordinate your work effectively.

Chapter 15, "Serving in a Facilitative Role in Your Own Organization." If you're an internal facilitator, consultant, or coach, you face different challenges than your external counterparts. In this chapter, I describe how your internal facilitative role develops, the potential advantages and disadvantages of the internal role, and specific strategies you can use to be effective in your role, including contracting with your manager.

Part Four: Working with Technology

In Part Four, I describe how to work virtually with groups.

Chapter 16, "Using Virtual Meetings." Increasingly, groups are meeting in virtual spaces rather than face-to-face. In this chapter, I describe when to use virtual meetings, how to decide among different virtual meeting technologies, identify the special challenges of virtual meetings, and explain how to effectively address the challenges.

FEATURES OF THE BOOK

This book offers several features that will help you navigate and learn the Skilled Facilitator approach:

- Key principles of the Skilled Facilitator approach are in **boldface** type, and key terms are in *italics* type.

- A book cannot substitute for the skill-building practice of a workshop (which is why we offer The Skilled Facilitator Intensive Workshop). Still, throughout the book I give verbatim examples that show you how to put the principles into practice. This includes real cases of how group members act ineffectively and how you can intervene in such cases.

- I share my own stories and my colleagues' stories to illustrate how to apply the Skilled Facilitator approach—and how not to apply it. There are examples of my own ineffective facilitation; I have learned from them and assume you will, too. In all the examples and stories, I have disguised the name and type of the organization, as well as the names of individual members. I have sometimes created a composite of several stories to quickly illustrate a point.

WHAT'S DIFFERENT IN THE THIRD EDITION

If you've read the second edition, you may be wondering how this edition is different. There are a number of significant differences:

- I focus more on the consultant, coaching, and trainer roles. In this edition, I explain throughout the book how you would approach a situation differently depending on your facilitative role.
- There is a new chapter on using virtual meetings.
- All of the models are completely revised. The unilateral control approach and mutual learning approach have new core values and assumptions, behaviors, and results. The Team Effectiveness Model has new core values and results.
- The mutual learning approach and the Team Effectiveness Model are completely integrated. The mutual learning approach is completed embedded in the Team Effectiveness Model.

PART ONE

THE FOUNDATION

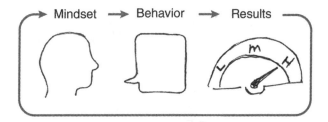

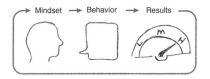

CHAPTER ONE

The Skilled Facilitator Approach

This book is about helping groups get better results. If you're reading this, you may be exploring how to or are already working with groups. You may be serving as a facilitator, consultant, coach, or trainer. In any case, you want to develop facilitation skills to help groups become more effective.

THE NEED FOR GROUP FACILITATION

Groups are the basic work unit in many organizations. Organizations are too complex for individuals alone to have all the information they need to produce products and services, or make key decisions, without creating unintended negative consequences. So, organizations create groups to get all the needed information in the same room, resolve different and conflicting views, and commit to a common course of action. Groups need to work effectively. But if you've worked with groups, you know they're often less than the sum of their parts; they make poor decisions, create mistrust and low commitment, and leave members demotivated and stressed. It doesn't need to be this way. This book will show you how to help groups achieve what they want and need to achieve.

MOST PEOPLE WHO NEED TO FACILITATE AREN'T FACILITATORS

If you work with groups, you need facilitation skills. Most people who work with groups don't think of themselves as facilitators, and technically, they're not. Essentially, a group facilitator is a content-neutral third party who helps a group improve how to work together to get better results. **But even if you're not a facilitator, you can still use the same approach—the mindset and skill set—that facilitators use to help groups get better results.** At its core, facilitation is simply a way of thinking and working with groups that increases the chance that they'll perform well, develop strong working relationships, and maintain or improve members' well-being. It's valuable for any relationship worth your time. If you serve in any of these roles, you'll benefit from facilitation skills:

- **You're an internal or external consultant, providing expert advice to organizations.** You may be an expert in the area of strategy, finance, accounting, IT, HR, marketing, logistics, organizational change, or any number of other areas. Your purpose isn't to facilitate groups, but you need to work with groups to understand your clients' challenges and needs, and propose and implement solutions.

- **You're an internal or external consultant whose purpose is to help groups improve their results by improving their process in some way.** You may specialize in process improvements such as Lean, Six Sigma, value engineering, quality improvement, or other related approaches. You may feel challenged when dealing with problems that stem from the soft side of groups, like resistance to change. Or you may specialize in a key element necessary for effective groups such as managing conflict productively, building trust, increasing diversity, or demonstrating leadership.

- **You're a coach, now working with teams.** You generally work with individuals but increasingly find yourself working with teams. You realize that helping a team requires more skills than working with someone one-on-one.

- **You're a trainer who helps people develop knowledge and/or skills in a group setting.** You need to actively engage people as you meet their learning needs while simultaneously making sure you stay on task and on time.

If you're a member or formal leader of the group you're trying to improve, facilitation skills are also essential for your work. I've written the book *Smart Leaders, Smarter Teams* (Jossey-Bass, 2013) for people in your role. It uses exactly the same mindset and skill set I describe in this book, and it includes specific examples to help you in your formal and informal leadership tasks.

IS THIS BOOK FOR YOU?

This book is for anyone who works with groups to help them get better results. It provides a comprehensive approach to facilitation that you can apply in a variety of roles. When you've finished reading the book, you'll have answers to the five main questions that anyone who wants to work effectively with groups must address.

Should I Be a Facilitator, Consultant, Coach, or Trainer to a Group?

How do I decide what role to play? What do I do if I need to help the group by using more than one role? You can help a group as a facilitator, consultant, coach, or trainer. Selecting the appropriate facilitative role is important. In each role, you help a group in a different way. The role you select depends on the type of help the group needs. If you select the appropriate role, you help the group achieve its goals. If you select an inappropriate role, you hinder the group and can hamper your working relationship with them.

The Skilled Facilitator approach defines six of these helping roles, describes how you use each role to help the group, and the conditions under which it's the most appropriate role for you to use (Chapter 2). It also explains when and how to move between the roles.

What Should I Pay Attention to to Help a Group?

Do I watch who speaks to whom or how much people speak? What role each member plays in the group? How people state their views and ask questions? How group members with different personality types interact? When you're working with a group, there are so many things you might focus on to figure out what the group is doing that is productive and unproductive. It's not possible to pay attention to everything, so how do you decide what's important to pay attention to and what's not? And how do you do this in real time so that you can respond immediately, instead of figuring it out after the meeting has ended?

When you ask yourself these questions, you're asking for a diagnostic model to guide what you pay attention to and how you make sense of it. The Skilled Facilitator approach uses a multifactor diagnostic model that enables you to identify what is occurring in a group that is increasing or decreasing its effectiveness. The approach describes eight behaviors (Chapters 5 and 10) that you can use each time a group member speaks, to analyze exactly how he or she is making the conversation more or less productive. The approach also describes two mindsets (Chapters 3 and 4) that group members use—one effective and one ineffective—so that you can infer when group members are thinking in ways that lead them to act less effectively.

Finally, the Skilled Facilitator approach includes a Team Effectiveness Model (Chapter 6) that describes how a group or team's design, including its structures and processes, affect its results. Structure includes the group's task and goals, the ways in which group members are interdependent as they accomplish the task, and the roles that group members fill as they work together. Process includes how the group solves problems, makes decisions, and manages conflict. By analyzing a group's underlying structures and processes, you identify powerful but invisible forces that affect the group.

The Skilled Facilitator diagnostic model enables you to attend to a range of factors (that is, mindset, behavior, structures, and processes) that make significant differences in the three results that every team needs to achieve: (1) solid performance; (2) strong working relationships; and (3) positive individual well-being.

What Do I Say When the Group Isn't Working Effectively?

When should I intervene with the group? What exactly should I say? Who should I say it to? After you've diagnosed what's happening in a group, you have to decide whether to intervene; that is, whether to share what you're seeing and what you think it means for the group, and see if the group wants to change its behavior. You can't intervene every time you see something that may reduce the group's effectiveness; if you do, the group may not accomplish its work and may lock you out of the room.

When you decide to intervene, you need to decide what kind of intervention to make, exactly what to say, and to whom. To accomplish this, the Skilled Facilitator approach includes a six-step process called the mutual learning cycle (Chapters 7 and 9). The cycle is a structured and simple way for you to think about what's happening in the group and then to intervene effectively. It enables you to intervene on anything that is occurring in the group, including when group members' behavior is ineffective (Chapter 10), when group members are using some process ineffectively (Chapter 11), and when emotional issues arise (Chapter 12).

How Do I Develop an Agreement to Work with a Group?

How do I figure out who my client group is and what kind of help they need? What agreements do I need to make to increase the chance of success, and which group members need to be involved in the agreement? What do I do if group members tell me things they want me to keep confidential? Addressing these questions and many others will enable you to reach an agreement about whether and how you and the group will work together. This is the contracting process, and how well you manage it affects the course of your work with the group. Manage it well and you and the group have created the conditions for an effective working relationship; manage it poorly and unresolved issues will continue to plague your work with them.

The Skilled Facilitator approach provides a five-stage contracting process. It describes the purpose and tasks for each contracting stage, the type of information to obtain and share with the group, the decisions you and the group need to reach, and who needs to be involved at each stage.

What Do I Do When a Group Is Difficult to Deal With?

How do I work with group members who aren't participating, are openly hostile with each other, or are resisting me? How do I deal with a group leader who is trying to control the facilitation? What do I do when the group is really frustrating me? Being able to effectively address challenging situations—ones in which the stakes and emotions are high and members have very strong and different views—is a sign of a skilled facilitator, consultant, coach, or trainer. That includes situations in which the stakes are high for you, you think you understand the situation and the group doesn't, and you have strong emotions.

At the heart of the Skilled Facilitator approach is the fundamental and powerful principle that how you think is how you facilitate—or consult, coach, and train. Although the tools, techniques, and behaviors that you'll learn in this book are necessary and important, ultimately your effectiveness stems from your mindset, the values and assumptions that drive your behavior and ultimately create your results. Even if you have a set of effective tools, techniques, and behaviors, you'll get poor results for yourself and the groups you're helping if you apply them using an ineffective mindset.

Unfortunately, when we find ourselves in challenging situations, almost all of us use the same ineffective mindset—unilateral control (Chapter 3). The specifics may differ for each of us, but when we feel psychologically threatened or embarrassed, research shows that 98 percent of us operate from this. As the name suggests, the core values and assumptions of this approach are designed so we unilaterally control the situation to get the outcome we want. Ironically, the unilateral control mindset leads you to act in ways and get the very results you're trying hard to avoid: lower-quality decisions, mistrust, unproductive conflict, defensive reactions, lack of commitment, strained relationships, decreased motivation, and increased stress.

The Skilled Facilitator approach operates from a different mindset that research shows is more effective—the mutual learning mindset (Chapter 4). The mutual learning mindset comprises the core values of transparency, curiosity, informed choice, accountability, and compassion. When you operate from the mutual learning mindset, rather than assuming you understand and are right while others who disagree don't understand and are wrong, you assume that each of us is missing information and that differences are opportunities for learning. You recognize that you may be contributing to the very problems you're complaining about.

Throughout the book, I will help you recognize when you may be operating from a unilateral control mindset and show you how to shift to a mutual learning mindset. My clients consistently tell me this is the most powerful part of the Skilled Facilitator approach—and the most challenging as well. The more you're able to do this, the more you'll be able to help groups, even in the most challenging situations.

THE SKILLED FACILITATOR APPROACH

The Skilled Facilitator approach is one approach to facilitation. It's an approach I've been developing since 1980, when I began teaching facilitation to others. The Skilled Facilitator approach is based on a theory of group facilitation that is grounded in research on groups. Its elements have been borne out by more than 35 years of research.[1] Here are the main characteristics of the approach.

It Answers the Questions: What Do I Do? How Do I Do It? Why Do I Do It That Way?

The approach accomplishes this by integrating theory and practice. Knowing what to do and how to do it—the specific behaviors, tools, and techniques—are necessary, but they're not sufficient. If you don't understand why you're doing what you're doing—the underlying principle—you won't be able to spontaneously redesign your behavior when you're faced with a new situation. By understanding the underlying theory and principles, you move from being a novice cook having to dutifully follow a recipe to a creative chef who can use the knowledge of ingredients and cooking chemistry to create any dish from the available ingredients.

A Systems Approach

Facilitators often tell me stories of how, despite their best efforts to help a group in a difficult situation, the situation gets worse. Often this happens because the facilitator isn't thinking and acting systemically.

For example, in your facilitative role, if you privately pull aside a team member whom you assume is dominating the group, in the short term it may seem to improve the group's discussion. But it may also have several unintended negative consequences. The pulled-aside member may feel that you're biased against him, thereby reducing your credibility with that member. If the group doesn't think the member is dominating the conversation, then you've unilaterally acted at odds with the group's needs, which undermines your relationship with the group. Even if you're reflecting the other group members' opinions, talking to the member individually shifts the group's accountability to you and inappropriately increases the group's dependence on you for sharing their views and solving their own problems.

When you *think* systemically, you see the group as a social system—a collection of parts interacting with each other to function as a whole. You understand that although every group is different, because all groups are systems, under the same system conditions they generate predictable system results, such as slow implementation time, deteriorating trust, or continued overdependence on the leader. You can predict what's likely to happen in a group based on how the group is structured and how members are interacting.

When you help a group, you enter into this system. Your challenge is to understand the group's functional and dysfunctional dynamics, and help it become more effective, without becoming influenced by the system to act ineffectively yourself. When you *act* systemically, you recognize that any action you take affects the group and you in multiple ways that have short-term and long-term consequences. Your interventions are more helpful to the group, and you avoid or reduce negative consequences for the group and you.

All the Parts Fit Together

Because the Skilled Facilitator approach is a systemic approach, it takes a comprehensive approach to helping groups—and all the parts fit together. Many facilitators develop their approaches by collecting tools and techniques from a variety of other approaches. There's nothing inherently wrong with this, but if the different tools and techniques are based on conflicting values or assumptions, they can undermine your effectiveness and the groups you're trying to help. For example, if you say that your client is the entire group, yet you automatically agree to individual requests by the group's leader, you may soon find yourself in the middle of a conflict between the group and its leader, rather than helping to facilitate the entire group.

The Skilled Facilitator approach starts with an internally consistent set of mutual learning core values and assumptions. Together they create the mindset upon which all the Skilled Facilitator tools, techniques, and behaviors are based. Consequently, when you use the approach, you're acting congruently. You won't be giving the group mixed messages or otherwise creating problems for the group.

It's the Same Approach for You and Group Members

One of the things that makes the Skilled Facilitator approach powerful is that, aside from the fact that your facilitative role differs from that of a group member, the approach is the same for you as it is for the groups you're helping. **The Skilled Facilitator approach states that effective facilitators, consultants, coaches, trainers, and group members operate from the same mutual learning mindset and use the same set of behaviors.**

There is no secret set of facilitator tools, techniques, or strategies. I wrote *Smart Leaders, Smarter Teams* so leaders and their teams could benefit from the same mutual learning mindset and skill set as facilitators, consultants, coaches, and trainers. If you want the groups you're working with to understand how to get better results by developing a mutual learning mindset and skill set, you can ask them to read *Smart Leaders, Smarter Teams.* Not only will it will help them become a more effective group, but also they'll better understand how you're using the same mutual learning approach to help them.

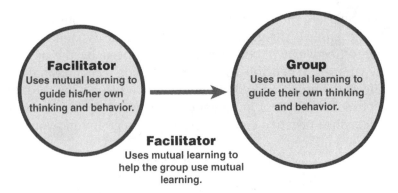

Figure 1.1   Using Mutual Learning Three Ways

This means that there is a common mindset and skill set, no matter what your role. When you act effectively in your facilitative role, you're modeling effective behavior for leaders and groups. This makes the transfer of learning from you to the group quicker and easier. Consequently, you can use the mutual learning approach in three ways, as Figure 1.1 shows: (1) You can use the mutual learning mindset and skill set as the basis for your thinking and behavior; (2) the group can use the mutual learning mindset and skill set as the basis for their thinking and behavior; and (3) you can use the mutual learning mindset and skill set to diagnose and intervene to help the group get better results using mutual learning.

You Can Use the Approach Almost Anywhere

Although this book is about helping work groups, many of my clients tell me that they use the mindset and behaviors of the Skilled Facilitator approach outside of work, with their families, friends, and community, and see positive results. You can use the approach in almost any situation—in any role—because it's based on principles of effective human interaction. For me, the principles underlying the Skilled Facilitator approach are simply the way I want to be in the world, as a facilitator, consultant, spouse, father, friend, or in any other role.

EXPERIENCING THE SKILLED FACILITATOR APPROACH

My clients consistently tell me that the Skilled Facilitator concepts and tools are easy to understand. And then, after practicing a little, they often add, "But it's harder than it looks." When you read the many verbatim examples I share in the book, you'll probably and reasonably think, *That's not difficult.* After all, the examples I share use everyday language that you've already mastered, even if you've never combined the words in the way that I have. It's not like you're watching me perform magic and wondering, *How did he do that?*

But it's harder than it looks for several reasons. First, you need to pay attention to many aspects of a group simultaneously. Second, you need to quickly make sense of what you're seeing. To do this efficiently and without feeling overwhelmed, you need instant access to your diagnostic models. Finally, you need to quickly decide what intervention to make with the group. All of this is cognitively challenging.

But here's the most challenging part: When you start to use the approach with real groups, you'll sometimes find it difficult to speak the words you have read in the book and maybe even committed to memory. It's not simply that you haven't learned the phrases; it's that you're dealing with challenging situations—ones that trigger your own unilateral control mindset. You may feel frustrated or annoyed with group members, anxious about conflict within the group, worried about whether you can help the group, or any mix of emotions.

Furthermore, because how you think is how you facilitate, when you're operating from a unilateral control mindset it trumps your ability to use mutual learning behaviors. In short, the most challenging part of facilitation is not the group—it's your mindset and how the group affects it.

I'm telling you this not because I'm trying to dissuade you from reading this book, but to let you know this is normal. All those who use the Skilled Facilitator approach find that their own mindset is the main challenge to their effectiveness—including me.

Now, here's the good news. If you regularly practice the approach and get rigorous feedback, you'll become more effective. You'll be able to operate from the mutual learning mindset more often. When you slip into unilateral control, you'll be able to realize it more quickly and move back to mutual learning more quickly. One of the joys of hearing from readers of *The Skilled Facilitator* and clients who I have taught is that they are much more effective than they used to be and their clients and colleagues tell them that. They also tell me that their effectiveness spills over to other roles in their life because they use the mutual learning approach in general.

MAKING THE SKILLED FACILITATOR APPROACH YOUR OWN

Part of learning the Skilled Facilitator approach is integrating it with your own style—making it your own. Throughout the book, as you read examples of what I would say in various situations, sometimes you may think that the words are natural and make sense; other times, you may think, *This sounds awkward;*

I can't imagine myself saying those words. You're likely to have the same experience as you begin to practice using this approach with groups. This awkward feeling is common, stemming partly from learning a new approach.

But it can also stem from trying to force-fit my style to yours. You can't be me (and I don't assume you would want to). When I was first learning how to use the mutual learning approach in facilitation, I tried hard to imitate Chris Argyris, from whom I learned the approach (he called it Model II) in graduate school at Harvard. As deeply as I respected Chris, our styles were different; I could not intervene exactly as he did and still sound like me. It was not until I found my own voice that the approach became mine. I assume the same is true for you. Learning to use the core values and behaviors is a journey; part of the journey is finding your own voice. Welcome to the journey.

SUMMARY

Most people who need to use facilitation skills aren't facilitators. The Skilled Facilitator approach is an approach for helping groups that you can use as a facilitator, consultant, coach, or trainer. It's a comprehensive, systemic approach that is based on theory and is supported by decades of research. It begins with a set of mutual learning core values and assumptions (called a mindset) that generates tools, techniques, and behaviors, all of which fit together. Together, the mutual learning mindset, the Team Effectiveness Model, the eight mutual learning behaviors, and other tools help you identify what is happening in a group and intervene to help the group increase its effectiveness. The approach enables you to explore and change your mindset, to improve your ability to help groups, even in increasingly difficult situations.

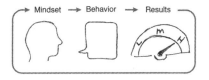

Mindset → Behavior → Results

CHAPTER TWO

The Facilitator and Other Facilitative Roles

I n this chapter, I begin by describing six facilitative roles—facilitator, facilitative consultant, facilitative coach, facilitative trainer, facilitative mediator, and facilitative leader—and explain when to serve in each role. I also explain how these roles are similar to and different from other helping roles, such as group coach and team coach. Next, I describe how to select the appropriate facilitative role(s) to fill and how to serve in several facilitative roles at the same time. For the rest of the chapter, I explain how to perform these roles in a way that is congruent with the core values of mutual learning.

CHOOSING A FACILITATIVE ROLE

As I described in Chapter 1, **most people who need to use facilitative skills don't need to be facilitators**. If you serve in any of these roles, you can apply the same mutual learning mindset and behaviors I describe throughout the book.

A note on terms: Unless I specifically distinguish between the facilitator role and other facilitative roles, I use the term *facilitative* to refer to any role in which you apply the mutual learning approach as a nongroup member. In a case in which a facilitator would approach a situation differently from someone who is in another facilitative role, I'll describe the differences.

It's important to understand the purpose of each facilitative role and how they are similar and different. This will enable you to select the appropriate facilitative role—the one that you and the client agree best fits his or her needs. If the client sees your facilitative role as appropriate, values your expertise, and considers you trustworthy, you'll be better able to help that client. However, if clients think you're serving in an inappropriate facilitative role or acting outside the role you said you would fill, then you'll have more difficulty helping them. Exhibit 2.1 summarizes the six facilitative roles I describe in this section.

The Facilitator Role

Unfortunately, developing a clear understanding of the facilitator role has become more difficult in recent years because organizations now use the word *facilitator* to indicate many roles. Human resources experts, organizational change consultants, trainers, coaches, and even managers have sometimes been renamed facilitators.

Defining the Facilitator Role. Expanding on my brief definition in Chapter 1, **a *group facilitator* is a person who (1) is not a member of the group, (2) is content neutral, (3) has no content decision-making authority or input, (4) is acceptable to all the members of the group, and (5) diagnoses and intervenes in a group, to (6) help it improve the processes by which it identifies and solves problems and makes decisions, in order to increase the group's effectiveness.**

Many elements of the definition are designed to ensure that all members of the group, not just the group's leader or the person who contacted the facilitator, see the facilitator as trustworthy and credible. Unless all group members trust the facilitator, the facilitator can't effectively fill the role and help the group. Let's clarify each of these elements of the definition.

Not a Member of the Group. You can't be a facilitator for a group you're a member of because you can't be completely neutral about issues in your group. Even if the issues you're facilitating don't directly affect you, your membership in the group can indirectly influence your neutrality. If you're a group member or leader, other members will reasonably expect you to be involved in the content of discussions and, depending on the topic, have a role in decision making.

The facilitator needs to be a *third party*, but it's not always clear what this means. Even if you aren't a member of the immediate group that requests facilitation, members still may not consider you a third party. For example, if the group is seeking facilitation to address concerns with the division it is part of and you're an internal facilitator working in the same division, group members may consider you a member of the larger group and not a third party. To serve as a facilitator, the group requesting help needs to consider you a third party.

Content Neutral. By *content neutral*, I don't mean you have no opinions on the issues that the group is discussing. That would be unrealistic. Rather, I mean that you facilitate the discussion without sharing your views, so group members cannot infer your views on the group's topics. Consequently, you don't

	Facilitator	Facilitative Consultant	Facilitative Coach	Facilitative Trainer	Facilitative Mediator	Facilitative Leader
Purpose	Help group use effective process to make decisions and increase its effectiveness	Provide expert advice on client's issues	Help an individual, group, or team achieve goals and increase effectiveness	Help people develop knowledge and skills	Help two or more people resolve a dispute	Influence a group to achieve goals and increase its effectiveness
Group Member	No	No	Can be	Can be	No	Yes
Involvement in Content	Content neutral	Content expert	May be involved	Content expert	Content neutral	Involved in content
Involvement in Content Decision Making	Not involved	May be involved	Not involved	May be involved	Not involved	Involved

Exhibit 2.1   Six Facilitative Roles

influence the group's decisions, directly or indirectly. Group members are easily and justifiably annoyed by a facilitator who claims to be neutral and then acts in a way that isn't neutral.

For example, if you're helping a group decide what new markets to enter, you don't share your opinion about which markets would be more profitable, give examples of what markets other organizations have pursued, or cite research on the topic. You don't even agree or disagree with other members' views. For example, responding "Good point" to a group member's comment breaks your facilitator content neutrality. By being content neutral, you increase the chance that all group members, regardless of their views on the topics, will see you as trustworthy. In addition, content neutrality ensures that the group remains responsible for solving its problems and making decisions. There is one content area in which mutual learning facilitators are not neutral. I'll describe this in the next section.

To remain neutral requires listening to members' views and remaining curious about how their reasoning differs from others (and from your private views) so that you can help the group engage in productive conversation. If you trade your curiosity for a belief that some members are right and others are wrong, or that the group as a whole is going in the wrong direction, you give up your ability to help group members explore their own views and differences and replace it with your desire to influence the content of the discussion. If you find yourself invested in an issue or in having the group reach a particular outcome, or if you have expertise on the subject that makes it difficult for you to remain neutral, then consider serving in one of the other facilitative roles.

No Decision-Making Authority or Input. This is an extension of the facilitator's content neutrality. *Content decision-making authority or input* means you have the ability either to make or participate in decisions regarding the group's topics of discussion. Even if you haven't expressed your view on the topic, the facilitator role prohibits you from being part of a vote or other decision-making process on the group's topics.

Acceptable to All Members of the Group. Requiring that you are acceptable to all members of the group is another way to ensure that you meet each group member's criteria and that the group will be open to your facilitation.

Diagnoses and Intervenes in a Group. A group facilitator works with the entire group. At times, you may meet with subsets of the group, including individuals, but the group is the basic venue in which you work. You watch the group in action, diagnose what is happening, and intervene to help the group become more effective in its problem-solving and decision-making processes.

Improves the Processes. *Process* refers to how a group works together. It includes how members identify and solve problems, make decisions, and handle conflict. In contrast, *content* refers to the topic a group is discussing. The content of a group discussion might be whether to enter a new market, how to provide high-quality service to customers, or what each group member's responsibilities should be. Whenever a group meets, you can observe both content and process simultaneously. For example, in a discussion about how to provide high-quality service, suggestions about providing special services to loyal customers or giving more authority to those with customer contact reflect the content of a discussion. However, members responding to only certain colleagues' ideas or failing to identify their assumptions reflect the group's process.

A facilitator is content neutral but also a process expert and advocate. As a process expert, you know what kinds of mindset (values and assumptions), behavior, process, and underlying structure are more or less likely to contribute to high-quality problem solving and decision making, and contribute to the three results of effective groups: performance, working relationships, and individual well-being. If you ask a group to use certain ground rules or if you identify certain ineffective behaviors in the group, it's on the basis of this process expertise.

As a process expert, you advocate that the group adopt a mindset and behaviors that improve its effectiveness, at least for the time you're actively facilitating the group. But being a process advocate does not mean you make these decisions for the group. You ask the group whether it sees any problems with your design for the facilitation, including the process you're advocating. For all of these decisions about the facilitation process, you are a partner with the group.

The Myth of Total Facilitator Neutrality: When Process Is the Content. It's a myth that facilitators are always neutral about the content of the group's discussions. Remember that "content neutral" means that a facilitator conveys no preference for any solution the group considers. When the content is group process, facilitators are not neutral. Not only do they have a point of view; they also are—or should be—experts. As a skilled facilitator, you know what kind of behavior and processes lead to effective problem solving and other important group outcomes, and you use this knowledge to facilitate the group. This is why groups hire you as a facilitator.

Every action you take and intervention you make with the group signals your beliefs about what makes for effective process. When you ask group members to use certain behaviors or ground rules, or when you intervene to help members act consistently with these behaviors, you're implicitly stating your belief that these behaviors and related processes will make the group more effective.

If you use a mutual learning approach, you're transparent about what you believe makes effective group process. You tell your clients that you will be modeling the mutual learning mindset and behaviors and ask them to tell you if they believe you're acting incongruently with them. As you intervene, you explain your interventions. All of this should leave no doubt about your views regarding effective group process.

Consequently, when the group's content turns to how to work effectively as a group, not only do you have a point of view on the topic, but also you've already declared and modeled your views. In these situations, your responsibility as a facilitator (or facilitative consultant) is to ask the group if it wants you to describe how the mutual learning approach can help improve the group's effectiveness. If the group chooses to pursue this, then you can shift into a facilitative consultant role, to help the group understand how it would use mutual learning in its context.

Don't Choose the Facilitator Role Unless It's Absolutely Necessary. The most common mistake when selecting your role is trying to serve as a neutral facilitator when you're a member of the group, have a stake in the issue, or have expertise to share. It's very difficult, if not impossible, to be effective in these cases.

HR business partners and facilitative leaders often make this mistake. Let's assume you're an internal HR business partner who provides HR support to part of your organization. As part of your role, you're asked to facilitate meetings of the leadership team you support. The topics of these meetings may be directly related to HR issues (for example, management succession), indirectly related (for example, business strategy), or unrelated (for example, technical production challenges). If you serve as facilitator on topics that are either directly or indirectly related to HR, you're likely to try to subtly influence the team with your expert views. When you realize that team members have ideas different from your own—ones that don't seem to reflect solid HR practice—you may begin asking leading questions in order to influence the team members' views without saying so explicitly, or you may simply identify some problems with others' proposals. At this point, you've left the facilitator role. Team members may begin to feel that they have been set up, believing that you're not filling the role you agreed to fill. At the same time, you're likely to become frustrated because you can't openly influence the team's ideas while serving in the facilitator role. By contrast, serving as a facilitative consultant or facilitative leader enables you to share your subject-matter expertise, be involved in the decisions, and still use facilitative skills.

The principle here is to serve in the facilitator role only when you're not a member of the group, don't have a stake in the issue, and don't have content expertise that is unique among the group members and that can benefit the client.

The Facilitative Consultant Role

Unlike a facilitator, a facilitative consultant isn't content neutral. If you're a *facilitative consultant*, an organization seeks your expertise in a particular content area. You're a third-party expert whose purpose is to help the client make informed decisions. You accomplish this by applying your area of expertise (marketing, management information systems, service quality, and so forth) to the client's particular situation, recommending a course of action, and in some cases implementing it for the client.

Any substantive decision-making authority you hold results not from your role per se, but from the client delegating decision-making authority to you. A facilitative consultant uses facilitative skills while serving as an expert in a particular content area. Like a facilitator, your facilitative consultant role may be external or internal to the organization. Human resources, organization development, or Lean and Six Sigma consultants often serve as internal and external facilitative consultants.

Facilitative skills are essential for expert consulting. Even if your client isn't a group, you're likely to find yourself working with one or more groups. These groups may not be asking you to improve their problem-solving and decision-making processes, but how well you work with these groups and how well the groups themselves work to solve problems and make decisions will have an impact on your ability to help the organization.

The issues on which clients seek your expert consultation are also ones on which organizational members often have strong and differing views. Consequently, your ability to help groups address these issues depends on your ability to effectively facilitate conversations. To paraphrase one of my clients, who is an expert consultant, "What do I do when I'm talking to the client about what I found and what I recommend, and people start disagreeing with each other in front of me?" When this occurs, you can facilitate the conversation while still being a participant and expert in the content of the discussion. By integrating facilitative skills with your expertise, you increase your value to clients.

The Facilitative Coach Role

In recent years, organizations have increasingly provided coaches for their executives, managers, and even groups and teams. At the heart of the facilitative coaching role is the ability to use a mutual learning mindset and skill set to help people increase their effectiveness by helping them learn to rigorously reflect on their behavior and thinking and to make better choices for themselves. **Rather than simply answer clients' questions, in** *basic facilitative coaching,* **you help clients figure out the answers for themselves. In** *developmental facilitative coaching,* **in addition to helping clients figure out the answers for themselves, you help them learn how to identify and ask these questions for themselves.** Depending on your background, you may bring subject-area expertise to your coaching and include a teaching role as part of your coaching.[1]

As a *group facilitative coach*, you work with more than one person during coaching sessions. Each person is working on his or her particular goals, which may or may not be similar. The purpose of group coaching is essentially the same as individual coaching, whether you're providing basic or developmental facilitation. In either type, group coaching provides the ability for group members to give feedback to and coach each other. This is a particularly important aspect of developmental group coaching.

Although members in a group-coaching group may be from the same work team, the purpose of group coaching is not to work with the participants as a team to improve their team. That is the role of developmental facilitation.

When I coach clients—whether they are facilitative leaders, consultants, facilitators, coaches, or trainers—we explore difficult situations that they face, the outcomes they seek, and what it is about the situation that makes it difficult for them. Using the core values and principles described in this book, I help them think about how the way they are thinking and acting (or have thought and acted) contributes to the outcomes they seek as well as creating negative unintended consequences. Over time, clients develop the ability to do this kind of analysis themselves and produce the outcomes they seek with few unintended consequences.

As a facilitative coach, you jointly design the learning process with the individual instead of assuming that you know how the person can best learn. You also model mutual learning by exploring with the person how your coaching methods are helping or hindering the client's ability to learn. You and the client explore the coaching relationship itself as a source of learning for both the client and you.

Finally, it's helpful to understand how the role of developmental facilitation is similar to the emerging field of team coaching. In recent years, the field of individual coaching has created the field of team coaching. **I consider team coaching to be very similar to developmental facilitation.** As a new field, there is lack of agreement about the definition of team coaching.[2,3] However, writers in the field of team coaching often consider team coaching to be significantly different from facilitation because they compare team coaching to basic facilitation and not developmental facilitation. For example, Clutterbuck defines team coaching as "Helping the team improve performance, and the processes by which performance is achieved, through reflection and dialogue."[4] Hawkins defines systemic team coaching this way: "A process by which a team coach works with a whole team, both when they are together and when they are apart, in order to help them improve both their collective performance and how they work together, and also how they develop their collective leadership to more effectively engage with all their key stakeholder groups to jointly transform the wider business."[5] Both of these authors describe how team coaching differs significantly from facilitation— from what I define as basic facilitation. However, their definitions of team coaching could serve as definitions of developmental facilitation. If you're interested in team coaching, the developmental facilitation role provides a systemic approach for helping teams achieve these goals.

If you want to learn about mutual learning coaching tools and techniques beyond those in this book, read *Facilitative Coaching: A Toolkit for Expanding Your Repertoire and Achieving Lasting Results* (Jossey-Bass, 2009) by Dale Schwarz and Anne Davidson.

The Facilitative Trainer Role

Trainers teach their clients knowledge and skills in a particular content area. One difference between consulting and training is the focus. As a consultant, you focus on solving—or helping the client solve—a specific problem or addressing a specific opportunity that the client is facing. As a trainer, you focus on teaching clients a set of skills and the knowledge that will enable them to solve a type of problem or address a type of opportunity. In practice, good consultants provide informal training in the moment and good trainers design their training so clients practice applying their new knowledge and skills to the real problems or opportunities that led to the training.

As a *facilitative trainer*, you use the mutual learning mindset and skill set to design and deliver the training. You work with the participants to design or customize the training so that it meets their needs. During the training, you regularly ask whether the training is meeting the participants' needs, and if it's not, you're skilled and flexible enough to modify the design in the moment. You also consider the training setting an opportunity for you to learn. You're open to changing your views and invite participants to challenge your assumptions. You use facilitative skills to enhance the interaction and learning among participants.

In recent years, some trainers have changed their title to facilitator or say they are facilitating a course. To the degree that this signals a shift in trainers' recognizing the value of facilitative skills and integrating them into their work, it makes me hopeful. Yet calling trainers facilitators obscures the fact that they are expert in and have responsibility for teaching some particular topic. I use the term *facilitative trainer* to acknowledge both sets of responsibilities and skills.

The Facilitative Mediator Role

According to Christopher Moore,

> Mediation is a conflict resolution process in which a mutually acceptable third party, who has no authority to make binding decisions for disputants, intervenes in a conflict or dispute to assist involved parties to improve their relationships, enhance communications, and use effective problem-solving and negotiation procedures to reach voluntary and mutually acceptable understandings or agreements on contested issues. Specifically, mediation and mediators help disputing parties to (a) open or

improve communications between or among them, (b) establish or build more respectful and productive working relationships, (c) better identify, understand, and consider each other's needs, interests, and concerns, (d) propose and implement more effective problem-solving or negotiation procedures, and (e) recognize or build mutually acceptable agreements."[6]

Facilitation and mediation are similar in several ways. Both involve intervention by a neutral third party who is acceptable to the clients and who has no content decision-making authority. Both seek to help people reach a decision acceptable to all who are involved. Facilitators and mediators use many of the same skills and techniques.

I see several distinctions between facilitation and mediation. Parties seeking a mediator have a conflict they've been unable to resolve, so traditionally the objective of mediation has been to help the parties reach an agreement to a particular conflict, and the mediator becomes involved after the dispute has occurred. Some parties seeking a facilitator may need help addressing a conflict, but conflict isn't the focus of all facilitations. Even when facilitators are helping to address a conflict, they often become involved before an impasse; the group or groups recognize they lack the skills to have a productive conversation on an important, high-conflict topic.

In general, mediation is more similar to basic facilitation than to developmental facilitation; mediators use their skills to help disputants resolve a particular issue, not to teach disputants how to resolve any issues they might encounter. However, an approach called transformative mediation moves beyond standard mediation by focusing not only on seeking a solution to the immediate conflict but also on transforming relationships among the participants.[7]

Having described the differences between classic mediation and facilitation, don't assume every mediator uses the same approach or that a potential client who asks you to mediate is expecting classic mediation. Ask them what they mean by mediation.

If you're a *facilitative mediator*, you apply the mutual learning mindset and skill set to your mediator role. Mediators I have worked with find this a relatively easy transition to make. One part of the transition that some mediators can find challenging is that mutual learning takes a different approach to conveying information between people. Mediators often talk with disputants alone, helping each understand the other disputant's situation and what the other may be willing to settle for. This go-between role (*mediate* comes from a Latin word meaning "to come between") is inconsistent with mutual learning because it shifts accountability for conveying information from the source (the disputants) to the mediator. In mutual learning, everyone is responsible for sharing their own information directly with those who need to hear it. In other words, everyone carries their own water.

The Facilitative Leader Role

Facilitative leaders use the mutual learning mindset and skill set to increase their own effectiveness and to help individuals and groups increase their effectiveness. This includes creating the conditions in which group members can also learn to use the mutual learning approach. **Unlike the other facilitative roles, you're not a third party when you serve as a facilitative leader. You can be a facilitative leader whether you are the formal leader of the group, a group member, or an individual contributor.**

In any case, the facilitative leader role is the most difficult facilitative role to fill because you need to use facilitative skills at the same time you're deeply involved in the content of the conversation and the decision-making process. The more you're involved in the content of a conversation, the more difficult it is to simultaneously pay attention to and help manage the process of the conversation. And the more you're involved in the content and the stronger your views on the content are, the more difficult it is to be curious about others' views and ask others to identify any gaps or problems in your reasoning. My book *Smart Leaders, Smarter Teams* shows how leaders and team members use mutual learning to get better results.

BASIC AND DEVELOPMENTAL TYPES OF ROLES

I divide facilitation, consulting, coaching, and mediation into two types—basic and developmental (Exhibit 2.2). In the basic type, you're giving a person a fish; in the developmental type, you're teaching a person to fish.

	Basic Role	**Developmental Role**
Client Objective	Solve a substantive problem or address an opportunity.	Solve a substantive problem or address an opportunity while developing the mutual learning mindset and skill set to apply to other situations.
Facilitative Role	Help group improve its process; take primary responsibility for managing the group's process.	Help group develop its process skills and mutual learning mindset and skill set; share responsibility for managing the group's process.
Process Outcome for Client	Same dependence on facilitative role for addressing future situations.	Reduced dependence on facilitative role for addressing future situations.

Exhibit 2.2   Basic and Developmental Types of Roles

In *basic facilitation*, **consulting, coaching, and mediation, the group seeks your help to solve problems or address opportunities, such as reducing the time for responding to customers, improving work relationships, or developing a strategy for marketing a new product.** You use your facilitative skills to help the group temporarily improve its process to solve the problem or create the opportunity. After the group solves its problem or creates the opportunity, they have achieved their objective. But the group hasn't learned how to do for itself what you did for it—apply mutual learning to reflect on and improve its process, and get better results. Consequently, if other difficult problems or opportunities arise, the group is likely to require your facilitative skills again.

In *developmental facilitation*, **consulting, coaching, and mediation, the group seeks your help to solve problems or address opportunities *and* to develop its mutual learning mindset and skill set so, in the future, it can identify and address other situations on its own.** In other words, developmental facilitation, consulting, coaching, or mediation enables a group to become self-facilitating, self-consulting, self-coaching, or self-mediating. The developmental form requires a group to reflect on and change its mindset and behavior. In this sense, the developmental form is more systemic and produces deeper learning than the basic form. In practice, helping occurs on a continuum from purely basic to purely developmental, rather than as two discrete or pure types.

But developmental facilitation, consulting, coaching, or mediation isn't worth the investment for every client. It reduces the individual's or group's dependence on you, but it also requires significantly more time and discipline for the individual or group to learn.

For a team, developmental facilitation becomes a better investment when it needs to work closely together over time on challenging, high-stakes issues, in which members have strongly held different views. Developmental facilitation is essential for some groups given their stated identity. For example, a truly self-directed work team must be self-facilitating; an organization that purports to be a learning organization has to have groups that can reflect on their mindset and behavior in a manner consistent with developmental facilitation.

Finally, as challenging as it is to provide skilled basic facilitation, consulting, coaching, or mediation, you need considerably more skill to provide the developmental form. For example, developmental facilitation requires that you think on more levels and dimensions simultaneously and in real time, about what is occurring in the group and how best to help the group. Throughout this book, I continue to describe how you would approach situations differently depending on whether you were using a basic or developmental approach.

SERVING IN MULTIPLE FACILITATIVE ROLES

At times, you may serve in two or more facilitative roles. You may serve in different roles in different settings or need to serve in more than one role in the same meeting. You may be a facilitative leader in your own group, a facilitator or facilitative consultant to other parts of the organization, and a facilitative trainer as well. I recently talked with an internal HR business partner who supports a leadership team by serving as a facilitator, facilitative consultant, facilitative trainer, facilitative coach, and facilitative leader—as a leadership team member and as a project manager with decision-making authority. If you're an external consultant, you may be moving between the roles of facilitative consultant, facilitative trainer, and facilitative coach. Because all six facilitative roles are based on the same mutual learning mindset, by using the Skilled Facilitator approach, you can move seamlessly and with integrity between the roles as necessary.

If, during a meeting, you think it would help the group for you to switch roles and the new role is appropriate for you to play, here are the steps to follow:

1. Identify the new appropriate role you want to switch to.
2. Explicitly describe to the group the facilitative role you want to switch to and explain your reasoning.
3. Seek agreement with the group to fill the new role.
4. Fill the role according to the agreement.
5. When you need to switch roles again, return to step 1.

WHEN IT'S APPROPRIATE TO LEAVE THE ROLE OF FACILITATOR

I've emphasized how important it is to clarify your facilitative role and to act consistently with it. Yet sometimes it's appropriate and helpful to temporarily leave your facilitative role and serve in another one. Leaving the facilitator and facilitative mediator roles is the most challenging because it means giving up content neutrality or other elements of the role that lead groups to see you as objective and trustworthy. This section describes when it's appropriate and beneficial to switch from the facilitator role to another facilitative role, and what risks you face in doing so. If you decide to move from the facilitator role to another facilitative role, remember to use the five-step process above.

Moving to the Facilitative Mediator Role

There are three common situations in which part of the client group is likely to ask you to serve as a mediator, by asking to meet with you alone and/or by asking you to convey information to another group or subgroup: (1) in the beginning of a facilitation, when subgroups have concerns either about working with you as a facilitator or about working with the other subgroups; (2) during a facilitation, when a member or members want information raised in the group or some action taken without it being attributed to them; and (3) in a conflict, when the facilitation breaks down and one or more subgroups are unwilling to continue.

If you serve as a facilitative mediator in these situations, you risk acting inconsistently with at least two mutual learning core values by (1) taking accountability for sharing information for which you're not the source and (2) acting on information that you received outside the group and without being transparent about doing so.

When members share information with you outside of the group conversation, they often want you to use it to intervene in the full group. But because the members often don't want the full group to know that they're the source of the information (or even that it was shared with you), they ask you to share the information for them or else act on their information without explaining that you're doing so. If you explicitly or implicitly agree to this, then you can't explain why you're intervening, and so you're not being transparent and accountable with the group. In addition, if the people who shared the information with you are unwilling to identify themselves in the full group, neither the group nor you can determine whether the information is valid. On the other hand, if you don't share or act on the information given you, the group and you may miss an opportunity to get the group together initially, to get an important issue raised, or to keep the group from completely breaking down.

In these situations, you can temporarily move to a facilitative mediator role without reducing the integrity of your facilitator role, if you meet several conditions. First, try to serve as a facilitative coach, helping one or more members of the group to raise their concerns or questions about the other members in the full group (I illustrate this in the section below on avoiding collusion). This role is still consistent with the facilitator role, as long as you're helping the group members raise their own issues and not raising the issues for them.

You can also meet with subgroups when you're beginning to work with a group and one or more subgroups have a concern about whether you're impartial and sensitive to their needs. Initially, ask the subgroups what makes them reluctant to share this information in the full group, share your reasoning on the advantages of doing so, and ask what would need to happen for them to be willing to do so. If they are not yet willing to share these concerns in the full group, it's reasonable to meet separately with them to hear their concerns. If the concerns are relevant for the other subgroups, help the subgroup members figure out how to share these concerns in the full group, if they are willing.

You also can temporarily act as a facilitative mediator if conflict between subgroups threatens a complete breakdown in communication. I facilitated a union-management cooperative effort in which the seven union members of the union-management committee simultaneously stood up and walked out in the middle of a meeting. The discussion had become tense, and union members were frustrated by what they perceived to be management's efforts to undermine the process. As the facilitator, I saw two choices. I could stay in the room, let the union leave, and see the process unravel, along with the progress the committee had made. Or I could temporarily assume the role of facilitative mediator, talk with the union members, and try to find a way to help union and management members work together again. I chose the latter course. I spent the next six hours mediating in meetings and phone calls. The next morning, the union and management subgroups were back in the room, discussing why the process had broken down and exploring ways to prevent it from recurring.

When you meet with a subgroup, especially if you decide to mediate by conveying information between subgroups, it's essential to state clearly that you will be serving in the facilitative mediator role. Develop a clear agreement with the subgroup about what information, if any, you will share with the other subgroups. Without this agreement, a subgroup can easily feel that you haven't acted neutrally, have violated confidentiality, or have colluded with another subgroup.

Moving to the Facilitative Consultant Role

Earlier in this chapter, I discussed when it's appropriate to serve as a facilitative consultant rather than as a facilitator. But even if you decide to serve as a facilitator, the client may still treat you as a facilitative consultant, asking you questions about subjects in which you have expertise (marketing, performance management systems, finance, and so on).

Sometimes it's appropriate and beneficial to the group for you to share your expertise. When you serve as a content expert, the group can quickly obtain valuable information and reduce the time it takes to make a decision. But there are also risks. The group may start to see you as a *non*-neutral third party, which reduces your credibility and ultimately your effectiveness. A second risk is that the group becomes dependent on you. Group members may grow sensitive to whether you approve of their decisions, which then affects the decisions they make.

In this situation, you can take several steps to reduce the risk that sharing expert information will negatively affect your facilitator role when you return to it. First, act as a content expert only when asked to by the group and only when the group reaches a consensus to do so. This reduces the chances of meeting the needs of only some group members. Second, avoid serving as a content expert in the early stages of working with a group. This reduces the likelihood of the group coming to depend on you in this role.

People who facilitate groups in their own organizations are often asked by group members to play an expert role. In Chapter 15, I discuss how an internal facilitator can offer expert information and facilitate effectively.

The Facilitator as Evaluator

Serving as an evaluator isn't a facilitative role. As a facilitator, you face a role conflict whenever someone in the organization asks you to evaluate the performance of one or more members in the group. For example, a manager who is outside the facilitated group may be concerned about the performance of one of the members. She may ask you to evaluate the member to help her decide whether to take any corrective action. Alternatively, she may be considering promoting one of several members of the group and ask you to evaluate the members to help her make the promotion decision.

You face a potential role conflict in this situation because evaluating group members can jeopardize the members' trust in you. One reason members trust you is that the facilitator has no authority and adheres to the principle that **the facilitator does not use information obtained within facilitation to influence decisions about group members that are made outside facilitation, except with the agreement of the group**. Evaluating group members increases your power in the organization and therefore decreases the likelihood of members discussing openly information that they believe could prove harmful to them.

One way a manager can obtain this information from you in a manner that is consistent with the mutual learning core values is to have the group member about whom the evaluation is being sought agree that you can share your observations with the manager. In this case, you provide specific examples that you observe about the group member's behavior. You share these observations in the presence of the group member—ideally, in the presence of the entire facilitated group—and ask the evaluated group member (and other group members) whether they would have made a different evaluation. Making your information available to all group members, so they can validate or disagree with it, enables the members to make an informed choice about whether you have shared valid information with the manager. This can reduce member concerns about trust to the extent that they are based on concern about your sharing valid information. In the course of your facilitation, if you have shared all relevant information with the group, it's likely that the information that you would share during the evaluation session has already been discussed with group members.

THE GROUP IS YOUR CLIENT

One significant principle of the mutual learning approach as applied to group facilitation is that **the group is your client.** When you choose the group as your client, you're telling your client that your responsibility is to help the group as a whole rather than only the formal team leader, a subset of the group, or even someone outside of the group. This simple choice has many implications. In practice, it means that you offer the group an informed choice about whether to work with you. It means that you don't automatically agree to the group leader's requests (say, to use a certain agenda or process) simply because they come from the group leader.

Facilitators often have concerns about treating the group as their client. The group leader has more authority and often more power than other group members. You may be concerned that if you try to meet group members' needs, you may not be able to fully meet the group leader's needs, and this may alienate the leader and jeopardize your future work with the group or the larger organization. But if you meet the leader's needs at the expense of other group members' needs, you lose your credibility with the group and your ability to facilitate. Viewed in this either-or way, you find yourself in a dilemma; either choice creates problems. The challenge is to recognize that the leader's role in the group is different and still treat the group as your client. I describe how to do this in Chapter 13, on contracting.

WHAT IS YOUR RESPONSIBILITY FOR THE GROUP'S RESULTS?

One challenging part of the facilitator role is deciding what responsibility you have for the group's results. As a basic facilitator, you fulfill your responsibility to the group by using a mutual learning approach to (1) design an effective process with the group to accomplish its work, (2) identify for the group when members have acted inconsistently (or consistently) with principles of effective group behavior, and (3) enable the group to make informed choices on the basis of your interventions. In addition, as a developmental facilitator, you help the group members learn how to (1) identify when they have acted inconsistently with the mutual learning mindset and behaviors, (2) explore the conditions that create this, and (3) change these conditions to generate better results.

Although you're not directly responsible for *what* the group decides, you are responsible for helping the group consider *how* its process affects the results it achieves. If a group is trying to decide what data to use to predict the size of the market for a service, as a facilitator, you don't offer an opinion about which are the best data to use (as a facilitative consultant with expertise in this area, you would offer your view). But you do help the group consider which criteria it uses to make the decision. If members disagree about the best data to use, you help them design a way to test their disagreement.

Given the difference between process and outcomes, some facilitators believe they aren't responsible for the client's results. These facilitators reason that their job is to focus on the group's process; if the client doesn't use this to achieve their results, the facilitators aren't responsible.

Other facilitators believe they are responsible for the client's results. These facilitators reason that they're hired to help the client achieve its objectives and if the client fails, they fail. If you're an internal facilitator, you may have even heard this message directly from managers who ask for your help, saying something like, "I need you to get this team to . . ." These managers finish the sentence by identifying a team outcome for which they have now made you responsible.

The problem with these approaches is that they assume either too little or too much responsibility for the group's results. Consequently, they fail to recognize the four possible relationships between whether the client achieves its results and whether you as the facilitator act effectively: (1) the client achieves its results because of the facilitator's actions, (2) the client achieves its results despite the facilitator's actions, (3) the client doesn't achieve its results despite the facilitator's actions, and (4) the client doesn't achieve its results because of the facilitator's actions.

The Skilled Facilitator approach recognizes all of the four possible relationships. It assumes that if a client achieves its results, you have contributed to this positive outcome only to the extent that you have acted effectively as the facilitator. It also assumes that if a client doesn't achieve its results, you have contributed to this negative outcome only to the extent that you have acted ineffectively as the facilitator. Acting effectively as a facilitator means operating from a mutual learning mindset and appropriately diagnosing and intervening in the group, within your facilitator role. These same assumptions apply if you're a facilitative consultant, facilitative coach, or facilitative trainer.

Here's an example in which you would bear some responsibility for a team's negative outcomes: You're working with a senior leadership team that is deadlocked about whether to release some survey results showing that employees have significant concerns about management. Instead of helping the team understand members' different views to determine the source of the conflict, you reinforce it by having the team list pros and cons for releasing the survey results. (I describe this example in detail in Chapters 4 and 5). You share responsibility for the team's outcomes, to the extent that it makes poor decisions based on your pros and cons process.

If you're wondering why a client may not achieve its goals even if you have facilitated effectively, there can be a couple of reasons. First, the group may make decisions based on incomplete information. As facilitator, you're responsible for helping the group raise and discuss all the relevant information. But if the group doesn't know that it's missing some relevant information and you don't have the content expertise to identify that missing information and ask whether it's relevant, then the group can make low-quality decisions.

Second, even if the group has all the relevant information and you have facilitated the conversation effectively, members can still make what you consider low-quality decisions. Even if you point out flaws in their reasoning process, they may still choose to make decisions based on the flawed reasoning. The group may have different values or assumptions about the situation than you do or consider different needs more important. Watching a group make what you consider a poor decision may be the most difficult part of acting congruent with the mutual learning core values and the facilitator role.

Evaluating Your Performance Independent of the Group's Results

Because the Skilled Facilitator approach distinguishes your facilitative effectiveness from the client's results, you need a method of evaluating your facilitative performance that is objective and independent of the client's results. The Skilled Facilitator approach enables you to do this by comparing your group interventions to specific criteria.

Colluding with the Group

Collusion is cooperation or a secret agreement between parties that affects others negatively. When you collude with a group, you're explicitly or implicitly asked (or you ask others) to act in a particular way but not to reveal that you're doing so, or why. Collusion is inconsistent with any facilitative role. It requires you not to be transparent and to unilaterally place the interests of some group members above the interests of the group as a whole, which prevents the full group from making an informed choice.

You can collude in several ways: (1) with one or more members against one or more other members, (2) with one or more members against a nongroup member, and (3) with a nongroup member against one or more group members. Here are examples of the three forms of collusion:

1. Jack, a group member, approaches you before a meeting. Jack says he wants to raise an issue in the meeting but doesn't want the group to know it's his issue. He's concerned that the issue won't get the attention it deserves if the group thinks he's raising it. Jack asks you to raise the issue "at an appropriate time" but to not tell the group where it originated. You agree.

2. A project team that you're facilitating is about to meet with Erika, the executive who sponsors the project but who isn't a member of the project team. Everyone has agreed that you will facilitate the meeting. The project team members are concerned that Erika is going to get into

too much detail and start doing the team's work. However, team members are concerned about saying this to Erika, so they ask you to subtly bring Erika back to the appropriate level of detail if this happens. You agree.

3. Sven, a manager, tells you that a team that reports to him (and that he isn't a member of) is spending too much time on an issue. Sven is especially concerned that the team is spending time discussing issues that aren't in its charge. He asks you to attend fewer group meetings and, when facilitating, to steer the group away from those issues. You say, "Okay, I'll see what I can do."

Colluding with group members is a solution that creates new problems and often makes the situation worse. In an attempt to help the group, by colluding you act inconsistently with the core values you espouse, reducing your effectiveness and credibility and the group's effectiveness. By shifting the accountability for raising issues from a group member to you, the group misses the opportunity to develop its skills for dealing productively with difficult issues, and you reinforce ineffective group behavior. Over time, you may wonder why the group is overly dependent on you, without realizing how your own actions contributed to the very outcome you set out to avoid.

In any of the situations described previously, you may feel a lot of emotion. You may feel angry if you believe members are asking you to collude with them. You may feel trapped if faced with choosing between meeting the request of a powerful member (who might pay your bill or salary) and acting inconsistently with your role and not helping the group. If members ask you to raise issues for them because they're worried about the consequences if they raise the issue themselves, you may feel sorry for them and want to protect them. In some of these situations, you may be naturally more compassionate than in others. Your challenge is to respond out of compassion when it's not your immediate response—and to do so in a way that doesn't shift member accountability to you because of how you are feeling about yourself or about others. We explore how to do this in Chapters 12 and 13.

Dealing with Collusion

One way to avoid colluding with a group is to discuss the issue as part of your contracting process with the group (Chapter 13). When you discuss the role you will play when helping them, you can describe what you can and can't do within your role, explaining how colluding creates negative consequences for the group and you. You can give examples of requests that you can't fulfill because they would lead to collusion.

If you receive a request that requires you to collude with the group, you can explain again how accepting the request would create negative consequences.

You can then ask the individual if he sees the situation differently. In this way, you can work with the person making the request to find a way for him to raise the issue directly with the relevant individuals. You might begin by saying, "I think it's important that the group hear your concern, and I think it's appropriate for you to raise it with the group because it's your concern. People may have questions that only you have the answers to. In addition, if I raise the issue in my role as facilitator, people may think I'm steering the conversation and acting outside my role, which can reduce the group's trust in me and make it harder for me to help the group. I can't raise the issue for you. But as soon as you raise it, I'll actively facilitate to help you and the other group members have as productive a conversation as possible. What do you think about what I'm saying?"

SUMMARY

In this chapter, I have described six facilitative roles in which you can use the mutual learning approach: facilitator, facilitative consultant, facilitative coach, facilitative trainer, facilitative mediator, and facilitative leader. The role you choose depends on the type of help the group needs. When the group needs multiple kinds of help, you may find yourself moving between one or more of the facilitative roles. You can implement most of the roles in either a basic or developmental form. In the basic form, you use your skills to help the group learn and/or solve one or more problems, or pursue an opportunity. In the developmental form, in addition to helping the group learn and/or solve one or more problems or pursue an opportunity, the group also learns how to do for itself what you are helping the group do. Central to all of the facilitative roles is the principle that the group is your client rather than the leader of the group, some subset of the group, or even a sponsor outside the group. Although temporarily leaving your role of facilitator is appropriate at times, it may also jeopardize the group's and your ability to act consistently with the mutual learning core values and reduce your ability to help the group. Finally, when a group's topic is improving its group process, you are not content neutral, even if you're serving as a facilitator. In all of the facilitative roles, you model and serve as an advocate for effective process using mutual learning.

In the next chapter, I will explain that how you think is how you facilitate—or consult, coach, or train. I will then explain how you undermine your ability to help groups when you operate from a unilateral control mindset.

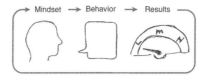

CHAPTER THREE

How You Think Is How You Facilitate

*How Unilateral Control Undermines
Your Ability to Help Groups*

T his chapter and the next one are about the most fundamental part of your facilitative role your mindset. I contrast two mindsets and the approaches they create—unilateral control and mutual learning. In short, the unilateral control mindset undermines your effectiveness and the mutual learning mindset increases it.

In this chapter, I focus on unilateral control. I describe the values and assumptions that constitute the unilateral control mindset, the behaviors that inevitably flow from them, and the poor results you get. Altogether, I refer to the mindset, behavior, and results as the unilateral control approach.

In this chapter, we focus on how *you* are less effective when you use the unilateral control approach, *not* how the group you're working with is less effective when it uses the unilateral control approach. Of course, when you're ineffective, the group you're helping suffers too. Still, keep in mind that the unilateral control approach that undermines your effectiveness is the same approach that undermines the effectiveness of groups you're trying to help. For a detailed description of how the unilateral control approach applies to teams, see my book *Smart Leaders, Smarter Teams*. When you help groups become aware of their unilateral control mindset and shift to the mutual learning mindset,

---

Parts of this chapter are adapted from Chapter 2 in *Smart Leaders, Smarter Teams*.

you're helping the group transform itself. But before you can help groups get unstuck from their unilateral control approach, you need to work on yours.

HOW YOU THINK: YOUR MINDSET AS AN OPERATING SYSTEM

At the heart of this book is the premise that how you think is how you facilitate—or consult, coach, train, and mediate. Everything you do starts with your mindset. Your mindset is the way of seeing that shapes your thoughts, feelings, and behaviors. **Your *mindset* is the core set of values and assumptions that drives your behavior.** Your mindset is what ultimately shapes the results you get for yourself and the groups you're trying to help.

Your mindset is like a computer operating system. Every computer needs one to run, whether it's a desktop, laptop, tablet, or smartphone. A computer operating system—whether it's Windows, Macintosh, or another kind—organizes and controls your computer's hardware and software so that the computer acts in a flexible but predictable way. Without an operating system, your computer is useless.

In a similar way, you use your mindset to act and get results. Your mindset controls the decisions you make, the statements you make, and the questions you ask. Like any good operating system, your mindset enables you to take action quickly, effortlessly, and skillfully. It does this by using your core values and assumptions to design your behavior. It uses principles such as, "When I am in situation X and Y happens, I should say or do Z." For example, "If I'm facilitating a group and one member is talking too much, I should intervene to equal out the participation." Like any computer operating system, your mindset works very quickly so you can assess the situation and make split-second decisions without having to take time to think about them.

Just as you rarely think about your computer's operating system—unless there's a problem—you're also usually unaware of your mindset. When you're intervening to stop a group member from participating too much, you're not aware that you may be thinking, *This guy doesn't get it. He doesn't see how he's dominating the conversation.* You just respond, seemingly without thinking. The fact that your mindset operates out of your awareness is a good thing—until your mindset becomes the cause of problems.

To continue the computer analogy, if your mindset is like an operating system, then your behavior is like application software, which helps you accomplish a specific task. Think of the different types of applications on your computer, for example, Microsoft Office, Google Search, or iTunes.

But how well a software application works depends on the version of the operating system you're running. You know this if you've ever tried to run a new software program, like a video game, only to discover that your operating system doesn't support it. If you're trying to run the most current version of iTunes or your favorite video game and you're using the current version of your operating system, your application will probably operate fine. But try to run a new program on an out-of-date operating system like Windows 95, and you'll be out of luck.

It's the same with your mindset and behavior. **If you want to adapt new behaviors, your mindset needs to be congruent with those behaviors.** If your mindset doesn't support the new behaviors, ultimately your mindset will trump your behavior and you won't be able to get the results or sustain the change you want.

TWO MINDSETS: UNILATERAL CONTROL AND MUTUAL LEARNING

Throughout this book, I describe two basic mindsets: unilateral control, which undermines your effectiveness, and mutual learning, which enhances it. If you facilitate from a unilateral control mindset, you'll contribute to the ineffectiveness of the groups you're trying to help, you'll undermine your relationship with them, and your well-being will suffer. If you facilitate from a mutual learning mindset, you'll help groups get better results, you'll develop stronger relationships with the group, and your well-being will improve.

Working from a mutual learning mindset is harder than it looks. When you find yourself in challenging situations, the research shows that 98 percent of us use the ineffective unilateral control mindset.[1] Challenging situations are ones in which the stakes are high, you have strong views and strong feelings, or you feel psychologically threatened, frustrated, or potentially embarrassed. In your facilitative role, there are many common and challenging situations that can lead you to operate from the unilateral control mindset. You may be working with a very important client group, working with a group for the first time, or believe that you're responsible for ensuring that the group achieves its goals. You may find yourself disagreeing with clients about how best to help their group. You may find yourself caught between what the group leader wants you to do and what other group members want you to do. Inevitably, you'll work with groups or group members who push your hot buttons. All of these situations are likely to activate your unilateral control mindset.

HOW YOU THINK IS NOT HOW YOU THINK YOU THINK

A second factor that makes it difficult to operate from a mutual learning mindset is your lack of awareness about your mindset. Research in psychology and economics often finds that we don't accurately describe how we make decisions to take action.[2] We say we're using one set of values and assumptions to guide our behavior, but when psychologists dig deeper, they find we're using a different set. It's not simply that we have a set of values and assumptions that we are aware of but don't tell others about; it's that we ourselves are unaware of the values and assumptions that are driving our behavior.[3]

If you aren't aware of the values and assumptions that guide your behavior, you can't identify when you're acting inconsistently with the values and assumptions you want to follow. This makes it very difficult to change your mindset. Fortunately, others can often see you being inconsistent with the mindset you're espousing and help you become aware of what's going on.

In my experience, the mindset that facilitators say they are operating from reads like a good group-process textbook. They often espouse the need for group members to operate from a common pool of information, to understand and appreciate different perspectives, and use a decision-making process that can generate commitment to a group decision. In addition, they often espouse that the team itself has the right answers. Yet, after analyzing thousands of cases in which facilitators faced challenging situations, almost all operated from a mindset at odds with the one they espoused and believed they were using.

THE CIO TEAM SURVEY FEEDBACK CASE

To see how the way we think is the way we facilitate, consider a real case. Barbara (she has chosen this pseudonym) is a member of an external consulting group helping a new chief information officer (CIO) and his leadership team address long-standing management and performance problems in his office. The CIO had asked Barbara's consulting group to conduct interviews and focus groups to generate data regarding the issue. In the meeting described below, the consulting group is presenting its findings. One of the group's main findings was that employees were waiting to see if the new CIO's team would release the results of the interviews and focus groups. Because of conflict within the CIO's team, Barbara expected that this would be a difficult conversation for the CIO team. As a member of the consulting group, she facilitated the meeting of the CIO and his team. (When Barbara assumed the role of facilitator, she created a role conflict problem for herself and the CIO team—a problem I described in Chapter 2.)

In this case, which Barbara wrote about as a participant in one of my workshops, she said her goals were "to allow the group to discuss whether to share the findings without the discussion degenerating into out-and-out warfare, and to guide the group to what we saw as the right decisions without appearing to take sides ourselves."

Exhibit 3.1 reproduces the conversation Barbara had with the CIO (Frank) and his leadership team. It includes two columns. In the right-hand column is a

Barbara's Thoughts and Feelings	The Conversation
Uh oh, this wasn't supposed to happen until this afternoon. I never thought they'd bring it up themselves! There goes the whole agenda.	MIKE: My God, we can't possibly let this stuff out of this room. It's dynamite. We'll look like idiots. I for one don't want to have anything to do with it!
Looks like it's going to get ugly real fast. This guy Joe just doesn't get it!	JOE: This just goes to show why we can never get the work done around here. The people are more interested in sitting on their butts and blaming their managers than in actually doing their jobs.
	SANDY: Well, wait a minute; these results are so striking I don't see how we can ignore them . . .
He's gonna be real trouble. If he doesn't have a stroke first, with those veins popping out. . . Time to do something so Sandy can get some support if there is any. Why isn't Frank saying something?	JOE: We don't have to let them make our decisions for us, though! (Continues with a lengthy diatribe about why people today don't have the same values and work ethic they used to.)
	BARBARA: Okay, let's do a process check here. I think this an important conversation for you all to have, but it might take some time. You can do it now, or wait until we work on the action plan this afternoon. What's the sense of the group?
	SUSAN: Let's get it out there now! (Some expressions of agreement around the table.)
Finally! Why'd he wait until now to speak up? Some leadership style!	FRANK: I think we need to take the time to do this now. It's pretty important.
This ought to flush everyone out up front so I know what we're dealing with here. I need to get this thing back under control.	BARBARA: Okay, then. Here's what I propose: let's go around the table and ask everyone for their views before we get into the discussion.
I wonder if I should have set a time limit for each person. This is turning into a debate, and no one is really listening to each other.	(The group does that, but it takes a lot longer than expected, and some people really hog the floor, on both sides.)
This ought to get some structure into the conversation and maybe tone down some of the emotional content.	BARBARA: Now that we have a sense of where you are as a group on this issue—and you're about one-third for release and two-thirds against—it's a good time to step back and look together at the pros and cons. I'll divide a flipchart into two columns, and you can brainstorm on that. Here goes . . .

Exhibit 3.1   Unilateral Control Approach: The Survey Feedback Case

Barbara's Thoughts and Feelings	The Conversation
No one is listening to anyone else; they're just hardening their positions. The clock is ticking, and the group really hasn't started its work yet. I wonder how much longer I should let them go? But if they can't even deal with this issue, how are they going to do any of the hard work down the road?	(The group charts the pros and cons, and although the discussion becomes more orderly, it is no less heated and no closer to a conclusion.)
Oh no, now they're going to move in for the kill against her. I don't want to break my neutral stance, but she's going to need some help here soon.	SANDY (near tears): I just can't believe we're even having this discussion! Who are we kidding? The employees already know what they think—who would we be hiding it from? If this group can't face up to the truth, what right do we have to be in our jobs? (Eye-rolling from Joe.) Frank, don't you agree?
This guy is absolutely hopeless!	FRANK: Well, I think you have a real point there, but . . .
Well, I guess this is my opening. Should I tell them what I really think? I might lose them all if I do.	MIKE: I'd like to hear from the consultants what they think. After all, they work with a lot of other organizations. What do other people do about things like this?
	BARBARA: Thanks, Mike. I have to say that you all are not the first to face this issue, and it's always tough. But Sandy is on to something: Your people know what they think, but they don't think you do. They want to know that they've been heard, and because there's so little trust here, they want more than just your assurances on that. By responding to their request to release the results, you'd be sending them a big signal that you really mean business about changing the culture. They're handing you a big opportunity. And in our experience with other groups, you need to make a clear gesture up front to get people's attention if you want to move ahead with change.
Oh, that's great. He obviously thinks I'm an idiot and doesn't want to release the stuff.	FRANK: How about a break now? I'd like us to mull this question over and revisit it this afternoon.

Exhibit 3.1   Unilateral Control Approach: The Survey Feedback Case (*continued*)

difficult part of the verbatim conversation that Barbara had with the team, as best she recalled it. In the left-hand column are Barbara's thoughts and feelings—her internal conversation—that she experienced during the conversation, whether or not she expressed them. As you read the case, notice how Barbara is thinking and feeling about the situation and how she chooses to act as a result.

Barbara's Contribution to the Team's Problems

What may be difficult to see at first reading is that Barbara contributes to the very problems she is privately complaining about. When Barbara wrote up her case, she didn't realize she was doing this. Even with the best of intentions, she was undermining her own effectiveness by operating from a unilateral control mindset. Barbara is typical of almost all the facilitators, consultants, coaches, and trainers I've worked with and taught: When they find themselves in a situation that they consider frustrating, threatening, or embarrassing in some way, they operate from a unilateral control mindset.

How do you undermine the very results that you say you're trying to create? To answer this question, I'll analyze Barbara's case through the lens of the unilateral control approach. I'll start with the mindset, then the behaviors it generates, and the results those behaviors produce.

THE UNILATERAL CONTROL APPROACH

The unilateral control approach has three parts: (1) mindset, (2) behaviors, and (3) results (see Figure 3.1). When you use the unilateral control approach,[4] you try to achieve your goals by unilaterally controlling the situation: You try to get others to do what you want them to do without being influenced by them. **When you apply a unilateral control mindset to working with people who see things differently from you, your essential perspective is:**

- **I understand the situation; you don't.**
- **I'm right; you're wrong.**
- **I will win.**

VALUES OF THE UNILATERAL CONTROL MINDSET

The unilateral control mindset comprises a set of core values and assumptions, summarized in Figure 3.2. Core *values* are end-states we think are worth striving

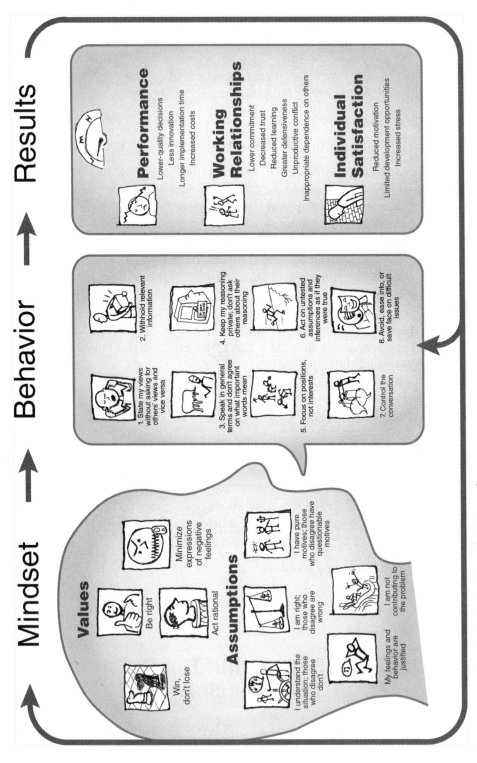

Figure 3.1 The Unilateral Control Approach

Mindset

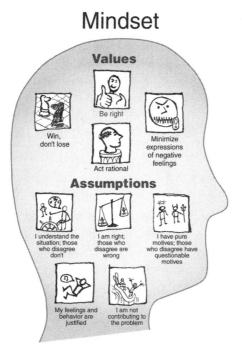

Figure 3.2   **Core Values and Assumptions of the Unilateral Control Mindset**

for. *Core assumptions* are fundamental beliefs we hold. This section expands on the values; the next will discuss the assumptions.

When you use a unilateral control mindset, you mix these values to differing degrees and unconsciously design your behavior based on them.

Win, Don't Lose

Having goals can make you more effective. But when you operate from the unilateral control mindset, achieving your goals as you have defined them becomes an end in itself. You frame the situation as a contest in which there are winners and losers; therefore, you must be one of the winners. When you watch or listen to others, you privately assess whether they're helping you achieve your goal or hindering you. You consider things that others say or do that don't support your view as getting in your way. You consider it a sign of weakness either to change your goals or not achieve them as you originally envisaged them.

In Barbara's case, she stated that one of her goals was "to guide the group to what we [the consulting team] saw as the right decisions without appearing to take sides ourselves." She frames the meeting outcome in win/lose terms; if the CIO group adopts the solution that her consulting team has already developed, Barbara's team wins. If not, Barbara's team loses.

Be Right

Being right is a corollary of "Win, Don't Lose." When you value being right, you take pride in showing others that your views are accurate. If you have ever taken satisfaction in thinking or saying to someone, "I told you so" or "I knew this would happen," you know what it feels like to value being right.

Barbara's goal, "to guide the group to what we saw as the right decisions without appearing to take sides ourselves," explicitly emphasizes this need to be right.

Minimize Expression of Negative Feelings

Minimizing expression of negative feelings means keeping unpleasant feelings—yours and everyone else's—out of the conversation. This value stems from a belief that expressing anger or frustration—or allowing others to express them—for instance, are incompetent behaviors. Expressing negative feelings may be seen as a sign of weakness or may hurt someone's feelings, both of which may make it difficult for you to accomplish your goals. In the unilateral control approach, raising negative feelings can lead to things getting out of control. In short, you believe that little good can come of people airing their feelings on a topic; it only leads to tension, wounded sensibilities, and strained working relationships.

Barbara hints at this value when she describes her strategy as allowing "the team to discuss whether to share the findings without the discussion generating into out-and-out warfare." Preventing "out-and-out warfare" is a laudable goal. By itself, it doesn't mean Barbara wants to avoid the expression of negative feelings. However, when the CIO group starts to share its negative feelings about whether to release the findings, Barbara suggests a pros and cons approach, partly to tone down the emotional content, rather than to better understand what leads the group members to feel strongly about their views.

Act Rational

When you value acting rationally, you expect yourself and others to remain purely analytical and logical. You believe that if you simply lay out the facts, others, if they're being reasonable, will agree with you. You try to present issues as being purely objective, regardless of how you or others are feeling about them. You consider feelings as a barrier to good problem solving and decision making instead of as another source of important information. The more you value acting rational, the more you want to be seen as having thoroughly thought through the matter at hand. When you discover gaps in your thinking, you try to prevent others from recognizing those gaps.

ASSUMPTIONS OF THE UNILATERAL CONTROL MINDSET

Figure 3.2 also summarizes the assumptions you make in the mindset of unilateral control.

I Understand the Situation; Those Who Disagree Don't

This assumption states that whatever information and understanding you bring to the situation is accurate and complete, and so are the conclusions you draw from them. In other words, the way you see things is the way things really are. If others hold different views, they just don't get it, are confused, misinformed, or simply clueless. If they understood what you understand, they would agree with you.

Barbara operates from this assumption explicitly when she thinks, *This guy Joe just doesn't get it!* She operates from this assumption implicitly when she thinks, *Why'd he [Frank] wait until now to speak up? Some leadership style!* and *This guy is absolutely hopeless!* Embedded in these thoughts are Barbara's assumptions that she understands what leadership looks like in this situation, that she fully understands what Frank is doing as a leader in this meeting, and that it doesn't measure up to effective leadership. If he really understood what leadership was, he would advocate releasing the findings.

I Am Right; Those Who Disagree Are Wrong

This assumption is an extension of the previous one. Here you assume that situations come with right and wrong answers and that your answer is, of course, the right one. People who disagree with you or see it differently are simply wrong. When you hold this assumption, it's not possible that you and the people with whom you are disagreeing can both be right.

Barbara doesn't consider that how she is making sense of the situation is based on less than a full understanding and therefore she may not be entirely right.

My Motives Are Pure; Those Who Disagree Have Questionable Motives

You consider yourself to be an earnest seeker of truth, acting in the best interests of the group and organization. At the same time, you question the motives of those who disagree with you. You assume they may be motivated by self-interest or some other inappropriate concern. Maybe they're trying to increase their power, control more resources, or even undermine your efforts.

Barbara seems to be operating from this assumption when Joe is speaking about how people today have different values and work ethics than they used to have, and she thinks, *He's gonna be real trouble.*

My Feelings and Behaviors Are Justified

Because others don't understand the situation as it really is (meaning, as you see it), because others are wrong, and because others may have questionable motives, you consider your feelings and behaviors justified. If you're annoyed or frustrated, if you need to act in a manner that is inconsistent with your values, or if you need to depart from your role, it's all justified. Although you may have preferred not to do these things, others' behaviors have left you no choice.

Barbara operates from this assumption when she thinks, *I don't want to break my neutral stance, but she's [Sandy's] going to need some help here soon.*

I Am Not Contributing to the Problem

In the unilateral control mindset, you see your feelings and the behaviors that result from them as the natural and inevitable results of others' actions toward you. You don't consider the possibility that you're contributing to the very problems you're privately complaining about. It doesn't occur to you that your thoughts and feelings may lead you to act ineffectively. In your view, all interactions go like this: Others do things that are ineffective, and you respond to their mistakes accordingly and appropriately. As a result, you see others as needing to change, not you. The only sense in which you may see yourself needing to change is that you may need to develop new ways to get others to change their ineffective behaviors.

In Barbara's case, she comes close to considering that she may have contributed to the problem when the group is listing pros and cons and she thinks, *No one is listening to anyone else; they're just hardening their positions. I wonder if I should have set a time limit for each person*, and later when she thinks, *I wonder how much longer I should let them go on?* But she stops considering her contribution to the problem when she thinks, *But if they can't even deal with this issue, how are they going to do any of the hard work down the road?* Barbara doesn't consider that people aren't listening to each other and hardening their positions as a result of her process for listing pros and cons. (I'll address the problem of pros and cons in Chapter 11.)

UNILATERAL CONTROL BEHAVIORS

You use the above mindset—the core values and assumptions—to design your behavior. When you work with a group and assume that you understand and are right and that those who disagree with you don't understand and are wrong, you think you need to convince others. Figure 3.3 shows eight behaviors you use to do that. Here is a brief description of each behavior and their results.

Behavior

Figure 3.3   Behaviors That Arise from the Unilateral Control Mindset

1. **State views without asking for others' views or vice versa.** With this behavior, you either state your views without asking others what they think or you ask others questions without sharing your view. As a result, you and the group end up talking past each other and you don't reach genuine agreements. When you ask questions that aren't genuine, you often "ease in," indirectly conveying your point of view. Easing in involves asking others questions or making statements that are designed to lead others to figure out what you're privately thinking without your having to say it. It's an indirect approach to get others to see things your way.

   Barbara does state her view and ask a genuine question when she says "let's do a process check." But she gets answers only from Sandy and Frank—both of whom agree with her privately held view—before assuming that everyone is in agreement. When Barbara proposes that the team list pros and cons, she doesn't ask team members' reactions before moving ahead.

2. **Withhold relevant information.** Because winning is paramount, you share the information that will advance your views and withhold relevant information that won't. Barbara withholds her private thinking that the conversation has turned into a debate and that people aren't listening to each other. By withholding that information, she misses the opportunity to learn whether CIO team members are seeing the same thing and, if so, to change it. But because Barbara is operating from the value of being right, sharing that information leaves open the possibility that others will disagree with her.

3. **Speak in general terms and don't agree on what important words mean.** When you make general statements like "I think it would be good to hear from some people who haven't spoken as much," the group doesn't know exactly which people you're talking about. As a result, some members whom you believe have been talking too much may speak up, believing that they weren't speaking much. Facilitators, consultants, and trainers often speak in general terms because they're concerned that by naming individuals, they may create defensive reactions.

4. **Keep my reasoning private; don't ask others about their reasoning.** You don't explain why you're saying what you're saying and asking what you're asking. Sharing your reasoning would make you vulnerable to people challenging your thinking, which could reduce the chance that your view would prevail. Asking others about their reasoning might surface information that's at odds with your views and

increases the chance that they'll ask you to explain your views, both of which decrease the chance that you'll win.

Throughout the case, Barbara fails to share her reasoning and intent: She is trying to guide the CIO team to the decision that her consulting group thinks is the right one without appearing to be doing so. Of course, Barbara can't share this intent because if she did, she would reveal the very strategy she is trying to keep private. Many facilitators and consultants do the same thing. It's a major part of unilateral control, and it creates significant problems for you and the groups you're trying to help.

5. **Focus on positions, not interests.** By focusing on a particular solution instead of the underlying needs you're trying to address, you and the group dig into your positions and fail to craft solutions that meet group members' needs and generate broad commitment.

Barbara focuses on the position of releasing the findings and attempts to get the CIO team to adopt her solution. She also encourages the CIO team to focus on positions rather than interests by having the team identify pros and cons.

6. **Act on untested assumptions and inferences as if they were true.** Because you assume that you understand the situation and are right, there's no need to test any assumptions or inferences you're making. As a result, when your assumptions or inferences turn out to be wrong, you make poor decisions.

Barbara assumes that Sandy needs support for her position (which is the same as Barbara's position) when Barbara thinks, *Time to do something so Sandy can get some support if there is any* and when Sandy is near tears and Barbara thinks, *Oh no, now they're going to move in for the kill against her.* In neither case does she ask Sandy whether she needs support. Barbara also makes negative inferences about Joe when she thinks, *This guy Joe just doesn't get it* and *He's gonna be real trouble,* and about Frank when she thinks, *Some leadership style* and *This guy is absolutely hopeless.* Finally, she makes untested inferences when she thinks about Frank, *He obviously thinks I'm an idiot and doesn't want to release the stuff.*

7. **Control the conversation.** To ensure that you win, you make sure that the conversation moves in the direction you think it should move. You make sure that people talk about topics that you consider relevant and that further your point of view. When people don't stay on topic—as you define "on topic"—you find ways to bring them back on topic. As a result, the group you're helping doesn't get all the relevant information on the table.

Barbara subtly controls the conversation by deciding that the group should talk about the issue after hearing only Susan's and Frank's view on this, even though she asked "What's the sense of the team?" She does the same thing when she answers Mike's question, "What do other people do about things like this?" even as she thinks she might lose the team if she answers the question and breaks her neutrality.

8. **Avoid, ease into, or save face on difficult issues.** Because you want to minimize the expression of negative feelings, you don't address issues that could make the group or you uncomfortable. As a result, you don't help the group get to the root cause of issues, and the issues continue to reduce the group's and your effectiveness.

Barbara has created an undiscussable issue with the group. She believes that the group should release the findings, and she also believes that she can't say this because she is supposed to be a neutral facilitator in this meeting.

RESULTS OF UNILATERAL CONTROL

Mindset leads to behaviors, and those behaviors produce results. The unilateral control approach identifies three types of results: (1) performance, (2) working relationships, and (3) individual well-being. Unfortunately, the results you get from unilateral control are the very ones you've been trying hard to avoid. Instead of achieving high performance, you get lackluster performance. Instead of getting improved working relationships, you get strained relationships. Instead of developing well-being, you create stress for yourselves and others. Figure 3.4 summarizes these results.

Lackluster Performance

You're trying to perform well so you can better help the groups you're working with to perform well. But if you're operating with the unilateral control mindset and behaviors, you undermine your own performance.

Lower-Quality Decisions and Less Innovation. The quality of the decisions you make in your facilitative role affect how well you help groups. Even though facilitators don't offer their views on the content of a group's decisions, facilitators are continually and deeply involved in making decisions with the group about how the group and the facilitator move through the process they're engaged in. If you're a consultant providing some kind of subject matter expertise, you are also deeply involved in the content of a group's decisions.

Results

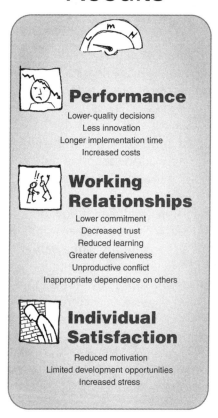

Figure 3.4   Results of Behaviors for a Unilateral Control Mindset

To make high-quality decisions, you need relevant information and an accurate understanding of the situation that you and the group face. This includes understanding the different group member needs that have to be met so that you can intervene in a way that meets those needs. This requires that you be transparent with clients about what you're observing in the group and why you're making your interventions. You also need to be curious about what they're thinking, including testing inferences that you make about the group. Unfortunately, none of this is possible if you're operating from a unilateral control approach. As a result, your decisions will be compromised by inadequate information and untested inferences.

Innovation requires creating something new, original, or creative. To innovate in the course of facilitation, you need to become aware of and challenge the assumptions that have constrained your previous interventions. But if you operate from a unilateral control mindset, you'll have difficulty identifying, let alone challenging, your own assumptions. Being open to group members' ideas and concerns will also increase your ability to facilitate innovatively. However, if you're operating from the assumption, "I understand, they don't," you'll miss these opportunities.

Longer Implementation Time.   When you seek to minimize the expression of negative feelings and avoid undiscussable issues, you may help groups reach a decision faster, but you also contribute to extending the time it takes the group to effectively implement its decision. The issues that aren't addressed before the group makes a decision will rear their heads during implementation and slow the implementation process until they are resolved. Group members whose needs haven't been adequately addressed may not actively support the implementation or may even block it after the meeting.

Increased Costs.   Poor decisions, reduced innovation, and longer implementation time often lead to increased costs. Longer implementation time increases costs as the group spends extra time revisiting earlier "agreements." If you're working with the group through the implementation process, the group is also paying for your fees (directly or indirectly) for a longer time than necessary.

In Barbara's case, her own value about winning and her assumption that her position was right led to a pros and cons process in which she focused the CIO team on positions. The team members dug into their positions, each arguing for his or her own view, which prolonged the decision-making process unnecessarily and reduced the team's ability to think innovatively about how to address its challenge.

Strained Working Relationships

Working relationships is the second type of results that suffer from a unilateral control approach. It decreases commitment, reduces team learning, and also promotes inappropriate dependence on others.

Lower Commitment.   People commit to decisions when they believe the decision will address their needs. Unilateral control undermines commitment by reducing the chance of meeting people's needs—including your own. You and the group focus on positions rather than on the interests underlying these positions. This leads to decisions in which you and the group are choosing between competing solutions, rather than crafting solutions that are likely to address all the identified interests. To the extent that the solution doesn't meet someone's interests, that person is likely to be less committed to the decision.

If you reach a decision with a group that doesn't meet the group members' needs, you're likely to find yourself monitoring group members to make sure they follow through on their commitment. It may be as small an issue as feeling you need to round up group members when they don't return on time from breaks or as large an issue as group members going through the motions of working with you because they have not genuinely committed to the process.

By focusing the CIO team on pros and cons, Barbara increased the chance that the team would limit its thinking to only two opposing solutions and increased the chance that some team members would not be committed to the decision.

Decreased Trust. If group members don't trust you, you simply cannot facilitate effectively. If any group member believes that you're partial to certain group members, that you're not understanding group members, that your interventions aren't helpful, or that your actions are inconsistent with the role you agreed to play, you may lose that member's trust. Operating from unilateral control increases this probability because you act on untested assumptions you make about the group and don't explain the reasoning and intent for your interventions.

Unilateral control can also lead you to distrust group members, which, in turn, can lead group members to distrust you. To the extent that you make negative attributions of group members' motives and don't test them, you generate your own mistrust of others.

By leaving her facilitator role without an agreement to do so, to share her views on whether the group should release the findings, Barbara risks losing the team's trust. She does this even as she wonders whether she will *"lose them all"* if she shares her view. Had Barbara been serving in a consultant role during the meeting, it would have been appropriate to share her views, but it is not appropriate as a content-neutral facilitator.

Reduced Learning, Greater Defensiveness, and Unproductive Conflict. To increase your effectiveness, you need to be able to learn with and from the group you're helping. This includes learning in the moment so that you can quickly modify your approach and meet the group's needs. Unfortunately, the unilateral control mindset undermines learning. When you assume you understand and are right and that group members who see things differently don't get it and are wrong, you have little interest in learning from them. Instead, you treat your own assumptions and inferences as facts, which adds to misunderstanding. Because you see your feelings and behaviors as justified and not contributing to the difficulty, you blame others for your mistakes and defensiveness.

Barbara's lack of curiosity about Joe's view, which she privately disagreed with, and her inferences about his being real trouble, prevented her and the team from learning more about Joe's concerns.

Similarly, the untested inferences and attributions that you make lead you to react defensively. When you tell yourself a negative story about what someone is doing and why they're doing it, it's easy to create your own defensiveness. You can see the beginning of a defensive reaction at the end of Barbara's case when Frank calls for a break and Barbara thinks, *He obviously thinks I'm an idiot and doesn't want to release the stuff.*

People get into conflicts when they pursue actions or solutions that are incompatible. If you operate from a unilateral control mindset, you see conflict as something to win rather than a puzzle to solve together. If you don't engage in conflict productively, you avoid it, smooth over it, or end up in battles. If you address the conflict at all, you end up with stalemates, escalating conflict, or compromises in which everyone is dissatisfied, and "losers" disengage or seek to even the score.

Barbara's pros and cons suggestion that led to a lower-quality decision and less learning also structured the conversation so that it created unproductive conflict for the team. It ensured that the conflict would escalate by asking people to frame the discussion in either/or, win-lose terms.

Inappropriate Dependence on Others. When you help a group, they are dependent on you. You have some expertise they need to become more effective. The challenge is to help groups in a way that doesn't create any more dependence on you than necessary. Ideally, as in developmental facilitation, your goal is to leave the group with greater capacity and less dependence on you. This means that group members manage their working relationships directly with each other, rather than depend on you to serve as an intermediary. When you operate from a unilateral control approach, you're less concerned about reducing dependency and more concerned about having your point of view prevail.

When Barbara moves to support Sandy's view, believing that Sandy cannot support herself in the group, Barbara subtly creates unnecessary dependence on herself. The belief that others need our help and can't be effective without our intervention stems from the unilateral control assumption that we understand the situation and the value of minimizing expression of negative feelings. In other words, we often believe that our job is to prevent group members from feeling hurt by others, rather than helping group members learn how to respond effectively to others' ineffective behavior.

Less Individual Well-Being

The third type of result is well-being, which includes a sense of satisfaction, motivation, and a lower level of stress. The unilateral control approach also reduces your well-being. Because unilateral control often leads to strained working relationships with the groups you're trying to help, the work can be less than satisfying and sometimes demotivating. It can be stressful to realize that if you share what you're thinking, you may create negative consequences. It's stressful if you make untested inferences and attributions about others that lead you and others to become defensive. Barbara shows a glimpse of this reduced well-being when she makes the untested inference that Frank thinks she is an idiot.

GIVE-UP-CONTROL APPROACH

There is another form of unilateral control that people use, called *give up control*. Sometimes people use the give-up-control approach when they recognize the poor results they get from using the unilateral control approach. Unfortunately, they are simply shifting from one form of control to another.[5]

The core values of the *give-up-control approach* are (1) everyone participates in defining the purpose, (2) everyone wins and no one loses, (3) express your feelings, and (4) suppress using your intellectual reasoning.[6] An assumption in the give-up-control approach that differs from the unilateral control approach is that in order for people to learn and be involved and committed, they must come to the right answer by themselves. Of course, the right answer is the one you have already come up with. When others don't see the answer that you see, you ask easing-in or leading questions to help them get the answer by themselves. This is the strategy that Barbara was using when she wrote that the goal of her meeting was "to guide the group to what we saw as the right decisions without appearing to take sides ourselves." The results of the give-up-control approach are the same as those of the unilateral control approach: poor performance, strained working relationships, and reduced well-being.

The easing-in strategy of the give-up-control approach is often part of the unilateral control approach. I think of the give-up-control approach as a subset or variation of the basic unilateral control approach.

Facilitators and consultants often move back and forth between the unilateral control approach and the give-up-control variation. If you're working with a group and get frustrated with the group's repeated inability to stay on track, you may intervene in a unilaterally controlling manner to get them back on track. If this approach doesn't keep the group on track, you may switch to a give-up-control approach and think to yourself, *They seem not to want my help. I'll just let the group continue to get off track. Eventually, they'll get frustrated with their lack of progress and figure out something's wrong.*

In the unilateral control approach, you take control; in the opposite model, you give up control. But because you take control and give up control unilaterally, fundamentally both models are unilaterally controlling.

HOW UNILATERAL CONTROL REINFORCES ITSELF

The insidious thing about the unilateral control mindset is that it both leads to and reinforces the very results you're trying so hard to avoid. In an effort to be right and win, instead of developing high-quality decisions, you get poor decisions that others are reluctant to implement. Instead of improving working relationships with others and creating individual well-being, you create defensiveness, strain these relationships, and create stress for yourself and others.

Just as your unilateral control mindset led you to get these poor results initially, it also sends you into a reinforcing vicious cycle. As the feedback arrows bordering Figure 3.1 indicate, the frustration you feel when you get these poor results reinforces your unilateral control assumptions that others—not you—are the cause of these poor outcomes and that your feelings and unilateral behavior are justified. Instead of considering how you might be contributing to these poor results, you continue to use the same unilateral control behaviors. You believe that if you persist, you'll eventually get better results. But pushing harder—or checking out in frustration—simply leads to more of the same poor results. The harder you try, the less things improve.

Although you don't intend to create these poor results, they are predictable. As systems thinkers like to say, systems are perfectly designed to get the results they get. Your unilateral control operating system enables you to efficiently and skillfully be ineffective. To make matters more challenging, you're typically unaware of your unilateral control mindset as you're operating from it. Like a good computer operating system, it works in the background, quickly and out of your awareness.

If you do become aware that you're contributing to the poor results you're getting, you're likely to think the cause is using ineffective strategies or behaviors. So, you may try to modify them. For example, if you're trying to get a group to recognize something they're doing that's unproductive, you might begin by easing in, asking them a series of questions in the hope they'll get what you're hinting at. If you recognize that the group isn't responding to your easing-in questions, you might switch your strategy to simply telling them what you think they're doing that's unproductive. However, shifting from asking easing-in questions to telling them your views is simply substituting one unilateral control behavior for another. Both lead to the same poor results because they don't change the root cause.

The root cause is your mindset. As long as you are using a unilateral control mindset, you won't be able to consistently create the kinds of results you need for yourself and the groups you're trying to help.

HOW DID WE LEARN UNILATERAL CONTROL?

If 98 percent of us use the ineffective unilateral control approach in challenging situations, how did all of us come to adopt such an ineffective approach? There are two ways.

First, almost all of us have been socialized to use unilateral control. We went to schools that used a unilateral control approach and had teachers that modeled unilateral behavior. Although we may have rebelled against it (I spent more than my share of time in the principal's office), by the time we graduated from high school, we had adopted it ourselves. By the time we took our first jobs, we were skilled in ways to indirectly push our own views, withhold information when sharing it didn't serve our needs, and guide conversations so they avoided topics we didn't want to address.

We joined organizations that were built on unilateral control and that rewarded it. Leadership and management research and practice began with trying to control behavior. That tradition continues, but today's organization uses more sophisticated language to hide it. **Keep in mind, few of us consciously set out to adopt an operating system that gets poor results, but it happens nevertheless, and we learn how to apply it "better" over time.**

The second way we learn unilateral control is even more deep-seated: Our brains are wired to use the unilateral control mindset in difficult situations. In short, our brain is designed to react immediately to threat before we can even think about what that threat is. I explain this further in Chapter 12, on emotions.

You might wonder why the brain is designed so that we sometimes act before we can think. The answer, from an evolutionary perspective, is that it's helped us survive. When our distant ancestors encountered what could be a large, threatening animate object, they were much more likely to survive if they could react—either flee or fight—before having to figure out exactly what the potential foe was. This makes sense from a risk management perspective. For example, if you run away from an apparent threat that turns out to be nothing, you're just out of breath. But if you fail to run away from a threat that's real, you may end up permanently out of breath. So we're programmed to err on the side of survival, whether that means fleeing or fighting. Although there are few large, literally life-threatening objects in our office environments, our brain still responds to modern-day "threatening" stimuli as though our survival were at stake.

To return to our computer analogy, you could say that we're dealing with out-of-date biological hardware that sometimes creates problems for us, but we can't replace that hardware (at least not yet, and I personally wouldn't want to be the guinea pig). Instead, we can change how we think so we can better deal with our out-of-date hardware; we can upgrade our operating system software by changing our mindset.

MOVING FROM UNILATERAL CONTROL TO MUTUAL LEARNING

To improve your practice, your most challenging—and powerful—work is to rigorously think about how you are thinking. This means identifying and exploring the core values and assumptions that drive your behavior and understanding how they differ from the values and assumptions you espouse; to rigorously reflect on how the values and assumptions you use increase or decrease your effectiveness; and to develop or adopt a new set of values and assumptions to increase your effectiveness. For the Skilled Facilitator approach, the more effective set of values and assumptions is mutual learning.

Understanding how unilateral control works will also directly help you help groups get the results they need. The unilateral control approach that reduces your effectiveness is the same approach that reduces the effectiveness of the groups who are seeking your help. To the extent you're able to identify how group members' mindsets and skill sets undermine their effectiveness, you can help them create the fundamental change they seek.

In the next chapter, you'll see how the mutual learning mindset differs from the unilateral control mindset and how it enables you and the groups you work with to get better results.

SUMMARY

How you think is how you facilitate—or consult, coach, train, or mediate. Your mindset leads to behavior, which leads to results. In challenging situations, when others hold different views, almost all of us use the same ineffective mindset—unilateral control. The essence of the unilateral control mindset is this: *"I understand the situation; you don't. I'm right; you're wrong. I will win."* Unilateral control creates the very results you're trying hard to avoid: poor performance, strained working relationships, and reduced well-being. When you operate from a unilateral control mindset, you reduce your effectiveness as well as the effectiveness of the groups you're hired to help.

Simply changing your behavior is insufficient to get out of unilateral control. To move from unilateral control to the more effective mutual learning approach requires that you shift your mindset—the core values and assumptions that drive your behavior. That is the topic of the next chapter.

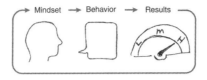

Mindset → Behavior → Results

CHAPTER FOUR

Facilitating with the Mutual Learning Approach

I n the previous chapter, I described how the unilateral control approach undermines your ability to help groups. In this chapter, I describe an alternative—the mutual learning approach. Everything in the Skilled Facilitator approach is based on the mutual learning approach. **In your facilitative role using the Skilled Facilitator approach, your greatest asset—and your greatest challenge—is to operate from the mutual learning mindset and approach.**

In this chapter, we're focusing on how *you* can use the mutual learning approach to be more effective, *not* about how the group itself can use the mutual learning approach. Still, keep in mind that the mutual learning approach applies equally to the groups you are helping. If they choose to use the approach, they will also greatly enhance their results. For a detailed description of how the mutual learning approach applies to teams, see my book *Smart Leaders, Smarter Teams*.

THE MUTUAL LEARNING APPROACH

Like the unilateral control approach, the mutual learning approach begins with a mindset, moves to behaviors, and ends with results (see Figure 4.1). Unlike the unilateral control approach, the mutual learning approach creates positive results in performance, working relationships, and individual well-being.

Parts of this chapter are adapted from Chapter 3 in *Smart Leaders, Smarter Teams*.

60

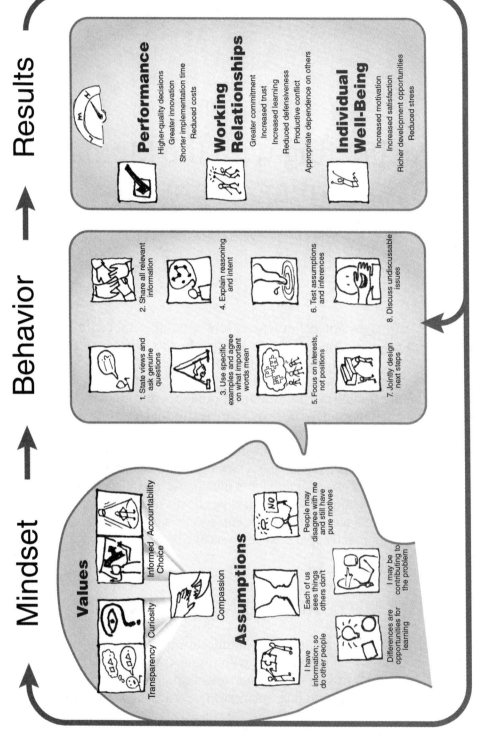

Figure 4.1   The Mutual Learning Approach

I have adapted the mutual learning approach from the work of Argyris and Schön (1974), who developed it and called it Model II, and Robert Putnam, Diana McLain Smith, and Phil McArthur at Action Design, who adapted it and called it the mutual learning model.

To see what mutual learning looks like in action, Exhibit 4.1 shows what Barbara's left-hand column might look like if she used a mutual learning approach. The comments to the right of the conversation show the unilateral control mindset and behaviors that Barbara diagnoses and the mutual learning mindset and behaviors she uses to intervene. The bolded words in the comments identify specific elements of unilateral control and mutual learning. As you read this, you may wonder why Barbara would say or think certain things. I explain this in the rest of the chapter as I describe the mutual learning approach.

Now let's look at the mutual learning approach, using Barbara's case.

VALUES OF THE MUTUAL LEARNING MINDSET

The mutual learning mindset has five core values (see Figure 4.2): Transparency, curiosity, informed choice, accountability, and compassion.

Transparency and Curiosity: Creating a Common Pool of Understanding

Together, transparency and curiosity help you create a common pool of information and understanding between yourself and the group you're helping. Everything you do relies on combining the two. When you're transparent, the group understands what you're doing and why. When you're curious, you learn what group members are thinking and feeling and why.

Transparency means sharing all relevant information, including your thoughts, feelings, and strategies with the appropriate people at the appropriate time. It means explaining why you're saying what you're saying, why you're asking what you're asking, and why you're doing what you're doing.

If you think a meeting is going off track and you want to bring it back on track, rather than just unilaterally switching the topic back to what you think it should be, you may say this to the team: "Once you started talking about staffing levels, it looked like you moved from identifying and agreeing on the key goals for this year to discussing how to achieve one of the goals. Does anyone see that differently? If not, my understanding is that you agreed that in this meeting you wouldn't address how to achieve the goals. Does anyone have a different understanding?"

If you're thinking that one member is being interrupted, you say something like what Barbara says in the redesigned CIO case: "Sandy, it looked like you weren't finished talking when Joe started to talk, yes?"

Barbara's Thoughts and Feelings	The Conversation	
Uh oh, I didn't expect this to happen until this afternoon. I never thought they'd bring it up themselves! This will change the agenda. I need to see if they want to discuss this now or later when it's scheduled.	Mike: My God, we can't possibly let this stuff out of this room. It's dynamite. We'll look like idiots. I for one don't want to have anything to do with it!	Barbara operates from the core value that the group should make an **informed choice**.
Mike is taking a position on this and assuming that they'll look like idiots if they release the data.		
I wonder what his underlying concerns and interests are. I wonder how he thinks it will blow up if they share it.		Barbara infers that Mike is focusing on a position, rather than an interest and is making an assumption.
Joe's also taking a position. He's also attributing some negative motives to employees. Does he think the data aren't valid? This conversation is not going to get any more productive if Joe and Mike are hunkered down in their positions and making untested assumptions.	Joe: This just goes to show why we can never get the work done around here. The people are more interested in sitting on their butts and blaming their managers than in actually doing their jobs.	Barbara operates from the mind-set, **I have some information; others have other information**. She is curious about Mike's reasoning, suspending judgment about it.
Should I intervene now or first see what Sandy and Frank think? Good —Sandy's speaking.		
	Sandy: Well, wait a minute, these results are so striking I don't see how we can ignore them. . . .	Barbara identifies the elements of Joe's behavior that makes the conversation less effective. She remains curious about Joe's reasoning, suspending judgment about it.
Joe's started to interrupt her midsentence, and she's just pulled back from the table. If she isn't finished, she doesn't look like she's going to finish talking. I want to get out her views, whatever they are; otherwise the conversation is going to be even less productive.	Joe: We don't have to let them make our decisions for us, though!	
	Barbara: Sandy, it looked like you weren't finished talking when Joe started to talk, yes?	
	Sandy: Yeah, he just cut me off.	
	Barbara: Sandy, would you be willing to ask Joe to let you finish?	
	Sandy: Yeah, Joe, can I finish?	
	Joe: Go ahead.	
Sandy's also taken a position. She sees it differently from Joe and Mike. She's asking some questions, but they sound rhetorical.	Sandy: The employees already know what they think—who would we be hiding it from? We have to share the results. If this group can't face up to the truth, what right do we have to be in our jobs?	Barbara identifies Sandy's behavior that contributes to making the conversation less productive.
Let me see if the group is ready to have this conversation now. If they are, I'm going to suggest they focus on interests and identify their underlying assumptions so they can explore each others' reasoning.	Barbara: Okay, let's do a process check here. I think the conversation you're having about whether to share the data is an important conversation. Before you go further, I want to see if everyone is ready to have this conversation now. I think it's important that everyone be clear on what the feedback data say so you can have a more informed conversation about whether to share the data. Anyone see that differently?	Barbara plans to give the group an **informed choice** about how to proceed and will also advocate a process, which is part of her facilitator role.
	(People nod in agreement).	Barbara checks for different views.
	Okay, so are there any questions about the results?	
	(People say "no").	
	Then, what do each of you think—do you want to continue the conversation now, save it for later, or take another approach?	Barbara gives the group an **informed choice** about how to proceed.

Exhibit 4.1 Mutual Learning Model: The CIO Survey Feedback Case

Barbara's Thoughts and Feelings	The Conversation	
	Susan: Let's get it out there now!	
	(Some expressions of agreement around the table.)	
Okay, everyone wants to talk about it. Now I can suggest the process.	Frank: I think we need to take the time to do this now. It's pretty important.	
I think Mike has assumed that they won't look like idiots if they withhold the information. But I think it's premature to ask him about this. It's more relevant to discuss when they are exploring their interests.	Barbara: Okay. Right now those of you who have spoken on the issue – Joe, Mike, and Sandy – have taken a position to either not share the data with employees or to share it. Does anyone see this differently?	Barbara identifies an assumption that she thinks Mike has made, but decides not to test it out at this point.
	(People agree she is correct).	
	The reason I ask is that right now I think you're about to get stuck because you are starting to go back and forth arguing for position—either sharing the data or withholding it.	
	But your positions may be in conflict even when your underlying interests or needs are compatible. So, by exploring your interests, together you have a better chance of crafting a solution that meets all the interests.	Barbara **explains her reasoning** for advocating a different process
	Given that, let me propose a different process and get your reactions. I suggest that as a group you develop a list of interests or needs underlying your positions. In other words, each of you identify the needs you are trying to address in dealing with the data. For example, Mike when you said earlier that you thought by sharing it you would look like idiots, it sounded like one of your interests is that whether you end up sharing the data or not, you want to do it in a way that the team looks competent rather than incompetent. Did I get your interest correct?	
	Mike: Absolutely, I don't want us to look like fools.	
	Barbara: So, we would list all of your interests on the board. Then, you would clarify what each of your interests meant so everyone understands them the same way. You'll get a chance to ask each other why your interests are important. Next I'll ask each of you if there are any interests on the list that you think should not be considered in coming up with a solution. Assuming everyone considers all of the interests legitimate, then I'll ask you to brainstorm some ways to meet all the interests. What questions do you have about what I'm proposing?	Barbara assumes that differences are opportunities for learning.
Good question, even if it's rhetorical.	Joe: Why don't we just list the pros and cons?	
I wonder what Joe thinks of this.	Barbara: In my experience, listing pros and cons encourages people to come up with as many reasons as possible to support their initial positions. Each "side" tries to build the longest list and both "sides" try to convince the others they are wrong. I'm asking you to do something different. By focusing on your interests, I'm asking you to temporarily suspend focusing on whether to share the data or not and instead identify what needs you are trying to meet in the data feedback process. Then you can figure out how to meet those needs whether or not you share the data. It turns out that people's needs are often compatible even when their positions are in conflict. What's your reaction, Joe?	Barbara **combines transparency and curiosity** by advocating for a process, **explaining her reasoning**, and then asking Joe for his reactions.
So, they've been in this situation before.	Joe: Sounds like you've seen some of our other meetings. I'm willing to try it, but I'm not sure how we'll close the gap between us.	

Exhibit 4.1   Mutual Learning Model: The CIO Survey Feedback Case (*continued*)

Barbara's Thoughts and Feelings	The Conversation	
	Barbara: I agree, Joe. I think it's too early to know how you you'll close the gap. By identifying all of your interests, we can find out what's causing the gap. Then you will have a better idea of whether and how you can close it.	
I want to make sure I address any questions before I ask for their commitment.	Barbara: Any other questions or concerns? (Everyone shakes their heads "no"). Let me check with each of you to see if you're willing to use this process: Joe, Sandy, Mike, Frank, Susan? (Each nods agreement.)	**Informed choice.** Barbara assumes that people need to make an informed choice in order to be committed to the process she's suggesting.
Well, this raises questions about my role. I was supposed to be the neutral facilitator in this meeting. If I answer his question, I'm leaving my role. But, Mike's question is a fair one, and it deserves an answer. Let me lay out the options and my concerns and see what they want to do.	Mike: I'd like to hear from the consultants about what they think we should do. After all, they work with a lot of other organizations. What do other people do about things like this?	Barbara assumes that **sharing all relevant information** will enable the group to make a better decision.
	Barbara: Your question's a fair one and deserves an answer. Before the consultants answer it, let me describe our situation, and then as a group we can figure out how to answer your question.	Barbara identifies that they will **jointly design the decision**.
	The group and I agreed that I would be a neutral facilitator in this meeting today, which means I wouldn't get into the content of your discussion. If I answer your question, I think I'm getting into the content and may be seen as taking sides, which may reduce my ability to help you as a facilitator. Does anyone see that differently?	**Each of us may see things that others do not.** Barbara describes the situation as she sees it and checks for differing views.
I agree.	Mike: It is content, but it's also what we hired your consulting group to help us with.	
	Barbara: I agree. So I can think of two options. Fred and Elise can answer your questions, and I can still serve as the substantively neutral facilitator. Or, I can step out of my facilitator role and become a facilitative consultant, sharing my views on the issue while still facilitating. I'm okay moving to a facilitative consultant role as long as the group recognizes that I'll be involved in the content of the conversation at the same time I'm facilitating your conversation.	Barbara shares relevant information so the group can make an informed choice.
	The other point I want to make is that the mutual learning core values and eight behaviors you have been using today provide some guidance to answering the questions of whether and/or how to share the feedback data. Again, if the group is interested, I'm happy to explain how you could use the core values and eight behaviors to guide your decisions.	
	So, given this, would you rather I continue to serve as a neutral facilitator, temporarily shift to the facilitative consultant role, or do something else?	

Exhibit 4.1   Mutual Learning Model: The CIO Survey Feedback Case (*continued*)

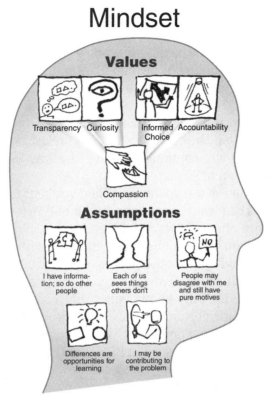

Figure 4.2   Core Values and Assumptions of the Mutual Learning Mindset

If you're asking a group whether they want to take a break, you explain why you're asking. You may say, "I'm asking because I noticed a number of you—Ellie, Bruce, and Quinn—standing up and walking around."

You value transparency because you realize that when others understand what you're thinking, you increase trust and others can respond to you more effectively. When everyone is transparent, you and the group create a common pool of information and can move forward together. This is true especially when people hold different views.

It's difficult to be transparent when you're using a unilateral control mindset; you have to share information that doesn't support your solutions, disclose why you really want to know what you're asking, and reveal that you are, in fact, trying to unilaterally control the situation. Sharing this information would undermine your approach and your ability to win. But being transparent when using a mutual learning mindset actually increases your effectiveness and your strategy because your strategy is to learn and move forward together rather than to control the situation.

But transparency isn't simply sharing exactly what you're thinking. You have to be thinking in a form that's useful to share. At times, each of us has thoughts and feelings about the people we work with that wouldn't be helpful to share in the way we're thinking or feeling. Sharing these thoughts isn't being transparent; it's a recipe for creating defensiveness in others and unproductive conflict. In Barbara's original case, her problem wasn't that she was withholding her thoughts that Fred was hopeless; it was that she was thinking in a way that was unproductive and that she couldn't share. Until Barbara shifts her mindset to mutual learning, she will continue thinking in a way that blocks her from being able to be transparent.

Curiosity is the partner of transparency. When you're transparent, you share information so others can learn about your thinking. When you're curious, you ask questions to learn about others' thinking.

If you realize that you have only some of the pieces of the puzzle and that people you're working with have other pieces, you'll be curious to know more. You'll realize that much of what you think you know about others is just an educated guess at best; to really know, you need to ask them.

The mechanics of curiosity are simple: You ask questions that you don't already know the answers to. Sometimes, you're simply asking team members what choice they want to make, as when Barbara asks, "Then, what do each of you think—do you want to continue the conversation now, save it for later, or take another approach?" Other times you're asking a question to understand what's leading someone to ask you a question. If you're wondering why a team member is asking what you think about team members who don't follow through, instead of simply answering the question, you might say, "What leads you to ask? This way I can answer your question better."

Developing a mindset of curiosity is more difficult than understanding the mechanics. In challenging situations, we usually believe that we understand and are right; those who disagree don't understand and are wrong. As experts hired to help others, our difficulty seeing others' perspectives can be compounded by the curse of knowledge.[1] Our expert knowledge makes it more difficult to think about issues from a nonexpert perspective.

I know this curse well. I've written three different books on increasing team effectiveness. The book in your hands—or on your screen—is the third edition of one of these books. I think I'm pretty expert about what makes teams effective and how to help them. So, I have to work to be genuinely curious when my clients have different views about how to increase their effectiveness. There is a Talmudic expression: "Who is wise? He who learns from everyone." I keep that in mind, asking myself, "What can I learn from my clients in this situation—about my work, myself, and how to better help them?"

When we're not curious, we can easily become frustrated, as we wonder why others don't understand what is obvious to us. That leads us to ask uncurious, rhetorical "questions" to make a point, such as, "Do you really think employees will accept your not releasing the results?"

The Power of Transparency and Curiosity. The numerous footnotes in this section cite research showing that transparent and curious people produce the three main outcomes of the mutual learning approach that I'll discuss later in the chapter: improved performance, better team relationships, and greater individual well-being. There is much more research on leader and team outcomes using the mutual learning core values and very little on facilitators or consultants using the core values. And the little research that focuses on facilitators and consultants is not nearly as rigorous. However, my clients have found that using the mutual learning core values creates positive outcomes regardless of the role in which they use them. And as you help groups use the mutual learning core values, they will create these positive outcomes for themselves. So, throughout the book, I draw on the research from all of these populations, showing the results of using the core values. Let's start with transparency.

- Leaders who are more transparent instill higher levels of trust in their employees.[2]
- Leader transparency is linked to higher employee motivation[3] and job satisfaction.[4]
- When leaders are more transparent, followers are more accepting of difficult organizational changes, a key element in reducing implementation time.[5]
- Teams that share more information with each other perform better.[6]
- When team members are more transparent with each other, they create a more collaborative culture and consider their team more effective.[7]
- In teams where there are significant power differences, when team members with less power are better able to speak up, the team has more success implementing new technology changes.[8]
- Teams that share more information among their members have less unproductive conflict.[9]
- Teams of physicians more accurately diagnosed patients when the team members explicitly shared their reasoning.[10]

Regarding curiosity, people who are curious:

- Have a higher tolerance for dealing with uncertainty.[11]
- Have an advantage detecting others' emotions and connecting with other people.[12] They are comfortable working through doubts and mixed

emotions in relationships.[13] In emotionally challenging situations, they are able to remain open and engaged.[14] They are also less likely to deny conflicts than people who are less curious.[15]

- Not only ask a lot of questions, but also reciprocate by sharing information about themselves.[16]

- Are more curious about the other side's needs and interests and are more likely to get more gains for both parties in negotiations.[17]

- Experience greater well-being. They report greater satisfaction and meaning in their lives.[18]

- Are less dogmatic in their ideas, more willing to consider different opinions, and more likely to consider the quality of the other person's reasoning.[19]

In contrast, people who are less curious feel threatened when they learn new information that is inconsistent with their beliefs. They quickly shift from trust to mistrust of others and engage in other forms of black-and-white thinking. All of this makes it difficult to manage complex and quickly changing situations.[20]

Combining Transparency and Curiosity. I talk about transparency and curiosity together because each requires the other. Research shows that in more effective teams, members move back and forth between being transparent and curious, without getting stuck in just one of these modes.[21] By being simultaneously transparent and curious in your facilitative role, you learn what others are thinking and they learn what you're thinking. This creates the common understanding you need to make quality decisions that generate commitment.

Informed Choice and Accountability: For Better Decisions and Commitment

The common pool of information you create through transparency and curiosity is necessary but not sufficient. You and those you work with need to transform that information into high-quality decisions that generate commitment. That's the role of informed choice and accountability.

Informed choice means making decisions and maximizing others' abilities to make decisions based on relevant information in a way that builds commitment. When you value informed choice, you create situations in which decisions are based on information you and the group have pooled together. Not only are you informed, but so, too, are those with whom you're working. When people make informed choices, they're more committed to the decisions.

When you're working with a group, many of the decisions you make are made jointly with the group because you're a third party and the group is ultimately responsible for choices that affect them. However, informed choice doesn't mean that the team needs to make its decisions by consensus. The field of facilitation has some of its roots in participative decision making. This has led some facilitators to consider consensus decision making as an end in itself. They have advocated, unrealistically, that teams make all of their decisions by consensus. I used to hold that view. Over time, I realized that requiring teams to make all their decisions using the same decision-making rule—no matter what that rule is—fails to take into account the complexity of teams. Some decisions don't require consensus to be implemented effectively. And there are times when even high-performing teams are unable to reach consensus and the team needs a decision to move forward.

The mutual learning approach doesn't require the group you are working with to use any particular decision-making rule. The group can use the full range of decision-making options, ranging from the leader making the decision himself or herself without consulting with others to the group making decisions by consensus. **What distinguishes mutual learning from unilateral control is not the decision-making rule that a group uses—it is the mindset that the group leader and members operate from before, during, and after the decision making.** Mutual learning seeks to maximize informed choice, along with transparency, curiosity, accountability, and compassion.

When you operate from a unilateral control mindset, you think informed choice threatens your chances of winning: If people get to make informed choices, they may choose differently from the way you want. But when you operate from a mutual learning mindset, you see that maximizing informed choice for all increases the chances of a high-quality decision you and the team will commit to.

In your facilitative role, you're providing the group with informed choices throughout the conversation, not simply at the end of conversation. In the CIO survey feedback case earlier in this chapter (Exhibit 4.1), Barbara offers the group an informed choice each time she shares her thoughts about possible next steps and then asks the group how they want to proceed. If you value informed choice, you build it into these "small" decisions along the way.

Accountability is the partner of informed choice. When people make informed choices or when they make decisions with others, they're also accountable to others for those choices. In your facilitative role, you're accountable to the group for the decisions you make by yourself and with them. When you're *accountable*, you meet several expectations:

- You willingly accept the responsibilities inherent in your position to serve the well-being of the organization. You're expected to serve the well-being of the client and the larger organization or context in which it functions.

- You expect that your name will be publicly linked to your actions, words, or reactions.

- You expect to be asked to explain your beliefs, decisions, commitments, or actions to your team and others you work with.[22]

Having your name publicly linked to your actions, words, or reactions means that people can easily know that what was said, done, or decided was what *you* said, did, or decided. This kind of accountability shows up in small but powerful ways. It's the difference between saying, "It was decided" and "I decided." It's the difference between saying, "Don't tell anyone I said this" and "If you talk to anyone about this, please let them know what I said."

Accountability also means that you're expected to explain your reasoning, decisions, and actions to others. It's not sufficient to simply tell the group what you said, what you did, or what you decided. It's necessary to explain what led you to say what you said, do what you did, or decide what you decided. Barbara demonstrates this when she explains to Mike why she can't simply offer her recommendation without first getting agreement to do so from the full group. By helping others understand your thinking, you reduce the chance that people will make up inaccurate stories about your intent.

Someone once said, "To those who have more power than us, we give explanations; to those who have less power, we don't. And those with less power can tell the difference."[23] In your facilitative role, you owe your explanations not only to the person paying for your services, the formal group leader, or your boss, but also to the other team members.

When you operate from a unilateral control mindset, you may try to hold others accountable without making yourself accountable. Or you may not even ask team members to be accountable because you don't want them to hold you accountable. But when your mindset is mutual learning, not only do you want to hold others accountable, but also you want to be held accountable. You don't see accountability as a burden, but rather as a way to honor commitments you've made that will help you and others achieve results. When Barbara was transparent about how answering Mike's question would be inconsistent with the agreement she had with the group, she was also being accountable to the group and enabling the group to make an informed choice about the role it wanted her to play.

The Power of Informed Choice and Accountability. The research shows that when teams create informed choice and accountability, results are better for performance, working relationships, and individual well-being. Regarding informed choice:

- When people are involved in decision making, they have greater commitment.[24] Their satisfaction also increases, and they become involved earlier and in more depth.[25] The earlier that people are involved in decision making regarding a change process, the more likely they are to accept it and adjust better to it.[26]

- Top management teams that use participative decision making—creating more informed choice—have more effective decisions and better organizational performance.[27] Team performance is greater when members are involved early in decision making and are given more in-depth information.[28]

- Top management teams that share more information, collaborate more, and jointly make decisions report better organization performance, attract and retain talented employees, and have better working relationships between managers and nonmanagers.[29]

- When team members are involved in decision making, they have higher job satisfaction.[30]

Regarding accountability:

- When teams and individuals have greater accountability, they perform better.[31]

- When there is greater accountability, teams seem to consider more information and review it more carefully.[32]

- When people are accountable for the reasoning they used to reach a decision, they make more accurate decisions.[33]

Accountability also affects team member relationships.

- People who are held accountable make less-biased decisions and ones that are less judgmental.[34]

- When people are accountable for how they reach their decisions, they make fewer inappropriate inferences and attributions about the attitudes and personalities of others.[35]

Compassion

Compassion is the fifth core value. It's also the emotional glue that holds all the core values together. *Compassion* has three parts. When you operate from compassion:

1. You are aware of the suffering that people you work with face.
2. You internally connect to their suffering, cognitively and emotionally.
3. You respond to the suffering.

When I say suffering, I'm talking about the daily frustrations and challenges people encounter, the emotionally difficult decisions they need to make, and the stress that results from this. Compassion means temporarily suspending judgment so that you can genuinely understand others and appreciate their situation. It doesn't mean taking responsibility for solving other people's problems or pitying them.

In your facilitative role, compassion enables you to help the group in situations when you might otherwise withdraw or act out in frustration. Without compassion, the mutual learning approach feels hollow and robotic. People see you as just going through the motions, using the right words but not seeming genuine. But when you're compassionate, others experience you as being genuinely concerned and operating from a spirit of generosity. This enables you to give clients very difficult feedback and still have them see you as supportive.

Compassion affects how you use the other core values. When you operate with compassion:

- You're *transparent* not because you simply want to tell people what you think, but because you want them to be able to make sense of your behavior.

- You're *curious* about others not because you want to use their responses to show them how they're wrong, but because you want to appreciate the situation from their perspective.

- You create *informed choice* for others not only because informed choice leads to greater commitment but also because informed choice is a fundamental way of respecting others.

- You hold others and yourself *accountable* not because you believe that people won't follow through unless you do so, but because accountability is a way of honoring one's commitment to others and the results you jointly seek to achieve.

Being compassionate doesn't mean rescuing people—doing things for them that they could and should do for themselves. That's what Barbara did in her original case when she tried to protect Sandy from others in the group instead of helping Sandy protect herself, if necessary. Nor does it mean avoiding transparency and accountability, and preventing informed choices—by ducking important but difficult conversations because you don't want people to feel bad. **Withholding information from others because it may be difficult for them to hear isn't being compassionate; it's being cruel.** Genuine compassion includes sharing information that is difficult to hear and even difficult to share, because you want to make an informed choice with others that will improve performance, working relationships, and well-being. In this way, compassion means temporarily suspending judgment about others, including their lack of ability to hear difficult information or feedback even as you hold each other accountable.

The first clients to whom I introduced the core value of compassion were high-tech leader-engineers developing computer chips. Their organization had come to dominate its market though logical, analytic research and development. Its culture drove hard. I was concerned that these leaders would summarily dismiss the idea of compassion. To my surprise—and great relief—they applauded compassion. They had seen how focusing purely on logic without compassion led to a workplace in which strained, mistrustful relationships made working together more difficult.

I have purposely chosen the word *compassion* over words like *empathy* or *understanding* because I want to emphasize the value of the heart—or more precisely, feelings—in decision making. Until recently, many people (myself included) believed that thoughts and feelings were in a battle over the quality of decision making. Our thoughts represented logic and analysis, which we considered the pure elements of decision making. Our feelings were merely distractions or contaminations of thought. In that model, considering what we or others were feeling only compromised the quality of purely logical-based decision making.

There were some people who believed that integrating thoughts and feelings into decision making generated better decisions than focusing only on logic, but the research wasn't there to support their views. Now we know they were right. Recent neuroscience research shows that leaders and teams make better decisions when they pay attention to thoughts and feelings. The seventeenth-century mathematician and philosopher Blaise Pascal was ahead of his time when he said, "The heart has its reasons, which reason does not know. . . . We know truth, not only by the reason, but also by the heart."

The Power of Compassion. Although philosophies and religions have extolled the virtues of compassion for thousands of years, researchers have just recently begun to identify how compassion at work makes a difference. For example:

- People who respond compassionately reduce punishing behaviors that can create further negative consequences.[36, 37]
- Negotiators who have low compassion have less desire to work with each other in the future and generate fewer joint gains.[38]
- Early findings also suggest that compassion can increase commitment to the organization.[39]

In my own experience, when people in facilitative roles operate from compassion, they create a psychologically safe environment for clients to learn, develop, and get better results. They more quickly identify the underlying, often previously undiscussable issues that prevent clients from achieving the results they want. In short, compassion creates trust between you and the group, which is essential for helping the group.

Blocks to Compassion. Some of us are naturally more compassionate than others. But for all of us, it's harder to be compassionate when we're frustrated, disappointed, or annoyed with someone. When this is the case, we're inclined to distance ourselves from others and their pain by telling ourselves that the person doesn't deserve compassion. As Diane Berke writes, "The major block to compassion is the judgment in our minds. Judgment is the mind's primary tool of separation."[40] Here are some judgmental messages we tend to think or convey when we are working with a group:

- *"Your suffering isn't that serious."* You're likely to work with groups that face a broad range of challenges and frustrations. Your job is to approach each person's suffering with the appreciation that it is real and significant for that person, not to judge whether the person's suffering reaches a level adequate to warrant a compassionate response from you.

- *"You contributed to your problem."* In this version of judging, only the faultless person earns your compassion. If a person is feeling frustrated because the team isn't including him in key problem-solving meetings, and you observe that this person is routinely interrupting others in meetings and dismissing others' suggestions, you might think to yourself, *Of course, they don't involve you; you act like a bully.* This may lead you to not respond compassionately. But most of us contribute at least somewhat (if not largely) to our own challenges. If you extend compassion only to those who have made no contribution to their problems, you'll exclude most of the people you work with—and yourself. Mutual learning means that you respond with compassion even when— and especially when—people have caused or contributed to their problems.

- *"You're acting like a victim."* A victim is, by definition, someone who is not able to help himself or herself. People act like victims when they discount their ability to help themselves or blame others for their problems. It doesn't mean they're not suffering; it only means they don't see the extent of their ability and responsibility to do something about a problem. If you believe that a person is acting like a victim—even if that's not the case—you'll probably either get angry at or feel pity for the person. In either case, you won't be able to respond with genuine compassion. In Barbara's initial case, she saw Sandy as a victim, unable to hold her own in the conversation. As a result, she tried to unilaterally protect Sandy, which could lead other team members to see Barbara as taking sides on the issue.

When I was growing up, I was regularly frustrated by my teachers and the school administrators. I was an excellent student, but I was frustrated with how teachers taught, with school policies that didn't sufficiently take into account student interests, and with the lack of responsiveness to student concerns. I found myself regularly trying to create organizational change in my schools— and was just as regularly rebuffed. The administrators dismissed my requests; they showed little compassion for my concerns. On the positive side, my frustration with these administrators motivated me to become an organizational psychologist.

Fast-forward 15 years. I was a professor teaching school system superintendents and principals in an executive education program. My topic was managing change and conflict. I remember looking out at my class of school administrators and thinking, *Finally, the tables are turned. Now you're in my school, and I've got the power.* I had quickly distanced myself from the people I was there to help, and they hadn't even done anything to me. As a result, they didn't get the learning or compassion they deserved—and my evaluations rightly showed it.

Looking back, I realized that payback was more on my mind than compassion. All of the above messages share the destructive assumption that people must *earn* your compassion. If someone has to earn it from you, it's not compassion.

When you assume you have to choose between either showing compassion or holding someone accountable, you get stuck in *either-or* thinking. The mutual learning approach enables you to get unstuck by using *both-and* thinking. Showing compassion doesn't mean giving someone a free pass. You can show compassion at the same time you hold the person accountable for his actions.

The good news is that you can be compassionate even if you have no expertise about the situation that is causing the person's or group's suffering. That's because **compassion isn't about solving problems. All you may need to do is listen, share your concern for the person, and extend an appropriate offer to help**.

ASSUMPTIONS OF THE MUTUAL LEARNING MINDSET

Along with the core values, there is a set of assumptions that you operate from in the mutual learning mindset. Take a moment now to look back at Figure 4.2 to notice again the set of values you just covered and to note the five assumptions.

I Have Information; So Do Others

With this assumption, you recognize that others are likely to have relevant information. Unlike in the unilateral control mindset, in which you assume you have all the information you need, in the mutual learning mindset, you assume that, because people have different responsibilities and experiences, they'll naturally have different information. That information may be the same as or consistent with the information you have, it may be complementary, or it may even be at odds with your current information. Operating from this assumption leads you to help the group get all the relevant information on the table.

Each of Us Sees Things Others Don't

If each of us may have different information because of our different expertise, responsibilities, and experiences, then it makes sense that we may see things that others don't. Even when you and the group are in the same meeting and hear the same information, the mutual learning mindset recognizes that each of you may see different implications or consequences. Operating from this assumption leads you to help the group identify the places in which people see things others miss.

One problem teams face is that they don't give enough consideration to information that only one member has. Teams tend to give more weight to information that more than one member holds. But teams make higher-quality decisions when they incorporate information that only one person holds.[41] Helping groups to integrate all knowledge in their decisions is an important part of your facilitative role.

Differences Are Opportunities for Learning

With a unilateral control mindset, you're either reluctant to explore differences because you know you're right and see nothing to be gained from it, or you want to engage others to show they are wrong. But with the mutual learning mindset, when you realize that you're seeing things differently from others, you become curious and explore what has led to your different views. Your curiosity leads to learning that generates better results and relationships. Whether you're identifying differences between you and the group or within the group, you recognize that this is the beginning of a creative process that will lead to better solutions. The sooner you're able to identify differences, the more time you have to help explore and resolve them.

People May Disagree with Me and Still Have Pure Motives

Because you assume that different views are natural and lead to better results, you can have significant disagreements with others and still believe that each person is approaching the situation with pure motives. This assumption works together with the core value of compassion; both are essentially about suspending judgment in order to learn. As a result, unlike the unilateral control mindset, you're not spending time and energy wondering about and trying to protect against the possible harmful motives of others. Notice that, in Barbara's revised case, unlike in her initial case, she doesn't make attributions about Joe being real trouble and Frank being absolutely hopeless because he doesn't want to release the documents.

When you operate from this assumption, something wonderful happens—there are fewer difficult people in the world. This isn't a naive mind game in which you wish away people you don't like. It's that when you change your mindset, it changes your behavior, and that can change how others respond to you.

I May Be Contributing to the Problem

In the mutual learning mindset, **you recognize that you may be contributing to the very problems that you're complaining about.** You see the working relationships between you and the group as a complex set of causal relationships rather than as a one-way street in which others act ineffectively and you respond effectively. Just as others may be thinking and acting ineffectively, so too may you. You recognize that others' ineffective behavior may actually be a result of (and reaction to) your ineffective mindset and behavior, and you realize your reactions to others' ineffective behaviors either aid or impede mutual learning.

In a unilateral control mindset, only others need to change. In a mutual learning mindset, you realize that everyone may play a role that prevents the team from achieving its goals. Consequently, everyone—including you—may need to change.

MUTUAL LEARNING BEHAVIORS

Mutual learning behaviors convert the mutual learning mindset into action. In a mutual learning mindset, you're able to generate behaviors that aren't possible from a unilateral control mindset. You're able to share all the relevant information about a situation, find out what others are thinking, test assumptions that you and others are making, develop solutions that address people's interests, raise what might have been undiscussable issues, and jointly design the next steps.

There is not a one-to-one relationship between the mutual learning core values and assumptions on the one hand and the eight behaviors on the other. Many of the behaviors result from a combination of the core values and assumptions. Figure 4.3 shows the eight mutual learning behaviors, which are the opposite of the eight unilateral control behaviors. In this section, I'll briefly describe each behavior. We will explore them in more detail in Chapter 5.

1. **State views and ask genuine questions.** With this behavior, you combine transparency and curiosity and operate from the assumption that people have different information, and differences are opportunities for learning. You share your views (using behaviors 2 through 5 to

Behavior

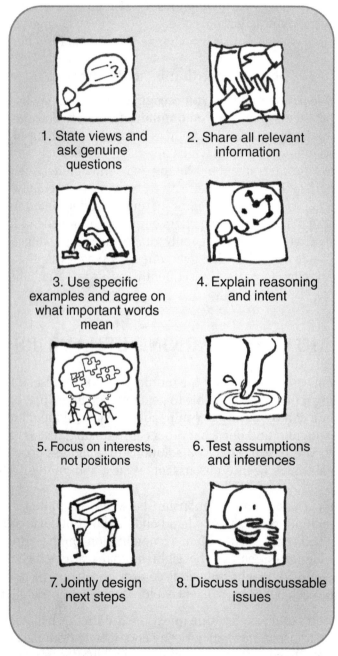

1. State views and ask genuine questions

2. Share all relevant information

3. Use specific examples and agree on what important words mean

4. Explain reasoning and intent

5. Focus on interests, not positions

6. Test assumptions and inferences

7. Jointly design next steps

8. Discuss undiscussable issues

Figure 4.3   Behaviors Generated by the Mutual Learning Mindset

explain your views) and then ask others what they think about your views or another relevant question. As a result, you quickly learn where you and others see things the same way and where you see things differently. Barbara uses this behavior each time she speaks in the revised case, checking to see what others think about what she has said.

2. **Share all relevant information.** Being transparent means sharing all relevant information so that everyone involved has a common pool of information with which to make, understand, and implement decisions. Barbara shares relevant information about the unintended consequences of focusing on pros and cons and the effects of her staying in or leaving the facilitator role.

3. **Use specific examples and agree on what important words mean.** Using this behavior increases the chance that you and the group you're working with are using the same terms to mean the same thing. It combines transparency and accountability, and it makes differences opportunities for learning. Barbara uses this behavior when she points out that she would be acting outside the definition of neutral facilitator if she answered Mike's question about what Barbara thinks the group should do.

4. **Explain reasoning and intent.** As I said in Chapter 1, people are hard-wired to make meaning. This behavior helps people understand what leads you to make the comments you make, ask the questions you ask, or take the actions you're taking. It reduces the need for people to make up stories—possibly inaccurate ones—about what you are doing and why. Sharing your reasoning and intent is a fundamental way to be accountable to others. Barbara uses this behavior when she describes the reasoning underlying the focus on interests rather than positions.

5. **Focus on interests, not positions.** Positions are solutions. Each of us generates solutions that meet our needs. Interests are simply the underlying needs that we want met in any solution. Focusing on interests enables you and the group to craft solutions that everyone can commit to, even when people's positions are in conflict. By focusing on interests, you and the group learn about the causes of differences, which enables you and the group to resolve these differences. This is possible because, as Barbara explained in the revised case, people's interests are often compatible even when their positions are in conflict.

6. **Test assumptions and inferences.** When you test assumptions, you learn whether what you're thinking is accurate. This ensures that you act on valid information, rather than a story you have told yourself,

which may or may not be true. When you use this behavior, you are using all of the mutual learning core values and assumptions.

7. **Jointly design next steps.** When you jointly design the next steps, you design them *with* others instead of *for* others. Joint design is a way to be transparent and curious, and enables you and others to make informed choices. It increases the chance that you'll get a better solution and that people will be more committed to implementing it. Barbara jointly designs each next step with the group, asking whether members want to move ahead or take a different direction.

8. **Discuss undiscussable issues.** Undiscussable issues are issues that negatively affect the group's results and that are often discussed in many settings except in the group—the one place they can be resolved effectively. When you use this behavior, you're using all of the mutual learning core values and assumptions, as well as all of the mutual learning behaviors. In Barbara's original case, she faced the undiscussable issue of trying to influence the team as a consultant at the same time she presented herself as a neutral facilitator. In Barbara's revised case, she made this issue discussable and jointly designed a solution with the group.

Keep in mind that **the mutual learning behaviors are necessary but not sufficient for achieving better results**. The behaviors need to be used with a mutual learning mindset to be useful. Without this mindset, the behaviors become, at best, less effective, and, at worst, tools for unilaterally controlling others.

RESULTS OF MUTUAL LEARNING

The results you and the group get with a mutual learning mindset and the behaviors that follow from it are the opposite of those you get with unilateral control. Let's look at the same three types of results we considered for unilateral control: team performance, working relationships, and well-being (see Figure 4.4).

Better Team Performance

Whatever your facilitative role, if you're working with groups, they're almost always seeking better performance. Even if group members are concerned about their working relationships or individual members' well-being, it is often because these either are now or may soon negatively affect performance. With the mutual learning mindset and behaviors, you help the group improve

Results

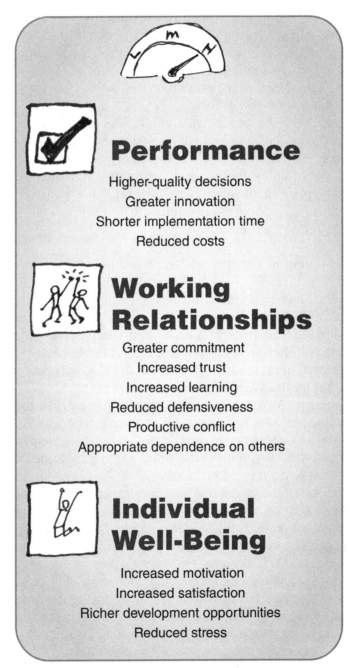

Figure 4.4   Results of Behaviors from a Mutual Learning Mindset

performance in several ways: higher-quality decisions, increased innovation, faster decision-plus-implementation, and lower costs.

Higher-Quality Decisions and Greater Innovation. When you use the mutual learning mindset and behaviors, you create higher-quality decisions with others because you're more likely to have identified the relevant information and created. a shared understanding of the situation. In addition, you approach decisions as a steward for each person's interests, rather than your trying to win or collude with a team member to win.

You can also help the group with whom you are working make more innovative decisions—creating something new and original. You make innovative decisions when you identify the accepted assumptions that are unnecessarily constraining the range of solutions, and then suspend those assumptions or replace them with different assumptions. Mutual learning gives you the ability to identify these assumptions and how they may be unnecessarily constraining high-quality decisions.

Shorter Implementation Time. Some people worry that using mutual learning adds to the time it takes to make decisions. My response is, "More time than what?" Is it more than quickly making a decision with the group and then having to meet numerous times because members aren't really committed to implementing it? Is it more than quickly implementing a decision only to learn that the implementation plan has to be reworked several times because team members didn't share important information or because the plan was based on incorrect assumptions that the team didn't check out?

Mutual learning uses the systems thinking principle: **go slow to go fast.** I first learned this principle from my father, an executive who was an engineer by training. Above the large wooden workbench in our basement workshop, he hung a sign that read: "If you don't have time to do it right the first time, how will you find time to do it the second time?"

Going slow to go fast recognizes that the finish line isn't when you and the group have made a decision; it's when the decision has been implemented effectively, even if you're not involved in the implementation. Mutual learning reduces the overall time of decision making and implementation by addressing issues that you and the group know will become problems if they aren't addressed before implementation. Sometimes mutual learning adds more time to to the process of making a decision but can then recoup it by reducing the time for effective implementation. In addition, sometimes mutual learning also saves time in making the decision; some groups spend a lot of time making low-quality decisions.

Reduced Costs. Mutual learning enables you and the group to reduce costs while maintaining high-quality decisions. Sometimes reduced costs stem from shorter implementation time, which includes spending less time in meetings. Sometimes, cost savings are a by-product of more innovative solutions. Other times, the cost savings are part of the purpose of the work itself, as in Lean, Six Sigma, or other kinds of process improvement work.

Better Working Relationships

The second area of results is working relationships. Here mutual learning generates greater commitment, increased trust, increased learning, and appropriate dependence on others. It also reduces defensiveness and makes conflict more productive.

Greater Commitment. Mutual learning behaviors generate greater commitment to decisions and to the group itself. By commitment, I mean promising to take action to support something. Creating commitment is a simple, if not easy, process. A group becomes committed to a decision when its members believe that their interests have been considered. When you operate from a mutual learning mindset, you're curious about others' interests and jointly design solutions that address them.

Increased Trust. Trust provides the foundation for relationships, but you can't build it directly. Trust develops when people depend on each other, take risks with each other, expect things of each other, and find that their dependence and risks pay off, and their best expectations are fulfilled. Initially, you and the group may grant each other some level of trust, but ultimately it must be earned.

The mutual learning core values and assumptions set the stage for increased trust. You operate from a spirit of generosity and trust when you assume that people can disagree with you and still have pure motives and when you assume that differences are opportunities for learning. You increase the chance that group members will trust you when you're transparent about your intent and genuinely curious about theirs, and when you're accountable to them and seek to help them make informed choices.

Increased Learning, Reduced Defensiveness, and More Productive Conflict. Your ability to improve as a facilitator, consultant, coach, or trainer depends on your ability to learn in the moment from and with the groups you're helping. Not surprisingly, all of the mutual learning core values, assumptions, and behaviors work together to increase learning. When you're transparent and curious, you learn what group members think about how you're working with them and how you can be more effective. Because you're compassionate and assume that you may be missing things, that you may be contributing to a problem, and that people can disagree with you and have pure motives, you use conflict productively—to learn what is causing it and to jointly agree on how to reduce or eliminate the causes. This enables you to approach your learning without becoming defensive, so you're less likely to contribute to making group members defensive.

Appropriate Dependence on Others. Whatever facilitative role you play, the groups you're helping are dependent on you to become more effective. Your challenge is to help them without their becoming unnecessarily dependent on you. Maintaining appropriate dependence on you increases the chance that the groups will work effectively when you complete your working with them.

You increase the chance that the group is appropriately dependent on you when you operate from the core value of accountability—acting accountable yourself and asking group members to do the same. A key principle for ensuring accountability is that **all are responsible for sharing their information directly with those they want to hear it**, rather than having you share members' information for them. In short, don't act as an intermediary. I discuss this in detail in Chapter 13.

Greater Individual Well-Being

The third type of result is well-being, which includes a sense of satisfaction, motivation, and a lower level of stress. Because mutual learning improves working relationships with groups you are trying to help, you experience your work as more satisfying and motivating, and so do group members.

Mutual learning also reduces your stress and anxiety. The mutual learning approach enables you to share what you're thinking in the form you're thinking it, rather than spending time and energy figuring out how to say what you're thinking without making your clients defensive. Instead of becoming anxious about what group members might think about you, mutual learning enables you to learn what they're thinking—and to reduce the stories you tell yourself that make you anxious in the first place. Even though facilitation is challenging work, it should maintain or enhance your mental health, not reduce it.

THE REINFORCING CYCLES
OF MUTUAL LEARNING

Like unilateral control, mutual learning creates reinforcing cycles, but unlike unilateral control, they are virtuous cycles. The first type of reinforcing cycle occurs between the three kinds of results. The positive results in your working relationship with the group affect your ability to help the group achieve better performance. The better performance also increases your well-being, because part of your well-being stems from your ability to help the group achieve the results it needs. And the decrease in your stress and anxiety can also positively affect your performance.

In the second type of positive reinforcing cycle, the results you achieve through mutual learning are reinforced using the mutual learning mindset and behaviors. Figure 4.1 shows these two reinforcing loops. The more you use the mutual learning approach, the easier it becomes to use it, even in increasingly challenging situations.

ARE THERE TIMES WHEN UNILATERAL CONTROL IS THE BETTER APPROACH?

This is a common and important question. If you're like many others, you may be thinking, *There are situations when I need to use unilateral control: Sometimes there isn't time for the group to make a decision; sometimes, it's my decision to make, not the group's; and other times, even if there were time, the group and I wouldn't be able to reach consensus.*

If you're thinking this, you are conflating the mutual learning approach with a consensus decision-making rule. As I described in the informed choice section of this chapter, t**he mutual learning approach doesn't require you to use any particular decision-making rule.** You can use the full range of decision-making options, ranging from one person making the decision without consulting with others to the group making decisions by consensus. **What distinguishes mutual learning from unilateral control is not the decision-making rule that you use—it is the mindset that you operate from before, during, and after the decision making.** This means that you're transparent about the reasoning for your decision and curious about whether the decisions you're about to make (or have made) have a negative impact on others.

Although mutual learning doesn't require that you use any particular decision-making rule, your particular facilitative role does create options and limits for your participation in decision making. Just as the role of facilitative leader vests the leader with authority to make decisions for the team, the role of facilitator prohibits the facilitator from even offering a view on the content discussions, let alone participating in the actual decision making. If you're a facilitative consultant, you're hired to share your views on the content of the group's discussions, but ultimately the group is responsible for making the decisions.

However, when it comes to the process you use to help the group address the content, you do have a role in decision making. As a facilitator, you're hired as a group process expert; the group expects that you will propose a process for working together. As a facilitative consultant, depending on your area, you may be considered a process expert in strategic planning, process improvement, or succession planning. Here, too, the group expects you to propose a process for working together on these topics.

In your facilitative role, there are many small decisions you make and implement, such as interventions, without checking first with the group. That's not necessarily unilateral control either, as long as you explain your decisions afterward and ask for feedback. There are many times when the situation is so routine that you don't have to actively confer with others or explain why you are asking the group something that is obvious.

Using mutual learning effectively means that you use the behaviors to the degree needed in a given situation. In general, your need for mutual learning behaviors increases as the situation becomes less routine, the stakes become higher, emotions run higher, points of views increasingly differ, or something unexpected happens. Even when you don't actively need to use specific mutual learning behaviors, you are still operating from a mutual learning mindset, ready to engage in specific behaviors as soon as you need them.

SUMMARY

In this chapter, I have described the mutual learning approach that is the foundation of the Skilled Facilitator approach. Everything you do in your facilitative role stems from this approach. The mutual learning mindset and behaviors create three kinds of results: solid performance, strong working relationships, and positive individual well-being. The difference between unilateral control and mutual learning is not what decision-making rule you use; it's the mindset you're using as you apply any decision-making rule. In the next chapter, we will explore the eight mutual learning behaviors in detail, and we will learn to use them with groups.

CHAPTER FIVE

Eight Behaviors for Mutual Learning

I n this chapter, I describe the eight behaviors of mutual learning, describe what each behavior means, and show how you can use them to help a group become more effective.[1]

USING THE EIGHT BEHAVIORS

The eight behaviors for mutual learning describe specific behaviors that improve group process and lead to the three mutual learning results: solid performance, stronger working relationships, and individual well-being. The behaviors stem directly from the mutual learning core values and assumptions.

Three Purposes for the Behaviors

The eight behaviors (Figure 5.1) serve several purposes. First, **they guide your behavior in your facilitative role**. To help groups become more effective, you need to act effectively. You use the behaviors to guide your talk, increase your own effectiveness, and help the group better accomplish its goals. By modeling the behaviors, you demonstrate how group members can do the same.

Second, **the behaviors help you diagnose group behavior and intervene**. By becoming familiar with the behaviors, you can watch a group in action and immediately identify when group members are reducing their effectiveness by

---

Parts of this chapter are adapted from *Smart Leaders, Smarter Teams*.

Behavior

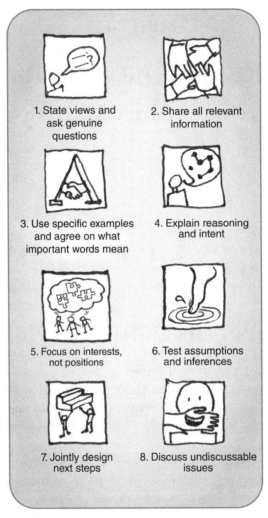

Figure 5.1   Eight Behaviors for Mutual Learning

not using one or more of the eight behaviors. Then you use the behaviors to intervene with the group to help increase its effectiveness.

Finally, **the behaviors can serve as ground rules for the groups you work with**. In the Skilled Facilitator approach, the behaviors that are effective for your facilitative role are the same behaviors that are effective for group members. When a group understands the behaviors and commits to using them, they become the ground rules—expectations for how members will interact with each other.[2] This enables the group to share responsibility for improving its process, a goal of developmental facilitation. In other words, when a group commits to using the behaviors as ground rules for interactions between group members, you can help the group learn to use the behaviors just as you do: to guide its own behavior and to serve as a diagnostic frame for improving that behavior.

In this chapter, we will focus on the first use of the behaviors—using them to increase your effectiveness. In later chapters, we will explore how to use the behaviors to diagnose and intervene, and how groups can use them as their ground rules.

Although the behaviors are numbered, you don't use them in any particular order. You use the behavior that is called for, often using several at the same time. I think of them as dance steps to be combined in a variety of ways, depending on the specific situation.

BEHAVIOR 1: STATE VIEWS AND ASK GENUINE QUESTIONS

When you state your views and ask genuine questions together, you are being both transparent and curious. **To use this behavior, you do three things: (1) express your point of view, (2) explain the reasoning that leads to your view, and (3) ask others a question about your view.**[3] As a facilitator, the view you're expressing is often a process you're recommending that the group follow or an observation about what's happening in the group. For example, you might say, "As a first step, I suggest you identify the needs that you believe have to be met for any solution you agree on. This will give you a set of criteria from which you can generate and evaluate potential solutions. Any concerns about doing this as the first step?" If you're a facilitative consultant, you will also be stating your views about the content of the group's discussions, because the content is your area of expertise. In this role you might say, "I recommend you give division heads their own budgets to manage. This will create a level of accountability and decision-making autonomy that is commensurate with their current level of responsibility. What are your thoughts about this? What, if anything, do you see differently?"

What Stating Your View and Asking a Genuine Question Accomplishes

Stating your view and asking a genuine question accomplishes several goals. First, it helps others understand your thinking and helps you understand what others are thinking. When you share your view, others understand what you're thinking. When you ask others questions, you understand what they're thinking. When everyone understands what everyone else is thinking, you and the group have the relevant information to better solve problems.

If you only inquire, you don't help others understand your reasoning and why you're asking. Alone, either stating your view or asking a question are both ways of unilaterally controlling the conversation; both can easily contribute to defensive behavior in others.

Second, stating views and asking genuine questions shifts a meeting from a series of comments to a focused conversation. If you watch meetings, people take turns saying what they think, but often members make comments that don't build on the previous person's comments, and in some cases they make comments that don't even seem to be related. This happens partly because when one person finishes talking, he or she doesn't ask others what they think. When you finish your comment by asking the group an explicit question, you immediately increase the probability that the person who responds will address your question. If everyone follows their statements by a question, then the group creates a focused conversation.

Third, the behavior increases the speed at which you and the group can learn. One of the mutual learning assumptions is that differences are opportunities for learning. **One of the mutual learning principles is to move toward the differences.** When you share your view and your reasoning and then ask others about it, group members can determine whether they agree with your reasoning or see parts of it differently. By identifying where members' reasoning differs from yours, you can help the group explore what leads to the different reasoning. Are they using different data, are they considering different interests, are they using different assumptions or values, or are they assigning different priorities to certain issues?

Whatever your facilitative role, it's essential that you know whether the group shares your views and if not, why not. If it doesn't share your views, it is unlikely to accept your action or any recommendations that are based on it.

Some facilitators, consultants, and trainers tend to avoid or minimize differences in the group, including differences between them and the group. If you minimize differences, you may be concerned that focusing on different views creates unnecessary conflict and defensive behavior that you won't be able to handle effectively. You may have learned inaccurately that by first focusing on common ground, you build the group's ability to deal with any differences. This will lead you to spend unnecessary amounts of time on what the group agrees on, which reduces the amount of time for identifying the differences and resolving them. The sooner you identify the differences, the sooner you can help the group address them.

Finally, stating views and asking genuine questions reduces defensive behavior. If you state your view without asking a genuine question, others will respond in kind by stating their own point of view, which leads you to respond in kind. This creates a negative reinforcing cycle in which each person is stating his or her view, trying to convince the others. But when you state your views and ask a genuine question, others see your comments not as a challenge, but as an invitation to share a different view. Therefore, they have less need to respond defensively. Your ability to increase learning and reduce defensive reactions depends on how you ask questions.

Make Sure Your Questions Are Genuine. Not all questions are genuine. And only genuine questions increase learning and reduce defensive behavior. A *genuine question* is one you ask with the intent of learning something you don't know. A nongenuine or rhetorical question is one you ask to indirectly make a point. The question, "Why don't you just try it my way and see how it works out?" is not genuine because embedded in the question is your implicit view, "just try it my way." In contrast, a genuine question would be, "What kind of problems do you think might occur if you were to try it the way I'm suggesting?" Notice that with the genuine question, you're not embedding your own point of view in the question.

The difference between genuine and nongenuine questions is not simply the words; it's also a difference in your intent and the kind of response you help to generate. If you use nongenuine questions, people infer (usually correctly) that you're trying to judge or persuade them with your question. In the extreme, if you ask several nongenuine questions in a row, others can feel like you're interrogating them, and they will become cautious, withhold information, and turn defensive.

One form of nongenuine question is called easing in. When you ease in, you indirectly try to raise an issue or advocate your point of view. One way of easing in is to use your question to get the other person to see your point of view without explicitly stating it. For example, you might ask, "Do you think it would be a good idea if we . . . ?" while privately thinking, *I think it would be a good idea if we. . . .*

You may ease in because you're concerned that explicitly sharing your view first will influence or simply reduce the input from others. But easing in telegraphs your view. It leads people to believe (again, usually correctly) that you're simply stating your view in the form of a question. This can lead people to respond defensively because you aren't being transparent about your thinking and you're asking others to be transparent about theirs. By stating your view and asking a genuine question, you're less likely to make others defensive.

Determine If Your Question Is Genuine. We typically ask nongenuine questions when we're feeling frustrated with whoever is not agreeing with us. We're usually thinking that the person doesn't understand the situation, is just plain wrong, has questionable motives, or all three. How can you tell if your questions are genuine or not? If you answer yes to any of the following questions, the question you're about to ask isn't genuine.

- Do I already know the answer to my question?
- Am I asking the question to see if people will give the right (preferred) answer?
- Am I asking the question to make a point?

Take the "You Idiot" Test. Another way to figure out if you're about to ask a nongenuine question is to apply what I call the "you idiot" test. It's a thought experiment you can do in the privacy of your own mind. Here's how it works:

1. **Privately say to yourself the question you plan to ask.** For example, team members have just said that they don't need to spend time agreeing on the purpose of the meeting because everyone understands it and agrees. You've seen a pattern of the team taking an inordinate amount of time to get things done because it hasn't agreed on what it is trying to accomplish. You're tempted to respond, "Why do you think your team takes so long to get anything done?"

2. **At the end of your private question, add the words "you idiot."** Now you're saying to yourself, "Why do you think your team takes so long to get anything done, you idiot?"

3. **If the question still sounds natural with "you idiot" at its end, don't ask it.** It's really a statement—a pointed rhetorical question. If you ask your question, people will hear the words *you idiot* even if you don't say them. Change the nonquestion to a transparent statement that appropriately (1) expresses your view, (2) explains your reasoning, and (3) immediately follow it with a genuine question. You might say, "I'm thinking that spending time agreeing on the meeting purpose will save you time in the long run. In previous meetings, when you were frustrated about not accomplishing the task, you didn't have agreement on the meeting purpose. Do you see that differently? If you get agreement on the purpose, then anyone can quickly identify when he or she thinks the conversation is off purpose and save team time. If you're correct that everyone agrees on the purpose for this meeting, then that conversation will be very short. What are your thoughts about my suggestion?"

In this behavior, we have explored how to state your view and how to ask genuine questions, but we haven't fully considered what to say when you explain the reasoning that leads to your view. Behaviors 2 through 5 address that question.

What to Be Curious About

When you become genuinely curious, you will naturally find the questions you want to ask. Until then, here are some examples of types of questions that are useful to ask.

Questions to Create Shared Understanding. Shared understanding of a situation or a problem is the foundation of effective problem solving and decision making. This begins with asking group members how they understand the situation and how it differs from others' understanding:

- What is your understanding of what X is saying?
- How do you understand the situation?
- What do you see as the differences between the ways you and others see the situation?

Questions to Explore Reasoning. The solutions and decisions that group members prefer result from their reasoning. This includes the relevant information and interests they consider and the assumptions and values they hold. But unless group members make public their private reasoning, other group members won't understand each other's reasoning. Here are questions that help others explain their reasoning and respond to your reasoning:

- Can you help the group understand the reasoning you used to get to your preferred solution?
- What are the relevant pieces of information, interests, and assumptions and values that you think are important to consider when solving this problem?
- What, if anything, in X's reasoning do you see differently?
- Given that you have different views about X [a piece of relevant information, an interest, or an assumption or value], how can you jointly design a way to decide what view to include in deciding how to solve the problem?

Questions to Determine Support. At the end of the conversation, the group needs to know if it has sufficient support to reach a decision. The following questions explore this and identify what needs to occur to develop that support if it doesn't currently exist.

- Are you willing to support the proposal?
- What concerns, if any, do you have about supporting this?
- What would need to happen for you to support this decision?

- Is this a decision you can support and implement, given your role in the organization?
- Are you open to being influenced about this decision?

General Purpose Questions. Sometimes you know you should be curious, but you're not sure what to be curious about. These questions are useful in many situations.

- How do you see it?
- What do you think?
- Can you tell me more about that?
- What led you to _____?

BEHAVIOR 2: SHARE ALL RELEVANT INFORMATION

Behavior 2 means that you share with the group all the relevant information you have. When you share all relevant information, you're being transparent and accountable to the group. Sharing relevant information also ensures that group members have a common base of information on which to make informed choices. If the group members make a decision and later find out that you prevented them from making an informed choice by withholding relevant information, they may feel frustrated, annoyed, or angry. They may also implement their agreement with little commitment or may even withdraw their agreement. You've probably withheld some information if a group member says, "I wouldn't have agreed to do that if you had shared this information with us before we made a decision."

What's Relevant Information?

Relevant information is any information that might affect the decision that you or others make, how you go about making the decision, or your thoughts and feelings about it. Sharing relevant information doesn't necessarily mean that you say everything you know about a topic or everything that enters your mind during a conversation. For each situation, you need to make some judgments about what is relevant information.

Unfortunately, in challenging situations, people use a unilateral control approach. That leads you to strategically withhold information, leaving a significant gap between what you're saying and what you're thinking and feeling. Sharing relevant information means reducing that gap in a way that's productive. Here are several principles for deciding whether you're sharing all relevant information.

- Share information consistent with your facilitative role.
- Carry your own water; have other people carry theirs.
- Share information that doesn't support your view.
- Share your feelings.

Share Information Consistent with Your Facilitative Role

If you're a facilitative consultant, trainer, or coach, your content expertise is relevant information to share. That's why groups hire you. But, as I described in Chapter 2, if you're a facilitator, sharing your content expertise is inconsistent with your role, unless you and the group have explicitly agreed when you can temporarily leave your role as a content-neutral facilitator to share your expertise on a particular topic. If you share information—even relevant information—that is at odds with your role, you risk reducing your credibility and the group's trust in you, and undermining your effectiveness. The same is true for facilitative coaches.

Don't Carry Others' Water

Share information for which you are the source, but don't share others' information for them. When you share information that others should be sharing, you are carrying their water. This reduces their transparency and accountability and inappropriately shifts it to you. In addition, because it's not your information, you can't fully answer questions people have about the reasoning underlying the information. For example, if a senior leader asks you to convey to one of his teams his purpose in having you work with the team, he's asking you to carry his water.

The information that others are asking you to share is usually relevant; it's just not *your* relevant information—it's theirs. The way to address this is to talk with the persons who are asking you to carry their water. We'll explore this in Chapter 13, on contracting.

Share Information That Doesn't Support Your View

Sharing relevant information includes sharing information that doesn't support your preferred solution. If you believe that the group would be better served by taking more time on the current agenda item and not discussing all the scheduled topics, you share your reasoning and you also explain the potential risks of not completing the scheduled agenda. If you're a facilitative consultant discussing a particular performance management plan that you strongly support, you also share the potential challenges of the plan. When you share information that doesn't support your preferred solution, it's fine to put it in context. You might say something like, "Even though there are a couple of challenges to using the X performance management plan, on balance I think it's the best option for you because . . ."

Share Your Feelings

There is no place for feelings in unilateral control—especially negative feelings. But in mutual learning, feelings are an essential part of the conversation and solving problems. When you share your feelings appropriately, you are sharing an essential and often ignored part of relevant information. You're also modeling effective behavior for the group that may seem counterintuitive to the group. Sharing your feelings helps people better understand how you view the content of the conversation.

Are you surprised—pleasantly or unpleasantly—when the group does something? Are you frustrated when the group seems not to follow through on commitments it made to you? Do you feel empathy for the challenge that the team is facing? Feelings are a natural and important part of the human condition; sharing them helps the groups you work with better understand and respond to you.

The challenge with sharing your feelings is to make sure you're sharing them effectively. As Aristotle wrote in the *Nicomachean Ethics*, "Getting angry is easy. But to get angry with the right person, in the right way, for the right reasons . . . that is not easy." Sharing your feelings effectively means that the feelings you're expressing are based on what has happened with you and the group, not on assumptions, inferences, or attributions you're making about the group. It means not only *sharing* the appropriate degree of feeling but also *feeling* the appropriate degree of feeling. Feeling annoyed, angry, or enraged are increasing degrees of the same basic feeling. There have been only a few times when I have felt very angry toward a group I was working with, but even those times were unwarranted. When faced with emotionally difficult situations, a unilateral control mindset leads us to feel stronger negative feelings and weaker positive feelings than are sometimes warranted based on the facts. We'll explore addressing feelings—group members' and yours—in Chapter 12, on emotions.

The next three behaviors are about the types of relevant information to share.

BEHAVIOR 3: USE SPECIFIC EXAMPLES AND AGREE ON WHAT IMPORTANT WORDS MEAN

In any conversation, it's essential to make sure everyone is talking about the same thing. That means everyone is using the same words to mean the same thing. Behavior 3 ensures that this happens.

When we don't agree on what important words mean, there are several causes: (1) We are using different words to mean the same thing, (2) we are using the same word to mean different things, or (3) we are not saying exactly what we mean to say. Here are several steps to take to reduce these problems:

- Say what you mean to say.
- Name names.
- Use specific examples.

Say What You Mean to Say

Facilitators, consultants, coaches, and trainers sometimes don't say what they really mean. We use indirect language and create misunderstanding. Trainers often ask participants whether they completed an assignment by saying, "Did you get a chance to . . . ?" I used to ask this question too, until a group of police chiefs broke me of the habit. I was helping the group learn how to manage conflict and started by asking, "How many of you had a chance to read the article I asked you to read?" To my pleasant surprise, all 50 hands went up. "That's impressive," I said. "This is the first group I've worked with where everyone has read the article." One of the police chiefs spoke up. "Roger, you didn't ask us if we read the article; you asked us if we had a chance to read it. We all had a chance." "You're right," I said. "Let me try this again. How many of you read the assignment?" This time only about one third of the police chiefs raised their hands. At that moment, I realized I had asked, "Did you have a chance to . . . ?" because I was trying to save face for those people who might not have completed the assignment. But, in doing so, I wasn't asking what I really meant and I wasn't asking people to be accountable.

It's easy to literally speak the words, "Did you read the assignment?" but to be willing to say them, you may need to change your mindset. Instead of thinking that by directly asking people if they completed an assignment you're putting them on the spot, when you operate from mutual learning, you see this as being transparent, accountable, curious, and compassionate.

Name Names

If you want the group to understand whom you are talking about, it helps to name names. If you're concerned that Erin and Eduardo haven't shared their view and Joan is speaking repeatedly on the topic, saying, "Let's hear from some people who haven't spoken yet" doesn't tell people whom you want to hear from. Even if you say, "Erin and Eduardo, I'd like to hear what your thoughts are," you're omitting the point that Joan's frequent comments seem to be hindering their speaking. To be transparent and accountable, you would say, "I haven't heard Erin and Eduardo's thoughts yet. Joan, you've spoken a number of times on this topic—have I missed anything? If not, would you be willing to let Erin and Eduardo share their thoughts at this point?"

If you're concerned about saying what I suggested, it may be because you see my comment as criticizing Joan, and you may be operating from the principle "praise in public, criticize in private." Unfortunately, the principle stems from a unilateral control assumption: Discussing your concerns about others' behavior is criticism, and criticism in the group is at odds with minimizing the expression of negative feelings. The principle is based on saving face—for others and for yourself. But, as you shift toward a mutual learning approach, you begin to think of these situations differently—as an opportunity to learn something you may have missed and to help members understand how they may have acted in a way that, perhaps without intention, reduced the group's effectiveness.

Use Specific Examples

Ironically, people often disagree on the meaning of words that they most commonly use. In a strategy meeting, people often have different definitions of *strategy*. In HR meetings, people often have different meanings of the word *accountability*. And people often have different definitions of what it means to start a meeting on time. In your facilitative role, you probably use terms from your field that have a meaning that is different from the general meaning of that term.

One way to determine whether you're using a word to mean the same thing as others is to give an example. If you suggest that the group make a decision by consensus, it's likely that members will have different definitions of *consensus*. To some members, it may mean that a simple majority of people support the decision; to others it may mean that most people support it; and to still others it means unanimous support. The first time the group agrees to make a decision by consensus and the decision has majority but not unanimous support, you'll discover that people have different definitions.

To agree on what consensus means, you can say,

When I say *consensus*, I mean unanimous support and not majority support. In practice, this means each of you can say you will implement the decision, given your role in the organization. If the decision is about IT, supporting it means that you, Pradeep, will have a significant implementation job, given your role as CIO. For Angie and Yosef, as heads of marketing and sales, supporting it may mean that your folks simply use the new system. My definition doesn't mean that you can't tell your direct reports about any concerns you might have about implementing the decision. It does mean saying something like, "Even though I have these concerns, I support the decision to implement it." Does anyone have a different definition of *consensus*?

Notice that giving an example with specific behaviors is part of describing what a word means and that it helps also to give an example of what it does not mean.

BEHAVIOR 4: EXPLAIN REASONING AND INTENT

Human beings are hard-wired to make meaning from what others do and say. If you don't explain your reasoning, group members will generate their own explanations of your reasoning, and their explanations may differ greatly from yours. *Explaining reasoning and intent* means explaining what leads you to make a comment or ask a question or take an action. Reasoning and intent are similar but different. Your intent is your purpose for doing something. Your reasoning represents the logical process that you use to draw conclusions and propose solutions based on the relevant information, your values and assumptions, and your interests.

Explaining your reasoning and intent includes making your private reasoning public so that others can see how you reached your conclusion and can ask you about places in your reasoning where they may reason differently. It's like when your fifth-grade teacher told you, "Show your work." If your answer to the math problem didn't match hers, she wanted to see if you used incorrect information, misapplied some formula, or made a mathematical error. In short, she wanted to see where her reasoning differed from yours.

To explicitly highlight your reasoning, you can follow your statement or question with something like this:

- "The reason I'm *suggesting* this is . . ." or "I'm *suggesting* this because . . ."
- "The reason I *say* this is . . ." or "I'm *saying* this because . . ."
- "The reason I'm *asking* is . . ." or "I'm *asking* because . . ."
- "The reason I'm *doing* this is . . ." or "I'm *doing* this because . . ."

For example, you might say, "Rather than have the group address each of your concerns as you raise them, I suggest we find out everyone's concerns and then quickly decide the order in which you want to address them. I'm suggesting this so you'll know all the concerns up front and be able to address them in an order that makes the most sense. Any concerns about doing it this way?"

Be Transparent about Your Strategy

One of the most important types of reasoning to be transparent about is the strategy you're using to work with and influence the group. This includes the process you're using to help a group solve a problem, how you move from topic to topic, and even how you handle ineffective behavior in the group. In your facilitative role, you're often responsible for designing and managing the group process. If the group doesn't know why you are doing what you're doing, you're not being transparent about your strategy. In Chapter 3, Barbara's strategy was to use unilateral control strategies that she would have found difficult to share with the group.

When you're not being transparent about your strategy, group members may become concerned that you're trying to manipulate them—even if you're not. When you're being transparent about your strategy, group members can understand the reasoning for your actions and you build trust with them.

Often you may not share your strategy simply because you think it's too much detail. When you operate from a unilateral control mindset, you withhold your strategy because sharing it reduces your ability to implement it. If people knew your strategy, they might not agree to follow it.

Take the Transparency Test

Here's a simple and powerful three-step thought experiment to figure out if you're about to use a unilaterally controlling strategy. I call it the transparency test. To show you how to use it, I'll use one of my favorite examples of strategies that people don't explain—the sandwich approach to negative feedback. If you've learned this approach, you know that when you have negative feedback to give someone, you sandwich it between two pieces of positive feedback. Here are the three steps for determining if your strategy is a unilateral controlling one:

1. **Identify the strategy you're using to have the conversation.** In the sandwich approach, the strategy when you have negative feedback to give is to start off on a positive note to make the person or people feel more comfortable and to make it easier to hear your negative feedback without getting defensive. Next, give the negative feedback, which is the reason you wanted to talk. Finally, give some more positive feedback, so the person or people will leave the meeting with self-esteem in place and won't be as angry with you.

2. **Imagine explaining your strategy to the ones you are using it with.** Also, imagine asking them how the strategy will work for them. Let's imagine you're using the sandwich approach with a group: "I called you in here to give you some negative feedback, and I want to let you know my strategy for having the conversation and see if it will work

for you. First, I'm going to give you some positive feedback to make you feel more comfortable and get you ready for the negative feedback, because I think you're going to get defensive. Then, I'll give you the negative feedback, which is why I called you in here today. Finally, I'll give you some more positive feedback so you'll feel better about yourself and won't be as angry with me. How will that work for you?"

3. **Notice your reaction.** If you find yourself laughing at the absurdity of what you're thinking, or if you're thinking *I could never share* that *strategy*, you've probably identified a unilateral control strategy that keeps you from being transparent. You keep your unilateral control strategies private because they work only when others don't know what you're doing or when they agree to play along.

The solution here isn't being transparent about your unilaterally controlling strategy; it's shifting your mindset so you begin using mutual learning strategies that become more effective when you share them with others.

BEHAVIOR 5: FOCUS ON INTERESTS, NOT POSITIONS

Focusing on interests is another way of sharing relevant information. *Interests* are the needs and desires that people have in regard to a given situation.[4] *Solutions or positions* are how people meet their interests. In other words, people's interests lead them to advocate a particular solution or position. The reason for focusing on interests is that often people's positions are in conflict even when their interests are compatible. By focusing on interests, you make it possible to agree on a solution or to solve a problem even when people have conflicting positions.

If you're part of a group buying a car and you say you want a Honda Accord and another group member says she wants a Toyota Prius, those are positions. If I ask you, "What is it about buying a Honda Accord that is important to you?," you will probably answer by describing your interests—the needs you are trying to meet. You might say that you want a Honda Accord because it's a reliable car, with low repair costs, and high resale value. Those are the needs you are trying to meet. If I ask the group member what it is about a Toyota Prius that's important to her, she may say that she wants a car that gets good gas mileage and that she can easily maneuver in tight spaces. If each of you agree that the other's needs are reasonable to take into account, then your joint task becomes finding a vehicle that meets both sets of needs. Because groups are often trying to develop solutions rather than choosing between two predefined alternatives, identifying interests enables them to get creative about how to meet the set of agreed-upon interests.

Explaining your interests is a central part of sharing your reasoning. When you recommend that a group use a particular process to discuss an issue or, as a facilitative consultant, when you recommend a solution for a problem a group is facing, you're implicitly offering recommendations that meet what you believe are the group's interests. Using this behavior means stating the interests explicitly.

As a facilitative consultant, you might say, "I'm recommending this solution because I think it meets the two interests you've identified—a solution that can be implemented within your current budget and that can be scaled up or down if your budget changes in the next few months. Did I hear your interests correctly, and, if so, do you think this solution meets your interests?

Here are four steps to help a group develop a solution based on interests:

Step 1: Identify interests. Ask group members to complete this sentence as many times as possible: "Regardless of the specifics of any solution we develop, it needs to be one that . . ." Record the answers in a single list of interests. If people keep identifying positions instead of interests, ask them, "What is it about your solution that's important to you?" This helps them to identify their underlying interests.

Step 2: Agree on interests to consider in the solution. In this step, you help the group clarify what each interest means and reach agreement on which interests it will consider in developing solutions. One way to ask this question is, "Are there any interests that someone thinks we should not take into account when developing a solution?" "Take into account" doesn't mean that everyone agrees that a given interest is important; just that everyone sees it as relevant. In the end, the group won't necessarily be able to craft a solution that meets all the relevant interests, though that is the ideal outcome. At the end of this step, the group will have a single list of the interests that an ideal solution would address.

Step 3: Craft solutions that meet the interests. Help the team generate solutions that meet as many of the interests as possible—ideally, all of them. At this step, you can say something like, "Let's come up with some possible solutions that meet all of your interests. You're not committing to any of these solutions yet; you're just getting them on the table." The group begins to identify possible solutions. This is a time for you to help members to play off and build on each other's ideas, seeking solutions that incorporate as many interests as possible. If the group members can't find a solution that meets the agreed-upon interests, help them explore whether all the proposed solutions have a common unnecessary assumption embedded in them. For example, if every proposed solution assumes that the work has to be performed only by full-time employees, ask whether that assumption is necessary to make. If it's not, ask them to generate other solutions without that assumption. If this doesn't help, then the team can prioritize or weight the different interests to find a solution that addresses the most important ones.

Step 4: Select a solution and implement it. Using this approach doesn't guarantee that the group will reach a decision that meets everyone's interests. It does, however, increase the chance that you will help the group find a solution that everyone can support.

BEHAVIOR 6: TEST ASSUMPTIONS AND INFERENCES

I said in discussing behavior 4 that human beings are hard-wired to make meaning. Behavior 6 explains how you make meaning; how, if you're not careful, you can create problems for yourself and the groups you are trying to help; and how you can test out the meaning you're making to help groups become more effective.

There are several kinds of meaning you can make. When you make an *assumption*, you believe that it is true without any proof. When you make an *inference*, you draw a conclusion about something you don't know based on things that you do know. Finally, when you make an *attribution*, you are making an inference about someone's motives—why that person is acting in a particular way. Here is an example of the differences between the three:

1. *Assumption:* The team leader will lead the meeting (because that is what team leaders do).
2. *Inference:* The team leader isn't telling people what needs to be done; therefore, she's not leading the meeting.
3. *Attribution:* The team leader isn't leading the meeting because she doesn't care about this project.

Assumptions, inferences, and attributions work in the same way. If you act on them believing you're right and it turns out you're wrong, you create problems for yourself and the group. Everyone makes assumptions, inferences, and attributions. That's not the problem. The problem is your lack of awareness. If you're not aware that you're making an assumption or inference, then you can't test whether it's true before you act on it and potentially create negative consequences. In this section, I'll be using the term *inference* to substitute for the lengthy phrase assumptions, inferences, or attributions.

Behavior 6 uses several skills. The first skill is becoming aware when you're making inferences—at the time you are making them. The second skill is deciding whether to test your inference. It's neither possible nor desirable to test every one. If you decide to test your inference, the third skill is testing it in a way that doesn't contribute to people getting defensive.

We'll start with the first skill—becoming aware of how you make meaning—by using a tool called the ladder of inference.

How You Make Meaning: The Ladder of Inference

To understand how we make meaning, let's consider a facilitator called Tye who is making a high-level inference about Cheryl, who is part of the team he is facilitating. The short left-hand column case (Exhibit 5.1) shows Tye's conversation with Cheryl and his thoughts and feelings. We'll use this example to explain the ladder of inference and how to test an inference you make.

How you make meaning is illustrated in the ladder of inference (Figure 5.2), which I have adapted from Argyris and Schön and also from Action Design, which built on Argyris and Schön's work. Like a real ladder, you start at the bottom of the ladder of inference and climb up.

At the bottom of the ladder of inference is all the observable information available to you. As you climb the ladder, you encounter three rungs: (1) observe

The Facilitator's Thoughts and Feelings	The Conversation
I need to get some specific examples, otherwise this is going to deteriorate into a "he said, she said" discussion.	TYE (THE FACILITATOR): Cheryl, you said that Jim and Lena are slowing down your marketing project. Can you give some specific examples of what they have done or not done that leads you to say they've slowing down your project?"
All right, shake your head. It's your choice. I'm just trying to help you. I'll move on.	CHERYL (A TEAM MEMBER): [Shaking her head] No. I told you earlier, and you didn't respond. They know what they've done.
	[Twenty minutes pass, and the team conversation moves on.]
Cheryl hasn't said a word for 20 minutes. All I did was to ask her to give some examples of how Jim and Lena were slowing down her marketing project. She just got annoyed and shut down. I'll try to get her back into the conversation.	TYE: Let's hear from some others. Cheryl, what are your thoughts about Lena's and Jim's suggestion to start their marketing project next quarter?
Now, I'm annoyed. You're not fine. You're fuming. Now you don't want Jim and Lena's project to start at all. You're just trying to get back at Lena and Jim for not supporting your earlier proposal.	CHERYL: Whatever they want to do is fine. I don't really care.
Okay. I gave you a chance. I'm done.	TYE: Okay.

Exhibit 5.1   Making a High-Level Untested Inference

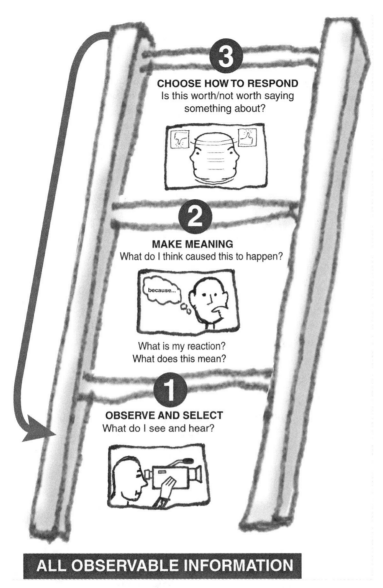

Figure 5.2   The Ladder of Inference

Source: Adapted from Argyris, C. (1985). *Strategy, change, and defensive routines.* Boston: Pitman, and Action Design (1997). Notebook materials, www.actiondesign.com.

and select information, (2) make meaning, and (3) decide how to respond. Let's start at the bottom and explore each part. Figure 5.3 shows Tye's ladder of inference during his conversation with Cheryl.

All Observable Information   In a conversation or meeting, you're faced with a lot of directly observable information. Think of directly observable information

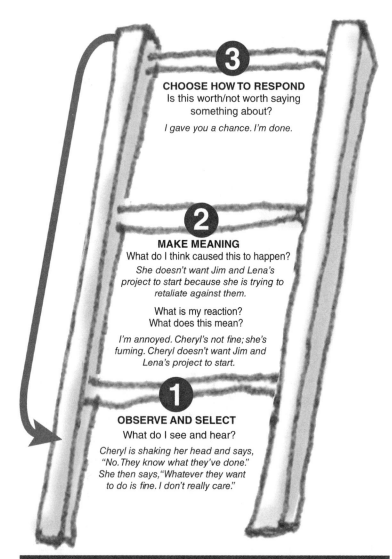

3

CHOOSE HOW TO RESPOND
Is this worth/not worth saying
something about?

I gave you a chance. I'm done.

2

MAKE MEANING
What do I think caused this to happen?

*She doesn't want Jim and Lena's
project to start because she is trying to
retaliate against them.*

What is my reaction?
What does this mean?

*I'm annoyed. Cheryl's not fine; she's
fuming. Cheryl doesn't want Jim and
Lena's project to start.*

1

OBSERVE AND SELECT
What do I see and hear?

*Cheryl is shaking her head and says,
"No. They know what they've done."
She then says, "Whatever they want
to do is fine. I don't really care."*

ALL OBSERVABLE INFORMATION

Cheryl is shaking her head and says, "No. I told you earlier, and
you didn't respond. They know what they've done." Later, when I
asked her, "What are your thoughts about Lena's and Jim's
suggestion to start their marketing project next quarter?," she
replied, "Whatever they want to do is fine. I don't really care."

Figure 5.3   Tye's Ladder of Inference

as whatever you can capture on video. This includes what people are saying and their nonverbal behavior, and spreadsheets and other documents, whether in hard copy or on a screen. In our example, everything that Tye and Cheryl have said is observable information and so is Cheryl's shaking her head.

Observe and Select Information At this first rung, it's as if you're answering your own question, "What do I see and hear?" I say *as if* because you do it unconsciously. Even in a one-on-one conversation, there is too much observable information to attend to. So, you observe and select certain data while ignoring other data. In our example, Tye pays attention to Cheryl shaking her head and saying, "No, . . . they know what they've done," but he doesn't select the part in which she says, "I've told you earlier and you didn't respond."

Make Meaning At the second rung, you begin to infer meaning from the information you selected, for example, *what's my reaction?* What does it really mean when this person says or does this? When Cheryl says, "Whatever they want to do is fine. I don't really care," Tye gets annoyed. He infers that Cheryl is not fine but is fuming. He then infers that Cheryl does not want Jim and Lena's project to start. Notice that Cheryl never said she didn't want Jim and Lena's project to start. After answering your own questions, you ask yourself, *What do I think caused this to happen?* As human beings, we like causal explanations because they help us figure out how to respond. In our example, Tye attributes to Cheryl that she doesn't want Jim and Lena's project to start because she is trying to retaliate against them.

Decide How to Respond At the third and final rung, you decide whether and how to respond. In unilateral control, if you decided to respond, you might make a comment or perhaps ask a question. In mutual learning, if you decided to respond, you would test your assumption or inference to see if it was accurate.

In our example, Tye is thinking, *I gave you a chance. I'm done.* He chose not to respond. Tye might have chosen to respond by telling Cheryl that her behavior wasn't helpful—a response that would also not be helpful.

Your Inferences Become Data

The ladder of inference is self-reinforcing. Notice the arrow on the left side of the ladder? It's called a reflexive loop. It turns the untested assumptions, inferences, and attributions you make into "facts" that lead you to look for data that confirm your "facts" and to also interpret ambiguous data as confirming your "facts." For example, Tye will use his inference—that Cheryl doesn't want Jim and Lena's project to start—to systematically select data from future interactions with the team to confirm his inference and attribution about Cheryl. If Cheryl makes an ambiguous comment, Tye is likely to interpret it as another example of the same. This reflexive loop leads you to create what you *think* is a solid basis for a conclusion. However, you create a large set of untested inferences that may be completely flawed.

Lower Your Ladder: Make Your Inference Testable

The main rule for using the ladder of inference is the same as a real ladder: Don't climb any higher than you need to. Just like a real ladder, the higher you climb, the more dangerous it becomes. We climb up the ladder higher than we need to when we make an inference that is further removed from the data than necessary. I call these high-level inferences. You've probably seen others make these high-level inferences. Imagine that you make a suggestion for how to improve a project and a group member responds, "You're just trying to make me fail!" You're probably thinking, *How did he possibly reach that conclusion? That's so far removed from what I said!* In the CIO case in Chapter 3, Barbara made several high-level inferences, including one at the very end of the case. When Frank said, "How about a break now? I'd like us to mull this question over and revisit it this afternoon," Barbara thought, *Oh, that's great. He obviously thinks I'm an idiot and doesn't want to release the stuff.* Her inference that Frank obviously thinks she's an idiot is greatly removed from the data she used to reach the conclusion. Similarly, in our example above, Tye's high-level inference was that Cheryl wanted Jim and Lena's project to fail and his high-level attribution was that Cheryl was seeking retaliation.

When you make a high-level inference, your final inference is supported by many other intermediary inferences. Like a house of cards, if one of the intermediary inferences is false, the logic collapses and the final inference can't be supported. We have a clinical term for people who routinely make certain types of very high-level negative inferences (and attributions) with little or no data: *paranoid.* Still, all of us make high-level inferences at times, especially when we are faced with challenging situations, including ones that make us anxious. Although you may make positive high-level inferences about others (she gave me a big smile—she's attracted to me), in challenging situations, our high-level inference is usually negative (as in Barbara's case: *Frank asked for a break; he obviously thinks I'm an idiot*).

With practice, you will make fewer high-level inferences that you need to lower. But you will still make high-level inferences at times. To test these inferences without getting others defensive, you need to realize when you're making a high-level inference and convert it to a low-level inference. I call this lowering your ladder. Figure 5.4 shows the two-step process. First, after you have made meaning and before you choose how to respond, ask yourself, *What did the person say or do that leads me to believe this?* This leads you to climb back down the ladder and recall and reexamine the data you used to make your inferences. You may realize that the person didn't say what you thought she said or that you didn't pay attention to something she did say. In Tye's case (see Figure 5.5), he would discover that Cheryl had also said, "I told you earlier, and you didn't respond."

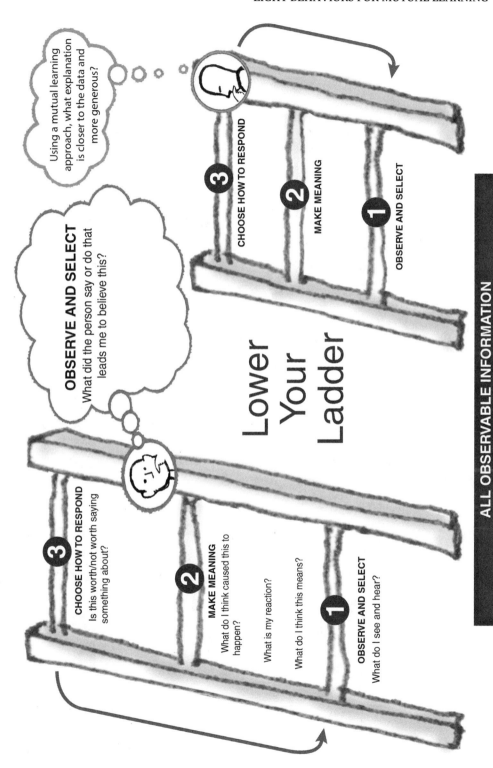

Figure 5.4 Lowering Your Ladder of Inference

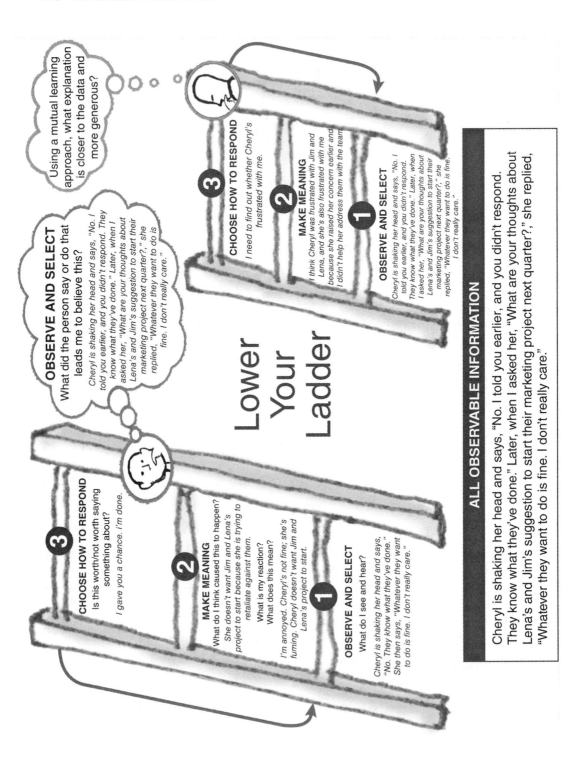

Figure 5.5   Tye Lowering His Ladder of Inference

Second, ask yourself, "Using a mutual learning approach, what explanation is closer to the data and more generous of spirit?" In other words, what inference would be reasonable to make using mutual learning and generosity as your guide? I'm not asking you to abandon reality or to be naïve. Your new inference still needs to fit with the data. In Tye's case, he might have inferred that Cheryl was frustrated with Jim and Lena and also frustrated with him because Cheryl had raised her concern earlier and Tye hadn't helped her address it with the team.

Decide Whether to Test Your New Inference

After you've made a new inference based on mutual learning and a generosity of spirit, you can decide whether you want to test it to see if it's true. You may decide it's still worth testing or it's not necessary. You can't test out every inference you make. If you did, you would drive people crazy.

To decide whether to test an inference, I ask myself, *What are the consequences if I act on my inference as if it is true and it is false?* Tye might decide that he needs to test out his inference because he needs to determine if he did not respond to Cheryl's earlier concern.

Testing Your Inference: The Mutual Learning Cycle

The mutual learning cycle (see Figure 5.6) is a tool for productively testing your inferences. The cycle has two sides. The left side is what you are thinking and feeling, and the right side is what you say. You've already learned the left side; it's your ladder of inference using a mutual learning approach.

Once you've completed the left side, the right side is easy to complete. You take your thoughts and feelings from the left side and share them on the right side (Figure 5.7). Here is how it works, step-by-step, using Tye's example:

Step 4:
"Cheryl, you said that you told me earlier about what Jim and Lena had done that led you to say they were slowing down your project, but I didn't respond to you. Did I get that right?" [If Cheryl says yes, Tye continues.]

Step 5:
"I'm thinking you're frustrated that I didn't follow up with you as well as frustrated with Jim and Lena. Is that what you're feeling, or am I wrong?" [If Cheryl agrees this is what she is feeling, Tye continues.]

Step 6:
"I didn't mean to not respond or frustrate you. I suggest we go back to your concern and find out what Jim and Lena's thoughts are. How does that sound to you?"

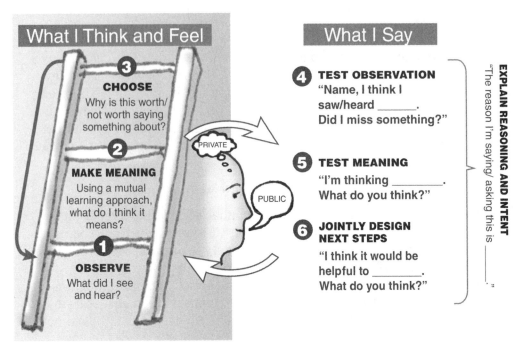

Figure 5.6 The Mutual Learning Cycle

The Mutual Learning Cycle Uses Most of the Eight Behaviors

The mutual learning cycle is powerful in part because it uses most of the eight behaviors. In step 4 of the cycle, you test your observation by using specific examples so you can agree on what important words mean (behavior 3) and you share all the relevant information (behavior 2) that leads you to make your inference. Step 5, testing your meaning, is the same as testing inferences and assumptions (behavior 6). In step 6, you jointly decide with others how to move forward (behavior 7, which we will explore next). Steps 4, 5, and 6 each have two parts. In the first part, you state your view, and in the second part, you ask a genuine question (behavior 1). Finally, the right side of the cycle states, "Explain reasoning and intent" (behavior 4). By using the mutual learning cycle, you are naturally using a mutual learning approach.

A note about language: You don't have to use the words *infer* and *inference*. If these words sound unnatural or like jargon, you can say, "I'm thinking that . . . ," "It sounds to me like . . . ," or something similar. Honor the meaning of the words and find your own voice.

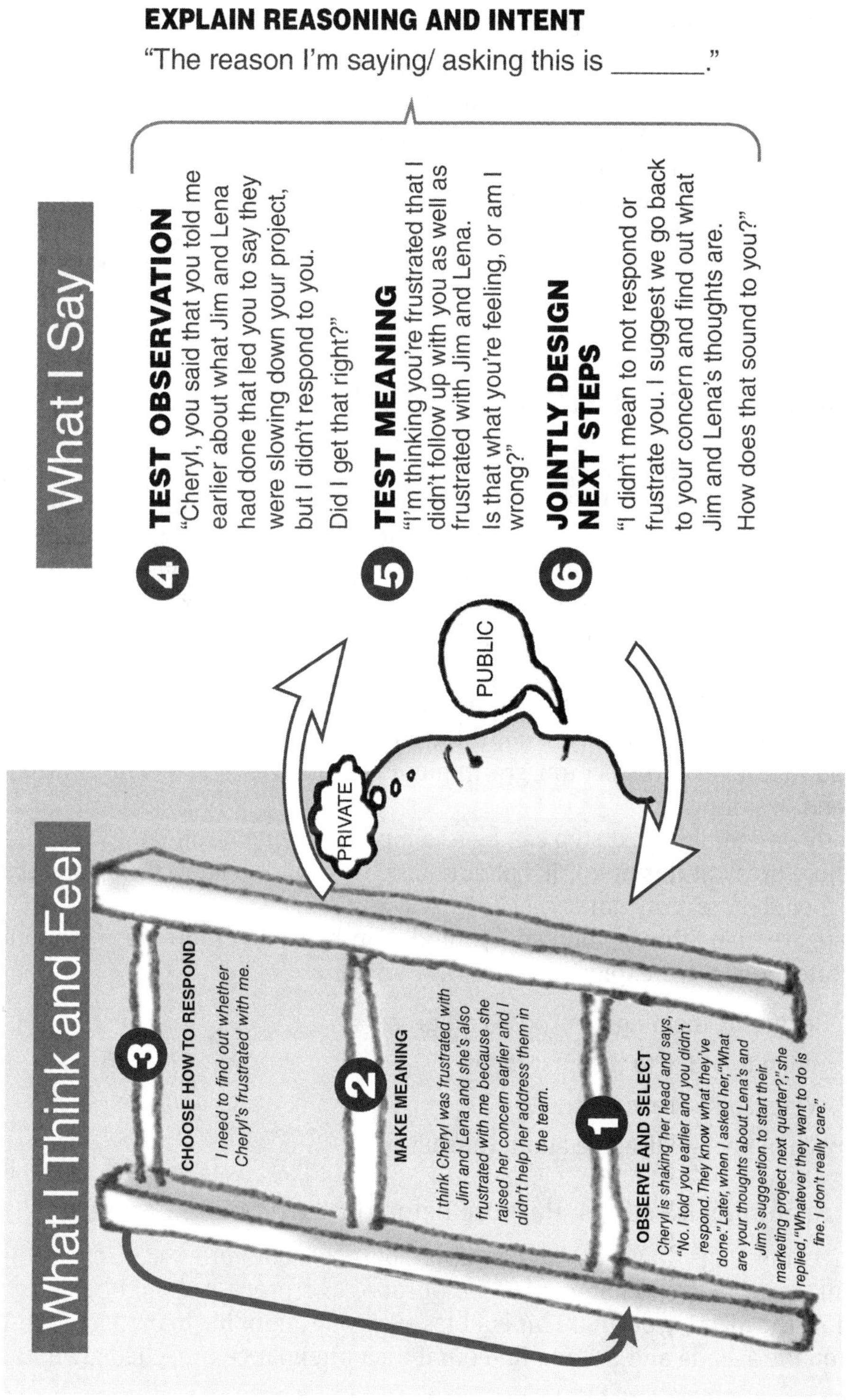

EXPLAIN REASONING AND INTENT

"The reason I'm saying/ asking this is _____."

What I Say

4 **TEST OBSERVATION**

"Cheryl, you said that you told me earlier about what Jim and Lena had done that led you to say they were slowing down your project, but I didn't respond to you. Did I get that right?"

5 **TEST MEANING**

"I'm thinking you're frustrated that I didn't follow up with you as well as frustrated with Jim and Lena. Is that what you're feeling, or am I wrong?"

6 **JOINTLY DESIGN NEXT STEPS**

"I didn't mean to not respond or frustrate you. I suggest we go back to your concern and find out what Jim and Lena's thoughts are. How does that sound to you?"

PUBLIC

PRIVATE

What I Think and Feel

3 **CHOOSE HOW TO RESPOND**

I need to find out whether Cheryl's frustrated with me.

2 **MAKE MEANING**

I think Cheryl was frustrated with Jim and Lena and she's also frustrated with me because she raised her concern earlier and I didn't help her address them in the team.

1 **OBSERVE AND SELECT**

Cheryl is shaking her head and says, "No. I told you earlier and you didn't respond. They know what they've done." Later, when I asked her, "What are your thoughts about Lena's and Jim's suggestion to start their marketing project next quarter?," she replied, "Whatever they want to do is fine. I don't really care".

Figure 5.7   Tye Using the Mutual Learning Cycle

Using the Mutual Learning Cycle to Diagnose and Intervene in Groups

In the beginning of this chapter, I said that you can use the eight behaviors to guide your own behavior as well as to diagnose and intervene in the group. The mutual learning cycle is the fundamental tool you use to diagnose and intervene, no matter what behaviors you're diagnosing and intervening on, and no matter what your facilitative role. The mutual learning cycle structures how you think and how you say what you're thinking. In Chapters 7 through 10, I show you how to use the cycle to diagnose and intervene with groups.

BEHAVIOR 7: JOINTLY DESIGN NEXT STEPS

Jointly designing next steps means deciding with others, not for others, when and how to move forward. When you jointly design next steps, you're being transparent about your strategy, developing mutual accountability for the process, and enabling the group to make an informed choice with you.

Jointly designing next steps is a specific form of behavior 1: Make statements and ask genuine questions. In joint design, you (1) state your point of view about how you think the group should proceed; (2) explain your reasoning, including your interests, relevant information, and assumptions; (3) ask others how they may see it differently; and (4) jointly craft a way to proceed that takes into account group members' interests, relevant information, and assumptions.

Jointly designing a next step can be as simple as saying, "I suggest we take a 15-minute break at this point. It's about halfway through the morning, and the break food is here. Any concerns?"

There are many things you can jointly design with the group. Here are four main categories we'll explore:

1. Beginning meetings: purpose and process
2. When to move to the next topic
3. When someone is off track
4. When people disagree about the facts

Beginning Meetings: Purpose before Process before Content

Effective meetings have an agreed-upon purpose and process. Unless the meeting was called spontaneously, the purpose and process should be agreed on before the meeting occurs. This enables everyone attending to prepare for the items on the agenda and even to find out if their attendance is needed given the topics. Meetings can have more than one purpose, and each agenda topic can reflect a different purpose. If you're a facilitator or facilitative consultant, you may be responsible for recommending a process to accomplish the meeting purpose and you may even be involved in helping the group shape the purpose of the meeting.

While effective meetings begin with an agreed-upon purpose and process, you may need to revisit and modify the purpose and/or process during the meeting. Sometimes a group discovers that it needs to accomplish another purpose before it is able to achieve the original purpose of the meeting. Sometimes, a group discovers that the process they are using to achieve a purpose fails to address all the issues that need to be considered to achieve the purpose.

Whether you are setting the purpose and process initially or modifying them during the meeting, the key point is to design them jointly with the group. Even if you're the person drafting a recommendation, you would share the meeting purpose and process with the group, explain your reasoning for structuring the purpose and process, and then ask, "What changes, if any, do you think we need to make to the proposed purpose and process?"

Agreeing on Whether Someone Is Off Track

Keeping a group focused on their topic is an important part of your facilitative role. But you may be doing this unilaterally. For example, consider a group discussing how to increase sales to current customers. If group member Yvonne says, "I think we have a problem with our billing cycles," and you respond, "That's a different topic," you're unilaterally controlling the conversation. Your comment assumes that Yvonne's comment is unrelated to the current topic. If she thinks her comment is on topic, she may stop participating in the meeting. As a result, the group doesn't get the benefit of using her relevant information in deciding a course of action. In addition, she may end up not being committed to the course of action that the group decides on.

If you're using the behavior of jointly designing next steps, you would say something like, "Yvonne, I don't see how your point about the problem with billing cycles is related to increasing sales to current customers. Maybe I'm missing something. Can you help me understand how you see them being related?" When Yvonne responds, you and the group members might learn about a connection between the two topics that you and they haven't previously considered. For example, the organization's billing cycles may create a long enough time lag that salespeople don't have real-time data about their customers' inventory. If there is a connection, the group can decide whether it makes more sense to pursue Yvonne's idea now or later. If it turns out that her comment isn't related, you can ask the group whether and when it wants to address it.

Designing Ways to Test Differences about the Facts

Sometimes groups get stuck when they can't agree on what the facts are. Without agreement on the facts—a key part of relevant information—it's difficult to make decisions that all group members are committed to. Unfortunately, when groups find themselves in this situation, they often create an escalating cycle in which each member tries to convince the others that his or her own position is correct. Each member offers evidence to support his or her position. Each doubts the other's data, and none are likely to offer data to weaken their own positions. Even after the disagreement is over, the "losers" are still likely to believe they are right.

When you help a group jointly design a way to test disagreements about the facts, you help it move forward in a way that all members agree on the facts. When I think of this behavior, I imagine two scientists with competing hypotheses who are able to design only one experiment to test their competing hypotheses. To conduct the experiment, they need to jointly design it so that it is rigorous enough to meet both of their standards and for them to accept the data and the implications that result from the data.

Consider an IT leadership team in which members disagree about the amount of time that it currently takes IT support staff to respond to and resolve employee IT problems. As a facilitator or consultant, you might begin by asking, "How can you jointly design a way to figure out what the current response time is?" You can begin helping the team develop a joint design by agreeing on what it means by the words *current*, *respond to*, and *resolve*. Next, you might ask the team how it can analyze available data and/or collect new data to answer the team's question.

It's essential that the team jointly design the methods it will use to answer its question. If the team doesn't, when the results are generated, some team members are likely to state that the team used a nonrepresentative sample, didn't collect the right data, or analyzed the data incorrectly. It's also important to have the team agree in advance on what kinds of results will lead the team to take certain actions. For example, what percentage of the IT problems would have to take longer than a certain amount of time for IT staff to resolve for the team to agree that there was a problem that needed to be solved.

Some disagreements are easier to address than others. Deciding what a particular memo says may be as simple as opening the file and looking at it together. Agreeing on what has been said in previous meetings may require talking to a number of people and trying to reconstruct the conversation. Particularly difficult is deciding what the effects will be of implementing a strategy or policy. Still, if the effects of the choice are significant, group members can collect data from other organizations that have already implemented a similar strategy or policy; or you can help the group simulate the effects by using systems-thinking modeling.

Degrees of Joint Design

No matter what your facilitative role, there is a continuum of joint design. At one end of the continuum, you design the next step on your own with no input from group members, except to ask if they have any concerns. This is often the case with simple next steps, such as suggesting that it looks like a good time to take a break or to recommend how the group get out all the relevant information needed for the decision. At the other end of the continuum, you and the group are full partners in designing the next step. This is often the case, when a group realizes it needs to change the purpose of the meeting or when a team is concerned that the current meeting process is not helping it accomplish the meeting's purpose.

BEHAVIOR 8: DISCUSS UNDISCUSSABLE ISSUES

Undiscussable issues are issues that are relevant to the group's task and are having or will have a negative effect on the group's results, but that individuals believe they cannot discuss openly in the group without some negative consequences. People often talk about undiscussable issues before and after meetings with others who have similar views, but not in the one place they can resolve them—in the group meeting.

Part of your facilitative role is to help the group address undiscussable issues that are reducing its effectiveness. We'll discuss how to do this in Chapter 10, on intervening with the mutual learning behaviors. For now, let's focus on undiscussable issues that you may have with a group you're working with.

Here are examples of undiscussable issues that you might face working with a group: (1) The group consistently doesn't follow through on its commitments, making it difficult for you to perform your role effectively during the meetings; (2) the group consistently asks you to share your view on the topics it is discussing or to behave in ways that are outside your facilitative role; and (3) you infer that the group does not have the knowledge, skills, or motivation necessary to accomplish its stated goals, even with your help. Keep in mind that these issues are not inherently undiscussable. You make the choice whether they are undiscussable.

The Problem with Not Discussing Undiscussable Issues

You create undiscussable issues when you operate from a unilateral control mindset. If you value minimizing the expression of negatives feelings, you're concerned that if you raise these difficult issues, others may get defensive, you may get defensive, and you will negatively affect your working relationship with the group you're supposed to be helping. Ironically, by not discussing the undiscussable issue, you create the negative effect you're trying to avoid.

If you value minimizing the expression of negative feelings, you also want to save face for others—and often for yourself, too. In short, you see discussing undiscussable issues as putting people on the spot and not being compassionate. But when you don't discuss undiscussable issues, you withhold relevant information from others and prevent them from making an informed choice. Here, too, you might ironically create the opposite of what you're trying to create. Instead of being compassionate, you create problems for others. In the extreme, preventing the group from making an informed choice can be cruel instead of compassionate.

Finally, if you're also operating from the unilateral control value of "win; don't lose," you may be concerned that raising an undiscussable issue will reduce the chance that you will win.

In short, unilateral control teaches us to praise in public, criticize in private. That prevents us from discussing undiscussable issues with the group.

How to Raise Your Undiscussable Issue

Using mutual learning means raising the undiscussable issue in the place where the relevant information is and the people who are present can address the problem. If the undiscussable issue involves the group and you, you raise it with the full group.

Discussing undiscussable issues doesn't involve any new mindset or behaviors. I made this a separate behavior only because it feels much more difficult to use. But to use the behavior, you use the mutual learning mindset and behaviors that we've already discussed. You assume that you may be missing things that others are seeing and that you may be contributing to the problem you're privately complaining about. You also assume that others' motives are pure, and value compassion for others and yourself. When you raise and discuss an undiscussable issue, you share relevant but difficult information with the group so that you and the group can jointly make an informed choice about what if anything to do differently. You state your views and ask genuine questions, use specific examples, agree on what important words mean, share your reasoning and intent, focus on interests, test your assumptions and inferences, and jointly design next steps with the group.

Here is what you might say if you were raising the undiscussable issue of the group not completing work that makes it difficult for you to perform your role:

> I want to raise an issue that I think is keeping me from helping you achieve your goals. I've noticed in the last three meetings that, as a group, you've

not completed the assignments you committed to get to me before the meetings, and as a result I haven't been able to adequately prepare to help you make decisions in the meetings. Is each of you willing to discuss this issue? [If yes, continue.] Okay, I want to suggest a process we can use to discuss the issue and check to see if it works for everyone. First, I'd like to provide a few examples of the issue and check to see whether each of you is seeing what I saw or is seeing it differently. I want to make sure we agree on what's happened before we move forward. Second, if we agree this is happening, I'd like for us to explore what is causing the behavior. I'm open to the possibility that I'm doing things that are making it difficult for you to complete the assignments you agreed to. Third, I'd like for us to identify the interests we need to meet for any solution to work. Finally, I'd like us to craft a solution that addresses the root causes and meets everyone's interest. Does anyone have any concerns about the process I'm suggesting or want to suggest an improvement? [If not, continue.] OK, is each of you willing to use this process?

Notice that when I raise the undiscussable issue, I am jointly designing next steps with the group, stating my views and asking genuine questions, explaining my reasoning, and identifying people's interests.

LEARNING TO USE THE BEHAVIORS

The behaviors are like individual dance steps. I have focused on the eight behaviors individually as a way to introduce them and show how to use each one. But the power of the behaviors comes from using them together, much like you would combine dance steps in different ways to move gracefully across the dance floor. When you use the behaviors, you are almost always using several of them at the same time.

You may feel awkward as you start using the behaviors. You may feel that it doesn't sound like you; instead, it sounds like you imitating something you read in a book (well, actually you have) or heard in a workshop. It's natural to feel unnatural as you begin to use the behaviors. The unnaturalness comes from a number of sources, notably trying to translate your left-hand column into sentences that use the grammatical structure of the behaviors, trying to integrate the behaviors with your own natural speech pattern and word choice, and trying to put it all together so you can talk at the speed of normal conversation.

It takes practice to find your own voice in using the behaviors. With regular practice, you will find that you can use the behaviors so it sounds like you are talking at your normal speed.

SUMMARY

In this chapter, I have described the set of eight mutual learning behaviors at the heart of the Skilled Facilitator approach. I explained how to use the behaviors to put into practice the mutual learning mindset. In the next chapter, we will explore what it takes to create an effective group and how you can help groups design themselves to be more effective. We have already discussed two of the three main factors: (1) a mutual learning mindset and (2) a set of mutual learning behaviors.

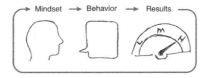

Mindset → Behavior → Results

CHAPTER SIX

Designing and Developing Effective Groups

I n this chapter, I describe how you can use the Team Effectiveness Model (TEM) to help the groups and teams you work with. I begin by describing why it's important to have a group or team effectiveness model as part of your work, whether you're a facilitator, consultant, coach, or trainer. Then I define the difference between a team and a group and why the difference matters so much for the teams and groups you work with and for how you work with them. I complete the chapter by describing the TEM and show how you can use it to design, diagnose, and intervene with teams and groups.

Groups and teams can be designed in different ways, even if they have the same task. Some designs lead to better results. If you're helping a new team design how it will work together or helping a current team figure out how it can work more effectively, it's probably obvious that how a team is designed will make a big difference in the results it can achieve. But if you're not helping teams and groups in this way, why should you care? The answer is that if a team or group is designed poorly, the poor design can hinder anything it tries to accomplish, including your ability to facilitate or consult with the team. Team design is an invisible but powerful force that shapes the system. If you don't know how the system works, you can't work effectively with it.

This particular section is adapted from the chapter "Designing for Mutual Learning" in *Smart Leaders, Smarter Teams*.

HOW A TEAM EFFECTIVENESS MODEL HELPS YOU AND THE TEAMS AND GROUPS YOU WORK WITH

If you're helping teams become more effective, you need a model of what an effective team looks like. That's true whether you're working with the full team, the team leader, or other members of the team. **A good team effectiveness model helps you and the team in three ways: as a design tool, a diagnostic tool, and an intervention tool.**

As a design tool, you can use the model to help a newly formed team design itself effectively. This work can and should be part of launching a new team. As a diagnostic tool, you can use the model with existing teams that are less effective than they need to be. Here, you and the team would compare the elements in an effective team model with the team's current design and functioning, identifying gaps that the team wants to close. As an intervention tool, you can use the model to watch the team in action. When you see behaviors that lead you to infer an ineffective team design, you can test your inference with the team, see if the members agree, and if so, ask whether they want to begin to redesign that element of the team.

Before looking at the TEM, it's important to understand the difference between a team and a group. That difference affects the team or group and how you work with the members.

THE DIFFERENCE BETWEEN TEAMS AND GROUPS—AND WHY IT MATTERS

As a facilitator, consultant, coach, or trainer, you're likely to be working with a variety of groups and teams. I have used the terms *group* and *team* interchangeably, but now I want to distinguish between the two. This is not an irrelevant abstract exercise. Teams and groups differ in fundamental ways. Those differences call for designing groups and teams differently, and require that you work differently with each. Let's start by distinguishing between the two.

What Makes a Team?

Team researcher J. Richard Hackman identifies four criteria for defining *a team*:

1. Members are interdependent around a team task.
2. Members know who is a member of the team.
3. Members know the extent of the team's authority.
4. Membership is stable over time.[1]

Hackman uses the term *real team* for teams that meet these criteria, as opposed to teams in name only. Where Hackman uses the term *real team*, I use the term *team*. Let's explore each of these criteria that make a team.

Team Members Are Interdependent around a Team Task. I consider interdependence the most important criterion for identifying a team. **To be a team there has to be a team task—a task that can be accomplished only by team members acting interdependently with each other.** Team researcher Ruth Wageman defines task interdependence as "the degree to which a piece of work requires multiple individuals to exchange help and resources interactively to complete the work."[2]

Many so-called teams aren't interdependent around a team task. For example, in many senior sales teams, each member is responsible for the sales of part of the organization's product line or services or for sales in some part of the world. Like a gymnastics team that has only individual events, members work largely independently of each other, without having to rely on each other to accomplish their task. At the end of the month or quarter, they report their respective sales to the team leader, who aggregates them for the total sales for that period. However, if the sales team sells as a team, jointly planning customer presentations and meeting together with potential customers, with each member contributing unique knowledge, skills, and resources to make a sale, the team would have significant task interdependence. Because a team's interdependence has a significant impact on how it needs to be designed and how you work with it, we'll return to this topic a little later, but first let's consider the three other criteria for a team.

Members Know Who Is a Member of the Team. If team members are interdependent around a team task, then they need to know who is on the team and who is not. One study found that fewer than 7 percent of the leadership teams they studied, when asked, could agree on who was on the team.[3] I have worked with executives who could not tell me exactly who was on the leadership team they led!

In my experience, when the team membership is unclear, there are two subgroups in the team: a core group of people, who everyone agrees are members, and a second group of individuals, who even among themselves aren't sure if they are team members. There are a number of reasons that team membership can be unclear. For example, the leader has never formally designated the team, has shifted members to new roles but is reluctant to move those people off or onto the leadership team, or has kept a member off the team who, organizationally, would be expected to be on the team. Whatever the cause, the lack of clarity undermines the team. If you're consulting to a team in which the membership is unclear, keep in mind that this can hinder your ability to help the team until the membership issues are resolved.

Members Know the Extent of the Team's Authority. Because teams have some decision-making authority, team members need to know the limit of their decision-making authority. What decisions are team members permitted to make, and what decisions are reserved for the team leader? Is the team allowed to make decisions only about executing the team task, or can the team also make decisions about how to monitor and manage work processes and progress? What about designing the team and its context or even setting the overall direction? Each of these areas gives greater decision-making authority to the team. Without this clear agreement, team members may either underuse or overreach their authority.

The Team Membership Is Stable over Time. Finally, a team needs to have a stable membership over time. There is a belief in popular culture that regularly changing the team membership infuses the team with new ideas and energy. That's an interesting idea, but research shows the opposite.[4] It takes time for a team to understand and agree on its purpose, agree on how it will work together, and then put those agreements into action, improving over time. If members are regularly joining and leaving the team, the team doesn't get to benefit from the shared understanding members created with each other: Members either spend too much time integrating new members or suffering when the team doesn't spend this time.

Why Interdependence Matters So Much

The reason that interdependence matters so much is that poorly managed interdependence becomes a root cause of many team and group problems. When team members are interdependent with each other, they need to rely on each other to produce a joint result. This leads team members to develop expectations for how other team members should work with them. These expectations lead members to hold others accountable. When team members' expectations or sense of accountability aren't met, it reduces their ability to achieve the joint result, and it also negatively affects working relationships and individual well-being.

Teams and groups accomplish their work and avoid these problems by dividing the collective task among members and, where they are interdependent, coordinating their work. The type and degree of interdependence and the type of coordination needed to manage it affect many elements of the team or group's design. As the level of interdependence increases, so does the level of expectations and accountability between team members. Teams have a greater need to coordinate, it's more difficult to coordinate, and their inability to coordinate well has a stronger negative impact on their performance and working relationships.[5,6] If the team elements are designed well—if they

Figure 6.1   Types of Interdependence

support the level of interdependence and coordination needed—the team can achieve better results.

There are different types of interdependence, which I've shown in Figure 6.1.[7] Each type of interdependence is created by designing some element of the team, and each influences team behavior in a different way. Let's begin by defining them and how they work. The two main types of interdependence are structural and behavioral. The first main type, *structural interdependence*, as its name states, refers to how elements of the team are designed or structured so that team members will work together to accomplish the task.

There are two kinds of structural interdependence—task interdependence and outcome interdependence. *Task interdependence* is the extent to which various elements of the team's work are designed so that team members need to interact with each other to accomplish the task, such as a sales team that sells as a team. The second type of structural interdependence is *outcome interdependence*, and there are two kinds. *Goal interdependence* is the extent to which performance is measured as a team, as individuals, or some combination. A team's goal interdependence increases the more that performance is measured as team goals rather than only individual goals. For example, if sales team members' goals were focused only on their parts of the sales, then goal interdependence would be low; if they were focused on the overall goals of the team, goal interdependence would be high. The second kind of outcome interdependence is *reward interdependence*—the extent to which rewards that individual team members receive depend on other team members' performance. If the year-end bonus a team member receives is determined only by that member's individual performance, reward interdependence is low. If the bonus is determined by the overall team performance, then reward interdependence is high. For example, if sales team members were rewarded only for how well they performed their part of the sales, reward interdependence would be low; if they were rewarded based on the sales for the entire team, reward interdependence would be high.

To create task interdependence and outcome interdependence, you design different elements of the team, which affect the team in different ways. You design the level of task interdependence by changing how the work itself is conducted; you design the level of outcome interdependence by changing the consequences that follow from accomplishing the work.

The other main type of interdependence, *behavioral interdependence*, is the extent to which team members *actually* interact with each other to accomplish their task. It's important to distinguish between structural and behavioral interdependence because designing a team with high structural inter-dependence—task interdependence, reward interdependence, and goal inter-dependence—doesn't necessarily ensure that team members will actually act interdependently. The opposite is also true. Sometimes teams with little structural interdependence choose to work together in a way that creates high behavioral interdependence.

When you're helping a team increase its effectiveness, interdependence is one of the first places to look. This includes understanding the main team tasks that need to be performed, and how task interdependence and outcome interdependence are designed into the team—or need to be designed into the team—to increase the three types of team results.

Teams Aren't Better than Groups: It's a Matter of Fit

A group that performs very well doesn't become a team. There are high-performing groups and high-performing teams. How well an entity (that is, team or group) performs doesn't determine whether it's a group or a team. What distinguishes a group from a team is the design. **If the work is designed so that members are interdependent around a team task, they are a team; if they're not interdependent, they're a group.** Whether a group or a team is effective depends partly on the fit between how the work is designed and how members act. If members are interdependent around a task but act as if they're not, they're a less effective team—but still a team.

Unfortunately, since teams became popular again in the 1990s, many organizations have pushed to make teams the default unit of work, even when the work could be better accomplished as a group. Simply telling a group that it's a team or exhorting it to act like a team doesn't make it a team.

Deciding whether to be a group or a team is an important decision; it affects the way many elements of the group or team are designed and the ability to achieve results. And whether to be structured as a group or a team isn't always clear. Often the task to be accomplished doesn't predetermine a certain degree of interdependence, especially among knowledge workers; the task could be designed with a little or a lot of interdependence. What matters is that there is a good fit between the task to be accomplished and the degree of inter-dependence used to accomplish it.

You can tell when there isn't a good fit. When a group is inappropriately made to work like a team, members don't see the need to attend team meetings. They consider them a waste of their time. When they do attend, they get frustrated being asked to solve problems that don't significantly involve them and to spend time deciding how to work together on issues that don't require the level of coordination being asked of them. As a result, they often tune out, unless the topic focuses on their particular part of the business. When members do participate, they focus on their own interests rather than also considering the needs of teammates or the larger organization. At other times, they are quiet or engaged on their smartphones. There is little curiosity and accountability because members don't consider that anything of consequence to them is on the agenda.

You can also tell when what should be a team is designed as a group, with little or no interdependence. The team spends its time listening to updates but not addressing the real issues that are affecting the team. Members become frustrated with other members because they don't get the information, collaboration, or other resources they need from each other. Their frustration mounts because they don't have a venue to solve these problems directly with each other; instead, they must work through their common boss or handle the issues one-on-one.

A Better Question: For What Tasks Do We Need to Be a Team?

I've been discussing interdependence as if an entity is either a group or a team, but that's an oversimplification. Even though a team may have a primary task, a team often has several tasks, some for which they need to be interdependent and others not. **Rather than asking whether we are a team or a group, a more useful question is: "What are the tasks around which we need to be a team and what are the tasks around which we need to be a group?"** This enables the team or group to design its elements to reflect different levels of interdependence, depending on the task. For example, effective teams solve problems and make decisions in different ways, depending on whether they are dealing with an issue on which they are interdependent or not interdependent.

HOW INTERDEPENDENCE AFFECTS YOUR WORK WITH TEAMS AND GROUPS

Whether you're working with a team or a group, and how well the members are managing their interdependence, can affect your work with them in several ways. First, it may affect how the group responds to you. If you're working with a group in which members believe the leader is requiring more interdependence than necessary, the members may see your work with them as another example of this unnecessary interdependence and may be disengaged or seem frustrated with you. Second, if the team or group members are having problems working together and getting the results they need, the issue of interdependence may be a root cause and one you want to explore with them. Third, if the team or group is new and looking for you to help it design how best to function, one of the first questions to explore is what degree of interdependence do the tasks require.

Toward the end of the chapter, I will explain how you can help teams and groups identify the appropriate level of interdependence for do the tasks, and how to design their team or group elements accordingly. To do this, we first need to understand all the elements that make a team or group effective.

THE TEAM EFFECTIVENESS MODEL

Until this point, I've been talking about team effectiveness models in general. Now I want to make the connection between team effective models in general and the TEM by describing what makes a practical team model. Remember that the Team Effectiveness Model applies to both groups and teams.

What Makes a Good Team Effectiveness Model

Models and theories are essential to your work. As the statistician George Box said, "All models are wrong, but some are useful."[8] Just as some teams are designed better than others, so are some team effectiveness models. To the extent that you use models that are well designed, you increase the chance of improving your practice and helping groups. A well-designed team effectiveness model will improve your ability to design, diagnose, and intervene with teams and groups. As the social psychologist Kurt Lewin said, "There is nothing so practical as a good theory." Here are some of the ways that the TEM is useful.

The TEM is a normative model, which shows you what a team *should look like* if it's effective. In contrast, a descriptive team model explains how teams function, not how they should function. It's not designed to help you identify whether the team is effective, and if it's not, what to do. A good example of a descriptive model is the widely cited, four-stage Tuckman model of group development.[9] Based on his review of 50 studies of mostly therapy groups, Tuckman identified four developmental stages: forming, storming, norming, and performing (he later added a fifth stage adjourning). Tuckman wasn't describing how these therapy groups should evolve, only how they did evolve. Unfortunately, many team practitioners have treated Tuckman's descriptive model as a normative model, assuming that for teams to be effective, they should move through all of these four stages in the order described. Because many descriptive models identify less than effective behavior, if you confuse a descriptive model with a normative model, you may be contributing to a group being less effective than it could be. In contrast, a normative model enables you to watch a group in action and identify gaps between how the team is currently functioning and how it would function if it were more effective.

The TEM is a causal model. It describes how the team elements interact to create the team results. This enables you to predict what's likely to happen to a team if you see certain structures, processes, or behaviors. It also enables you to help a team conduct a root cause analysis so it can make changes that solve problems instead of simply addressing symptoms. In other words, a causal model helps you identify the points of leverage for helping a team improve its effectiveness. A simple list of five or seven things that teams need to do to be effective isn't a causal model.[10] It may be easy to understand, but it doesn't help you understand what to do if a team isn't effective.

The TEM is internally consistent. If a model is internally consistent, then all of its parts fit together. They aren't in conflict. Internal consistency is important because it ensures that when you use the model to intervene and design, you don't create conflicts for yourself or the team you're helping.

The TEM is relatively comprehensive; it captures much of what the research has found to contribute to effective teams. Like any model, it's a simplified way to describe how something works, but it identifies the factors that explain most of what contributes to effective teams.

The Team Effectiveness Model: The Big Picture

The TEM (Figure 6.2) defines (1) the results an effective team achieves, (2) the elements that a team needs to achieve these results, (3) how each of these elements should be designed, and (4) how the elements are related to each other. Although it's called the Team Effectiveness Model, it's equally relevant for groups and teams. That's because **the elements that make work groups and teams effective are the same; what may differ is how the elements are designed**. You can use the TEM with a variety of groups and teams, including leadership teams, functional teams, cross-functional teams, project teams, and task forces. It's designed for groups and teams that discuss work issues and make decisions about them. You can use the TEM for groups and teams whose members come from one part of an organization, many parts of an organization, or more than one organization.

The TEM has three parts—mindset, design, and results—and incorporates the mutual learning approach. **The results of the TEM and the mutual learning approach are the same: (1) performance, (2) working relationships, and (3) individual well-being. The mindset of the TEM and the mutual learning approach are also the same** (see Chapter 4 to review the mutual learning and TEM results and mindset). However, the mindset in the TEM represents a collective team mindset rather than an individual mindset.

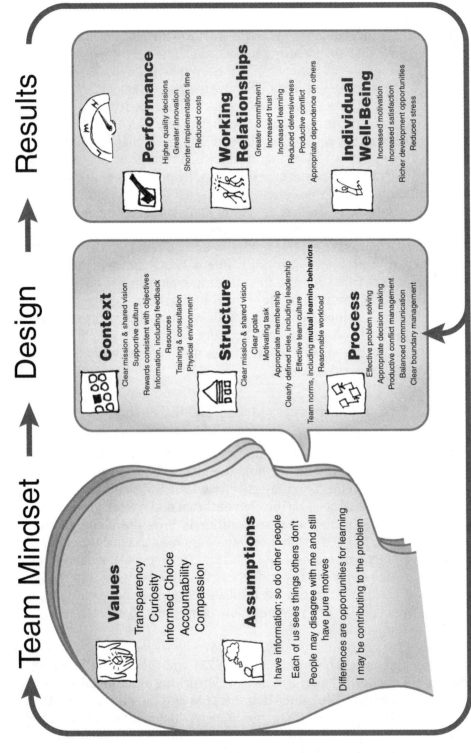

130

Figure 6.2   Team Effectiveness Model

The main difference between the TEM and the mutual learning model is their middle columns; in the TEM, it's design, and in the mutual learning approach, it's behavior. The TEM design column includes three factors that contribute to team effectiveness—context, structure, and process. These include organizational and team-level factors, indicating that it takes more than effective behaviors to create an effective team. Still, as Figure 6.3 shows, the TEM includes the eight mutual learning behaviors within the structure element called team norms, including mutual learning behaviors.

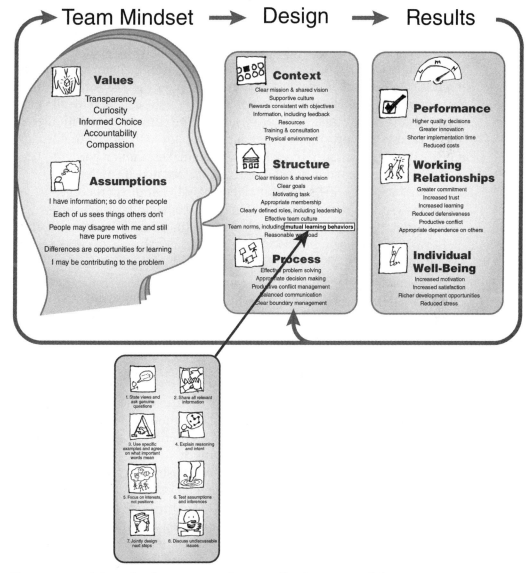

Figure 6.3 Eight Behaviors as Part of Team Effectiveness Model

WHAT'S YOUR MINDSET AS YOU DESIGN?[11]

How you think is how you design. If the people who design the team do so with a unilateral control mindset, then they will embed elements of unilateral control in the team structures and processes. This will create the results that the team is trying to avoid: poorer performance, weaker working relationships, and lower team member well-being.

Here are two performance management examples of how using a unilateral control mindset leads to ineffective team design:

- Many teams have a performance management process that leaders use to assess their direct reports' performance and to give them feedback. This process is usually designed so that, before actually meeting with the direct report, you assess that person's performance and generate examples to support your conclusion. Your leader approves your assessments of your direct report's performance before you have the conversation with the direct report. This preemptive oversight is supposed to ensure that leaders fairly assign performance ratings. But it also makes it much harder to be curious about what your direct report thinks, because if you learned that you'd missed some significant elements of your direct report's performance, you'd need to go back to your leader and correct yourself, and say that person deserved a higher rating than you'd thought. When a performance management process is designed like this, your curiosity easily gives way to defending your initial assessment.

- In many teams, the leader's assessment of a direct report comes from information that is provided by the direct report's peers or other managers. But there's no place in the process where the leader shares that with the person he or she is assessing or reveals the source of his information. As a result, team members and others working with the direct report aren't accountable to the person being assessed.

These examples describe how unilateral control core values and assumptions get embedded in one aspect of team design and how they can lead to unintended negative consequences. My point is that **every element of team design reflects the mindset of the person or people designing it.**

Just as leaders are usually unaware of how they're using their mindset to design behavior, they're unaware of how they're using their mindset to design elements of the team. They don't necessarily intend to design the team in a way that may undermine its effectiveness; it's just how their operating system works. That's one reason that leaders are often surprised when their teams aren't consistently following the core values they espouse. The team's design reflects and reinforces a different set of values and assumptions than the ones the leader may be espousing.

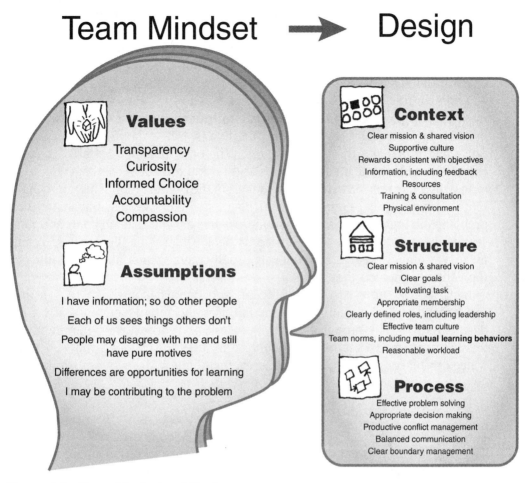

Figure 6.4 Team Mindset and Design

In addition to structures and processes, team design involves shaping the context in which the team exists, so the rest of this chapter will break down the design challenge into those three topics. Figure 6.4 reiterates the connection between mindset and team design and previews the discussions.

TEAM STRUCTURE, PROCESS, AND CONTEXT[12]

Team structure **comprises the relatively stable characteristics of a team.** When people think of structure, they usually think first of organizational structure—who reports to whom. But a team's structure also includes its mission and vision, the task, the membership, and the roles that each person plays.

Team process is *how* things are done rather than *what* is done. To be effective, teams need to manage a number of processes, including how they solve problems and make decisions. Structure is simply a stable, recurring process that emerges from team members continually interacting with each other in the same way.[13]

Team context includes elements that are usually designed or that emerge from the larger organization and that influence how a team works. This includes how clear the organization's mission is, how supportive the organization's culture is, and the extent to which the organization's reward system is consistent with the team's objectives and how the team works together.

In general, teams located at higher levels in the organizational hierarchy have more authority to design their team elements. Work teams may have their problem-solving and decision-making processes as well as team goals and roles set for them, whereas leadership teams decide these for themselves. Teams located at higher organizational levels usually have greater ability to influence the context in which they work.

Let's look at how structure, process, and context contribute to a team's results, and how the mutual learning mindset and interdependence affect the design. As you read through structure, process, and context, keep in mind that a team is a system. To get the best team results, all of the elements that constitute it need to be congruent with each other, including with the team's mindset.

TEAM STRUCTURE

These are the elements that make an effective team structure: (1) clear mission and shared vision, (2) clear goals, (3) motivating task, (4) appropriate membership, (5) clearly defined roles, including leadership, (5) effective group culture, (6) group norms, including mutual learning behaviors, and (7) reasonable workload.

Clear Mission and Shared Vision

The mission is the purpose of a team; it answers the question, "Why do we exist?" A team achieves its mission by accomplishing various goals, which in turn are achieved by performing various tasks. A vision is a mental picture of the future that an organization seeks to create. Whereas a mission clarifies why the team exists, a vision identifies what a team should look like and how it should act as it seeks to accomplish its mission. Together, a mission and a vision provide meaning that can inspire and guide the members' work. Many teams have mission and vision statements in their conference rooms. But the value of a mission and vision lies in the shared commitment that members make to achieving them, not in the laminated poster on a wall.

Ultimately, it's the team leader's responsibility to set or confirm the mission for the team. But mutual learning leaders don't simply lay out a compelling mission and then expect people to sign up for the trip. Using the mutual learning mindset, they are transparent about not only what the mission is but why it's that mission as opposed to other plausible missions. They're also curious about others' views of the mission and seek to incorporate their interests and ideas. When others make suggestions that the leader finally decides not to incorporate into the mission, the leader is accountable for explaining his or her reasoning. The leader also asks team members to be accountable by saying whether they are willing to commit to the final version of the mission the leader and the team developed. Assuming that members are committed to the team's mission simply because they're on the team is too big an assumption to leave untested.

Ultimately, mission and vision are personal. For team members to commit to them, the mission and vision need to speak to them directly. When members aren't able to commit to the mission and what's required of them to achieve it, mutual learning leaders respond with compassion rather than seeing this as an act of insubordination or organizational treason.

Clear Goals. The team's goals need to be clear enough that the team agrees on what they mean and can measure its progress toward them. The team's goals also need to be consistent with the larger mission and vision. Consistent with the research, in a mutual learning team, whether the goals are set by the leader or with team members, the reasoning underlying the goals is clear.[14] To increase goal interdependence, goal accomplishment is also measured at the team level, instead of only the individual level.

Motivating Task

Even when team members are interdependent with each other, team members can become disengaged because the team task isn't motivating. What makes a team task motivating isn't how charismatic or compelling the leader is or the rewards that follow from strong performance; it's the design of the team task itself. Some teams design members' work in ways that doing it becomes uninteresting; other teams design their work so that doing the work is itself motivating. Research shows that for a team task to be motivating, it should meet the following conditions:[15]

- It requires members to use a variety of their skills.
- It involves a whole and meaningful piece of work with a visible outcome.
- The outcomes have significant consequences, either for customers or others in the organization.

- It gives members significant autonomy over how they accomplish the task so that they feel ownership of their work.
- It generates regular and trustworthy feedback to team members about how well the team is performing.

For the team leader, providing informed choice means enabling the team to jointly design the task. It's difficult to know the variety of skills that members have and want to use, what they consider a meaningful piece of work, and what they consider autonomy. By jointly designing the task with the team and being curious, the team increases the chance that the task meets these conditions.

To increase the degree of task interdependence, the team designs the task so that multiple team members exchange help and resources interactively to complete the work.

Appropriate Membership

An effective team has a carefully selected membership. Of course, members need to bring an appropriate mix of knowledge and skills to successfully complete the team's goals. But there are also many team member characteristics that are strong predictors of team performance. Some of these include personality factors such as team member agreeableness, conscientiousness, openness to experience, and preference for teamwork.[16]

Selecting team members that prefer to work as a team is particularly important if a team is interdependent around its task. Research shows that teams whose members share egalitarian values create more interdependence than teams with shared meritocratic values.[17] Team members who prefer to work individually are not very influenced by team or organizational values that promote cooperation, but, unfortunately, team members who prefer to work cooperatively are influenced by individualistic cultures to become more individualistic.[18] This is one example of how building a team in which interdependent members actually work as a team is a multifaceted task that means taking into account individual characteristics, team design, and the context in which the team functions.

Teams also need to decide how many members will comprise the team. When Abraham Lincoln was asked how long a man's legs should be, he responded, ". . . long enough to reach from his body to the ground."[19] Similarly, the answer to the question, "How many members should be on a team?" is "Just enough to complete the task." A team with more members than it needs to complete the task will spend unnecessary time on coordination that could be spent working directly on the task. In addition, as the team grows, members can lose interest in the work and reduce their effort. Still, the research does not show a clear relationship between team size and team performance, perhaps because the appropriate size of a team depends on its task.[20]

As we discussed earlier in this chapter, a team must also have clear understanding of who is on the team and a team membership that is stable enough to have the time to learn how to work together well.

Clearly Defined Roles, Including Leadership

In many teams, team members consider the formal leader solely responsible for the team and the formal leader takes on this role. By formal leader, I mean the head of the team. As a result, the formal leader leads the meetings, sets team agendas, guides the flow of discussion, and identifies next steps. Members participate but leave the leadership roles to the formal leader. This is what I call a one-leader-in-the-room mindset. If you've consulted to a team like this, even if the team accomplished its goals, you probably saw that the team members were overly dependent on the formal leader.

In teams using mutual learning, team member roles are more fluid. Members may rotate chairing the meetings, taking responsibility for coordinating agendas, and identifying next steps. More important, leadership isn't confined to the formal leader. It's a shared role and responsibility. Operating from the assumption that each person may see things that others miss, each member is accountable for ensuring that the team is functioning well. When a member sees something happening in the team that may reduce its effectiveness, it's that person's role to raise it with the team, whether that person is a member or the formal team leader.

Research suggests that as teams have higher task interdependence, leadership behaviors have a more significant impact on team effectiveness.[21] This makes sense, given that teams with greater task interdependence require more complex coordination.

Effective Team Culture

Culture is powerful but intangible. *Team culture* is the set of values and assumptions that team members share and that guide their behavior. A team's culture can influence how it deals with issues of quality, timeliness, authority, or any other issue relevant to the team's work. For example, one leadership team I worked with shared—and operated consistently with—the belief that if you give intelligent people the right information and let them do their work, they will create a great product. As a result, there were very few complaints of micromanaging; people were given a large amount of autonomy. They produced innovative solutions that met their customer's needs. In contrast, other organizations have a belief that people need to be told exactly what to do or carefully monitored, or otherwise negative consequences can result. In these organizations, team members have little autonomy and feel underutilized.

The core values and assumptions that constitute a team's mindset can also be considered part of that team's culture, but I have identified them separately because they are so fundamental that they influence how a team engages other aspects of its culture. Still, it's fair to say that **changing a team's mindset is changing a team's culture**.

You can't identify a team's culture simply by listening to what members say they value or believe. We often espouse values and beliefs that are inconsistent with our actions, and we are often unaware of our inconsistencies.[22] The values and beliefs that constitute the team's culture have to be inferred by observing the artifacts of the culture,[23] including how members act.[24] Artifacts are products of the culture, including the policies, procedures, and structures that members create.

Culture affects everything a team does and gets reinforced through policies and behavior, but it generally operates outside team members' awareness, which makes it difficult to identify and change.

Mutual learning teams understand the power of culture. They understand that how the team thinks is how it leads. So they talk about the culture that they want to create and how it may differ from their current team culture. They identify the values and assumptions that are currently operating in the team and openly discuss whether they are helping or hindering the team. They are always asking themselves, "How does the decision or action we're about to take align with the values and assumptions we say we stand for?" This often involves discussing undiscussable issues. After they have identified gaps between their present culture and their desired culture, they jointly design ways to close this gap.

Team Norms, Including Mutual Learning Behaviors

Norms are expectations that team members share about how they should behave with each other. Norms are ways of putting the culture into action. Teams can have norms about anything, including who gets copied on e-mails, how to manage time, and who talks first in meetings.

One easily observed norm involves time. (Throughout the world, time is treated differently in different cultures.) For example, some leadership teams I work with place a high value on the precision of time and assume that honoring time commitments conveys respect. As a result, they have a norm that meetings start exactly at the designated starting time, regardless of who is absent. Other teams I work with have different values and assumptions about time. They have developed a norm that leads them to start meetings after everyone arrives, which could be 15 minutes later than planned.

Unfortunately, team norms often develop implicitly, just like the values and assumptions that give rise to them. When that happens, a team finds itself operating with a set of expectations that has mysteriously evolved over time and may not serve the team's needs.

One of the norms in many teams is that the formal leader, because of his authority, gets to play by a different set of rules than the rest of the team members. He may control or dominate the meeting, interrupt others, or switch the conversation when he thinks someone is off track. Other team members may find this behavior ineffective, but they don't raise this issue. But mutual learning teams operate from the assumption that all team members, including the formal leader, play by the same ground rules. That means that behavior that is considered ineffective for a team member is also ineffective for the team leader. This doesn't change the formal leader's authority to make decisions; it simply requires that person to use effective communication behavior in doing so.

The eight mutual learning behaviors—when adopted by a team—become team norms for putting the mutual learning core values and assumptions into action. Because mutual learning teams are transparent about their norms and make an informed choice to adopt them, they're able to hold each other accountable when they see others acting inconsistent with a team expectation. In fact, in mutual learning teams, it's a norm that *all* team members give feedback when they think others are acting inconsistently with a team expectation. In this way, team members share accountability for supporting each other in creating the behaviors they have agreed will lead to better results.

Reasonable Workload

Although technology has increased the speed at which we can perform many tasks, it hasn't increased the speed at which we think or can effectively discuss things with each other—two central tasks for leaders and teams. Effective teams have the ability to estimate when the demands on their time will become so great that the quality of their work will begin to suffer. More important, teams that are able to raise undiscussable issues explicitly address this when they see it coming.

TEAM PROCESS

Team process refers to *how* things are done rather than *what* is done. To be effective, teams must manage these processes: (1) problem solving, (2) decision making, (3) conflict management, (4) communication, and (5) boundary management. The two primary team processes are problem solving and decision making.

Effective Problem Solving

Many teams spend much of their time solving problems. A *problem* is simply a gap between a desired outcome and the current situation. Problem solving is the systematic approach a team uses to close the gap.

Teams have many systematic processes for solving problems, such as Lean, Six Sigma, and other continuous improvement methods. All of these methods can be very powerful, but only if team members are willing to be transparent, curious, accountable, and compassionate with each other. If team members withhold information or assume that they are right and others are wrong, these problem-solving processes become battlegrounds for unilateral control mindsets. Teams that use some formal type of problem-solving process are typically more skilled at the technical side than at raising and discussing challenging issues. As a result, they end up trying to solve problems without all the relevant information.

Appropriate Decision Making

When people first learn about mutual learning, they often assume that they'll need to make decisions by consensus. It isn't so. **The difference between a team that uses mutual learning and one that uses unilateral control isn't with the kind of decision-making rules they use—it's their mindset.**

Mutual learning and unilateral control have the same general decision-making rules: (1) The team decides either by consensus or another rule, including delegating it to a part of the team to decide; (2) the leader decides after discussion with the team; (3) the leader decides after discussion with individual team members; (4) the leader decides without discussion with team members; or (5) the leader delegates the decision to the team or certain members. Now let's explore how leaders using unilateral control and mutual learning might apply the same decision-marking rule but create different outcomes.

If leaders use unilateral control to approach a consensus decision, they're thinking, *How do I get my team members to buy in to the solution that I have already developed?* If they're using mutual learning, they're thinking, *How do I ensure that we get a decision that is based on valid information that ideally meets all stakeholders' needs?* The solution may be one that they thought of before the meeting, one that another team member suggested, or one that the team jointly crafted in the meeting.

If leaders are operating from unilateral control, they assume that they understand the situation and are right. When others offer views or solutions that disagree with their views, they privately question others' motives and discount others' views. But if leaders are operating from mutual learning, they assume that others may see things that they don't. They openly question others and try to learn from their various views.

Many times leaders need to make decisions without consulting others; this is not necessarily operating from unilateral control. They're operating from unilateral control if they consider their own needs only and assume they have most or all of the information needed to make a sound decision or if they don't tell their direct reports about these decisions, let alone how they arrived at them. In the same situation, leaders are operating from mutual learning if they act as a steward, thinking about all stakeholders' interests; make the decision recognizing that they have less than full information; and have a sense of accountability to their direct reports. They tell their direct reports the decisions they made and the reasoning underlying them. They ask if their decision may create any problems, recognizing that, in some situations, they may not be able to change the decision.

If mutual learning leaders have already made a decision, they tell people so. They don't go through the charade of getting input if they've made up their mind. They understand that going through the motions of getting input and then implementing the decision they had already made creates team member cynicism, not engagement. They understand that seeking input without genuine curiosity or openness to change is manipulative and reduces trust and commitment.

Team members don't expect to be involved in every decision; nor do they want to be. But they do expect the formal leader to be transparent with them about whether she's made up her mind about something or how open she is to being influenced. And team members expect that the formal leader won't waste the team's time by getting input on issues that have already been decided.

How a team makes decisions also reflects how it is accountable to others inside and outside the team. In one organization, a leadership team was voting whether to select a particular internal candidate for an HR position. One team member expressed some concerns about the candidate but recused himself from the vote because he didn't have any specific data to back up his concerns. A second team member said he had had concerns for over a year about some actions the candidate had taken. The president asked the second team member whether he had shared his concerns with the candidate. When the member said, "no," the president replied, "Then your vote doesn't count, either." That team member learned a lesson about accountability: he couldn't withhold feedback from an employee and then use that same information to vote against the employee's promotion.

Productive Conflict Management

Effective teams appreciate that conflict is a natural part of teamwork and organizations. They understand that conflict is sometimes simply what occurs when people advocate for different solutions that can't all be implemented. The mutual learning mindset makes it easier for a team to engage conflict productively. Because members assume that differences are opportunities for learning, they don't dig in to positions and try to win the conflict. Nor do they try to avoid the conflict or simply accommodate others' positions.[25]

Instead, they get curious, engage others, discover the source of their different views, and work to bridge the differences. Bridging the differences isn't the same as compromising. When you compromise, you can still operate from positions, seeking to maximize your own gain. When you bridge the differences instead of splitting them, you understand where your assumptions differ from others and where your interests are aligned, even when your positions are in conflict. This enables the team to generate solutions that aren't possible through compromise. Because team members assume that no one has all the pieces of the puzzle and that people can disagree without having questionable motives, they can address high-stakes conflicts without having them negatively affect working relationships.[26] In fact, mutual learning teams often report that after resolving a high-stakes conflict, they often have a better working relationship with the other parties. Teams that have higher task interdependence also require greater skill for managing conflicts.

Balanced Communication

Teams need to communicate so that members get the information they need when they need it and so that the team develops a common understanding of the issues it discusses. Without common understanding, team members can go off in different directions and can create conflicts even if they are acting with the best of intentions.

The mutual learning approach provides basic principles and specific guidance for balanced and effective communication. By balanced I mean that members communicate directly with the people from whom they need information and with whom they need to solve problems. In many teams, team communication operates from the assumption that members are accountable to the leader. As a result, when challenging situations arise, the leader often serves as the hub of communication, with each member sharing relevant information with the leader. But in mutual learning teams, communication operates from the assumption that each team member is accountable to the full team. As a result, members are accountable for sharing their own information directly with the relevant team members. The team leader doesn't serve as an intermediary for team members who are having conflicts with each other.

Teams that use a mutual learning mindset communicate about a wider range of issues. They're able to discuss issues that other teams don't know how to or aren't willing to discuss. As a result, they're able to address barriers to team effectiveness that other team members can't. Finally, because they understand that both thoughts and emotions are important for making good decisions, they talk about their feelings as part of problem solving and managing conflict, leading members to have a deeper understanding of each other.

The degree of interdependence also affects how a team communicates. Research shows that members of groups with high interdependence share more information with each other than do members of groups with low interdependence.[27] In addition, when group members have very different pieces of relevant information, it has a much greater effect on team performance when interdependence is high compared with when interdependence is low.[28]

Clear Boundary Management

Every team has to figure out how to work with the larger organization it is part of as well as individuals and groups outside of the organization.[29] This is managing a team's boundaries. When a team is working with other teams, it has to figure out (1) what information to share with other teams and what information it needs from other teams; (2) where its responsibility for a task ends and the other team's responsibility begins; and (3) which team gets to make which decisions. If a team doesn't manage these boundaries well, it can end up without enough information to accomplish the task or taking on tasks that are beyond its expertise, responsibility, or resources; alternatively, it could end up with another team performing its work. Finally, it could end up without appropriate control over its own area of responsibility.

When team members seek agreement on these issues with other teams, they're often doing so as peers; neither team has the authority to unilaterally decide these issues. In mutual learning, if the teams can't collaboratively reach agreement on these issues, they don't unilaterally escalate the issue to a higher level. They jointly escalate it to the two formal team leaders. Fortunately, mutual learning teams are less likely to have to jointly escalate these kinds of boundary conflicts with other teams, even when the other teams don't know about mutual learning.

TEAM CONTEXT

Every organizational team is influenced by the larger organization—even the most senior leadership team. Teams are more effective when their larger organizational context includes: (1) A clear *organizational* mission and shared vision, (2) a supportive culture, (3) rewards consistent with team objectives, (4) information including feedback, (5) material resources, (6) training and consultation, and (7) a physical environment that supports the work.

A team's ability to influence or even control its context varies with its level in the organization. In any case, mutual learning teams take an active approach to the larger organizational environment that influences their work. This means changing policies when a team has the authority to do so, influencing policy when it doesn't have the authority, and finding creative ways to minimize the unintended negative effects of the organization on the team when it can do neither.

Clear Organizational Mission and a Shared Vision

An organization has a mission and a vision that serves as the umbrella for all of its teams. Clearly, a team's mission and vision should be congruent with those of the larger organization. Still, a team may find times when others outside its team are acting in ways that seem at odds with the organization's espoused mission and vision. Mutual learning teams are willing to engage others with curiosity and compassion when this occurs.

As an organization undergoes significant changes in its mission, expect that teams will face challenges. A health care provider that began moving to an accountable-care organization model found that the shift in mission and vision led to key structural changes that required its clinical leadership team to redefine the team's roles and reporting relationships with other key leaders in the organization.

A Supportive Organizational Culture

Just as each team has a culture, so does the larger organization. Teams that work in an organization with a supportive culture have a greater chance of being effective because team members share the basic values and assumptions that guide organizational behavior in general. When a team has a culture at odds with the larger organizational culture, even simple work with other teams can be challenging.

Many organizations espouse values and assumptions similar to mutual learning, but few organizations, including those that espouse this kind of culture, act in ways that consistently demonstrate it. In practice, most organizations' cultures resemble unilateral control to a greater or lesser degree. One organization development manager told me that his organization had a great culture on paper but that leaders and teams didn't know how to live the culture every day. He saw mutual learning as a way to translate the company's compelling but abstract culture into everyday behavior. The teams you're helping may be in a similar situation.

Then again, the organizations you're helping may *espouse* a culture of unilateral control. If so, the challenge isn't simply developing new behaviors to put the culture into action; it also means changing the values and assumptions that are embedded in the organization. As difficult as it is to change a team's culture, it's exponentially more difficult to change the larger organization's culture, if only because of its size. If the team you're working with is senior enough, it may decide that the mutual learning core values and assumptions reflect the kind of organization culture that it wants the organization to embody. If so, modeling the values and assumptions in that team is a good start for others to learn what is possible.

But even if the team isn't in a position to formally influence the culture of the larger organization, when it works with people outside the team, it can influence how those people think and act. I've worked with many leaders who, after a particularly challenging but effective meeting, were approached by another leader who said something like, "How did you do that? I've been trying for months to get an agreement with that group, and you did it in a few hours." By modeling successful mutual learning and having people see the results, they are more likely to become curious about how to create similar results. These are opportunities for team members to explain what they were doing and the mindset that made it possible.

Rewards Consistent with Objectives

Designing rewards to obtain better team performance isn't straightforward—the best approach depends on the type of interdependence. If the team task doesn't involve interdependence, it doesn't matter whether the rewards are individual or team-based.[30] If the task involves high interdependence, team-based rewards are essential for obtaining strong performance. Teams that receive group incentives for an interdependent task outperform teams receiving individual rewards.[31] But if the team task is hybrid—that is, some tasks involve interdependence and some don't—rewards don't elicit better performance, even when they are congruent with how the team task is performed.[32] In general, it's difficult for hybrid teams to be effective.

One graphic design team in a financial company illustrates how a change in team rewards affects performance. This design team had an excellent reputation, having won a number of industry awards. Members were highly interdependent on projects; they worked closely together, not concerned about who got credit. The team leader rewarded the team as a whole for their work—a reward design consistent with the research above. But HR changed the reward system so that each team member had to be rated and ranked individually and given a merit bonus based on individual effort. The team found itself paying attention to who was doing what; henceforth, work that had flowed naturally among them now was in contention. To their credit, they recognized that the new reward system undermined their effectiveness, and they approached HR to describe their concerns and see if their interests could be met. Unfortunately,

HR maintained that the team could not have a team-based reward system. They had to divide the performance pay among the team, and they couldn't divide it equally among all of the members. Eventually, most of the team members left to start their own firm.

Rewards need to be congruent with the values that the organization espouses. When I introduced mutual learning to leaders in a global oil company, I first showed them the unilateral control approach. I asked, "Does anyone recognize this approach?" One leader said, "Yeah, that's basically what we use here." Another leader added, "Use it? We've been rewarded for it—I've been rewarded for it—for years!" The organization was concerned about the results that its leadership practices were generating but hadn't realized that it had designed the reward system so that it reinforced the unilateral control results.

Often organizations hope to create a certain culture even as they reward behaviors that are inconsistent with it.[33] Employees are exhorted to be transparent and accountable at the same time HR policy prohibits them from talking about their salaries with others. Leaders receive survey results evaluating their leadership in which the evaluations are anonymous so the leader can't know who has said what about him and those who said it don't have to be accountable to him for the accuracy of their statements. Ultimately, this leads to cynicism as people see the gap between what the organization says is important and what it rewards and prohibits. And cynicism is a first step toward apathy or exit.

Mutual learning teams identify how organizational systems are rewarding ineffective team behavior, and they try to change these systems. Even if a team is unable to change or influence them, it can discuss the negative consequences of the systems and explore ways to minimize their effects.

Information, Including Feedback

Every team needs information from the larger organization to accomplish its objectives and improve the way it works. Information is the lifeblood of informed choice.

Systems Information. As organizations use more sophisticated integrated planning systems, leadership teams increasingly have real-time information about finance and accounting, supply chains, manufacturing, sales and service, customer relations, and human resources. These integrated systems can enable a team to work effectively with others within the organization and with customers and vendors. Of course, a team's ability to use the information depends on its access to the information, the quality of the information, and the extent to which it captures data that a team needs.

Information from Other Teams. Much of the information a team needs isn't embedded in information systems; it's in the minds of the others that a team works with. Whether a team is working with another function, with suppliers, or with customers, its success depends on the ability to get all of the information on the table to make good decisions. Many leaders I've worked with complain that these other teams aren't forthcoming with information they need. They infer that others are withholding information. But this often changes when a team becomes more transparent with its information, more curious about what the other team's interests are, and more compassionate about the other team's situation. When others understand that you intend to use their information for them rather than *on* them, they become more willing to share what you need.

Feedback from Colleagues. One of the most pervasive ways that organizations fail their teams is by withholding feedback from team members or creating feedback mechanisms that aren't transparent or accountable. I gave an example of this problem earlier in the chapter when I described how managers did not give feedback to their peers' direct reports. In mutual learning, the simple principle is this: **If you work with people directly and have concerns about their work, you are accountable for sharing your concerns with them directly, whether they have more, less, or the same amount of authority as you**. You cannot abdicate or delegate this task. Everyone carries their own water.

Survey Feedback. One area in which almost all organizations fail to demonstrate transparency and accountability is in 360-degree feedback. In 360-degree feedback, a leader or a team learns how he or the team is doing from those who complete a survey. If the feedback is for an individual leader, that person receives the anonymous aggregated scores of some of the person's peers, some of the person's direct reports, and perhaps some of the person's customers—internal or external. The team leader's responses are identified because people usually have only one manager, and she is formally responsible for managing performance. If the feedback is for a team, the team receives the anonymous scores of peers on other teams, the team's direct reports, and perhaps the team's customers—internal or external. Again, the team leader's feedback is identified. But even the team members don't know how their fellow team members evaluated the team in the survey items.

All of this makes it difficult if not impossible for a team to improve how it performs and works together. If each team member doesn't know what the other members think about the team, it's difficult to talk about exactly what can be done differently to improve it. And it's difficult to be curious because, if members ask people specifically how they rated the team on a particular item, they're violating the agreement that individual responses will be anonymous. The anonymity that leads to the lack of transparency, curiosity, informed choice, and compassion stems from the assumptions that granting people anonymity will yield the truth and that it will save face both for those giving the feedback and receiving it. However, there isn't any research indicating that granting anonymity gets the truth; people can still distort their responses because they aren't accountable.[34] And researchers note that 360-degree feedback doesn't necessarily lead to behavior change.

When a team uses mutual learning with 360-degree feedback, all team members complete the survey and ask some direct reports, peers, customers, and the team leader's manager to complete the survey also. When the survey results come back to the team, each team member's responses are identified by name. Those outside the team are also asked to include their name on their surveys, so team members can follow up if they have questions. This makes the responses transparent and accountable. It facilitates curiosity and asking team members what led them to respond as they did and what needs to happen for the team to become more effective in that area. This is the level of conversation that's needed for teams to improve. Can it feel uncomfortable? Yes, at first, but **the goal is not to be comfortable; it's to be effective, even if you feel uncomfortable**.

Only when those giving feedback identify themselves can a team get to the level of behaviors that are specific enough to create change. **If team members don't trust each other enough to give transparent and accountable feedback, then you've probably identified the most significant problem the team faces; solve that problem, and every other team problem becomes much easier to solve.** If team members believe that they must first have trust before they can start moving to mutual learning, then they are confusing cause and effect, and will likely never build or rebuild trust. Trust develops when team members take risks by making themselves vulnerable—for example, by being transparent—and see that others do not use the vulnerability against them.

If the technology doesn't permit it, taking the initiative to identify oneself can take some effort. Tom, a director of a large metropolitan library system, found that when he was asked to complete 360-degree evaluations of his peers, the survey required that his responses be anonymous, even though he wanted his name associated with his feedback. To be transparent and take accountability, in the space provided to add comments, Tom wrote his evaluation of the peer and began each comment with "Tom thinks . . ."

Resources

Apart from information, a team needs other resources, including technology and material resources. For virtual teams, this includes the technology to work together across time and space. While using mutual learning may not increase a team's ability to obtain additional resources, it can increase the chance that it better understands the reasoning of those providing the resources.

Training and Consultation

Teams need training and consultation to periodically develop their skills and get help solving problems. But the training or consultation a team receives may be at odds with the mutual learning culture it's trying to create. Many leadership teams have told me the different unilateral control techniques they have learned at some point in their careers—either from internal or external consultants. They often mention the sandwich approach to negative feedback, talking last so they learn what their team members really believe and asking rhetorical questions to get people to figure out what you mean.

Often internal HR and learning and development units espouse mutual learning but provide tools and techniques that are unilateral. One organization described its performance management process as a conversation with the employee, but at no time did it teach leaders how to be curious about the inferences leaders made about the direct report or the direct report's reactions to the leader's plan for the direct report.

The approach that mutual learning teams use with training and consultation is the same one used by teams that focus rigorously on their team strategy. They assess every decision they make by asking if it's congruent with the strategy. If it's not, they make a different choice. Regarding training and consultation, mutual learning teams assess the training product or service and ask whether it's congruent with their core values and assumptions. They know that it will create problems for the team if they use training or consultation methods that aren't.

Physical Environment

Winston Churchill said, "We shape our buildings and then our buildings shape us." The physical environment that a team works in has subtle but powerful effects. One consumer products organization designed its new facility based on its desire to increase collaboration. It designed enclosed and open office spaces to meet the different leaders' needs; informal café-like places with tables and comfortable chairs located near stairs so that people could easily start or continue a conversation; a very prominent open staircase to encourage people to walk and therefore meet each other more frequently than on an elevator; conference rooms that people could reserve; and other conference rooms that could only be used spontaneously. All of these environmental decisions stemmed from the organization's specific values and assumptions about encouraging collaboration and spontaneous conversation within teams and across teams.

Contrast that example with a professional development organization that moved into a new building and assigned most of the conference rooms to key leaders so that others could no longer meet spontaneously. Or, worse, an agricultural equipment manufacturer that found out it had redesigned its building to include almost no spaces for people to meet.

How a team's space is configured reflects the values and assumptions of those who design the space. If a team has control over its space, it can ensure that it reflects how the team wants to work together. If it doesn't have control, it can try to influence those decisions or make ad hoc changes so the physical environment facilitates rather than hinders the team's ability to work together.

INTERORGANIZATIONAL TEAMS AND GROUPS

To simplify the discussion about what makes a team effective, I have assumed that all team or group members work for the same organization. Clearly, this is not always the case. You may be helping a team that comprises members from different organizations with a common interest in an issue, such as an industry association team, a task force of community organizations, or a team that is addressing environmental issues and includes representatives from business, labor, and environmental entities and government agencies.

An interorganizational team has structural and process elements that are similar to those of other teams. However, the interorganizational team is subject to the organizational cultural influences of each organization that is represented in the team. In short, an interorganizational team operates in a complex organizational context, which makes working with these teams more challenging.

HELPING DESIGN OR REDESIGN A TEAM OR GROUP

With an understanding of the TEM and how the degree of interdependence that a team or group needs influences how it should be designed, you can help the team or group. The process differs somewhat depending on whether you're working with a newly formed team or a team that has existed for a while.

Helping Design a New Team or Group

Here are the steps for designing a newly formed team or group:

1. **Agree on the team mission, vision of the team, mindset, and culture.** These four elements form the foundation that the team will use

to design the rest of the team elements. The team designs each of the other elements so they advance the mission and are congruent with the team vision, mindset, and desired culture.

2. **Agree on the main tasks that must be accomplished to achieve its mission.** This includes tasks that can be accomplished by individual team members or a subgroup of the team and that must include all team members.

3. **Agree on which of these tasks team members need in order to be interdependent.** Because a given team—especially leadership teams— can often be designed with more or less interdependence, if members don't agree about where and how they are interdependent with each other, this disagreement will spill over into most elements of the team's design. In one leadership team I worked with, the leader believed that the team task had a high degree of task interdependence, but most of his team believed there was a relatively low level of interdependence. Capturing their different views, at one point in the meeting the leader declared, "We need to agree: Are we a gymnastics team, or are we a hockey team?"

   The tasks around which teams are interdependent vary greatly depending on the level of the team in the organization. Work teams are interdependent around producing the organization's products and services or the functions that support them. But leadership teams don't make a product or deliver a service—they make decisions that define the products and services and how the organization functions to produce and deliver them. Senior leadership teams are often interdependent around the following tasks: setting the organization's mission and vision; defining organizational level strategy; approving major capital expenditures; shaping organization-wide change; ensuring organizational leadership; and serving as stewards of the organization's culture.

4. **Design the appropriate level of interdependence into the task.** Using the mission, vision, mindset, and team culture as a foundation, design how the task is performed so it has the appropriate level of interdependence. There are four ways to design a team task so it increases or decreases interdependence:[35]

   - **Design the physical technology of the task.** The team can increase interdependence by designing the physical technology so members must work simultaneously on the task or interact with each other. Alternatively, the team can design the task so it reduces or prevents simultaneous action, such as an assembly line.

- **Assign responsibility for completing the task.** To maximally increase interdependence, all team members can be collectively responsible for completing the full task. To reduce interdependence, individual members can be assigned responsibility for completing specific tasks.

- **Establish rules and processes.** To increase interdependence, rules and processes can be established that expect members to share information, communicate with each other, and solve problems and make decisions together. To reduce interdependence, the opposite kinds of rules and procedures can be established.

- **Distribute the resources necessary to complete the task.** To increase interdependence, the resources can be distributed among team members so they need to share these resources to complete the task. To decrease interdependence, resources can be allocated to individuals responsible for those individual tasks.

5. **Design the rest of the team structure and process elements.** With the four foundational elements and the task designed, the rest of the elements can be designed to be congruent. The design of the other elements will already have taken place in the previous step. For example, allocating responsibilities for tasks will naturally lead to designing team roles. Establishing rules and processes will naturally lead to designing better avenues of communication, conflict resolution, and problem solving.

Helping Redesign an Existing Team or Group

When you are redesigning an existing team or group, the process begins with identifying the gaps between the current and desired state. Here are the steps:

1. **Using the TEM, agree on the elements of results, then design, and finally mindset, where there is a gap between the desired state and current state.** Circle each of the elements where there is a significant gap. When you are considering team norms, remember to include the eight mutual learning behaviors.

2. **Starting with the elements of the results and working backward toward design and mindset, conduct a root causes analysis.** Agree on how the elements of structure, design, and context that the team circled in step 1 contribute to reducing each of the results elements that the team circled. Draw arrows to show these relationships. Next, agree on how the elements of mindset that the team circled in step 1 contribute to

each of the circled elements of structure, design, and context. Draw arrows to show these relationships.

3. **Identify and redesign the root cause elements.** In the design column, root causes often include unclear mission and goals, team task, roles, and decision-making authority. Any mindset elements that are circled are by definition root causes. When you are identifying root causes, look for incongruences between the degree of interdependence required and the way the team task is designed. **Keep in mind that interdependence is not an element in the model; rather, it is a characteristic that is embedded in elements throughout the model**. Also, remember that redesigning mindset elements is changing the team's culture; agreeing that team members want to shift their mindset is necessary but not sufficient for changing the culture.

4. **Identify and redesign the nonroot cause elements.** Even if team members change to a mutual learning mindset, there may still be elements of team structure, process, and context that need redesigning. Identify these needed changes so that the combination of the changes in mindset and team structure, process, and context significantly reduce or eliminate the gaps identified in step 1.

If you want to also focus on the team's strengths, create a second part for steps 1 through 3, in which the team identifies elements in which there are not significant gaps between the desired and current state.

In my experience, this process takes about three days, depending on the size of the team, whether the team is new or trying to improve its effectiveness, and the extent to which team members' views are similar or different. This is time well spent. A team can perform no better than its design makes possible.

SUMMARY

In this chapter, I described how you can use the TEM to help new and existing teams and groups get better results. I began by describing how a good team effectiveness model helps you design effective teams, and diagnose and intervene in teams. Next, I described the difference between teams and groups, the main difference being that teams have a team task, and team members must interact and coordinate with each other to accomplish it. Team interdependence is so important because poorly managed interdependence is a root cause of many team and group problems. Despite the popular emphasis on teams, teams are not better than groups; what matters is the fit between the task and team or group design.

I described the TEM, which shows how a team's mindset and design (structures, processes, and team context) lead to the three team results. The TEM incorporates the mindset, results, and behaviors of the mutual learning approach. Finally, I described a process you can use to help new teams or groups design themselves for strong results and a process for existing teams or groups to design their team elements to improve results.

In the next chapter, we begin the section on diagnosing and intervening with groups. The chapter provides an overview on how to figure out what is happening in a group and how to intervene.

PART TWO

DIAGNOSING AND INTERVENING WITH GROUPS

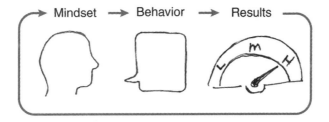

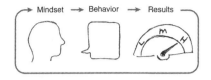

CHAPTER SEVEN

Diagnosing and Intervening with Groups

How do you watch a group in action and figure out exactly what is happening that is increasing or decreasing the group's effectiveness? This is the central question for diagnosing groups. After you figure out what's happening, what do you say to help the group become more effective? This is the central question for intervening with groups. If you're a facilitator, answering these two questions is your central task. If you serve in another facilitative role, answering these two questions is also essential to accomplishing your work with clients.

In facilitation, *diagnosis* is the process by which you observe a group's behavior and infer the meaning, based on your models of group effectiveness. The word *diagnosis* comes from the Greek word *diagignōskein*, meaning "to distinguish or discern."[1] In facilitation, *intervention* is the action you take, based on your diagnosis, to help the group improve its effectiveness. The word *intervention* comes from the Latin word *intervenire*, which includes *inter*, meaning "between," and *venire*, meaning "come."[2]

In this chapter, I describe, in big-picture terms, diagnosis and intervention. This includes what to look for while watching a group in action, how to make meaning of what you're observing, how to decide whether to intervene, and, finally, how to intervene. I'll reintroduce the mutual learning cycle—a tool I introduced to test inferences and assumptions—as a primary tool to guide your diagnosis and intervention process.

WHAT YOU NEED TO DIAGNOSE

Before you can intervene effectively to help a group, you have to diagnose what is occurring in the group. To diagnose, you use two sets of knowledge and skills. First, you need to know what to look for. When you watch a group in action, there are many behaviors that you could pay attention to. But you're limited in the number you can attend to at any time, and some behaviors are more important than others because they reflect dynamics that significantly influence the group's effectiveness. To be able to quickly understand which types of behaviors are important to focus on and why, it's useful to have models in your head of what makes an effective group and an ineffective group.

The good news is that you have already learned most of what to look for:

- The **unilateral control approach** describes a mindset, behaviors, and results that lead to ineffective groups.
- The **mutual learning approach** describes a mindset, behaviors, and results that lead to effective groups.
- The **Team Effectiveness Model** describes the design elements necessary for group or team effectiveness, as well as incorporating the mutual learning mindset, behaviors, and results.

These are the three main diagnostic frames you use to diagnose behavior using the Skilled Facilitator approach.

Second, you need a process for diagnosis—a method for observing and making sense of behavior you're seeing, regardless of the specific behaviors. The good news here is that you've already learned this process—it's the left half of the mutual learning cycle.

When you combine what to look for with the process for making meaning, you get what's shown in Figure 7.1. Each of the elements in the unilateral control approach, mutual learning approach, and the Team Effectiveness Model have behaviors associated with them. These are the behaviors you pay attention to in step 1 of the mutual learning cycle. When you see these behaviors, you infer the meaning associated with that element. Here are a few examples:

- One of the elements in the Team Effectiveness Model is clearly defined roles, including leadership. This would lead you to pay attention to comments in the group that reflected unclear roles. If you heard one team member saying, "I'm responsible for the budget," and another team member saying, "No, that's my job; you're only responsible for the projections," you might infer that these members have not clearly agreed on their roles.

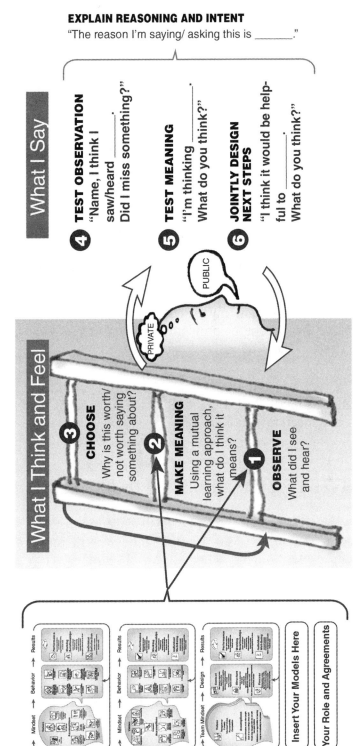

Figure 7.1   What to Look for to Diagnose Groups

- Two of the behaviors in the mutual learning approach are to share all relevant information and to explain reasoning and intent. If you heard the following team members' exchange, you might infer that Jeanne was not sharing all relevant information or explaining how she arrived at her conclusion.

> JEANNE: "I don't think the reorganization is going to happen."
>
> RICH: "Why not? Everyone I've spoken with says it's going to happen."
>
> JEANNE: "Let's just say not everyone wants it to happen."

- One of the elements of the mutual learning mindset is the assumption that I may be contributing to the problem. If you heard the following team members' exchange, you might infer that Lin assumed that she was not contributing to the problem.

> JAMAL: "You're right, Lin, my team is getting the design documents to you late. But part of the problem is that your team keeps changing the design specifications. We're constantly reworking the documents."
>
> LIN: "That's your team's job, Jamal. The customer has the right to change its mind. We're just meeting the customer's needs. Your job is to meet the deadlines."

WHAT YOU NEED TO INTERVENE

After you have finished diagnosing and have decided to intervene, you have to actually intervene. To do this, you use the right side—the public side—of the mutual learning cycle. You test whether you observed what you think you observed, test whether it means what you think it means, and decide with the group how to move forward. When you intervene, you use the mutual learning mindset and behaviors from Chapter 5.

Let's look at the diagnosis and intervention steps of the mutual learning cycle.

THE MUTUAL LEARNING CYCLE

The mutual learning cycle is a structured way to diagnose behavior and then intervene on it. The cycle (shown in Figure 7.2) has six steps: three for diagnosis, followed by three for intervention. The diagnostic steps (1 through 3) are

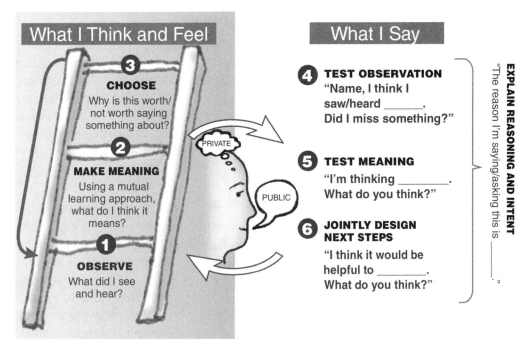

Figure 7.2 The Mutual Learning Cycle

private; they represent your thoughts.[3] The intervention steps (4 through 6) are public; they represent what you actually say to the group.

The mutual learning cycle is designed to help you make low-level inferences and to test whether they are accurate. In the intervention steps, you repeat the diagnostic steps. You state publicly what you were privately thinking and then ask the group whether or not they see it the way you do.

Here is a summary of the diagnosis steps and intervention steps.

Step 1: Observe Behavior

In step 1, you directly observe the behavior in the group. Directly observable behavior comprises the verbatim words that people speak and the nonverbal actions they take. I think of directly observable behavior as anything I can capture on video. For example, I might observe this interaction:

DON: I think we should hold off on the new project until the fourth quarter.

SHARON: That's too late. It has to start no later than the second quarter.

DON (*in a louder voice*): It just won't work to start so soon.

SHARON (*rolling her eyes*): Well, we don't have the luxury to do it later.

Step 2: Make Meaning

In step 2, you infer some meaning from the behavior. An inference is a conclusion you reach about something unknown, on the basis of some things that are known to you. In this example, I infer that Sharon and Don are acting inconsistently with several mutual learning behaviors. For example, they are stating their positions (start the project in the fourth quarter or, the second quarter) without sharing their interests, and they aren't explaining the reasoning underlying their statements. I might also infer from Sharon rolling her eyes that she's frustrated with Don's comment.

Step 3: Choose Whether, How, and Why to Intervene

In step 3, you decide whether, how, and why to intervene in the group. In this example, I need to decide whether the inferences I have made in step 2 warrant my intervening or whether I should remain silent. Is Sharon and Don's focus on positions, or is their failure to explain their reasoning or is Sharon's seeming frustration enough of a problem that I should intervene? If I decide to do so, I must design my intervention by deciding to whom I will address my comments, exactly what I will say, and when I will say it. In this example, I would decide to address their focusing on positions.

Step 4: Describe the Behavior

In step 4, you publicly describe the behavior that you observed and that led you to intervene. Then you ask the group member or members whether they observed the behavior differently. Here, I might say, "Don, a minute ago I think you said we should hold off on the new project until the fourth quarter. Do you remember it differently? And Sharon, I think you said that you needed to start the project in the second quarter. Am I correct?" If they agree with my descriptions, I have accurately described their behavior. Then I move to the fifth step.

Step 5: Test Your Inference

In step 5, you share the inference that you privately made in step 2 and test with the group member or members whether they have a different inference. I might say, "Don and Sharon, it seems to me that each of you is stating a position without explaining the interests that led you to take your position. How do you see that?" Or, if I choose to refer to the behavior without identifying it by name, I might say, "Don and Sharon, it looks like each of you has said what you want to happen but not what led you to favor that solution. Do either of you see it differently?" In any case, if neither Don nor Sharon sees it differently, then I move to the sixth step.

Step 6: Jointly Design Next Steps

In step 6, you and the group members jointly decide the next step to take. Here I might say, "Don and Sharon, I'm thinking it would be helpful if you would identify the needs you're trying to meet through the solutions you're proposing. Any concerns about doing that?" Assuming that they agree to do so, the cycle begins again, and I continue to observe whether their behavior (and that of the other group members) is contributing to or hindering the group's effectiveness.

Sharing Your Reasoning and Intent

At steps 4, 5, and 6 you may share your reasoning and intent. This helps the group members better understand why you are intervening at all, especially why you are asking them to redesign their behavior in a particular way. For example, at the beginning of step 4 you might say, "I want to make some observations about something that I think is slowing the group down, so I can get your reactions." Or at step 6 you might say, "Would you be willing to share your interests? The reason I'm asking is because if you can identify each of your interests, I think you will be better able to find a solution that integrates your different needs."

You repeatedly use the six-step cycle throughout facilitation with the group. In developmental facilitation, over time, the group learns to conduct its own diagnosis and interventions, becoming less dependent on you. In basic facilitation, the group usually relies on you to diagnose and intervene.

SUMMARY

In this chapter, I described the process of diagnosing and intervening, using the six-step mutual learning cycle. You use steps 1 through 3 of the cycle to diagnose what is happening in the group and use steps 4 through 6 to intervene. The cycle is designed so that when you use the intervention steps, you are stating to the group what you were privately thinking in the diagnosis steps and then testing whether group members saw things the same way, made the same meaning, and agree with the next step to take. To figure out what to diagnose, you use the unilateral control approach, mutual learning approach, and the Team Effectiveness Model to look for behaviors and infer what they mean.

In the next chapter, we'll explore in detail how to diagnose groups.

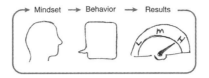

Mindset → Behavior → Results

CHAPTER EIGHT

How to Diagnose Groups

I n this chapter, we explore in detail how to diagnose groups. I explain how to use the first three steps of the mutual learning cycle: (1) observe behavior; (2) make meaning; and (3) choose whether, why, and how to intervene. Throughout the chapter, I describe the challenges you will likely face when you diagnose and how to overcome them.

STEP 1: OBSERVE BEHAVIOR

Diagnosing group behavior begins with direct observation. This seems obvious, but it has significant implications. For group members to understand the reasons for your diagnosis and intervention, you need to base your actions on the raw materials of group interaction that everyone can observe—the words and actions of the group.

Remember Behavior as Behavior

Observing behavior means listening to group members' words and watching their actions. Step 1 requires that you be able to remember the exact words that group members said and the nonverbal behaviors that accompanied them. The challenge is to be able to remember the behaviors without changing them or adding meaning.

If you see a group member roll her eyes and you describe her behavior to yourself as frustration or impatience, you have gone beyond describing her directly observable behavior and instead are inferring meaning. You can't directly observe frustration or impatience; you can only infer it. You can, however, observe people rolling their eyes, crossing their arms, or talking in a louder voice. Similarly, you don't directly observe people focusing on positions or withholding relevant information; you infer this from their specific words and actions. **Doing step 1 well means training yourself to distinguish between behaviors and the inferences you make from them.**

In practice, it is almost impossible to observe behavior without making meaning of it. The reason you notice certain behavior is you believe it *is* meaningful; that is, it makes a difference in the group's process. You use—and should use—the diagnostic models you have in your head, such as the mutual learning behaviors and the Team Effectiveness Model (TEM), to pay attention to and identify important behaviors.

Consider Felipe, who responds to a plan developed by his group by commenting, "Let's just say not everyone will be willing to support our plan." Using the Skilled Facilitator approach, you find Felipe's sentence meaningful because it suggests that he has relevant information to share (about who will not support the plan and why) that he hasn't shared with the group. In contrast, in a facilitation approach with another set of diagnostic concepts, the facilitator might initially make some other meaning out of the same sentence—perhaps considering Felipe to be undermining the solution.

For some of us, after we have made meaning of behavior, we have difficulty remembering the specific behavior that led us to make our interpretation. We may be able to remember that a member was frustrated but not recall her rolling her eyes that led us to infer it. Our brains are designed to quickly make meaning out of behavior because it is the meaning of behavior that seems important to us, not the behavior itself. But in your facilitative role, it's essential that you remember the behavior because it's the raw data for your inferences, diagnoses, and interventions. If group members don't agree with the inference you've made, and if you can't recall the behavior from which you made the inference, then you have no way of explaining how you moved from the data to your inference.

Use Diagnostic Models to Decide What Behaviors to Look For

What kinds of behaviors are important to attend to when you're observing a group? There are a huge number of behaviors you can look for, and it's beyond your (or any human's) cognitive capacities to catch every behavior in the group. Even if you were a human video camera—capable of remembering every word and action that every member said—that by itself would not tell you which behaviors were *important,* or how to use them. You need a way to categorize or code group members' conversation and actions so you can search for a few, general types of behavior.

As I mentioned earlier, the unilateral control approach, mutual learning approach, and TEM are three diagnostic models for identifying behavior that has a significant impact on the group's process and results. As Figure 8.1 shows, you use these diagnostic models in step 1 to attend to certain behaviors, and you use them again in step 2 to make particular meaning out of the behavior you've observed. In this way, steps 1 and 2 are inextricably linked.

Using the Mutual Learning Behaviors to Observe Groups. In the Skilled Facilitator approach, the eight mutual learning behaviors are a central part of observing and diagnosing group behavior. You use the eight behaviors as a template for observing behavior. As you watch group members, you mentally compare what team members are saying and doing to the eight behaviors and notice what is consistent or inconsistent with each of the mutual learning behaviors. In a given comment, a group member might act consistently with certain behaviors and inconsistently with others.

Take, for example, a team that's been trying to solve a problem of customers waiting too long to receive service. Having agreed on a definition of the problem and criteria for a solution, the team decides to move to the next step: brainstorming potential causes. After several members have each identified a potential cause, this conversation occurs:

AL: One reason may be that we don't have adequate coverage throughout the workday. For example, yesterday at 10:00 AM, using our standard response time analysis, we calculated an average wait time of 20 minutes for customers across all areas. I have the individual department numbers if you want them. That's 15 minutes longer than our acceptable standard for adequate coverage, and we had 10 percent fewer people covering the phones at that time of day.

TED: I agree that's the cause. Let's increase the coverage 10 percent, at least during the peak periods.

SUE: Yeah, I agree with Ted. That should make a big difference.

SAM: Well, I think our people are just tired of working.

AL: Well, I think we've just got some people who are burned out.

MIA: Al and Sue, it sounds like your suggestions to increase coverage are solutions, but I understood that we were still talking about causes. Do you see this differently?

AL AND SUE: No, you're right.

MIA: Are you willing to focus only on potential causes and hold the solutions until we finish identifying causes?

Analyzing the conversation, we see that Al begins by using a specific example of inadequate coverage with data and describes what he means by adequate

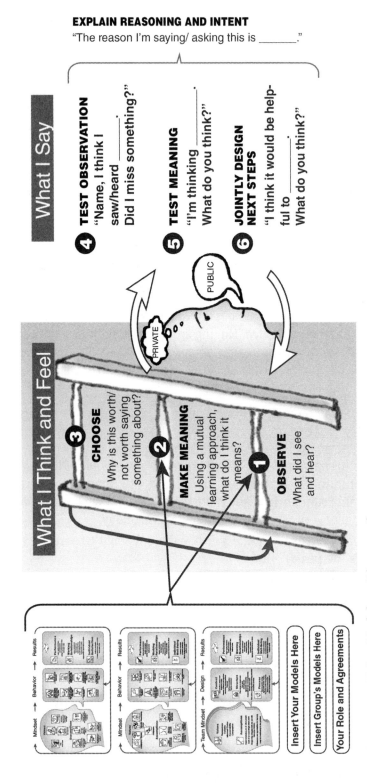

Figure 8.1   Using Models to Diagnose Groups

168

coverage (behavior 3). By doing so, he explains the reasoning behind his belief that the cause of the problem is inadequate coverage on the phones (behavior 4). However, he doesn't ask about whether others see any flaws in his reasoning or have different data (behavior 1, asking a genuine question). Next, Ted and Sue, by discussing solutions, switch the focus of the conversation without checking with the group (behavior 7). Sam returns to the focus of the conversation (behavior 7) by addressing another potential cause, but he makes an untested inference about people being burned out (behavior 6), and he doesn't share any specific examples (behavior 3) or the reasoning (behavior 4) that leads him to his conclusion. Like Al, he doesn't ask whether others have other information or see it differently (behavior 1).

In Mia's two comments to Al and Sue, Mia gives the specific example of their suggesting solutions (behavior 3) as a way of illustrating that they have changed the focus of the group (behavior 7). Notice that, having stated that Al and Sue seem to be off track, Mia specifically asks them whether they see it differently (behavior 1). After they agree with her, Mia asks if they are willing to refocus on discussing causes of the problem (behavior 7) instead of simply telling them that they are off focus and to refocus. Mia acts consistently with the behaviors; she is also using the behaviors to ask Al and Sue to act consistently with a behavior they have not used.

Using the Team Effectiveness Model to Observe Behavior. The TEM provides additional behaviors to look for. Each element of the TEM needs to be in place for the group or team to function well. Because the mindset and results columns of the TEM and the mutual learning approach are the same, the unique elements to look for in the TEM are the design elements listed in team context, team structure, and team process. For example, within team context, you can look for behavior that suggests the team is not receiving adequate information or other resources from the larger organization. Within group structure, you can look for behavior that suggests the group doesn't have clear goals, clearly defined roles, or even agreement on who is a group member. Within group process, you can look for behavior that suggests the group does not have an effective process for solving problems, making decisions, or managing its boundaries with the rest of the organization.

To take a simple example, consider a group conversation about a report that contains errors:

JACQUE: The numbers literally did not add up. We had blank cells and columns without totals. Ken, you were supposed to do the final check on the copy; what happened?

KEN: I was just handling the text. I got the tables from you; that was your job.

You might reasonably infer from watching this interaction that Ken and Jacque haven't clearly agreed on their roles and responsibilities for this project.

Using Mindset to Observe Behavior. Observing group members' behaviors to see if they indicate elements of unilateral control or mutual learning mindsets is a deeper and more powerful kind of diagnosis because mindset is often a root cause. Here, you look for the core values and assumptions group members use to design their behaviors and the structure and process elements of their group. Observing and intervening on group members' mindsets is a central part of developmental facilitation.

Consider, for example, a conversation in which members are trying to persuade each other to choose a particular solution. If a group member says, "You just don't get it. What you're proposing makes no sense!," we might consider that the member's behavior reflects core assumptions that he understands the situation and is right and that others who see it differently don't understand and are wrong. Of course, you usually need more than a single sentence to make this kind of inference.

Using Other Models to Observe Behavior. You can use the mutual learning cycle with almost any model you currently use to diagnose how a group is doing, as long as the concepts in the model can be connected to specific group behaviors. If you facilitate strategic planning efforts, you can use the mutual learning cycle with your strategic planning model. If you're a Lean or Six Sigma consultant, you can use the mutual learning cycle with these models and processes. If you're helping groups manage conflict, you can combine the mutual learning cycle with your process for managing conflict.

For example, if you're helping groups learn and use a problem-solving model, you can use that model with the mutual learning cycle to see whether the group is using the problem-solving model effectively. There are many variations of problem-solving models, and almost all of them include steps to follow in a particular order. For example, a simple problem-solving model might use the following seven steps: (1) agree on the problem statement, (2) develop criteria for a solution, (3) identify root causes of the problem, (4) brainstorm potential solutions, (5) select the best solution based on the criteria, (6) implement the solution, and (7) evaluate the implementation. For each step, there are specific actions that a group is expected to take. Given this, you can use a problem-solving model to watch for group behavior that indicates whether the group is following the model steps in sequence and whether it is performing each step effectively. In Chapter 11, I describe how to apply the mutual learning cycle to diagnose behavior in a variety of other models.

Using Your Agreement with the Group to Observe Behavior. The agreement you make with the group about how you will help them also affects what kind of behavior to look for. If a group seeks your help because members say they can't resolve conflict without argument, you look for behavior that lets you determine whether you agree with the group's diagnosis. If the group seeks your help because it spends a lot of time discussing plans but never accomplishes them, you look for behavior related to that diagnosis. However, as I discuss in Chapter 13 on contracting, although the agreement with the client may specify particular behaviors that the client wants you to focus on, it doesn't limit what you can observe and diagnose. To act consistently with the mutual learning approach, you consider all the behavior of the group so that you can help the group identify what is reducing its effectiveness, confirm or disconfirm the group's own diagnosis, and enable the members to make an informed choice about whether to change.

The agreement you reach with the group about your role and how you and the group will work together leads you to look for behaviors that are consistent and inconsistent with your agreement. For example, if you agree to serve as a content-neutral facilitator, you look for times when group members ask your opinion about a topic they are discussing—a request that would be inconsistent with your agreed-upon role.

STEP 2: MAKE MEANING

In step 2 of the mutual learning cycle, you use the diagnostic models to make meaning out of the behavior you observed in step 1.

Making Meaning

As I described in Chapter 5, an *inference* is a conclusion you reach about something you don't know based on things you do know. For example, if you observe a group leader tapping a pencil on the desk and saying "Go on, go on" in response to her direct reports' explanation, you may infer that the leader is impatient. You can't observe impatience; you infer its presence from the meaning you make of the behavior you observe.

Whatever your facilitative role, you need to make inferences because inferences create the meaning you use to decide whether and how to help the group. If, in the example of the leader, you infer that when she taps her pencil and says "Go on, go on," it's meant to encourage the direct report to talk, then you may choose not to intervene. If, however, you infer that the tapping means she is trying to move the conversation faster than other group members want to go, you may intervene.

Inferences can also save you time by aggregating and abstractly conveying a large number of behaviors. It can be more efficient to say, "She was very angry" than to describe the manager's multiple behaviors that led you to infer the anger ("In a loud voice she screamed, 'You've ruined the project'"; "She threw the report on the floor"; "She left, slamming the door"). Similarly, rather than saying, "It was 10:15 when I saw Frank enter his office and take off his trench coat. Frank is due at work at eight," you can say, "Frank was late this morning."

There are different kinds of inferences you make when working with a group. Following are some of the key types.

Inferring the Causes of Behavior. You use inferences to identify the causes of behavior. When an auto mechanic announces that "your car's timing is off" after listening to the engine and hearing complaints of engine hesitation, the mechanic has inferred the cause of a problem from its symptoms. Similarly, when you suggest that the group is lacking focus after observing failure to reach a decision within an hour, you are making a causal inference after observing a number of behaviors. A causal inference is about what has led to something happening. You need to make causal inferences because a group can solve a process problem only after identifying what caused the problem, and the cause is often not directly observable.

Inferring Emotion. Sometimes you may make inferences about members' emotions. Someone who has asked a number of questions that the group hasn't answered may respond by sitting back in her chair, crossing her arms, tightening the muscles in her face, and furrowing her eyebrows. You may quickly infer that the behavior reflects anger, but it may also reflect some other emotion.

By making an inference about (and intervening on) an emotion on the basis of behavioral cues, you both broaden and deepen how you observe and help the group. Because we generate our emotions from our experiences, embedded in group members' emotions are their stories about experiences in the group that have led them to feel whatever they feel. When you pay attention to members' emotions, you're attending to things that they consider important. In doing so, you're also attending to the third criterion of group effectiveness, the extent to which experiences in the group contribute to individuals' well-being. By inferring and intervening on emotion, you can quickly find out about important issues in the group that haven't been addressed, such as an unexpressed interest, an untested assumption someone is making about others, or an undiscussable issue.

Anytime there is a mismatch between the emotions you infer that group members are feeling and what you expect, you have an opportunity. For example, if you infer that a group member is feeling angry and you're surprised, essentially you are thinking to yourself, *Given the behavior I've seen in the group, I don't see how this would lead the member to respond with anger.* You can consider several possibilities. First, you may have missed important behavior in the group; had you observed it, you might not be surprised that the member is angry. Second, you may not have missed any behaviors in the group relevant to the feeling you have inferred; in this case, you might consider whether the member's feeling stems from concerns he hasn't yet expressed in the group, or from things that have happened outside the group meetings. Finally, you may have incorrectly inferred what the member is feeling.

In developmental facilitation, you can use emotions to help group members explore their mindsets. Embedded in every emotion is some element of mindset. By identifying what members are feeling, you can help them explore how their values and assumptions led them to make meaning of the situation and respond in a way that generated the emotion. You can also help them explore how their emotions are based on an event that occurred in the group, or on an event unrelated to the group, or on an untested assumption or inference they made.

Attending to emotion is part of bringing compassion into your work. Emotion is always part of the group conversation, whether or not members are aware of their emotions or expressing them. By attending to members' emotions, you may affirm what they are feeling, help them recognize that their emotions are natural, and advocate for discussing them as an important element of building effective group working relationships.

But you can also go beyond that. You can help them see how their thinking influences their feelings, how their feelings may be based on an untested inference or attribution about others, and if so, how by changing their thinking they have the ability to make new choices about what they are feeling. In short, by helping group members become more aware of their feelings and the sources, you strengthen their ability to make choices about their response. We examine this more in Chapter 12, on working with emotions.

I want to caution you about inferring what people are feeling based on their body language. A number of books describe various aspects of body language— the position of a person's arms, head, or hands—and describe what each position means. I hope it is clear that in the mutual learning approach, a given behavior doesn't necessarily always mean one thing. Across cultures, the same body language can have many meanings. Even within a culture, a particular nonverbal behavior can have numerous meanings. If each time you see me cross my arms in front of my chest you infer that I'm feeling defensive or am closing out your views (as some books suggest), your inference is often incorrect. Not that I never get defensive, but I also get cold easily, and I cross my arms to get warm. Other people cross their arms over their chest because it's simply a very comfortable position for them.

Attributing Motives. Sometimes, you make *attributions*. These are causal inferences about other people's motives—*why* they are doing something. Consider a facilitator who is helping an executive team that is experiencing several conflicts. At one point Hans, the team leader says, "Why don't we put this issue aside so we can give it some careful thought." This leads the facilitator to think—but not say—*Typical Hans. This isn't about time; he's not willing to take on the difficult issues.* In thinking this, the facilitator is attributing to Hans the motive of wanting to avoid difficult issues.

Attribution often involves high-level inference. After you have attributed a motive to a group member, you're likely to begin interpreting his behavior in a way that's consistent with the motive you have attributed to him. As with other inferences, it becomes important to test your attribution.

Making a Value Judgment. Many inferences also involve value judgment— that is, whether you consider the behavior in question to be positive or negative. If you observe a conversation and think, *Bob was obnoxious to Joan,* you not only are summarizing a large number of behaviors but likely are also stating implicit disapproval of Bob's behavior. In the example of the executive team, the facilitator's attribution of the leader's motivation includes a negative judgment about it; the facilitator doesn't approve of the leader avoiding a difficult issue and covering it up with a false explanation.

Making Process and Content Inferences

When you work with a group, you make inferences about both the process and the content of a conversation.

Making Inferences about Process. *Process inferences* are about the quality of conversation and the effectiveness of the group's process and structure. You make a process inference when you privately conclude that group members are acting consistently or inconsistently with a particular mutual learning behavior or mindset, having difficulty with an element of the TEM such as boundary management, not following some aspect of a problem-solving model, or acting inconsistently with some other group process model you use.

In making a process inference, you try not to focus especially on the content of the conversation. In other words, you're interested in how the group members say whatever they say. Whether the group is talking about problems with losing market share or retaining employees, you can make the same inference that the members are focusing on positions rather than interests.

Making Inferences about Content. As the name states, *content inferences* are about the substantive meaning of the conversation. For example, consider an interaction in a meeting about a project deadline:

SHERRY: We really need your cost projections by 5:00 PM Friday if we are going to get the final report to corporate by next Tuesday. Can you guarantee that you'll meet that deadline?

LEWIS: That's a stretch, but we'll do the best we can.

Hearing Lewis's response, I would infer that he has promised a good effort but not guaranteed meeting the deadline. Having made this inference, in step 3 of the mutual learning cycle, I might decide to intervene to test whether he *is* guaranteeing to meet the deadline. By making a content inference and then intervening on that basis, I could help group members clarify their meaning.

There is a link between making content inferences and group process. If I decide to intervene on a content inference, it is because I believe that if I do not, the untested inference may negatively affect the group's process.

Making Inferences about Others Making Content Inferences. Sometimes, as you observe a conversation, you think that a group member is making an inference; that is, you are inferring that someone else is making an inference about the content of the conversation.

Consider this brief interaction in a conversation about job performance:

ALEX: Sandy, I've got some concerns about your covering both of your regions. I want to talk about it and see if we can agree on something that will work.

SANDY: Well, if I can't handle both regions, I doubt anyone else will be able to do the job.

Here I would infer that Sandy is inferring that Alex thinks Sandy is not capable of handling both regions, even though Alex didn't say that.

When you infer that a group member is making a content inference and not testing it, then you may decide to intervene so that the members don't continue their conversation on the basis of what might be an incorrect inference. In this kind of situation, you are making both a content inference and a process inference; you are inferring that a group member is incorrectly inferring a particular meaning, and you're also inferring that the group member is doing so without testing the inference, which is inconsistent with the behavior test assumptions and inferences.

Recognizing Our Inferences as Inferences

Everyone makes inferences. Step 2 of the mutual learning cycle requires that you recognize the content and process inferences you are making as you make them. It's this awareness that enables you to reflect on whether your inferences have a basis in any data and decide whether you should intervene to test them. Without this awareness, you assume that your inference is accurate and intervene without testing it. You treat your untested inference as valid data, and if you are incorrect, you can create negative consequences.

Imagine that you're facilitating a group in which Juan is speaking each time after every other group member speaks. You infer that Juan is talking too much, but you're unaware that this is an inference you are making. You might say, "Juan, how about letting others share their thoughts?" If you've inferred incorrectly, other group members may respond, "No, Juan's not talking too much. He may be talking a lot, but we need to hear his information before we can make a decision." Using the mutual learning approach, you would recognize that your belief that Juan is talking too much is an inference (and a judgment) that is important to check with the other members of the group. You might say to the group, "I've noticed that during the last 10 minutes, Juan has made every other comment. Has anyone noticed anything different? If not, I'm wondering whether people feel that his comments are relevant and whether any of you have been trying unsuccessfully to share your thoughts."

Moving Back and Forth between Observations and Inferences

In practice, you don't always simply move from step 1 to step 2 to step 3 of the mutual learning cycle. Sometimes you use your diagnostic models to observe behavior, make an inference about what the behavior means, and return to observe more behavior to confirm or disconfirm your working hypothesis, until you decide whether to intervene. For example, you might observe a group and begin to infer that there's an undiscussable issue in the group. If you're uncertain, you may continue to observe the group, looking for more data that either confirm or disconfirm your inference. If you believe you have enough data for your inference, then you may choose to intervene.

Making Low-Level and High-Level Inferences

Just like a real ladder, the higher you go on the ladder of inference, the more dangerous it is. **When you use the Skilled Facilitator approach, you diagnose behavior by making inferences that are no higher than necessary.** Unnecessarily high-level inferences can reduce the effectiveness of your interventions because group members reasonably infer that your inferences aren't connected to the data. To reduce this problem, the eight mutual learning behaviors are designed to produce relatively low-level inferences.

In Chapter 5, I described the difference between low-level and high-level inferences. When you make a *low-level inference*, you add only a relatively small amount of meaning to the observable behavior. As you make *higher-level inferences*, you add more meaning about what members are feeling, the cause of their behavior, their motives, and your judgment about these things. Higher-level inferences are really made up of a number of inferences, each stacked upon the previous inference. If any one of the lower inferences is incorrect, then all of the inferences that it supports collapses, like a house of cards.

Exhibit 8.1 shows three levels of inference that a facilitator might make for both process and content. The observable behavior used to generate these

Facilitator's High-Level Inference	Leslie doesn't want Jack's project to succeed. (content inference) Leslie is trying to manipulate Jack. (process inference)
Facilitator's Mid-Level Inference	Leslie won't give Jack any of her people because she believes Jack's people can do the project themselves. (content inference) Leslie is unwilling to tell Jack her concerns. (process inference)
Facilitator's Low-Level Inference	Leslie wants to delay giving Jack a full-time person. (content inference) Leslie is asking questions but not explaining the reasoning for her questions. She is not sharing her own interests. (process inference)
Group Members' Observable Behavior	JACK: I really need a full-time person dedicated to this project. LESLIE: How soon will it start? Can it wait two months until next quarter? JACK: The project's got to be worked on right away. I can't wait any longer than I already have. LESLIE: Well, I know one of your people has the experience for this; how about if Jill works on it part time until next quarter? JACK: I don't think she wants to do that. LESLIE: Couldn't we have more people work on smaller pieces of the project instead of just one person?

Exhibit 8.1   Facilitator High-Level, Mid-Level, and Low-Level Inferences

inferences is at the bottom of the exhibit. Note that the mid-level and high-level inferences have assumptions embedded in them that cannot be directly linked to the observable data.

There are times when you need to make high-level inferences as part of your diagnosis. In developmental facilitation, if you infer a group member's core value or assumption as part of his or her mindset, you're making a relatively high-level inference. Suppose you infer from a member's behavior that he values unilaterally controlling the conversation to make sure that his solution prevails; you are actually making several high-level attributions about the cause of his behavior.

Issues of trust, power and control, equity, and defensiveness often involve making relatively high-level inferences based on behavior in the group. To the extent that you think these issues have a significant impact on a group's effectiveness and you have an agreement with the group to explore these issues, you should consider inferences of this kind.

When you make a high-level inference, it needs to be logically connected to the behavior observed. In high-level inferences, you're actually making a series of nested inferences, with each at a successively higher level and adding more meaning, attribution about motive, and judgment to the behavior you observed. For group members to understand how you arrived at your high-level inference, you have to be able to fully explain your reasoning. This means that you can describe each step of your inferential process—beginning with the level closest to the observable behavior—and that you don't make any inferential leaps to reach your conclusion. If you're not able to do this privately in step 2 of the diagnosis-intervention cycle, you won't be able to explain your reasoning when you intervene.

STEP 3: CHOOSE WHETHER, WHY, AND HOW TO INTERVENE

The final diagnostic step is to decide whether, why, and how to intervene. It's the transition step between the diagnosis and intervention parts of the cycle. In practice, *intervening* means entering the group's conversation to help it become more effective. An intervention is any statement, question, or nonverbal behavior of yours designed to help the group.

Step 3 is important because, practically, **you can't intervene every time you see group members acting less effectively than they could**. If you did this, the group wouldn't accomplish any of its substantive task and you would frustrate them. So, you need a way of deciding when it's worth intervening and when it's not.

Deciding Whether to Intervene

You consider whether to intervene after you've inferred in step 2 that the group can improve its effectiveness, on the basis of one or more of your diagnostic models. Members may be acting inconsistently with mutual learning behaviors or elements of the mutual learning mindset, or acting in a way that suggests a problem with an element of the TEM. Or they may be acting inconsistent with one or more elements in one of your own models.

Here is a set of questions you can ask yourself to decide whether to intervene.

Have I Observed the Behavior Enough to Make a Reliable Diagnosis? Sometimes you need to repeat steps 1 and 2 of the mutual learning cycle before you are relatively sure that your inference is worth testing. If you think that group members are focusing on interests rather than positions but aren't certain, then you may decide to observe the group a little more to either confirm or disconfirm your hypothesis.

However, waiting to intervene also has potential disadvantages. If you wait until you're quite confident about what you've observed, group members may infer that you are slowing the group's progress by not intervening sooner. In addition, early intervention shows the group what it can expect from you and can help members become quickly aware of behavior. You can reduce this potential problem if you state early in the facilitation why you may not intervene at times when others believe it would be appropriate. You can also invite the group members to intervene for each other.

To What Extent Is the Behavior Hindering the Group's Effectiveness? Not all ineffective behavior has the same impact on a group's effectiveness. For example, consider a group in which Tom is not fully explaining his reasoning and intent. Even if he's acting inconsistently with that behavior, you may choose not to intervene unless you observe some other behavior in the group that leads you to infer that not sharing his reasoning is contributing to a problem. You may notice other group members are making negative inferences about Tom's motives.

Sometimes you decide to intervene because you anticipate that the behavior will have a negative impact on the group in the future. Suppose you infer that group members are making plans on the basis of some significant untested inferences; that's an important time to intervene. Making this kind of judgment requires understanding how ineffective group process is causally connected to various negative group outcomes. Essentially you're thinking, *When I see this kind of behavior under these conditions, I can predict that it will have a negative impact on the group.*

Behavior that hinders the group keeps it from achieving any of the three team effectiveness results: (1) strong performance, (2) productive working relationships, and (3) individual well-being. Keeping in mind all three effectiveness results can help you decide whether an issue is critical enough to warrant intervention.

Is There Effective Behavior I Want to Acknowledge and Reinforce? Although almost all of this chapter focuses on identifying behavior that reduces a group's effectiveness, it's essential to help group members see when they are beginning to use mutual learning behaviors and elements of the mindset. This means simply pointing out what a team member has said and how it has made a difference.

What Are the Consequences If I Don't Intervene? There may be positive and negative consequences if you don't intervene. Here are two general issues to consider. First, if you don't intervene, will a group member do so? One principle of the Skilled Facilitator approach is to reduce unnecessary dependence on you as the facilitator. In other words, don't do for the group what the group can do for itself. This principle leads you not to intervene if group members can intervene themselves. Determining what the group can and cannot do at any point requires continual testing.

Not intervening can be a strategy for further diagnosis and group development. If you believe that members have the skills to recognize and intervene on their own behavior, you can give them time to intervene first. Especially in developmental facilitation, you may decide not to intervene immediately to determine whether members will intervene on their own. If a member does intervene effectively, you learn that the group has developed the ability to diagnose and intervene on that type of behavior or issue.

The second issue is this: If you don't intervene now, what is the probability that you can intervene later and still help the group avoid any negative consequences of its ineffective behavior? Ineffective group behavior diminishes a group's results. But in some situations, if you don't intervene, there are large negative consequences for the group, and they occur quickly; for example, the group's process may be growing increasingly more ineffective, the quality of the group's decisions is suffering, or there is insufficient commitment to implement a decision.

Consider, for example, a group that has made a decision without realizing it hasn't reached consensus and is about to move on to the next agenda item. If you don't intervene immediately, the group may realize it hasn't reached consensus only after it begins to commit resources and implement the decision.

In contrast, if members are discussing a problem and aren't giving specific examples to illustrate their points, the consequences for the group are likely to be less severe if you don't intervene immediately. Group members will probably have a more difficult time understanding what exactly each member means, and as a result, the conversation may take time. You will surely have other chances to intervene before the results of not sharing specific examples become severe. If, however, by not giving specific examples members begin to dig into their positions and make negative attributions about others, the consequences become greater.

Because group process repeats itself, like the horses on a merry-go-round, you have repeating opportunities to intervene on the same ineffective behaviors or patterns. If members don't test inferences on one issue, they are likely not to test those inferences throughout their discussion of the issue at hand, as well as other issues. However, once a group makes a decision on the basis of ineffective process (such as an untested inference), you may not have another opportunity to help the members deal with the content of their decision if you do not intervene at that time.

Have I Contracted with the Group to Make This Type of Intervention? Part of your agreement with a group is to delineate the kinds of interventions you will make with them. In basic facilitation, your agreement with a group may not include making an intervention about fundamental group dynamics or members' mindsets. Although you may see certain issues arise in the group, it may not be necessary to address them for the group to accomplish its stated objectives.

However, if you need to make a type of intervention that you haven't contracted for so the group can accomplish its stated objectives, you can recontract with the group in the moment.

Do I Have the Skills to Intervene? Some interventions, such as those dealing with defensive behavior, require significant skill. To be helpful, you need to intervene within the limits of your skills. This doesn't mean that you should totally avoid intervening if you're not completely proficient; that would prevent you from taking a reasonable risk to become more effective—a behavior worth modeling for the group. However, it's important to limit the risk by choosing interventions that are within reach of your current level of skills. If you decide to pursue an intervention that is new and challenging for you, you might begin by saying, "I'm going to take a risk here and do something I haven't tried before . . ."

Principles for Choosing among Possible Interventions

At any time, you may have the opportunity to make a number of interventions. How do you decide which one to make? There is no one correct answer. Faced with the same situation, two facilitators may make different interventions. In addition, making one intervention doesn't preclude your making another. In fact, the different types of interventions are often linked or nested within one another. For example, you may begin by intervening on several mutual learning behaviors, which then leads to teaching a concept on one of the eight behaviors, which then leads you to intervene on a group member's mindset. I know of no simple rule for mechanically deciding which intervention to make. Still, there are a few principles you can use to help you decide.

You Get More Than One Chance. Interventions are not one-step solutions. It's rare that you can make a single intervention that goes directly to the cause of a problem and helps the group improve. Don't misunderstand me; I love a well-crafted intervention, one that addresses the group's issues succinctly, power-fully, and compassionately. But if you think of crafting only the ideal interven-tion, you place unreasonable pressure on yourself to get everything right the first time you open your mouth. Ironically, focusing on getting it completely right distracts you from doing the good work you're capable of.

Instead, I find it helps to think of interventions as a series of unfolding steps. I start with one, and then depending on the members' responses, I move to other related interventions. Each time I intervene, I learn more about how the members are thinking and feeling and about how my interventions work, all of which enable me to better craft my next intervention. In shifting my thinking this way, I also show compassion for myself.

Address Concerns about Your Facilitative Role First. If a group member directly or even indirectly raises a concern about your facilitative role or performance, this is the first intervention you make before any others. People may be concerned that you're paying attention to some members more than others, that you're becoming involved in the content of the conversation (if you're a facilitator), or that you're colluding with certain members. Or the group members may be concerned that the process is not helping them achieve their objectives.

I refer to this situation as being in facilitator check. In the game of chess, if the other player puts your king in check, the only move you are allowed to make is one that gets your king out of check. If you can't move your king out of check, it becomes checkmate, and you've lost the game. Putting aside the inappropriate win-lose element of my chess analogy, you're in the same situation in your facilitative role. You can't perform your facilitative role when group members have unresolved concerns about how you are helping them.

It can feel threatening to have group members question your role and performance, but only by encouraging them to describe their specific concerns can you address them. Chapter 12 deals with the issue of handling your emotions as well as those of group members.

Consider Whether You Are Doing Basic or Developmental Facilitation. There are some interventions you would more likely make in basic facilitation than in developmental facilitation, and vice versa. Remember that in basic facilitation, you're helping the group temporarily improve its process so it can accomplish some significant task. In developmental facilitation, you're still helping the group accomplish a task, and in addition you're helping it learn how to essentially facilitate its own work, including being able to reflect on its thinking. Basic and developmental facilitation are not discrete categories; they reflect a continuum.

Basic Facilitation In basic facilitation, you choose interventions that are narrowly designed to help the group directly address the task at hand. This includes managing group process and structure, intervening on the behaviors, and focusing on elements of the TEM that are essential for the group to accomplish its task, such as clear goals and appropriate membership. While you help group members articulate their core values and assumptions about the task they are working on, you are less likely to intervene on their mindset in general. Nor are you likely to intervene on the more fundamental elements of the TEM such as group culture, in part because you may not have contracted to make these interventions, but also because they are often not required in helping the group accomplish its specific task.

Developmental Facilitation As facilitation becomes more developmental, you draw on the full range of interventions. You teach the group concepts and techniques for improving process, including helping it to become proficient in using the behaviors. If, for example, you find yourself intervening on the same mutual learning behaviors, this might lead you to begin to intervene on mindset to understand what people are thinking that leads them to continue acting inconsistently with the behaviors.

In basic facilitation, when a conflict arises in the group, you may choose to intervene by asking members to focus on their interests, test their assumptions, and share their reasoning. In developmental facilitation, you are likely to go beyond such interventions and examine the pattern of group conflict and how members contribute to creating the structure of the conflict. In doing so, you help group members learn how they create unproductive conflict in general and how they can change it.

Go Broad before You Go Deep. At any point, you can intervene by going broad or by going deep. When you go broad, you quickly find out what each member thinks about something. When you go deep, you explore a particular topic in depth, sometimes by engaging only one or a few members in your intervention. **The principle is to go broad before you go deep.**

For example, if a group is discussing barriers to implementing an organizational change, going broad would mean saying something like, "Let's go around the room and have each of you quickly identify the barriers you think need to be addressed. We'll build a list as we go. After you've completed generating the list, you can decide which barrier you'd like to discuss first in more detail." However, if you intervened by going deep you might begin by saying, "Let's discuss each of the barriers you think need to be addressed. What's the first barrier someone wants to address?" When the first person identified a barrier, you would ask the group to discuss it in detail. Going broad enables you and the group to quickly identify all the barriers that the group wants to address and then jointly plan the most efficient and effective way to address them. If you go deep first, the group may spend a lot of time on the first person's barrier, which the group may consider a lower priority, including the person who raised it. By going broad first, you help the group more effectively jointly design its next steps in the meeting.

Principles for Deciding with Whom to Intervene

Part of deciding how to intervene is deciding to whom you should address your interventions. Do you address your intervention to the person who engaged in dysfunctional behavior, to the person who was the recipient of the behavior, or to the entire group? Here are some principles to help you decide.

Intervene with the People Who Have the Data. The basic principle is to intervene with the person or people who have the data to respond to your intervention. For interventions on the mutual learning behaviors, this usually means intervening with the person or people whose actions are inconsistent with the mutual learning behavior. If you infer that someone hasn't shared her reasoning with the group, you would address your intervention to her, because she is the person who can best explain her reasoning. If several members are focusing on positions rather than interests, you would intervene with each of them, addressing each by name.

When intervening on a pattern of behavior—a behavior that has occurred at least two or three times—you would address all members who contributed to the pattern. First, you identify the full pattern so group members understand the point of the intervention. Then, in the order in which they have entered the pattern, you address each member's contribution. This allows the group to see how the pattern develops.

Identify People by Name. It may seem obvious, but **when you are making interventions, it's essential to identify the members by name**. This is being transparent and accountable, and it enables group members to make an informed choice. Some facilitators address the group in general terms when they observe certain members acting in a way they consider ineffective: "I notice some members focusing on positions rather than interests. I think it would be helpful if you would focus on your interests." These facilitators reason that by not addressing members specifically, they avoid embarrassing people or putting them on the spot. However, because these members haven't been addressed directly, they may not know that the facilitator is addressing them, and it prevents the facilitator from finding out whether the group members agree with the facilitator's inference. As a result, members may not respond to the facilitator's intervention, either because they don't understand it is meant for them or because they disagree with the facilitator's inference about their behavior.

There are times when it's not necessary to address specific group members, as when you are helping to manage group process and structure. You might say, "What are some ways to solve this problem?" When you are asking the full group if the members agree with something, you might say, "Does anyone have any concerns with the proposal?"

Deciding What Type of Intervention to Make

Part of deciding how to intervene is to decide what type of intervention to make. The type of intervention you decide to make will depend on the diagnosis you have made. We have already described a number of types of interventions: (1) identifying behaviors inconsistent with the eight mutual learning behaviors,

(2) identifying behaviors inconsistent with an element of the mutual learning mindset, and (3) identifying behaviors that suggest some element of team design has not been addressed or is not being used effectively. In this section, I describe additional types of interventions you can make.

Managing Group Process and Structure. In a group process or structure intervention, you decide with the group what process and structures to use during the facilitation. Because this is your area of expertise as facilitator, you make the decision jointly with the group. This entails advocating for a process that meets the group's needs, whether it's a particular problem-solving process, a strategic planning process, or some other. In a large group, managing process may also involve recognizing people to speak and monitoring their time.

Advocating structure includes helping the group clarify its meeting objectives and agenda, suggesting what kind of people may need to participate to generate valid information, and estimating how much time may be needed for various discussions.

Teaching Concepts and Techniques for Improving Group Process. At times, you may need to teach the group about a particular method or technique for improving process so that it can decide whether to use the method. You are doing this when you explain the mutual learning mindset and behaviors, and ask group members whether they want to use them during the facilitation and even after. Other examples include teaching a group to use the TEM or a general problem-solving model.

Technically, when you make this intervention, you're serving as a facilitative trainer. Still, this intervention is consistent with the facilitator's role if it focuses on improving group process. However, if you teach concepts related to the substance of the group's issues (such as marketing methods or product development), you are moving outside the role of facilitator and into the role of facilitative consultant.

Making Content Suggestions. In the content type of intervention, you share some information or suggest how the group can address some substantive aspect of the issue. As you saw in Chapter 2, this type of intervention is an essential part of the facilitative consultant's role, but it is technically inconsistent with the facilitator's role.

However, as I discussed in Chapter 2, **when the content of a group's discussion *is about* how to manage process effectively, you're not neutral about the content because you are a process expert**. Consequently, a content suggestion closely related to group or organizational process and therefore closely related to the group's behavior is appropriate for you to intervene on in your facilitator role.

It can also be appropriate for a facilitator to enter into the content when the group has tried unsuccessfully to identify a solution that meets all the members' interests. Here you may suggest a solution if you first receive the group's permission and afterward ask whether the suggested solution meets all the members' interests.

Here's how you might intervene in this kind of situation: "Tawana, you said your interest behind sending a memo now was to let the department know what progress the group has made. Is that correct? [Continuing, assuming Tawana agrees] Ted, you said your interest behind not sending a memo now was to avoid having people falsely conclude that the group has made a decision; correct? [Continuing, assuming Ted agrees] If the group sends out a memo stating very clearly that the memo reflects the group's current thinking but that the group has not made any decision, would this meet everyone's interests?"

Reframing. A *reframing* intervention helps members change the meaning they ascribe to an event. As the meaning of the event changes, group members' responses and behaviors also change.[1] For example, group members are often reluctant to give each other negative feedback, because they say they care about members and don't want to hurt them. I often help members address their reluctance by helping them reframe what it means "to care." I suggest that genuinely caring about members means *giving* others feedback about their behavior so that the data can be validated and the person receiving the feedback can make an informed free choice about whether she wants to change her behavior. Further, I suggest that by *withholding* information, members *hurt* each other by precluding each other from making an informed choice about whether to change ineffective behavior. When you help members reframe something, you are helping them change some assumption and/or value in their mindset.

Your Facilitative Role and Performance. In an intervention oriented toward the facilitator, your role or performance is the subject of discussion. This is the case of facilitator check I described earlier in the chapter. The purpose of this type of intervention is to identify whether and how you have acted ineffectively and, if so, to identify what if anything needs to happen for you and the group to continue to work effectively.

CHALLENGES IN DIAGNOSING BEHAVIOR AND HOW TO MANAGE THEM

As you develop your diagnostic skills, you'll likely face several challenges. Some are inherent in the nature of facilitation; others have to do with learning the mutual learning approach. Here are some common challenges and suggestions for how to manage them.

Observing and Making Meaning at Different Levels Simultaneously

As you watch a group and try to understand what is happening, the meaning you make will depend on the level you focus on. You can look at things at three levels: behavior and interaction, patterns of behavior, and structure.[2] Regardless of the level you focus on, you're still starting with the same directly observable behavior. So when you look at these three levels, you're not seeing different things; you are seeing the same thing in different ways. Yet, what level you pay attention to affects how you intervene with the group. As you move from seeing only behaviors or interactions to seeing structure, your ability to make high-leverage diagnoses and interventions increases.

Behavior and Interaction. At the first level, you focus on *behavior and interaction.* Focusing on this level, you notice who is saying what to whom, how others respond, and which mutual learning behaviors members are using and not using.

Consider a team conversation in which the leader begins the meeting by identifying a problem communicating with field staff: "The way to solve this problem is to upgrade everyone's software." The IT director responds, "That's not necessary. We're not going to do that." You notice other team members are rolling their eyes after the leader speaks, but you say nothing. Looking at the behaviors and interactions, you infer that both the leader and the IT director are focusing on positions and that other members are withholding some relevant information.

This might lead you to intervene by asking them to focus on their interests and share all relevant information.

Patterns of Behavior. At the second level, you focus on *patterns of behavior.* You take the behavior you noticed at the first level and note how it recurs over time. In addition, you pay attention to other behaviors and interactions and note how they recur over time.

Continuing with the example, you begin to note the frequency with which this type of interaction occurs and the other conditions that are present around the time of the interaction. You might, for instance, note that the leader and IT director focus on positions after the IT director shares information that the team is creating problems for IT. You might also note that members are silent whenever the team leader initiates a new conversation, but they speak up when the IT director initiates the conversation.

This could lead you to intervene by describing this pattern of behavior and interactions, which is a more powerful intervention than simply identifying a single occurrence of an ineffective behavior.

Structure. At the third and deepest level, you notice the underlying *structure.* Unlike focusing on behavior and interaction or on patterns, noticing structure means proposing a causal explanation for part of how the group is operating. The causal map uses the TEM, which has the mutual learning approach embedded in it. By focusing on structure, you help the group see how the mindset it is using leads it to design the elements of its group that, in turn, affect group members' behaviors and lead to diminished results in performance, working relationships, and well-being. By describing this causal map to the group, you can test its validity with the group, and the group can make a choice about changes it wants to make to reduce the negative results it is experiencing.

At this level of structure, you might infer that members are assuming that the IT director's motives are questionable, as they believe he is not likely to approve their IT requests if they disagree with him. You might also infer that members are trying to operate from the core value of minimizing the expression of negative feelings and are reluctant to state views differing from the IT director's if their own IT support is on the line. So they respond through nonverbal behavior. You might also infer that as a result of not raising their concerns with the IT director, they create a cycle in which the IT director makes decisions without the full input of the other members, which leads to lower-quality decisions and the members continuing to be frustrated with the IT director. The IT director may contribute to this by recognizing the members' discontent but not raising it for fear of precipitating the expression of negative feelings.

By intervening on this causal structure, you can help the group members explore how their thinking leads to action that creates unintended results, by contributing to maintaining the system that each is dissatisfied with. In this way, you help the group explore the underlying dynamics that keep their more superficial but ineffective behavior and pattern in place. This means engaging in developmental facilitation and intervening on mindset.

Diagnosing at the Speed of Conversation

To facilitate effectively, you need to be able to diagnose (and intervene) at the speed of the group's conversation. If there is a consistent delay between when the ineffective group behavior occurs and when you figure out what is happening and intervene, you will frustrate the group by having them backtrack.

When you first try to diagnose and intervene using the mutual learning cycle, you will have this delay. The conversation seems to move so quickly that, by the time you have inferred which behavior to intervene on, you have missed several comments that followed it. As you continue to practice, you will be able to immediately match the mutual learning behaviors to what group members are saying.

Needing to Attend Constantly to the Group

One reason facilitation, consulting, coaching, and training are so mentally demanding is that if you're doing it well, you're attending continuously to the group. If you're consulting or training, you have to learn to continually observe the group at the same time you're involved in the content of the discussions. Unless you are working with a partner and you can relieve each other, it's difficult to mentally take time out from the group.

One way to increase your ability to attend to the group is to reduce the distractions that fill up your thoughts. This may mean resolving issues unrelated to the facilitative work before it begins or resolving to put the issues out of your mind until you've finished the work. If possible, not having to respond to voice mails, e-mails, texts, and other interruptions during the facilitative work is a major way to reduce distraction. A second method is to increase your ability to focus for a long period of time by practicing your diagnostic skills. As your ability to diagnose behavior increases, you can do it with less effort and therefore attend to the group longer before tiring. Of course, you can explain to group members that you have temporarily lost focus and ask them to repeat what they have said.

The good news, as I mentioned above, is that if you miss something in the group, you're likely to have other opportunities to observe it. Fortunately, for you—and unfortunately for groups—ineffective group behavior is often repetitive.

Being Comfortable with Ambiguity

At times, you may be unable to make sense out of what you're observing in the group. You may feel uncertain, confused, or overwhelmed, and even wonder how you can help the group. This is a natural feeling for even an experienced facilitator, especially when you're just beginning to work with a group. A natural response to ambiguity and confusion is to try to impose some order. The challenge is to become comfortable with ambiguity and not impose order prematurely by rushing to inference and diagnosis. Diagnosing behavior prematurely reduces the probability that you understand important aspects of the group's situation.

One reason group behavior seems ambiguous at times is that you're observing a complex pattern, but the group has displayed only part of it. Like a mystery that seems impossible to solve until the last page of the book, the entire pattern may need to appear before you can interpret it. Sometimes, you may feel confused because you've missed the beginning of the pattern, much like starting to watch a movie that's already begun; a conflict between members just before the meeting begins might be played out during the meeting.

Apart from accepting that ambiguity and confusion are inevitable, you can try to make sense of the situation by generating alternative hypotheses about what is happening and by observing behavior that either confirms or disconfirms the hypotheses. Of course, you can also share your ambiguity and confusion with group members and ask them to jointly diagnose the situation.

Reducing Cognitive Bias

Cognitive bias occurs when people consistently think in ways that systematically distort some aspect of objective reality.[3] Cognitive bias reduces the quality of our decisions and actions. Some of our cognitive biases stem from what we pay attention to and what we don't; what and how we remember; and how we make inferences and reason. Cognitive bias represents the human condition; while some of us exhibit less cognitive bias than others, we are all subject to it.

Since the 1970s, psychologists have identified many cognitive biases.[4] Here are several types of cognitive bias that are particularly relevant in your facilitative roles:[5]

- **Fundamental attribution error:** The tendency to overemphasize personal factors and underestimate situational factors when explaining other people's behavior. As a facilitator, consultant, or coach, it will lead you to be less helpful to groups by paying less attention to how the group structures and the context in which the group works account for their behavior.

- **Confirmation bias:** The tendency to selectively look for or interpret information in a way that confirms your assumptions, inferences, or hypothesis. The reflexive loop in the ladder of inference shows how confirmation bias works. There is a saying, "We don't see things the way they are; we see things the way we are."[6]

- **Halo effect:** The tendency to extend your view of a person's positive or negative traits in one area of their personality to other areas of their personality. This leads you to evaluate group members more monolithically than they are and to see them as either positive or negative.

Becoming aware of your mindset and thinking process in general reduces the probability that you will be subject to cognitive bias and enables you to help a group make better decisions. By identifying your systematic personal biases and personal issues (need for control or approval; fear of being wrong; and so on), you can begin to monitor your behavior. Also, by working with a partner with whom you have discussed these issues, you can get feedback from the partner and also reduce the chance of your issues affecting the group.

Being Drawn in by the Content

In your facilitative role, you have to pay attention to the content of the conversation to help group members explain their views and test their assumptions and inferences about an issue. The challenge is to pay attention to the content without being drawn into it and without losing your ability to help the group.

When you're drawn in by the content, you stop attending to the group's process; you might even find yourself participating in the content of a conversation when it's not appropriate for your facilitative role. You can get drawn in if you're interested in the content, completely unfamiliar with it and trying to figure it out, or feel overwhelmed by the group's process and use the content to seek refuge.

One way to avoid being drawn into content is to attend to it for the purpose of examining the process. When you attend to the group, you're looking for whether group members are using the mutual learning behaviors. If you infer they aren't, then you attend more closely to the content to see specifically how the potential process problem is affecting the content. It's as if the group conversation is a piece of music. The group process is the melody, and the content is the specific notes. You pay attention to the melody until some part of it sounds off-key, at which point you listen to the specific notes.

Being Limited by Your Diagnostic Frames

Your effectiveness is determined partly by the range (and validity) of your diagnostic frames. The law of the instrument states that if the only tool you have is a hammer, everything will look like a nail to you.[7] Applying this to diagnosis, you naturally construe the behavior you observe to fit the diagnostic frames you have. If, for example, you're able to diagnose when group members are acting inconsistently with the behaviors, but you're less able to use the TEM to diagnose the group's problems or to diagnose problems that stem from members' mindset, then you may continue to make interventions that address only part of the cause of the behavior and that miss the root cause. In addition, if you have your favorite diagnostic frames, you may look for opportunities to use them, even when another frame may be more appropriate.

All of this reduces your ability to help a group. The challenge is to develop the ability to diagnose the comprehensive set of behaviors related to group effectiveness and to learn to use an equally comprehensive set of interventions related to these behaviors.

SUMMARY

In this chapter, we've explored in detail the diagnostic steps of the mutual learning cycle. This includes (1) how to use various models to guide what you look for when observing a group, (2) how to use those same models to make meaning of what you observe, and (3) how to decide whether, why, and how to intervene. We also explored various challenges to diagnosing and how to overcome them.

In Chapter 9, we will explore the details of how to craft an intervention so that it follows logically from your diagnosis. This includes identifying exactly what you might say at each intervention step of the mutual learning cycle.

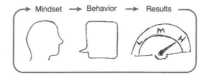

CHAPTER NINE

How to Intervene with Groups

I n the previous chapter, we explored how to diagnose groups using the mutual learning cycle and various models. In this chapter, I describe how to use the mutual learning cycle and various models to intervene once you've decided to do so. I describe each step of an intervention and explain what to say, how to say it, who to say it to, when to say it, and when not to say it. At the end of the chapter, I describe how to carefully choose your words when intervening.

KEY ELEMENTS OF THE INTERVENTION STEPS

The mutual learning cycle intervention steps have several key design elements. By understanding these elements, you will better understand how the entire mutual learning cycle is structured and the logic for using it.

The Intervention Steps Parallel the Diagnostic Steps

The three intervention steps of the mutual learning cycle parallel the three diagnostic steps (Figure 9.1). In short, in the intervention steps, you make public your private reasoning in the diagnostic steps and test whether group members agree with your thinking:

- In step 4, you describe to the group what you privately observed in step 1 that led you to intervene, and you test whether the group agrees with your observations.

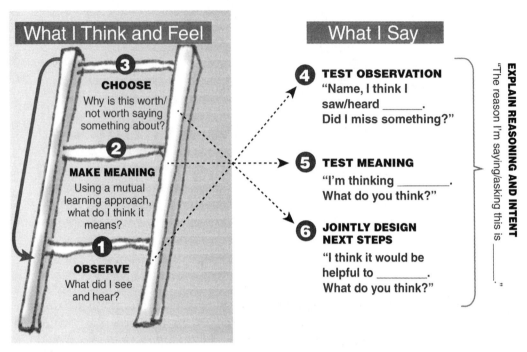

Figure 9.1 The Parallel between the Diagnostic and Intervention Steps of the Mutual Learning Cycle

- In step 5, you describe the inferences you privately made in step 2 and test whether group members agree with your inferences.
- In step 6, you and the group jointly design the next step.

Assuming group members have decided to change their behavior as a result of your intervention, the cycle begins again, and you observe whether the group members have in fact changed their behavior. You use the mutual learning cycle continually to determine whether there is any group behavior for you to intervene on.

Mutual Learning Behaviors and Mindset Are Embedded in the Intervention Steps

The mutual learning mindset and behaviors are embedded in the intervention steps of the cycle.

- In step 4, as you describe observable behavior, you are using the mutual learning behavior, "use specific examples and agree on what important words mean."

- In step 5, as you share your inference, you are using the behavior, "test assumptions and inferences."

- In step 6, when you are jointly designing next steps with group members, you are using that behavior: "jointly design next steps."

- In each step 4 through 6, you can use the mutual learning behavior, "explain reasoning and intent." In step 4, you use it to briefly explain why you are intervening. In step 5, you explain how the group member's behavior may be ineffective. In step 6, you explain how the next step you are suggesting can create a more effective process.

- Steps 4 through 6 each have two parts: In the first part, you explain your view, sometimes adding additional reasoning; in the second part, you ask a genuine question to learn what group members think about your view. These two parts make up the mutual learning behavior, "state views and ask genuine questions."

Because the mutual learning behaviors are a way of operationalizing the mutual learning mindset, when you intervene, you are using the mutual learning values and assumptions:

- You are being transparent about what you are observing, what it means to you, and why you are intervening.

- You are being curious about whether the people you are intervening with see things differently from you. You assume that others have information you might not have and that they may see things that you miss. You assume that differences between your and others' views are opportunities for learning.

- You are enabling group members to make an informed choice about how they proceed and are enabling yourself to do the same.

- You are being accountable to the group by moving forward only after having tested whether your data and inferences are correct. You are asking group members to be accountable by responding to your genuine questions.

- You are intervening with compassion, recognizing that group members have likely created their own unintended consequences. You also assume that you may be contributing to the problem you are observing.

Compassion is a fundamental element in intervening. It's relatively easy for group members to agree to use the behaviors and agree that you can intervene when they act inconsistently with the behaviors. But when you start intervening on their behavior, it can become difficult for group members. They may feel bad about their ineffectiveness or believe they've been put on the spot by your intervention. If you see the group members primarily as having promised to act effectively, then you may view your interventions simply as a way to police their transgressions. If they continue to act ineffectively, you may become frustrated with them for not having the skills that they hired you to help them with. At this point, your interventions shift from being helpful to being hurtful.

Instead, if you see the group members as simply trying to work together without the necessary skill set and mindset, you view your interventions as a way to provide (or teach them) the skill set and mindset they are missing. If they continue to act ineffectively, you can have compassion for them, thinking about the difficulty they are having in learning this approach, just as you learned it.

USING THE MUTUAL LEARNING CYCLE TO INTERVENE: AN EXAMPLE

Exhibit 9.1 shows a simple example of intervening using the mutual learning cycle. Three executives are discussing how to redesign part of the organization's performance management system. The right-hand column shows the conversation, and the left-hand column presents the facilitator's notes about the conversation. Now let's explore each of the intervention steps in more detail.

Facilitator's Notes	Conversation
I infer that Raul has stated a position and has begun to discuss an interest in being able to budget for the system (step 2). I consider whether to intervene to ask Raul to fully identify his interest. I decide to wait to see how others respond, given that he has begun to identify an interest (step 3).	RAUL: I think the performance management system needs to have a cap on the payout and a forced distribution with a predefined percentage of people who will be rewarded. This way we can budget for it in advance.
I consider whether to ask Kate to check whether others share her assumption (step 2). I decide not to make this intervention because she has clearly stated the assumption and the next person may respond to it without my intervening (step 3).	KATE: But a forced distribution assumes that only a predetermined number of people can be excellent performers. It's hypocritical for us to say that we expect everyone in this organization to be excellent and then design a system that assumes that's not possible.
I infer that Andrew may be discussing another topic and therefore unilaterally designing the next step in the conversation (step 2). I wait until the next person speaks to see if the conversation will return to what I understood to be the original topic (step 3).	ANDREW: Kate, if anyone is hypocritical, it's the employees. Remember how they were complaining last year that their managers didn't give them enough autonomy, and then when it was given to them, they said their managers were too distant?

Facilitator's Notes	Conversation
I infer that Raul continues on the same different topic as Andrew (step 2). I decide to intervene because the group seems not to be returning to the original topic as I understand it (step 3).	RAUL: Yeah, no matter what we did, it wasn't good enough.
I briefly explain my reasoning for intervening and then describe the directly observable data and test whether Raul and Andrew see it differently (step 4).	FACILITATOR: I want to check whether the conversation is still on track. A minute ago, you were talking about the forced distribution. Then Andrew, you said, "Kate, if anyone is hypocritical, it's the employees." You continued and then, Raul, you said that you agreed. Andrew and Raul, did I miss anything?
With Raul and Andrew agreeing that I have accurately described what they said, I move to step 5 of the cycle.	RAUL and ANDREW: No, that's right.
I share my private inference from step 2 that I don't see the relationship between Andrew and Raul's comment and the comments made before they spoke. I check to see if they see a relationship I don't see (step 5).	FACILITATOR: Andrew and Raul, I don't see the relationship between your comments and conversation about the forced distribution. Can you say how your comments are related, if they are?
Andrew agrees that his comment represents a different topic and that it is not going to affect discussion on the current topic (step 5).	ANDREW: Well, it's a different topic. We have to find ways of getting people to accept more responsibility, but I don't think that's going to affect whether we have a fixed distribution.
With Raul agreeing, I move to step 6.	RAUL: Yeah, I agree.
I ask the group whether they want to return to the distribution topic or continue on the shifting-responsibility topic (step 6).	FACILITATOR [Addressing the full group]: What do you want to do? Do you want to continue the conversation about distribution or shift to the issue of responsibility?
	RAUL: Let's go back to the distribution issue.
I check for consensus from the group (step 6).	FACILITATOR: Okay. Anyone have a different suggestion?
	ALL MEMBERS: No.
I ask Kate to take the next step to bring the group back to the original topic (step 6).	FACILITATOR: Okay. Kate, you were the last person to talk before the topic changed. Would you repeat what you said so people can respond?

Exhibit 9.1   Intervening Using the Mutual Learning Cycle

STEP 4: TEST OBSERVATIONS

In step 4, you describe to the group the information that you've observed in step 1 that leads you to intervene, and you test whether the group agrees with your observations. Sharing observations means sharing directly observable information. As I described in Chapter 5, directly observable information includes anything you can capture on a video, including all the group members' verbal and nonverbal behavior.

Begin by Addressing Members by Name

When you begin step 4, you address the group member by name so the group knows to whom you're speaking. It's also helpful to include a phrase such as "I think I heard you say . . ." or "I think you said . . ." Using such a phrase sets you up to complete the sentence by quoting what the group member said, which is exactly what you want to do in step 4.

Share Your Observations without Adding Meaning

It's important to share your observations without making an inference or attribution. If you've done step 1 of the cycle well, this won't be a problem. Exhibit 9.2 shows several statements you might make to share your observations

Nature of Inference	Facilitator's Statement
High-Level Inference and Attribution	
You infer that Andrew is shifting the topic unilaterally because he wants to control the situation.	"Andrew, you changed the subject. I think you are trying to control the conversation."
Medium-Level Inference and Attribution	
You infer that talking about responsibility is not talking about distribution, and you attribute the cause to Andrew's not listening to what Kate was saying.	"Andrew, you changed the subject. I don't think you heard what Kate was saying."
Low-Level Inference and Attribution	
You infer that talking about responsibility is not talking about distribution.	"Andrew, I think you're talking about a different topic than Kate."
Directly Observable Information	
"Andrew, you said, 'Kate, if anyone is hypocritical, it's the employees. Remember how they were complaining last year that the managers didn't give them enough autonomy, and then when it was given to them, they said their managers were too distant?'"	

Exhibit 9.2   Embedding Inferences in Sharing an Observation

with the group and to test whether the group agrees. The easiest way to avoid making an inference or attribution is to repeat the words you heard the group members use. Once you add an inference or attribution, you move beyond observation to interpretation. A video camera simply observes; it doesn't interpret.

It's essential to share your observations without making an inference or attribution, because the observable data are the basis of your intervention. If group members don't see the observable information as you see it, they're unlikely to agree with your inference that is based on the observable information.

Consider Explaining the Intervention You Are About to Make

At any point in steps 4, 5, or 6, you can explain why you're intervening. This is shown in Figure 9.1, with a bracket leading from the three interventions steps pointing to the line, "Explain Reasoning and Intent," and the opening line, "The reason I'm saying/asking this is . . ." This is an important part of the mutual learning cycle because it helps group members better understand how you're trying to help them.

At step 4 it's sometimes helpful to briefly explain the intervention you're about to make, before you share the directly observable information. You might begin your intervention by saying, "I want to check whether the conversation is still on track" before describing the observable behavior. This is particularly useful when you're about to describe a complex pattern that requires you to share and test a large number of behaviors. You might say, "I've noticed a pattern of behavior in the group that I think makes it difficult for you to reach consensus. Let me share what I've observed, check it out with you, and see whether you agree." The statement quickly helps members understand not only why you're intervening but also that you are going to check your understanding with them, which reassures group members. Without this context, you would be describing and testing many behaviors, and group members would be wondering where you're heading.

Be Prepared for Members to Disagree with You

Be prepared for group members to see things differently. The second part of step 4 involves asking the person whether you've accurately captured what the person said. If you ask, "Have I misstated anything you've said?" and the person simply answers yes, then follow up by saying, "What did I miss?" Finding out that you've misheard a group member is not a mistake; on the contrary, it's a success. Using the mutual learning cycle well means learning that others see things differently from the way you do.

After the person tells you what she actually said, you can then decide if it still makes sense to proceed with your intervention. If the corrected version no longer leads you to infer that the person has acted inconsistently with the mutual learning behavior, you stop your intervention. You can say, "I was going to follow up on what I thought you said, but given what was actually said, it's not relevant."

Sometimes, between the time a person has spoken and the time you start to intervene, you may forget exactly what the person said that led you to intervene. In this situation, you can simply say something like, "Sheryl, would you repeat what you just said? I wanted to follow up on it, but I forget exactly what you said." Group members don't expect you to be infallible; it's okay to occasionally ask people to repeat themselves.

STEP 5: TEST MEANING

In step 5, you state the inference that you have privately made in step 2 and test with the group member or members whether they have made a different inference. As I mentioned in Chapter 8, you might be testing one of many kinds of inferences: Whether the team member or members are behaving inconsistently with an element of mutual learning behaviors or mindset, agreements reached regarding elements of the TEM, agreements regarding your facilitative role, or agreements to use some other model, such as a process improvement model. You might also be testing whether team members made inferences about the content of the discussion.

Publicly testing inferences with the group prevents you from unilaterally acting on inferences that are inaccurate. This helps you avoid the confirmation bias I described in Chapter 8 that can also lead you to a self-fulfilling prophecy, in which you help to create the very behavior you expect to see.[1,2,3]

As I described in Chapters 5 and 8, it's important to avoid making inferences at a level higher than needed for your intervention. In the example with Andrew and Raul (Exhibit 9.1), the facilitator's inference that Andrew's comment doesn't seem related to Kate's comment is a relatively low-level inference. You don't have to make a higher-level inference to intervene on the behavior of jointly designing next steps.

There are times, particularly in developmental facilitation, when you do make high-level inferences—for example, regarding a group member's mindset. Under certain circumstances, you might, for instance, infer not only that Andrew's comment is unrelated to Kate's but also that Andrew is introducing this comment by design to purposely shift the conversation away from Kate's topic, which he finds challenging in some way.

However, to make such a high-level inference, you would need to share the data that led you to make it. The data might come from previous group conversations in which the group and you explored with Andrew his reasons for regularly shifting the topic of conversation before checking with group members. You also would have needed to see a pattern of this behavior before making the high-level inference. If Andrew has changed the topic of the conversation only once or twice in the meeting, the data are probably insufficient for you to make such a high-level inference. Also, to make a high-level inference intervention, you need an agreement with the group to do so. I discuss this in Chapter 13, on contracting.

When you do make a high-level inference or attribution about a group member's motives or emotions, attribute it to the person but not to his or her personality. For example, you might say, "David, given what you just said, I'm inferring the reason you don't want to give your consent is that you don't trust that Lucinda will help you complete the project. Is my inference off?" rather than "You are not very trusting toward Lucinda" or "You aren't a very trusting person." The difference is important. The former statement is more closely related to the observable behavior. It makes an attribution about trusting behavior in a particular situation rather than overgeneralizing and implying that the person has a mistrustful personality. Also, attributing the behavior to personality implies that it is less likely to change, because aspects of personality are relatively stable. Consequently, the former statement is less likely to elicit defensive behavior than the statements in parentheses.

Sometimes you state your inference in a way that identifies a behavior that you believe the group member is not using: "Brett, your statement sounds like a position rather than an interest. Do you see it differently?" If you want to emphasize the group's agreement to use the mutual learning behaviors, instead you might say, "Brett, one of the behaviors the group agreed to use is to focus on interests rather than positions. Your statement sounds like it's focusing on positions. How do you see it?"

Be Prepared for Group Members to Disagree with You

Be prepared for group members to see things differently. The second part of step 5 involves asking the person whether your inference is accurate. As with step 4, if you ask, "Is my inference off in any way?" and the person simply answers yes, then follow up by asking what meaning he makes of his statement. Here, too, finding out that a group member's meaning is different from yours is not a mistake; it's a success.

Whether you're testing an inference about content or process affects how you respond if a group member doesn't agree with the inference you have made. If you are testing a content inference—one about the meaning of the person's words—you are likely to accept the person's interpretation if it makes sense to you as a possible explanation. You accept it because it is difficult for someone other than that person to independently know what he or she means.

If, however, you're making a process inference—for example, that a group member is acting inconsistently with a behavior—then you pursue the differing interpretations because as a process expert, you have relevant information and can logically explain the reasoning by which you made your inference. For instance, if in step 5 you share your inference that Amal has stated his view and not asked a genuine question and Amal disagrees with your inference, you might then say, "Amal, would you explain how you see your statement as both making a statement and asking a genuine question so I can understand where we see it differently?" After listening to Amal's explanation, you may explain as a process expert how you think his understanding is incomplete, or you might learn from his explanation that he has, in fact, asked a genuine question and you missed it.

Don't State Your Inference as a Question

Some facilitators make their interventions in the form of a question.[4] The facilitator might begin an intervention by asking, "Andrew, do you think you're off track?" Author Edgar Schein states that the question format is generally more helpful "because it encourages, even forces, the client to maintain the initiative. If the goal is to help the client to solve his own problem, to own the responsibility, then the question is the best way to communicate that expectation."[5]

I share Schein's goal of helping the client to own responsibility, and I think his approach can be appropriate for a group in developmental facilitation that is becoming skilled at diagnosing its own behavior. However, I see several potential problems with the question format. First, it requires you to withhold relevant information. If you're thinking, *I heard Lois say "X," which leads me to infer that Lois is not explaining her reasoning,* but say to the group "Do you think Lois is explaining her reasoning?" or "What do you think of Lois's comment?" then you're withholding relevant information and easing in. Unless you state the relevant information, you can't check whether the group shares your point of view.

This leads to the second problem: The group can feel set up. If the group answers, "Yes, Lois is sharing her reasoning," then unless you share your differing view or drop the intervention, you need to continue asking leading questions until the group figures out the supposed answer. Eventually, the group may infer correctly that you are looking for the so-called right answer, but for whatever reason, you're unwilling to share it with them.

Finally, using the question format can send the message that the group needs to take responsibility for its observations but that you don't have to take responsibility for yours. This message is inconsistent with the mutual learning principle that the facilitator is supposed to model effective behavior. Therefore, unless the group understands that your question is designed to help the group learn to diagnose its own behavior, it is more effective to share your inference about the member's behavior and then ask whether the member or others view it differently.

Consider Explaining Why You Are Testing This Inference

As I mentioned in step 4, at any point in steps 4, 5, or 6 you can explain why you are intervening. At step 5, it's sometimes helpful to briefly explain the potential negative consequences that lead you to intervene.

You might say, "The reason I'm testing my inference that group members are raising issues and not following them through to a conclusion is that I think it's a major contributor to the frustration you've said you're feeling about not being able to get consensus." If a member is making an untested inference or assumption, you might explain by saying, "I'm inferring that you're thinking that the problem needs to be solved using the current staffing available. Is my inference correct? The reason I raise this is because if it turns out that your assumption is incorrect, you may end up designing a solution that makes it more difficult to implement."

STEP 6: JOINTLY DESIGN NEXT STEPS

In step 6, you jointly decide with group members what next step to take. What that next step might be depends on the behavior you and the group saw and the inference you and the group agreed on. If you intervened because a group member was making an untested inference, you would suggest that the group member test her inference. If you intervened because team members were unclear or had conflicting views of their roles, you might suggest that the members spend time clarifying their roles. If you intervened because you saw behavior that led you to infer that team members were wanting to minimize expression of negative feelings, you might suggest that the members discuss what leads them to hold this value and address the unintended negative consequences associated with it.

When you jointly design the next step, sometimes you propose the next step, other times you ask a group member or members what they would propose, and still other times, you're crafting the next step together. If you're proposing a next step, you might say, "I think it would be helpful to test your inference to see if it's accurate. Any concerns about doing that?" If you're asking a group member to offer the next step, you might say, "Eduardo and Elan, given that you have different expectations about the deadline, what next step do you think would be helpful to take?" If you're crafting the next step together, you might begin by saying, "Given that you all agree that it's not possible to achieve your original meeting purpose in the time remaining, I suggest we spend a few minutes jointly deciding how best to use your time. Does anyone have a different suggestion?"

Consider Explaining Your Reason for the Joint Design

In step 6, you might want to explain your reasoning for asking the person to take a next step, including changing his or her behavior to act consistently with the mutual learning behaviors. Generally, by step 6, there may be less need to explain your reasoning, especially if you have done so at steps 4 and/or 5. If you haven't explained in step 5 the potential problem with making untested inferences, you can do so in step 6. You might say, "The reason I'm suggesting this is that by testing your inference, you can be sure you are designing the solution on the basis of accurate information."

Help People Design Their Next Step If They Need Help

When group members choose to redesign their behavior to take the next step, sometimes they need help. If they've just been introduced to the mutual learning behaviors, they may not know how to test an inference, focus on interests, or combine stating their views with a genuine question. Here, you can help the members redesign their behavior either by coaching them or by modeling the behavior for them. Of course, you can jointly design how you help them by saying something like, "Do you want some help? If so, would you like me to coach you and/or model it for you?"

Even if members redesign their behavior, it may still be inconsistent with the desired behavior. In this situation, you use the mutual learning cycle again, sharing your observation, testing your inference that they are, for instance, still focusing on positions (explaining why you believe that), and asking the members whether they want to try again.

Honor People's Choice to Not Redesign Their Behavior

It's rare that group members choose not to redesign behavior that is inconsistent with the mutual learning behaviors if they've validated your observations and inferences. But what if, for example, a member says no when you ask whether he would be willing to give a specific example? First, you can ask, "Can you say what leads you to say no? I'm asking not because I want to pressure you or put you on the spot, but to find out if there is something that is keeping you from giving an example so people can better understand your concern. The choice is still yours." If the person is willing to share his concern, you can then explore that concern with the person and the group and ask, "What needs to happen for you to be willing to share an example?" Ultimately, to preserve the group's free choice, you must respect members' decisions about whether they want to change their behavior.

Viewing a reluctant group member as resistant is not a particularly useful frame. It attributes to the person that he is unreasonable—even if you don't understand his reasons—and questions his motives. Instead, if you view a reluctant group member as having unmet needs—needs that you may not fully understand—you can maintain your compassion even if he chooses not to change his behavior.

HOW TO MOVE THROUGH THE INTERVENTION STEPS

Although the intervention steps are numbered 4, 5, and 6, you won't always move through them in this order. There are situations in which you will repeat steps, skip steps, and use the steps in a different order. Here are the key factors to consider.

When to Skip Intervention Steps

So far, I have described how you can use the three intervention steps in their full form. Each of the steps has two parts: In the first part, you state your view, and in the second part, you ask a genuine question. In addition, for any of the steps, you can add an explanation of your view or question.

Although each step of the cycle serves a purpose, sometimes you can skip a step—or part of a step—and still intervene effectively. One reason to skip a step is that using the full mutual learning cycle repeatedly when it's not needed can sound unnatural, awkward, or laborious. However, skipping a step inappropriately can create problems.

Deciding when to skip a step is a judgment call. Steps 4, 5, and 6 are each designed to share your reasoning and check with group members to see if they see the situation differently. Skipping a step creates two risks. First, you increase the chance that group members will not understand part of your reasoning for asking them to change their behavior. Second, if you skip the part of the step that tests for differing views, you end up assuming that members agree with your observation or inference. If your assumption is incorrect, then you move to the next step of the cycle without the members having agreed to a previous step.

There are several conditions under which you sometimes skip a step.

A Member Has Just Spoken. If a group member has just said something and you intervene immediately after she has spoken, you can skip step 4 and begin with step 5. For example, in a group meeting discussing the effects of the economy on the organization, Tara says, "I've been through this before. Believe me, there will be layoffs." If you intervene immediately after Tara speaks, you can skip to step 5 and say, "Tara, hearing you say that, I'm thinking that you have some relevant information about previous situations like this one. Is my inference correct?"

However, if Tara has just spoken but said a number of things, it helps to repeat the part of what she said that you want to focus on so that she and others understand, but skip the part of step 1 in which you test for differing views. You could say, "Tara, you said a number of things just now. One thing you said was X. From that, I'm thinking that you have some relevant information about previous situations like this one. Is my inference correct?"

The Intervention Creates an Ordinary Request. If the group member has just spoken and you're asking him to use a mutual learning behavior that is a generally accepted request in meetings, you can skip directly to step 6. For example, if Ellis has said, "We miss the deadlines because we don't have full cooperation from other divisions," you might say, "Ellis, can you talk about a time when that happened?" Here, you're intervening to ask Ellis to use specific examples and agree on what important words mean. Because asking people for specific examples is typically seen as an ordinary request, your risk is relatively low if you skip to step 6. Other behaviors that may fall in this category, depending on the group culture, are explaining your reasoning and intent, and focusing on interests and not positions.

Group Members Have Agreed to Redesign Their Behavior. In developmental facilitation, when a general agreement exists that members will redesign their own behavior, you don't need to ask each time. Instead, in step 6 you can simply ask, "How would you say that so it is consistent with the mutual learning behaviors?"

You Want to Paraphrase What a Group Member Said. Paraphrasing involves taking a group member's words and using different words to convey essentially the same meaning. When you paraphrase, you are often combining steps 4 and 5, because by changing the words that a group member has used, you may be adding your own meaning. You can paraphrase in order to summarize and capture the essence of a person's comments: "Jessica, I'm going to paraphrase what I heard you say; then tell me if I misrepresented you in any way. I understood you to be saying that creating a new division will shift the responsibility for quality away from manufacturing without creating any benefits. Is there anything I said that didn't accurately capture what you meant?"

You might also paraphrase in order to emphasize certain points that the person has made, perhaps to contrast them with others' comments: "Jessica, let me see if I can paraphrase, emphasizing the key issue as you see it. These are my words, not yours; let me know if I misrepresent what you've said. You're saying that, unlike Ian, you do see a lack of cooperation between the units, and you are frustrated that he doesn't see it. Have I misstated anything?"

When Not to Skip Intervention Steps

There are also conditions under which it's not helpful to skip an intervention step.

Group Members Are Misunderstanding Each Other. When group members misunderstand each other, using both parts of all the intervention steps increases the change that you don't add to the misunderstanding. Using all the steps is particularly important in high-conflict situations, particularly if a group member is responding defensively. In this situation, you can begin step 4 by saying, "Pierre, I know you just said this a second ago, but I want to repeat it to make sure that I have heard it accurately, because there have been a number of times when people said they had been misquoted."

The Intervention Is Complex. A complex intervention requires that you share more of your reasoning than with a simple intervention. Discussing undiscussable issues and jointly designing next steps are complex mutual learning interventions. Testing assumptions and inferences can also be complex. Other complex interventions involve exploring group members' mindsets and reframing.

The Group Is Beginning Developmental Facilitation. Early in developmental facilitation, using the complete intervention cycle helps members learn all the steps. After members become familiar with the entire cycle, collapsing creates less of a risk of misunderstanding. Then members know which steps you have skipped and can respond if they believe the missing steps need to be discussed. If skipping a step creates a problem, you can return to using the full cycle.

When to Repeat Intervention Steps

I have described the mutual learning cycle as a one-way process in which you move from step 4 to 5 and 6 (sometimes skipping part of a step along the way). However, sometimes you repeat steps. For example, if you're intervening on a pattern of behavior, you may identify several people's observations and test them in step 4. This is essentially using step 4 each time to describe a behavior and test to see if you are seeing it the same way as the group members. After you have identified and tested all the observable information you are using to make your inference, then you move to step 5 and test the several inferences you have made from the observations.

When to Change the Order of Intervention Steps

Sometimes it's more helpful to start at step 5 of the cycle, stating your inference, and then move to step 4, describing the behavior you've observed that led you to make the inference. This is particularly helpful when you have observed a lot of behaviors that together form a pattern that you are intervening on. In this case, you might say, "Marc, you've said a number of things in the last few minutes that led me to think that you're frustrated with the amount of time it's taking the team to make a decision." At this point, you could skip the testing for agreement and go directly to step 4 and share the behavior you saw that led to this inference. You might say, "You said, 'This should have been done a month ago,' 'Guys, this is a simple decision,' and 'I don't have time for this.'" Then you can return to step 5 and ask, "Is my inference correct?" Notice that this combines changing the order of steps and skipping the testing part of step 4. As you start using the mutual learning cycle, you can experiment with skipping steps and changing the order.

If You Launch an Intervention, Land It

Whatever intervention you make, be sure to complete it. I think of an intervention as launching a plane into the air. Until you land it, you haven't completed the trip. Practically, this means several things. First, if you're asking a question or proposing something to the group, make sure you actually ask a question for people to respond to. Second, ensure that you get an answer from all the people you're asking. If you're asking group members whether they agree with your suggestion to move to the next topic, don't take a number of people saying yes as an indication to move ahead. Get a response from everyone.

If, while people are responding to your question, the group starts to discuss a different topic, ask the group to finish responding to your question. You might say, "Drew, I'm not seeing how what you're saying is responding to my question. Did I miss it? If not, can you answer my question about whether you think the group should move to the next topic so we can find out if everyone is ready to move on?"

Sometimes it's difficult to finish an intervention you've begun. Group members start by answering your question, and at some point the conversation shifts without your realizing it. If you're always thinking about whether the group is on the specific topic, including whether it is responding to your specific questions or requests, you increase the chance of landing the interventions you launch and helping the group become more effective.

CHOOSING YOUR WORDS CAREFULLY

The specific words you use in your interventions are important. A small difference in your choice of words makes the difference between being clear or vague, descriptive or evaluative, inclusive or divisive, and compassionate or unsympathetic. By using language that states exactly what you mean—no more and no less—you can intervene clearly, effectively, and compassionately. Here are some principles to consider when choosing your words.

Avoid Jargon

Some people find the language of mutual learning relatively jargon-free. To others it feels like jargon. For example, I use the term *inference* throughout the book, but if that sounds like jargon to you or you think it would sound like jargon to the people you are using it with, choose a different term. Instead, of saying, "I am inferring . . . ," you can say "I'm thinking that . . ." or "It sounds to me as if . . ." The purpose is to use words that are clearly understood and that reflect your own voice, not mine.

Use Words with One (Correct) Meaning

To avoid being misinterpreted, use words and phrases that have one meaning— the meaning you want to convey. Certain phrases carry more than one meaning. As part of a union-management cooperative effort, I served as the facilitator in a three-member training team that included union and management representatives. When an employee asked whether a workshop exercise could be approached in several ways, the union representative on our training team said, "I don't care which way you do it." Later, the employee said he was annoyed that the union representative wasn't interested in answering the question. He misinterpreted the union representative's statement to mean "I'm not interested in your problem." The representative could have avoided this misinterpretation if he had said, "I don't have a preference for how you conduct the exercise."

Use Descriptive Words

Use descriptive words if they can be substituted for evaluative words. Words that identify directly observable behavior are more easily validated than judgmental words. The behavior to "use specific examples and agree on what important words mean" is based partly on this principle. It's easier for a group to agree whether a member spoke during the meeting than to agree on whether he was engaged.

Descriptive words are consistent with the facilitator's neutral role. Judgmental words contain some built-in evaluation, implying that the facilitator either approves or disapproves of a behavior or idea. For example, in facilitating a conflict between teachers and administrators, I intervened to summarize the two alternatives posed by members, saying: "You have identified two alternatives. The radical one is X. The other alternative is Y." As soon as the word *radical* left my lips, I realized I had made a mistake, even though some group members had used that term. By labeling one alternative with the adjective *radical,* I loaded it with all the political connotations with which that word has come to be associated. For some group members, *radical* probably had a positive connotation, while for others it was negative. In any case, by framing the alternative as radical, I added an unnecessary evaluative component. Had I intervened in a purely descriptive way, I would have said, "You described two alternatives. One is X. The other is Y."

Use Proper Nouns

Use proper nouns or other nouns rather than pronouns. Consider this short exchange between José and a facilitator:

JOSÉ: I talked with Peter about how to handle my conflict with Fred. Peter said he wasn't the kind of person who was particularly good at resolving conflicts and that I should try to solve the problem on my own. Or, I could work something out with Jack, Beth, or Nancy. Frankly, I don't think I can get help from any of them.

FACILITATOR: Do you think you can solve the conflict without him?

By using the pronoun "him," the facilitator fails to clarify whether he is referring to Peter, Fred, or Jack. When pronoun confusion becomes complicated, it begins to sound like the famous Abbott and Costello routine, "Who's on First?" The pronoun *that* (or *this*) creates similar confusion. By using individuals' names or their distinct titles, you can avoid confusion.

Use Active Voice

Use active voice unless the identity of the actor isn't clear. Active voice identifies who or what is taking the action; passive voice doesn't. "Sue decided to promote Glen" uses active voice. "It was decided to promote Glen" uses passive voice. When you use active voice, you provide valid information to the group, reduce potential ambiguity, and act consistently with the belief that individuals should be accountable for their actions. As my eighth-grade English teacher repeatedly told our class, "Use active voice. I want to know who is doing what to whom!"

However, it can be helpful to intentionally use passive voice when it's not clear who the person in question is. If two group members are disagreeing about who told the director that the team task couldn't get finished today, you might ask, "When the director was told that the deadline couldn't be met, how did it create a problem?"

Use Words Bestowing Equal Recognition

Use words that give equal recognition to all members and tasks. To be credible with all subgroups, refer to each subgroup in a way that maintains its identity and doesn't subordinate it to other groups. **The principle is to refer to each subgroup in terms that reflect its independent identity rather than in terms that use another subgroup as a point of reference.** My colleague Peg Carlson and I used to be members of a university department faculty made up mostly of lawyers. At faculty meetings, faculty members would refer to "the lawyer faculty" and "the nonlawyer faculty." Peg, who like me is an organizational psychologist, commented that until she came to this organization, she had not realized that she was a nonlawyer. She then said that she realized that she was also a nonastronaut, a nonphysicist, and so on.

The point is that when you identify people in terms of a reference group that they don't belong to, you minimize part of their identity. The reference subgroup often consists of those with the highest status or power in the group, even if that reference group doesn't represent a majority. In the example with Peg, if you refer to psychologists as nonlawyers, you are also using the language of the high-power subgroup to define a low-power subgroup. In a subtle way, this can lead others to infer that you are aligning yourself with the high-power subgroup members, which can lead the low-power subgroup members to question your commitment to the full group and, if you're a facilitator, your neutrality.

Use Words That Distinguish Your Facilitative Role

Choose words that distinguish your facilitative role from group members' roles. Refer to the group as *you* or *the group* rather than as *we* or *our group*. If you're part of the decision-making process (for example, if the group and you are deciding about the meeting process), it's appropriate to use the term *we*.

Avoid Imperatives (Like This One)

An imperative is a command, such as "make a decision" or, more loosely, "you must make a decision" ("Avoid imperatives" is also an imperative!). One problem with using imperatives is that as a third party, you don't have the authority to give the group commands. As a facilitator, consultant, or coach to the group, you're an advisor, not in a decision-making or commanding role.

Another problem is that, in general, people don't respond well to being told what they must do. They are much more receptive to hearing what the options are and what the consequences are likely to be if they choose each option. This means talking with the group members about cause and effect—what the effect will be if they use or don't use a particular behavior. For example, rather than simply saying, "You need to check out your assumption before acting on it," you might say something like this: "When you act on your assumption without testing it, you may end up acting on incorrect information, and that can reduce your ability to make a more informed choice. Do you see it differently?" Focusing on cause and effect also helps people see the systemic nature of their actions.

Be Careful with Humor

Avoid humor that puts down or discounts members or that can be misinterpreted. Humor can be a valuable tool for relieving tension in the group, emphasizing a point, and helping members examine their behavior. However, certain types of humor can reduce your effectiveness. Sarcastic humor about a member's ineffective behavior can decrease trust in you because people are likely to interpret the humor as unsupportive. Sarcastic humor can create problems because it requires the listener to interpret your meaning as the reverse of the literal meaning of the words. The sarcastic statement, "I can see there is a high level of trust in this group," means "there is *not* a high level of trust in this group." If members don't detect the sarcasm, they will question your diagnostic skills if they believe there is low trust in the group. Even if they do detect the irony, you haven't modeled transparent communication.

SUMMARY

In this chapter, I have described the intervention steps of the mutual learning cycle: stating your observations, testing the meaning you've made, and jointly designing the next steps. The cycle is designed to publicly share your reasoning so you can test it with group members and ensure that you and the group are moving forward together. By using the cycle to intervene, you help the group create effective group process. In the next chapter, I will give examples of how to use the mutual learning cycle to intervene when group members aren't using the mutual learning behaviors.

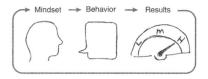

Mindset → Behavior → Results

CHAPTER TEN

Diagnosing and Intervening on the Mutual Learning Behaviors

O ne of the most common interventions you make using mutual learning is to intervene when group members are reducing their effectiveness by not using the mutual learning behaviors. In this chapter, I give verbatim examples of how to use the mutual learning cycle to make these interventions. Before offering the verbatim examples, I describe how intervening on the eight behaviors differs from intervening with other group ground rules and the agreement you need to reach with the group before making these interventions effectively.

HOW MUTUAL LEARNING BEHAVIORS DIFFER FROM MANY GROUND RULES

The mutual learning behaviors may differ from other ground rules or behaviors you have seen or used. Many groups have a set of ground rules they use to help their group work effectively. As a consultant, you may also have a set that you suggest that the group use.

The mutual learning behaviors differ from some other ground rules in several ways. First, some other behaviors or ground rules focus on procedural matters: "Start on time and end on time," or "turn off mobile phones." Procedural behaviors are useful, but they don't help the group create productive conversation. Second, some other behaviors describe some desired behavior but at an abstract level, such as "treat everyone with respect" or "be constructive." These ground rules often focus on outcomes without identifying the specific behavior that enables members to treat others with respect or to be constructive. As a result, these ground rules can create problems if group members have different ideas about how to act respectfully. For some group members, that may mean not raising any concerns about individual members in the group; for other members, it may mean the opposite. Third, some other group or consultant ground rules are often based on unilateral control, such as the common ground rule, "praise in public; criticize in private." Unilateral control ground rules usually create the opposite result the group is seeking to create.

CONTRACTING TO INTERVENE ON MUTUAL LEARNING BEHAVIORS

Before you can intervene in the group to help it use the mutual learning behaviors, you need an agreement with the group to make this kind of intervention.

Contract Questions to Answer

To reach this agreement, the group needs to answer three questions:

1. Does the group want you to intervene when you see them using behavior that could be more effective if they used mutual learning behaviors instead?
2. Does the group want to take responsibility for using the mutual learning behaviors themselves?
3. Does the group want to adopt the mutual learning behaviors as their own group ground rules?

Let's look at how the group's answers to these three questions affect how you work with them.

The group's answer to the first question is really about whether it wants to work with you, assuming that an essential part of your approach is to use the eight behaviors to diagnose group behavior and intervene with it. This includes asking group members to use the behaviors when you think doing so improves the process. You can't use a mutual learning approach without doing that. **If the group doesn't want you to use the mutual learning behaviors, it is essentially saying that it doesn't want to use your approach.**

If the group's answer to the first question is yes, then the answers to the second and third questions determine how you will intervene to help it use the mutual learning behaviors. Just because you're using the mutual learning behaviors to help the members become more effective doesn't mean that they want to use those behaviors on their own. If the group wants you to help them use the mutual learning behaviors but doesn't want to take responsibility for using them on their own, they are asking you to do basic facilitation. However, if the group wants you to help them use the eight behaviors *and* wants to take responsibility for using them themselves, you are doing developmental facilitation. If the group wants to adopt the mutual learning behaviors as their ground rules, they are making a formal commitment to themselves as a way of operating.

Helping a Group Decide Whether to Use the Mutual Learning Behaviors as Their Ground Rules

In the first two editions of *The Skilled Facilitator*, I refer to the mutual learning behaviors as ground rules. The term *ground rules* stems from the special rules that apply to a particular ballpark, originally called *grounds.* Unlike most sports, the playing area in baseball extends to the outfield fence and the seating in foul territory area. Because each baseball park is uniquely designed with different fences, railings, and domes, there need to be specific rules that address how to handle situations when the features of that ballpark (that is, grounds) interact with the play of the ball.[1] In this edition, I changed the term to recognize that **the mutual learning behaviors are not a group's ground rules until that group has agreed to use them as such.**

To help a group decide whether it wants to adopt the eight behaviors as its ground rules, you can distribute the free article "Eight Behaviors for Smarter Teams" located on the Roger Schwarz & Associates website at www .schwarzassociates.com/resources/articles. Then you can talk with the group about how the eight behaviors can increase the group's effectiveness, how the group would use them, and how you would help the group use the behaviors. You can also be curious and ask about concerns that it has about using the behaviors. This conversation is part of contracting with the group, which I discuss in detail in Chapter 13.

Why I Don't Ask Groups to Develop Their Own Ground Rules

Sometimes facilitators and consultants ask me why I don't recommend that groups develop their own ground rules. They reason that members commit to behaviors they develop and that they can develop useful ones. I have several reasons for introducing a set of behaviors rather than asking the groups to create them.

First, as a facilitator and consultant, I know that groups hire me for my process expertise—that includes knowing what kind of behavior helps a group become more effective. **Because I use these behaviors as the core of my diagnosis and intervention, changing the behaviors would also mean changing the types of behavior that I diagnose and intervene on.**

Second, in my experience, members are often not able to identify behaviorally specific behaviors—the kind needed to improve group process. In addition, they sometimes generate behaviors that are designed to unilaterally protect themselves and others and reduce the group's ability to make a free and informed choice.

Third, I don't assume that members have to develop the behaviors themselves to be committed to them as ground rules; rather, I assume that they can be committed to them if they make a free and informed choice to use them.

Finally, in basic facilitation, a group is reasonably asking the facilitator to manage its process. Asking a group to develop its own ground rules—ones that are behaviorally specific and based on research—is very difficult for the group to do, takes a lot of time, and may shift the group away from its primary task for which it has hired you.

Consequently, I choose to present the eight behaviors to the group, explain how they work, encourage members to raise questions and concerns they may have, and identify any behaviors they think might be missing or need to be changed. (For example, groups sometimes add a ground rule about keeping certain information confidential.) I use this approach for both basic and developmental facilitation, although in developmental facilitation, the group and I spend considerably more time exploring this issue.

If you do choose to ask the group to develop or modify the behaviors, the basic principle is that the rules should be consistent with the mutual learning mindset if you want to use the behaviors as a basis for diagnosing and intervening with the group.

How to Intervene with Basic and Developmental Facilitation

In both basic and developmental facilitation, you use the mutual learning cycle to intervene on mutual learning behaviors, but you intervene differently. One difference is that in basic facilitation, you state your inference about the mutual learning behavior you saw wasn't being used. In developmental facilitation, you are more likely to ask the group members what they saw that was inconsistent with mutual learning behaviors. A second difference is that in developmental facilitation, you often help the group members explore the mindset they were using to generate that behavior. In basic facilitation, you are less likely to intervene on the members' mindset that is generating ineffective behavior.

Here are two examples, the first one using basic facilitation and the second using developmental facilitation to ask the group member to make his own diagnosis.

3. Choose: *I think it's important that Ted confirm whether his direct reports are, in fact, withholding information and whether it's for the reason he is thinking. In addition, if he left the meeting, that would seem to address the symptom rather than the root cause.*

2. Make Meaning: *I'm inferring that Ted is inferring that people are withholding relevant information and that he is attributing it to the fact they are concerned about sharing this information with him because he is their boss.*

1. Observe: *Ted [the team leader] says, "I think I should leave the meeting so that the group can talk among itself. I sense that you're holding back saying things because I'm your boss."*

    Marlene says, "No, I think you should stay."

    Sue says, "Yeah, stay. It's not an issue."

4. Test Observation: "Ted, you said, 'I think I should leave the meeting so that the group can talk among itself. I sense you're holding back saying things because I'm your boss.' Did I get that right?" *[if yes, continue]*

5. Test Meaning: "I'm thinking that your conclusion that they are holding back and that it's because you are their boss are untested inferences. Do you see that differently?" *[If Ted agrees, continue.]*

6. Jointly Design Next Steps: "I think it would be helpful to share what specifically you saw that led you to infer they were holding back and what you saw that led you to attribute it to your being the boss. Then you can test whether your conclusions are accurate. What do you think about doing that?"

Exhibit 10.1   Intervening: Using Basic Facilitation

3. Choose: *I think it's important that Ted confirm whether his direct reports are, in fact, withholding information and whether it's for the reason he is thinking. In addition, if he left the meeting, that would seem to address the symptom rather than the root cause.*

2. Make Meaning: *I'm inferring that Ted is inferring that people are withholding relevant information and that he is attributing it to the fact they are concerned about sharing this information with him because he is their boss.*

1. Observe: *Ted [the team leader] says, "I think I should leave the meeting and let the group talk among itself. I sense that you're holding back saying things because I'm your boss."*
   Marlene says, "No, I think you should stay."
   Sue says, "Yeah, stay. It's not an issue."

4. Test Observation: "Ted, you said, 'I think I should leave the meeting so that the group can talk among itself. I sense you're holding back saying things because I'm your boss.' Did I get that right?" [if yes, continue]

5. Test Meaning: "I'm thinking you missed an opportunity to use one of the mutual learning behaviors. Do you see it, or do you want me to share what I'm thinking and see if you agree? *[If Ted identifies that he has made an untested inference and attributed it to his being the boss, continue.]*

6. Jointly Design Next Steps: "Yeah, that's what I was seeing. Do you see the next step or do you want me to suggest it?"

Exhibit 10.2   Intervening: Using Developmental Facilitation and Asking the Group Member to Identify the Behavior

INTERVENING ON THE MUTUAL LEARNING BEHAVIORS

In the rest of the chapter, I show examples of how to diagnose and intervene when group members could be more effective if they were using the mutual learning behaviors. For each of the eight behaviors, I show one or more typical comments that a group member or members might make and how you use the mutual learning cycle to diagnose and intervene on that behavior. If you want to remind yourself how each step of the cycle works, review Figure 10.1. For more detail you can refer back to Chapters 7, 8, and 9.

To save space, I have assumed that the team member agrees with the behavior that the facilitator or consultant has observed (step 4 of the cycle) and with the inference that the facilitator or consultant has made (step 5 of the

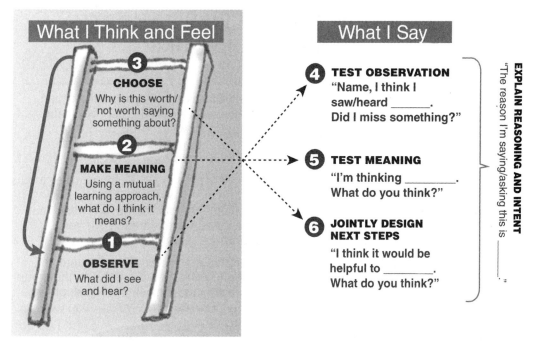

Figure 10.1   The Parallel between the Diagnostic and Intervention Steps of the Mutual Learning Cycle

cycle). In practice, if someone has a different view of the behavior or the inference you described, you stop at that point, ask how the person sees it, and proceed accordingly.

I have varied the examples to show how to skip and combine intervention steps. Each example can be thought of as a separate move that you make under particular circumstances. You combine these various moves to respond to the members' previous comments.

BEHAVIOR 1: STATE VIEWS AND ASK GENUINE QUESTIONS

3. Choose: *If Pat has an opinion on this, I think it's important for her to share that information explicitly so people know what she thinks and to ask others what they think.*

2. Make Meaning: *From the inflection in Pat's voice, I inferred that she has her own thoughts about the question.*

1. Observe: *Pat said, "Do you really think September is too late to roll out the new program?"*

4. Test Observation: "Pat, a minute ago, when you asked whether people thought September was too late to roll out the new program . . ." *[skip test to see if I heard her correctly]*

5. Test Meaning: ". . . from the inflection in your voice, it sounded like *you* think September wouldn't be too late. Is that what you were thinking?" *[if yes, continue]*

6. Jointly Design Next Steps: "I think it would be helpful to say that to the group, explain your reasoning, and ask others how they see it. Are you willing to do that?"

Exhibit 10.3   Asking a Member to State Views and Ask Genuine Questions

BEHAVIOR 2: SHARE ALL RELEVANT INFORMATION

3. Choose: *I want to test this out because if the data are not monolithic, it may change people's views.*

2. Make Meaning: *Amy presents the data in an overall conclusion. I'm wondering whether it is conclusive at the subgroup level.*

1. Observe: *Amy says, "The data we collected and analyzed support my view; people think we need to focus more on our core business."*

4. Test Observation: "Amy, you said that the data support your view that people think we need to focus more on our core business." *[skip test to see if I heard her correctly]*

5. Test Meaning: *[skip step]*

6. Jointly Design Next Steps: "Can you tell people the specific results so people can get a fuller picture of what you found?"

Exhibit 10.4   Asking a Member to Share All Relevant Information

3. Choose: *I want to check this out because if it is related to Julie's comment, that may identify an important issue. Even if it's not related, they may still be withholding relevant information that the group could benefit from.*

4. Test Observation: "I want to share an observation and get your reactions. Jennifer, Ted, and Sue, I noticed that you haven't spoken for the last 10 minutes, since Julie said, 'It's important that the group exceed the third-quarter revenue projections.' Did I miss anything?" *[if no, continue]*

2. Make Meaning: *I'm wondering what led them to become silent. I'm inferring that it may be related to Julie's comment.*

5. Test Meaning: "I'm thinking that you have had additional thoughts to share since Julie spoke. Am I off?" *[If members agree with my inference, continue.]*

1. Observe: *Jennifer, Ted, and Sue have been silent for a period of time. They haven't spoken since Julie, their manager, stated, "It's important that the group exceed the third-quarter revenue projections."*

6. Jointly Design Next Steps: "Would you be willing to say what led you not to share the information?"

Exhibit 10.5   Asking Group Members about Their Silence

BEHAVIOR 3: USE SPECIFIC EXAMPLES AND AGREE ON WHAT IMPORTANT WORDS MEAN

3. Choose: *I think it's important to find out what Jorge means so the group can determine if it sees it the same way.*

4. Test Observation: "Jorge, you said, 'You guys aren't taking initiative on the project. If I don't get the tasks started, it doesn't happen.' Yes?" *[If Jorge agrees, continue.]*

2. Make Meaning: *When Jorge says this, he hasn't said who "you guys" are, nor has he said what he means by "taking initiative."*

5. Test Meaning: *[skip step]*

1. Observe: *Jorge said, "You guys aren't taking initiative on the project. If I don't get the tasks started, it doesn't happen."*

6. Jointly Design Next Steps: "I think it would be helpful to say whom you mean by 'you guys' and give some examples of when you thought they didn't take initiative. Then people can figure out if they see it the same way you do. Any concerns about sharing that?"

Exhibit 10.6   Asking a Member to Use Specific Examples and Agree on What Important Words Mean

BEHAVIOR 4: EXPLAIN REASONING AND INTENT

3. Choose: *I think it's important for Don to see what Sandy's reasoning is, to find out if it makes sense to him or not.*

4. Test Observation: *[combine with step 5 as a paraphrase]*

2. Make Meaning: *Sandy states her conclusion without sharing her reasoning that led to it.*

5. Test Meaning: "Don, you're saying that you don't see any relationship between the software installation and people being trained by the end of the month. Have I got that right?" *[if yes, continue]*

1. Observe: *Sandy said, "We won't be able to have all the team members trained in managing conflict by the end of the month, given the new software system that's being installed." Don said, "I totally disagree; the two are completely unrelated."*

6. Jointly Design Next Steps: "I'm thinking that if you asked Sandy, she could explain how she sees them as being related. Are you willing?"

Exhibit 10.7   Asking One Member to Ask Another Person to Explain Reasoning

3. Choose: *I think it's important for Erik to share his reasoning so that others can understand it and can see whether it makes sense to them.*

4. Test Observation: *[skip step]*

2. Make Meaning: *Erik has stated his conclusion without sharing the reasoning he used to arrive at it.*

5. Test Meaning: *[skip step]*

1. Observe: *Erik said, "I've thought about everything people have said, and I think it makes the most sense to charge our services back to our internal customers."*

6. Jointly Design Next Steps: "Erik, would you be willing to share with the group how you arrived at your conclusion? I'm asking because I think it will help people understand how you used their comments to reach your conclusion."

Exhibit 10.8   Asking a Member to Explain His Reasoning

BEHAVIOR 5: FOCUS ON INTERESTS, NOT POSITIONS

3. Choose: *I think it's important for them to state their interests so they can find out whether their interests are compatible and, if so, how to craft a solution that meets all of them.*

2. Make Meaning: *When Hans and Ellen say this, they state their positions but not their underlying interests.*

1. Observe: *Hans said, "I want to outsource the printing rather than do it in-house." Ellen said, "No, we need to keep it in-house."*

4. Test Observation: "Hans, you said you want to outsource the printing rather than do it in-house. Yes? And Ellen, you said you want to keep it in-house. Is that correct?" *[If both agree, continue.]*

5. Test Meaning: "I understand the solution that each of you is proposing, but I don't yet know what your underlying needs are that have led you to propose your solutions." *[skip test for different views]*

6. Jointly Design Next Steps: "Can each of you say what it is about outsourcing it or keeping it in-house that's important to you? I'm asking because if you know each other's underlying needs, you may be able to come up with a solution that works for both of you."

Exhibit 10.9   Asking Group Members to Identify Their Interests

3. Choose: *I think it's important to intervene because if my inference is correct, they will probably need some help thinking about interests.*

4. Test Observation: "I want to share what I've been seeing and suggest a different approach, if it makes sense to you. I've been asking you to identify your interests, and when you responded, you said [quotes some of the members' comments]. Yes? *[if group agrees with the paraphrase of behavior, continue]* I've said that you were still identifying positions."

2. Make Meaning: *I'm inferring that group members are having difficulty thinking about what an interest is.*

5. Test Meaning: "I'm thinking that you are not sure what I mean by *interests* and that it would be helpful for me to walk you through identifying your interests. Am I off the mark?" *[Continue if everyone agrees with the inference.]*

1. Observe: *When group members are trying to agree on how to redesign the vendor procurement process, they have repeatedly returned to describing their positions instead of focusing on interests. For example, Darnell has said, "We absolutely need to use the same software we currently are using." Elsie has said, "No, we just need to have people handle a project from start to finish. No handoffs." And Dahlia has said, "None of that matters. We need to develop a preferred vendor list."*

6. Jointly Design Next Steps: "Okay. One way to identify your interests is to work backward from your positions or solutions. Think of the solution you have been proposing for this problem. Now ask yourself, 'What it is about my solution that's important to me? In other words, what is the need I'm trying to address in my solution?' For example, Darnell, is it that using the current software reduces the learning time to get people up to speed? Is it that the current system is also integrated with the rest of the ERP software? Or something else? Are there any questions about how to identify your interests? *[if no, continue]* Okay, are you willing to start to identify your interests?"

Exhibit 10.10   Helping Group Members Think about Their Interests

BEHAVIOR 6: TEST ASSUMPTIONS AND INFERENCES

3. Choose: *I think it's important for Ellis to test this out because it affects the project deadline.*

2. Make Meaning: *I'm inferring that Ellis has inferred that the group will drop the temporary employees from the project after the peak season ends and that bringing on new people will delay things.*

1. Observe: *Ellis said, "Don, we have to extend the project deadline because we'll need to restaff the project after peak season."*

4. Test Observation: "Ellis, I want to check something out. I think you said, 'We have to extend the project deadline because we'll need to restaff the project after peak season.' Yes?" *[if yes, continue]*

5. Test Meaning: "It sounds like you're thinking that the temps will be laid off after peak season even if they are working on the project. Are you thinking that or something else?" *[If Ellis agrees, continue.]*

6. Jointly Design Next Steps: "I'm thinking it would be helpful to test that with Don, since he handles temp layoffs. What do you think?"

Exhibit 10.11   Asking Someone to Test an Inference He Is Making

3. Choose: *I want to test this because eliminating it at all sites is very different from doing it at just one.*

2. Make Meaning: *I'm inferring that she means the group needs to eliminate the customized service at all sites if it eliminates it at one site.*

1. Observe: *Lucia said, "Eliminating the customized service will make us less attractive."*

4. Test Observation: "Lucia, I want to check something out. I think you said, 'Eliminating the customized service will make us less attractive.' Did I get that right?" *[if yes, continue]*

5. Test Meaning: "It sounds to me like you're thinking the group would need to eliminate the customized service at all sites if it eliminated it at one. Have I understood that correctly?"

6. Jointly Design Next Steps: *[Step 6 is not needed if the person with whom you are intervening is also the person about whom you are making the inference.]*

Exhibit 10.12   Testing an Inference You Are Making

3. Choose: *I need to test this because my effectiveness depends on their perceptions of me.*

4. Test Observation: "Drew, I want to check something out. When you said, 'We wouldn't be so far behind schedule in this meeting if we didn't have to look at everything we're saying . . .'" *[skip testing to see if Drew agrees he said this]*

2. Make Meaning: *I'm inferring that Drew thinks my facilitation is slowing the group down unnecessarily.*

5. Test Meaning: ". . . I inferred that you think it's my facilitation that is unnecessarily slowing the group down. Are you thinking that?"

1. Observe: Drew said, *"We wouldn't be so far behind schedule in this meeting if we didn't have to look at everything we're saying."*

6. Jointly Design Next Steps: *[If Drew says yes, then the facilitator says, "Can you say what you see me doing or not doing that's slowing the group down? I'm asking because I'm not seeing that, but I may be missing something."]*

Exhibit 10.13   Testing an Inference You Think Someone Is Making about You

BEHAVIOR 7: JOINTLY DESIGN NEXT STEPS

3. Choose: *I need to check it out because either Larry has changed the group's focus unilaterally or I am missing the connection between performance standards and his comment.*

4. Test Observation: "Larry, I want to check if you've switched focus. A minute ago, the group was discussing performance standards and you said, 'I think we need to figure out who will fill the open position we have.' Yes?" *[if yes, continue]*

2. Make Meaning: *I don't see the relationship between performance standards and Larry's comment. I wonder whether Larry is on the same topic or whether he has switched focus?*

5. Test Meaning: "I don't see the relationship between performance standards and your comment, but I may be missing something." *[skip test for agreement]*

1. Observe: *The group was discussing performance standards when Larry said, "I think we need to figure out who will fill the open position we have."*

6. Jointly Design Next Steps: "Can you say how your comment is related, or if it's not, can you talk with the rest of the group about which topic you want to discuss?" *[I skipped the statement and moved directly to the question.]*

Exhibit 10.14   Jointly Deciding Whether the Group Is on Track and What the Next Step Is

3. Choose: *If I intervene, I can help them jointly design a way to find out what the situation is.*

2. Make Meaning: *Both Gareth and Leila seem convinced that their data are valid. Unless they agree on this issue, I don't think they will be committed to a solution.*

1. Observe: *Gareth said, "The product meets our error tolerances." Leila responded, "No, it's outside our specs."*

4. Test Observation: "Let's see if you can figure out a way to resolve your differences. Gareth, you said, 'The product meets our error tolerances.' Correct? And Leila, you said, 'The product is outside your specs.' Yes?" *[If both agree, continue.]*

5. Test Meaning: "It sounds to me like the two of you need to agree on this in order to get a solution that both of you are willing to support. Am I correct?" *[if yes, continue]*

6. Jointly Design Next Steps: "Would you be willing to jointly design a way to test out whether the product is within the tolerances?" *[if yes, continue]* "Okay. Do either of you have an idea how you could design the test so both of you consider it a valid test?"

Exhibit 10.15   Asking Someone to Propose a Joint Design for Testing a Disagreement

3. Choose: *I need to intervene so the group can make a choice about how it uses its time.*

2. Make Meaning: *[no inference needed]*

1. Observe: *The group is about to exceed the amount of time it agreed to spend on a topic.*

4. Test Observation: "You agreed to discuss this topic for two hours until ten-twenty. It's now ten-fifteen . . ."

5. Test Meaning: ". . . and it looks to me as if you haven't yet identified a solution that will meet the interests you've identified. Does anyone see it differently?" *[if no, continue]*

6. Jointly Design Next Steps: "If you continue working on a solution, I think it will be difficult to accomplish the last task on the agenda, given that you have taken about a half-hour longer than you allocated for each issue." *[skip test for different views]* "What are your thoughts about continuing your discussion, moving on to the last topic, or taking some other approach?"

Exhibit 10.16   Helping the Group Manage Its Time

3. Choose: *I need to intervene because if Ian or Leslie doesn't agree and Chen thinks they do, there is a misunderstanding.*

4. Test Observation: "Chen, you said, 'We've got agreement.' But I didn't hear what you were asking for agreement on, and I didn't hear Ian or Leslie say they agreed. Did I miss something?" *[if no, continue]*

2. Make Meaning: *I'm inferring that Chen did not yet get agreement from everyone.*

5. Test Meaning: *[skip step]*

1. Observe: *Chen said, "We've got agreement." I didn't hear Bart say what he was seeking consensus on, and I didn't hear Ian or Leslie say they agreed.*

6. Jointly Design Next Steps: *[skip statement part of step]* "Would you be willing to say what you're asking for agreement on, and ask Ian and Leslie if they support it?"

Exhibit 10.17   Helping a Group Member Test for Agreement

---

3. Choose: *I need to intervene because if she is responding to pressure, she is not making a free choice. If she has changed her mind, it would help the group to understand what led her to change.*

4. Test Observation: "Adi, in the past hour, you have expressed concerns about implementing the proposed program and have identified some interests that may not be met by implementing it in its proposed form. For example, you've said, *[quote Adi's comments]*. Have I captured that accurately?" *[if yes, continue]* Just now, you said 'Okay, I'll support it,' but I didn't hear you say what's changed that led you to change your view. Did I miss that?" *[if no, continue]*

2. Make Meaning: *I'm thinking that she might be feeling pressure to support the proposal.*

5. Test Meaning: I'm thinking that either you have heard some things that have led you to genuinely change your view or that you might be feeling pressure to support the proposal now." *[skip test part of step]*

1. Observe: *Adi previously expressed concern about the proposal but has now said, "Okay, I'll support it."*

6. Jointly Design Next Steps: *[skip statement part of step]* "Can you say what led you to support the proposal now?"

Exhibit 10.18   Checking Whether a Group Member's Expressed Support Is Genuine

BEHAVIOR 8: DISCUSS UNDISCUSSABLE ISSUES

3. Choose: *I think it's important to raise this because if my inference is right, and Stephanie, Bob, and Juan's team has a concern about Allison that she doesn't know about and Stephanie, Bob, and Juan may have a problem getting their needs met that they don't seem able or willing to address.*

4. Test Observation: "I want to share some observations, raise what may be an undiscussable issue, and get your reactions. My intent isn't to embarrass anyone or to put anyone on the spot but to help you create the more effective working relationship you said you need. During this meeting, several of you— Stephanie, Bob, and Juan—have commented that your team needs some consultation on improving service quality. Am I correct?" *[if yes, continue]* "And each time Allison has offered her HR team to provide the service, at least one of you has said that the HR team is already overcommitted to other important work. Am I off?" *[if yes, continue]* "Stephanie and Bob, I also noticed one of you looking at the other before declining HR's offer. Yes?" *[if yes, continue]*

2. Make Meaning: *I'm inferring that Stephanie, Bob, or Juan has some concern about HR providing them consultation and may also be concerned about discussing that concern.*

5. Test Meaning: "From all of this, I am inferring that at least the three of you may have some concern about HR's providing the consultation. Is that what you're thinking, or is it something else?"

1. Observe: *During the meeting, Stephanie, Bob, and Juan said that their team needs some consultation on improving service quality. Several times, Allison has said her HR team can provide the service, and each time, Stephanie, Bob, or Juan said the HR team is already overcommitted to other important work. Stephanie and Bob also looked at each other before declining HR's offer.*

6. Jointly Design Next Steps: *[If Stephanie, Bob, or Juan agree that they have a concern, I will then ask them to explain their concern to Allison. If they say they don't have a concern, then I will say, "Okay. I'm still puzzled. If you're telling Allison that she's already overcommitted, and then you're looking at each other doesn't mean that you have concerns about HR, can you help me understand what it does mean?"]*

Exhibit 10.19   **Identifying a Possible Undiscussable Issue**

SUMMARY

In this chapter, I have explained the need to reach an agreement with the group about whether and how you will intervene when you infer that the group can improve its effectiveness by using the mutual learning behaviors. I have given verbatim examples of how to diagnose and intervene on each of the eight behaviors. The course of your intervention depends on whether the group member or members agree with your observation and inference. Whether you choose to skip or combine intervention steps or a part of a step depends on a number of factors.

In the next chapter, I will describe how you can use these interventions to help a group improve the ability to use any process tools its members are working with.

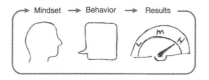

Mindset → Behavior → Results

CHAPTER ELEVEN

Using Mutual Learning to Improve Other Processes and Techniques

I n this chapter, I describe how to use the mutual learning approach to help groups improve almost any other process or technique they use. This includes techniques such as experiential exercises and processes such as Lean, Six Sigma, or other quality and process improvement approaches, strategic planning or innovation processes, performance management processes, or simply one of the many standard problem-solving processes. I begin the chapter by describing the different ways that groups may reduce their effectiveness when using other processes and techniques. This includes when groups use a process or technique that is incongruent with mutual learning and when groups use processes and techniques that call for mutual learning, such as Lean. I describe how to use the mutual learning cycle to determine the cause of the group's ineffectiveness and to intervene.

Throughout this chapter, I use the words *process* or *processes* or *other processes* when referring to the nonmutual learning processes, techniques, and exercises that a group uses to perform its work.

USING MUTUAL LEARNING TO DIAGNOSE AND INTERVENE ON OTHER PROCESSES

When a group is trying to use mutual learning and other processes, you can focus your interventions on both elements. A group can reduce its effectiveness because it is using a process poorly, because it's not using some element of mutual learning, or both. There are four ways that a group can reduce its effectiveness when using a process:

1. The group is using the process inconsistently with how it is supposed to be used.

2. The group is acting consistently with the process, but because the process is designed incongruently with mutual learning, the group is acting incongruently with mutual learning.

3. The group is using a process that is designed congruently with mutual learning, but the group is acting incongruently with mutual learning.

4. The group is using a process that espouses elements of mutual learning, but the group is not acting congruently with mutual learning.

To diagnose whether a group is facing any of these situations, you use the mutual learning cycle, as I described in Chapter 6. The box labeled "Insert Group's Models Here" on the far left side of Figure 11.1 shows that you use the models, processes, and techniques that the group is using along with mutual learning as the basis of your diagnosis.

In steps 1 and 2 of the cycle, you look for behaviors that lead you to infer incongruent use of the process or incongruence with mutual learning. If you infer that the group is acting incongruently with mutual learning, it's necessary to identify the cause. Is the group acting incongruently with mutual learning behavior caused by using the process, is the group simply acting incongruently with mutual learning, or both?

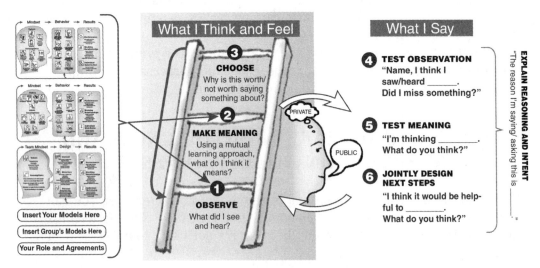

Figure 11.1 Using Mutual Learning to Diagnose and Intervene on Other Processes

Each of these situations requires a different intervention. To decide which interventions to make (which is step 3 of the mutual learning cycle), you can answer the questions in the flowchart shown in Figure 11.2. By answering the questions, you will be able to intervene on the root causes that are reducing the group's effectiveness.

Based on your answers to these questions, you're ready to intervene using the cycle. In step 4 of the cycle, you state the behavior you observe and test for different views. In step 5, you state the inference you've made—one of the three conditions above—and test for different views. In step 6, you jointly design the next step with the group.

In previous chapters, I've explained how to diagnose and intervene when the group is acting incongruently with mutual learning—situation 3 above. In this chapter, I provide examples of how to diagnose and intervene in the other three situations.

DIAGNOSING AND INTERVENING WHEN GROUPS ARE USING A PROCESS INEFFECTIVELY

Whether groups are using a process you provided them, one of their own, or one from their organization, it's important to intervene when they are using it ineffectively. Next, I identify several ways that groups predictably use processes ineffectively and how to intervene on them.

The Group Uses Part of the Process Incorrectly. If the group is using a process you introduced to it, you should have a detailed understanding of how the process works and how groups are likely to use it incorrectly. For example, when I introduce groups to the process of solving problems by focusing on interests rather than positions, I know that groups are likely to make certain mistakes: They state their interests in the form of positions; they use short phrases instead of complete sentences, which makes it difficult for them to agree on what the phrases mean; and they shift from developing a list of interests to lists of pros and cons for each potential position.

When you understand in advance how groups may use a process incorrectly, you can help them avoid these mistakes and quickly help correct misuses when they occur. Even if you're helping the group use one of its processes, it's important to know it well enough to understand how groups may use it incorrectly.

Group Members Follow Steps Out of Order or Focus on Different Steps. Many processes include a number of steps that are designed to be used in a particular order. Some processes are designed for groups to move through the steps iteratively. In both cases, group members sometimes skip steps, usually jumping prematurely to developing or even selecting solutions. Here, your intervention is

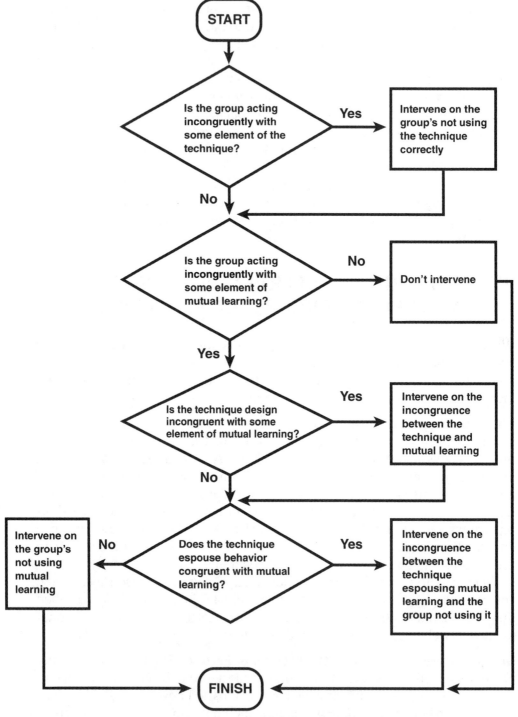

Figure 11.2   Questions to Answer for Deciding Which Interventions to Make

straightforward: Tell the team or individual members where you see them getting off track, check for their views, and jointly decide what step the team focuses on next.

The Group Engages the Process Superficially. If you've used a particular process or technique with different groups, you know that some groups get more out of the process than others. Some groups deeply reflect on and challenge their assumptions, look at situations from a wide number of perspectives, and develop innovative solutions. Other groups get less value from the same process.

This is a more difficult intervention to make because groups naturally bring different levels of skill and energy to the same task. That said, when you infer that the group has more energy, skill, or creativity to bring to the process, it's important to share your inference and ask for the group's reaction. This may lead the group to invest more in the process and you to receive a commensurate return.

DIAGNOSING AND INTERVENING ON PROCESSES THAT ARE INCONGRUENT WITH MUTUAL LEARNING

If you've been facilitating for a while, you've probably collected a figurative bag of tools, techniques, and processes for helping groups with different situations. If you're a new facilitator, you're probably looking to fill your bag. **For every tool you have or are thinking of adding to your toolkit, there's an essential first question to ask yourself:** *Can it be used so that it is congruent with the mutual learning mindset and behaviors?* You should answer this question before introducing a process to a group.

Facilitators often contribute to a group's ineffectiveness by recommending processes that are incongruent with mutual learning. If you facilitate using a process that's incongruent with mutual learning, you increase the chance of creating defensiveness, unproductive conflict, decreased trust, reduced learning, reduced commitment, or lower-quality decisions.

Some processes are inherently incongruent with mutual learning. If you try to redesign them to be congruent, you fundamentally change the purpose of the process. However, there are many processes that are incongruent with some element of mutual learning but that can be easily redesigned to be congruent and still maintain their purpose and effectiveness. Below I provide examples of commonly used processes that are incongruent with elements of mutual learning. For those approaches that are not inherently incongruent with mutual learning, I explain how to redesign them.

Next, I distinguish between processes *you* choose to use with the group and processes that are part of the organization's methods (for example, a team feedback system) that the group is asking you to facilitate. Of course, assuming that the process is not inherently incongruent with mutual learning, it's easier to redesign a process that you choose to use with the group compared with one that the group is using as part of its organizational methods.

Processes You Select

Because you select these processes, you have flexibility to avoid ones that are inherently incongruent with mutual learning and the ability to redesign those that are not inherently incongruent.

Pros and Cons. In a pros and cons process, the group is trying to decide between two or more potential solutions. You ask the group to list all the advantages (pros) and disadvantages (cons) of each potential solution. The group uses the outcome of the process to select the best solution.

This process is inherently incongruent with the mutual learning behavior focus on interests, not positions. It also encourages group members to reinforce their positions, based on a win, don't lose unilateral control mindset. As a result, the group finds itself in unproductive conflict and reduced learning.

Because a pros and cons process is inherently incongruent with mutual learning, you can't redesign it. However, you can substitute a process that will achieve the same purpose and be more effective. This is the four-step process for making decisions based on interests that I described in Chapter 5 in the section on behavior 5: focus on interests, not positions.

Experiential Exercises That Rely on Deception or Withholding Information. Many experiential exercises are designed to help a group learn about and improve its process by working on a nongroup task. Some experiential exercises are used as icebreakers to begin a meeting. There are hundreds of experiential exercises available online.

Many experiential exercises are congruent with mutual learning; however, some rely on deception or withholding information. One example is the missing square exercise that is designed to see how groups manage conflict (for reasons that will become clear in a minute, the name is not shared with participants). The facilitator divides puzzle pieces among team members and then asks them to jointly solve the jigsaw puzzle. The facilitator must not reveal that the puzzle cannot be solved because it is missing one piece, which another group possesses. Each group must figure out on its own that another group holds the piece it needs without being informed that cross-group collaboration is a possibility or requirement.

This exercise requires you to withhold relevant information and to deceive the group if any members ask whether the piece is missing. As a result, it increases the chance that the group will lose trust in you.

But even exercises that require you to withhold information can still be used with a mutual learning approach if you add one condition: You tell the group that the exercise requires you to withhold some information or use deception and then ask if the group is willing to participate. In this way, you're at least being transparent that you cannot be fully transparent and letting them make at least a somewhat informed choice.

Experiential Exercises That Don't Let Group Members Decide the Level of Risk They Are Willing to Take. Experiential exercises differ in the level of social and emotional risk that members are exposed to. By social and emotional risk, I mean the degree to which members are asked to reveal information about themselves, engage in behavior that reveals information about themselves, or otherwise makes them feel inappropriately vulnerable. Exercises that don't require members to speak or to act in unusual ways likely generate little risk. Activities that require members to reveal private information about themselves, such as their greatest regrets, failures, or most embarrassing situations generate much greater risk. So do exercises in which the facilitator asks group members to answer some simple questions or to draw something and then interprets their answers using high-level inferences and attributions that suggest personal things about them that they did not know they'd be revealing. In some exercises, how group members draw a pig or select a favorite figure is said to reveal something about their sex life.[1] These latter exercises also face the more fundamental problem of providing invalid information, which also undermines the facilitator's credibility.

Putting aside these exercises that are irrelevant and potentially harmful to group effectiveness, the paradox here is that for a group to learn about itself, it may need to be more transparent than it has typically been, and that can require greater risk. At the same time, if group members don't feel sufficient psychological safety, their learning is hindered.[2]

If you facilitate exercises that don't let group members decide whether they want to take the level of emotional risk generated by the exercise, you act incongruently with several elements of mutual learning. You're not accountable or compassionate toward participants, and you prevent them from making an informed choice. For group members to decide whether they want to take the level of risk associated with a given exercise, before they decide to participate, they need to know generally what they will be expected to do, what they will be expected to reveal about themselves or others, and what others may be expected to reveal about them.

I rarely use experiential exercises in my facilitation. I find that group members' own experiences trying to solve their problems create more than enough real data to help them learn about their dynamics and themselves as group members. Some facilitators reason that experiential exercises increase learning by enabling the group to learn about its process without becoming distracted by its real task issues. I believe that using experiential exercises to help intact teams learn about and improve their process bypasses the real challenges that they encounter and must address to be effective. Avoiding experiential exercises also eliminates skepticism about whether an exercise generates learning that the team can reliably apply to the real work, and it shortens the time for applying the learning to real teamwork. Still, I recognize that many facilitators find these exercises helpful.

Processes That Are Part of the Organization

As a facilitator or consultant, you may be asked to facilitate meetings in which the team is using a process that is part of its or the larger organization's methods. When elements of those methods are incongruent with mutual learning, a potential conflict arises. If the group is trying to use mutual learning as a team, members are now faced with a mismatch between their team values and assumptions and a method that they may be required to use. Groups are often quick to see these incongruences. Even if they don't aspire to using mutual learning as their basis for working as a team, you are now helping a team use a process—which is the team's process, not yours—that is incongruent with your approach.

So, what do you do? Ideally, you assess whether the processes that the group plans to use are congruent with mutual learning during the planning stage of the facilitation. But it's not always possible to learn about all of the processes that a group uses, especially if you will be working with them over a period of time.

If the group is trying to use mutual learning, you raise the incongruence and ask how members see the situation. You do this even if you're a neutral facilitator because, as I discussed in Chapter 2, facilitators using mutual learning cannot be neutral about team processes that are incongruent with mutual learning. If members share your view about the incongruence, then you can ask them what actions, if any, they want to take. If they're interested in eliminating the incongruence, you can help them identify ways to modify the method to be congruent with mutual learning and still be acceptable to the organization. Keep in mind that making these modifications often involves challenging deeply held unilateral control values and assumptions held by the larger organization, or at least by those who designed the process.

Team Feedback. you're a facilitator, consultant, or team coach, teams may call on you to facilitate a team feedback process. In most of these processes, team members complete an online survey about their view of the team and/or you interview team members individually. You provide the results to the team in the form of a presentation and/or report and facilitate a team discussion about what the results mean and what, if anything, the team wants to do differently, given the results.

As I explained in Chapter 3 in the section on information, including feedback, most team feedback processes are incongruent with the core values of transparency, informed choice, accountability, and curiosity because the individual team member data are anonymous. If the data are quantitative for any given result, such as degree of trust in the group, team members see only an average group score with a standard deviation or the distribution of scores. They don't see which team member gave which score. This same anonymity occurs in 360-degree feedback processes, in which a team member receives feedback from his or her peers, direct reports, customers, and manager. In this case, the person's manager is usually identified because the results are grouped by category and a person often has only one manager. This incongruence undermines the very results that the feedback is designed to help teams achieve, including increased understanding and trust, accountability, and performance.

Fortunately, you and the team can redesign team feedback processes, including 360-degree feedback processes, to be congruent with mutual learning. If the team is using a survey tool, see if you can select the option to identify each member's responses, an increasingly available option. (If you're choosing the tool, select one with that option.) In the Team Effectiveness Survey that Roger Schwarz & Associates designed and uses with its clients, the feedback results identify each team member. Figure 11.3 shows a feedback slide from a real

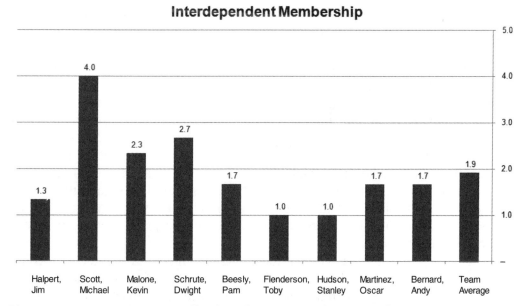

Figure 11.3   Team Survey Feedback with Team Members Identified

leadership team that was one of my clients. If you are familiar with the TV show *The Office*, you will recognize that I have replaced the leadership team members' real names with the names of characters from the show. This particular slide shows each team member's view of how interdependent he or she believes team members need to be with each other for the team to be effective. On a scale of 1 to 5, a score of 5 means that team members believe they need to be very interdependent to be effective.

Notice that you can quickly identify which team member gave which response. This quickly enables team members to become curious and ask each other the reasoning that led to their responses. In my feedback session with this leadership team, the formal team leader, identified in the figure as Michael Scott, began a conversation with his team about why people didn't think they needed to be as interdependent as he believed they did. It turned out to be an important conversation that identified some root causes of the team's reduced effectiveness. It's unlikely that the team could have had this conversation, or could have had it as efficiently as it did, without having team members' responses identified.

For these feedback conversations to be productive, the team needs to be transparent and curious with each other. That means introducing the team to mutual learning before the feedback so members understand the value of transparency and curiosity, and asking if they are willing to receive the feedback with each team member's results identified.

Performance Management Processes. Most large organizations have a process for assessing each individual's performance and having the manager and direct report meet to discuss the direct report's performance. You may be asked to be involved in this process as a trainer, consultant, facilitator, or coach.

These processes are often incongruent with the mutual learning core values of transparency, curiosity, informed choice, and accountability. In a number of organizations I have worked with, the method prohibits managers from telling their direct reports the sources of the data they are using to evaluate the direct report. If the direct report asks, "Where did you hear that?" the manager is supposed to respond, "That's not important" or "I can't say." But if direct reports can't know the source and the context of the data that are being used to evaluate them, they can't independently assess the data's validity and are more likely to dismiss them if they disagree with them. In addition, if they want to learn more about the situation so they can improve, the anonymity of the sources prevents it.

The performance management meeting also limits the managers' curiosity. One organization that asked me to help it integrate its performance management process with mutual learning, espoused the need for managers to be curious about their direct reports' views but had designed a meeting template that led to the opposite results. There was no time identified or allocated for managers to ask the direct reports' reactions to the evaluation.

The structure also made it difficult for managers to be curious. Before holding a meeting with a direct report, the manager's manager needed to approve the rating that the manager planned to give the direct report. The operating assumption was that the meeting would not—and should not—lead to a change in the direct report's rating. But, in order for this assumption to be valid, the manager had to have all the relevant information about the employee's performance before having the performance conversation with the employee. The purpose of the conversation was for the employee to learn but not necessarily for the manager to learn. If during the conversation between the manager and direct report, the manager was curious and learned some information that might lead her to want to increase the employee's rating, she had to make a case for the change.

If you encounter these incongruences, you can make the same kind of interventions that you might make in the case of team feedback above. If you believe that the process the team is asking you to train, consult on, or facilitate is significantly at odds with the values you use in working with groups, then you have to decide whether and how you will work with the group on this project.

Leadership Training. You may be working with groups that use behaviors or techniques they have learned in leadership training sessions provided by the organization, delivered either by internal or external consultants. It's common for me to find that leaders have been taught some element of leadership that is incongruent with mutual learning. One example is the sandwich approach to giving negative feedback that I described in Chapter 5. Another is speaking last so you won't inappropriately influence your direct reports' views on a topic.

Here, too, your responsibility is to point out the incongruences you see, ask for the group's thoughts, and enable it to make an informed choice about how it wants to proceed.

Sometimes clients who are trying to create a mutual learning organization ask me to review with them their organization's training programs. They want to determine how they are congruent or incongruent with the mutual learning approach. They recognize that it creates problems when people are unaware that two or more training courses are not only different but also incongruent. People feel that the organization is giving them a mixed message about how to lead. Worse, if people don't recognize the inconsistencies and try to apply techniques from two incongruent approaches, they can be ineffective and create conflict rather than improve the situation.

DIAGNOSING AND INTERVENING ON PROCESSES THAT ESPOUSE MUTUAL LEARNING: LEAN AND OTHER CONTINUOUS IMPROVEMENT APPROACHES

Some processes espouse a mindset and behaviors that are congruent with mutual learning, but groups using the processes don't exhibit it. This is often the case with Lean, Six Sigma, and similar approaches to continuous improvement. Lean teams focus on continuously improving some operational process by applying a set of technical problem-solving skills.

Even though the two pillars of the Lean approach are continuous improvement and respect for people, teams that use Lean tend to focus considerably more on the technical aspects. Some Lean experts have found that many Lean practitioners don't understand what respect for people looks like in Lean practice and describe respect for people as the missing piece of Lean.[3] At least one expert has explained that it's very difficult to define respect for people in the Lean context.[4]

That Lean teams often pay relatively little attention to effective group process—the foundation that enables them to solve continuous improvement problems—isn't surprising. Continuous improvement approaches are based significantly on engineering principles, and continuous improvement consultants often have an engineering or technical background.

In my consulting with organizations over the years, I've noticed a pattern with organizations that are engaged in some form of continuous process improvement. The consultants helping these organizations, both internal and external, often tell me that the approach works at first or works with what people call low-hanging fruit—the issues that are easy to address. But frequently, the teams have increasing difficulty in designing process improvements when it requires them to address challenging, often undiscussable, issues in the team.[5] One Lean expert has advocated for what he calls Lean behaviors, noting that Lean teams perpetuate ineffective group process that would be considered waste by Lean standards.[6]

Given that Lean is designed to solve problems by addressing the root causes of those problems, it's ironic when Lean teams are less effective because their group process hinders their ability to use Lean as effectively as possible. For example, Lean processes work better in teams where all team members consider it their responsibility to find and correct quality problems.[7] In mutual learning terms, this reflects the shift from a one-leader-in-the room culture to a lead-from-every-chair culture.

This is where mutual learning makes Lean and other continuous improvement processes more effective. Mutual learning describes the specific mindset and skill set needed to raise and address challenging issues in way that embodies respect for people. **In short, just as Lean improves quality and reduces waste in operational processes, mutual learning improves quality and reduces waste in group process.**

You can help Lean teams use mutual learning to put the respect for people pillar into practice throughout the 14 Lean principles that James Womack and his colleagues developed and organized into four categories.[8] Here are some examples:

- The first category of Lean principles is having a long-term philosophy that drives a long-term approach to building a learning organization.[9] At the heart of a learning organization are teams in which members use mutual learning to reflect on their own situation and behavior, identify the assumptions they hold that limit their effectiveness, and change their assumptions and behaviors to design more effective teams and organizations.

- The second category of Lean principles is that "the right process will produce the right results." The Team Effectiveness Model, which includes the mutual learning mindset and behaviors, describes both effective team process and team design, which shapes team process.

- The fifth principle—build a culture of stopping to fix problems, to get quality right the first time—is reflected in the mutual learning principle "go slow to go fast," which is adopted from the field of systems thinking.

- The seventh principle—use visual controls so no problems are hidden—is a way to call attention to problems that people might otherwise miss and to encourage them to respond. The analog in mutual learning is to "discuss undiscussable issues." Like production processes, group processes do have observable behaviors, but unlike production processes, there is no easy way to convert them into visual controls. The task of calling attention to otherwise unnoticed or unaddressed issues becomes shared by all team members.

- The ninth principle—grow leaders who thoroughly understand the work, live the philosophy, and teach it to others—occurs through the mutual learning behaviors, "state views and ask genuine questions," "explain reasoning and intent," and "test assumptions and inferences." By using these behaviors, leaders come to better understand the work themselves and to better help others understand it.

- The eleventh principle—respect your extended network of partners and suppliers by challenging them and helping them improve—occurs in part through the mutual learning behavior "test assumptions and inferences." By identifying any inaccurate or unnecessary assumptions that partners and suppliers are making, the organization helps them improve. Notice that the Lean approach frames challenging others as a sign of respect. This is consistent with the mutual learning mindset of being simultaneously transparent, curious, accountable, and compassionate.

- The twelfth principle—go and see for yourself to thoroughly understand the situation—is consistent with the mutual learning value of informed choice and operationalized partly by the mutual learning behavior, "use specific examples and agree on what important words mean."

- The thirteenth principle—make decisions slowly by consensus, thoroughly considering all options; implement decisions rapidly—also reflects the mutual learning principle, "go slow to go fast." Mutual learning includes consensus (defined as unanimous support) as one possible decision rule. The emphasis is on being certain that everyone is committed to implementing decisions. It accomplishes this by ensuring that team members share all relevant information, including their assumptions and interests, and jointly design solutions that meet these interests. Where team members have different views, they use mutual learning to jointly design tests to ensure the proposed solutions meet the needs of the process and the people involved, which is the eighth Lean principle.

Of course, with Lean, just as with mutual learning, how you think is how you lead. As many organizations have learned the hard way, you can't create a Lean organization by adopting Lean behaviors without understanding and living the underlying Lean philosophy. Because Lean's "respect for people" principle and mutual learning are very congruent, helping Lean teams develop a mutual learning mindset will increase their ability to implement the Lean principles.

SUMMARY

In this chapter, I have described how you use mutual learning to help groups increase the effectiveness of any process they are using. By using groups' processes as the basis for observing and making meaning in the mutual learning cycle, you can intervene to help them improve. By ensuring that the processes you select to use with groups are congruent with mutual learning, you avoid reducing the group's effectiveness.

I provided examples of how groups decrease their effectiveness when using a process incorrectly, when there is incongruence between mutual learning and a process, and when a process espouses mutual learning but the group does not manifest the mutual learning mindset or behaviors.

In the next chapter, I will describe the interventions you can make to address emotions in the group.

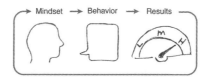

CHAPTER TWELVE

Diagnosing and Intervening on Emotions—The Group's and Yours

I n this chapter, I explain how to deal with emotions arising in groups, mostly difficult emotions. I begin by describing how people generate emotions and how they express them. Next, we consider how emotional discussion in groups can trigger your emotions and affect your ability to facilitate, as well as how you can intervene to help people express their emotions effectively. The chapter ends with a description of how you can respond when group members get angry at you and how you can use this as an opportunity for learning—for the group and you.

THE CHALLENGE

Part of serving in your facilitative role includes helping the group address difficult, conflict-ridden problems. In working on these problems, group members may experience a variety of emotions, including anger, fear, surprise, and sadness. *Emotion* refers to a feeling and the distinctive thoughts associated with it, along with the psychological and biological states that, all together, predispose a person to act.[1] Your challenge is to help group members identify their emotions and the source, and express them in a way that contributes to—rather than detracts from—group effectiveness.

This is difficult. Like the groups you're trying to help, many of the facilitators and consultants I teach or coach find it hard to deal with an emotional situation. This makes sense if you consider that most people employ a unilateral control mindset when they feel psychological threat or embarrassment. Faced with a group that's becoming emotional, you may have a similar reaction. You may fear that if the group gets out of control, you won't know how to help it. You may be overwhelmed by your own feelings and not able to think clearly. Part of the challenge of dealing with group members' emotions is dealing with your own. I address this challenge later in the chapter.

The ability to deal with emotions is what Daniel Goleman calls emotional intelligence.[2] Drawing on the research of Peter Salovey and John Mayer, who coined the term *emotional intelligence*, Goleman describes emotional intelligence as the ability to be aware of and manage your emotions, to use your emotions in motivating yourself to achieve goals, to have empathy for others, and to effectively deal with emotions in your relationships with others.[3]

Fortunately, people are increasingly coming to value emotional intelligence in the workplace. Organizational leaders are realizing that if a group doesn't deal with emotion productively, it negatively affects the group's performance, the ability to work together in the future, and individuals' professional and personal development. You can help group members shift from being afraid of dealing with their emotions to helping them use emotions to improve the quality of their work and their relationships.

Before you consider how people generate emotions and how to intervene, it's worth repeating an earlier point: Group facilitation is not therapy. **The purpose of dealing with emotions that arise in facilitation, consulting, coaching, or training is to help the group become more effective at its work, not to change people's personalities or to focus on emotions for their own sake.** To be appropriate, your interventions on members' emotional behavior must relate to some element of team effectiveness.

HOW PEOPLE GENERATE EMOTIONS

Understanding how you and group members generate and deal with emotions can help you work effectively. Here I present a very simplified version, drawing on recent research.

Converting Sight and Sound into Feeling and Thinking

How our brain converts what we see and hear into what we feel, think, and decide to do is an unsettled area of research. Researchers used to posit a dichotomous model in which different parts of the brain were responsible for emotion and cognition—feeling and thinking. In this model, the parts of the brain responsible for emotion reacted quickly and without precision, while the parts of the brain responsible for thinking reacted more slowly and with more nuance. For the emotion of fear, the amygdala, two almond-shaped parts of the subcortical brain, played the central role in the initial response; the prefrontal cortex, responsible for higher-order thinking, played a central role in the later response. Drawing on this research, Daniel Goleman introduced the term *amygdala highjack*, in which the initial amygdala response to perceived threat leads all of us at times to be less emotionally intelligent than we could be.[4]

Recent research calls into question this simple dichotomy between emotion and cognition being processed in different and discrete parts of the brain. It suggests that no brain region is dedicated to any single emotion; many different brain areas can produce the same emotional result; and emotions like fear and anger are constructed by multipurpose brain networks that work together. Regions like the amygdala are important to emotion but are neither necessary nor sufficient for it.[5] Although how we generate emotion is still being explored, there's no question that we often manage our emotions poorly. So, we are still faced with the same challenge: integrating our thoughts and feelings to increase our effectiveness with others.

Factors That Contribute to Generating Emotion

There are a variety of factors that can, in a group meeting, lead you or a group member to become emotional and respond in a unilaterally controlling way. Knowing what factors contribute to emotion helps you respond appropriately and, when possible, prepare yourself internally.

The Content of the Subject Being Discussed. Certain subjects are likely to be emotionally hot topics because they often evoke feelings of fear, anger, shame, or guilt; consider a performance appraisal, an organizational restructuring or layoff, a merger, violence, or sexual harassment in the workplace.

The Nature of Your Relationship with the Group. Even if you've clarified what the group can reasonably expect from you, it may still have unrealistic expectations of how you can help the group. Combine this with the fact that you aren't solving the problems for the group or giving it expert technical advice on how to do so, and this can cause group members to feel ambivalent about you. On one hand, they may very much want and need your help; on the other, they may feel disappointed that you don't solve the problems they need solved.

The Depth of Your Intervention. Deep interventions, such as mindset interventions, ask people to reveal information about themselves—their assumptions, values, opinions, and feelings—that is quite private. By revealing the information, they risk making themselves vulnerable. A member may share the fact that his ineffective behavior with a boss is based on his belief that the boss can't be trusted. Or, he may reveal that his ineffective behavior results from believing that another member isn't competent to do the job. Depending on what the member reveals, he or she may fear loss of support from peers, retaliation by a more powerful member, or loss of face. Consequently, the person can feel threatened by and react emotionally to interventions that ask for such information to be revealed.

Experiences That Trigger Past Emotional Responses. An individual's past experience triggers current emotional response. If people perceive the current situation as similar to a past situation in which their emotions were triggered, their emotions can be triggered again.

Cultural Diversity. People of different cultures, races, or genders can make divergent meaning out of the same event and have a range of emotional responses. For example, some Asian cultures place a high priority on "saving face." In a conversation in which group members are not saving face, an Asian member may respond more emotionally than a member from the United States, if each responds in a way stereotypical of his or her culture.

Our Story about Ourselves. All of us have constructed a story about who we are and are supposed to be. When we are too attached to our story and don't live up to it, it can lead us to feel anxious, angry, or sad. When I started consulting, I believed that I should be as competent as a seasoned consultant. I was anxious anticipating that I wouldn't intervene effectively with my clients. When I made a mistake with a client, I would dwell on it, which distracted me and made me less effective.

HOW GROUPS EXPRESS EMOTIONS

In the *Nicomachean Ethics,* Aristotle defined the challenge of dealing with emotions this way: "Anyone can become angry—that is easy. But to be angry with the right person, to the right degree, at the right time, for the right purpose, and in the right way—this is not easy." Your challenge is to help group members identify, express, and discuss their emotions to increase rather than decrease the group's effectiveness.

People express their emotions in two ways: directly or indirectly. In the former case, they describe what they are feeling: "I am really angry at you," or "I fear that someone will get back at me if I'm honest."

People express their emotions indirectly in two ways: verbally or nonverbally. Indirect verbal expression can take many forms, including raising or lowering the voice, immediately changing an opinion when pressured, and verbally attacking someone or denying that person's actions. Nonverbal examples include glaring at or looking away from other group members, slouching in or perching on a chair, folding or waving the arms, tightening facial muscles, and sighing.

In both indirect methods, you and other members can't identify the emotion without asking or making an inference, even if it's only a low-level inference. People express the same emotion in different ways, and even the same person can express the same emotion differently at different times. You may express anger by becoming hostile, while I may express anger by withdrawing from the conversation. Further, a given behavior can express different emotions. One person's outburst may reflect anger, while another's is from anxiety. Consequently, you can't reliably infer a person's emotions from his or her behavior.

Acting defensively—part of the unilateral control mindset—is a common way for group members to indirectly express emotion. *Defensive behavior* is a way of trying to reduce anxiety or stress that involves denying or distorting reality.[6] Examples are denial, blaming others, withholding relevant information, and suppressing emotions.

People express their emotions effectively when they express them directly and in a manner consistent with the mutual learning mindset and behaviors. Whether a person acts effectively doesn't depend on how frequently or strongly he or she expresses emotions.

Just as cultural differences affect how members of a group generate emotions, they also affect how members express them. Some organizations believe that discussing emotions is "touchy-feely" and don't see the relationship between productive discussion of emotion and the group's effectiveness. Consequently, people in such an organization feel pressure to avoid emotional discussion. In contrast, other organizations believe—and the research suggests—that unresolved issues of negative emotion, especially those that create defensive behavior, reduce the group's ability to maintain its working relationship and consequently the ability to perform tasks.[7] People in this sort of organization feel less pressure to avoid emotional discussion.

The group's culture within the organization also influences whether and how members express emotion. Even if the larger organization culture believes that expressions of emotion are inappropriate, a group within the organization may believe including emotions in the discussion is healthy.

The cultural makeup of group members also has an impact on how they express emotion. Although it's dangerous to assume that a person from a particular culture expresses his or her own emotions in a way that is stereotypical of the culture, nevertheless some cultures express their emotions more directly and emphatically, while others express their emotions more subtly. The same holds true for people with different levels of education, socioeconomic class, and hierarchy within the organization.

MANAGING YOUR OWN EMOTIONS

You're working with a group discussing roles and responsibilities, when Michelle starts to accuse Joe of slacking off. Immediately, Joe angrily tells Michelle that if she were competent, the group wouldn't be having problems. Walt jumps in admonishingly, saying that Joe is in no position to complain. With each comment, the group members get angrier.

Many of the facilitators and consultants that I teach or coach have a difficult time in a situation like this one, where group members get very emotional. It's hard to help the members manage their emotions effectively if your own emotions are getting in your way. If you start to get overwhelmed emotionally, you can do several things to manage your emotions and regain your effectiveness.

Slow Down

First, slow down. You don't need to immediately jump in when you see the group getting emotional. Intervening quickly out of anxiety or anger can be worse than making no intervention at all. By slowing yourself down, you have the chance to use your emotions to inform your thinking rather than to override it. The traditional advice of taking a deep breath and counting to 10 is useful. It gives you a chance to interrupt your purely emotional response and integrate your thinking with your emotions.

Treat Yourself with Compassion

Remember that the core value of compassion includes treating *yourself* compassionately. For most people, dealing with an emotional situation is challenging. Compassion for yourself means recognizing that you're also a learner in this process, that there will be times when you feel anxious, overwhelmed, afraid, stuck, and so forth, and that is part of what it means to grow and develop. As a "recovering perfectionist," I can tell you that when things are not working out as you would like, you don't earn extra points for getting down on yourself. Pay attention to your inner critic, such as telling yourself that you must make the situation better. Your own self-talk can be a sign that your self-compassion is slipping.

Notice, Experience, and Name Your Emotions

Notice your emotions. Because emotions involve a physical response, your body is often your first clue that you're feeling some distress. The more that you learn how you manifest feelings—for example, sweaty palms, racing pulse, clenched jaw, tight stomach—the more quickly you'll be able to use this early warning system to help you evaluate what's happening.

Name your emotions. Is it anger, fear, shame, surprise, disgust, sadness, joy, or some other emotion—or a combination of emotions? These are some basic emotions, but there are scores of them, including blends of emotion. Anger includes frustration, resentment, and annoyance; fear encompasses anxiety, nervousness, and wariness, to name a few. Increasing your emotional vocabulary makes it easier to clearly name your emotions, which makes it easier to work with them.

To name your emotions, allow yourself to experience them without judging. It's natural to have a range of emotions when facilitating, consulting, or coaching; don't berate yourself for having them. If you think to yourself, *I'm feeling anxious and that's bad,* you add another layer of emotion, which makes it more difficult to identify your initial emotion and creates distraction. Instead, try reframing your thinking so that you're curious and compassionate with yourself: *Hmmm, this is interesting; what am I feeling here?*

Identify the Source

Identify the source of your emotion. By continuing to remain curious and compassionate, you can reflect, *I wonder where my reaction is coming from?* Ask yourself what specifically people have said or done that generated the emotion. Is it something that has happened in the present conversation? Is it something from a previous conversation with group members? Is it something from a relationship with other people that you're carrying over to this group?

Ask yourself if something is happening that's triggering your own issues. Knowing what your own issues are helps you identify this quickly. For example, if you generally set unrealistically high standards for yourself and keep on raising the bar, you may react emotionally if a group member begins to discuss this topic emotionally. Ask yourself: *Is the level of my emotion in proportion to the situation, or not?* Getting annoyed with group members is different from being outraged at them. Here, too, remaining curious and compassionate with yourself helps you identify the source of your emotion.

Use the answers to your questions to help diagnose the situation. Consider that your own emotions may be mirroring what one or more group members are feeling.[8] For example, if you're annoyed at a team member's comment and think that it has something to do with an interaction between group members, consider the possibility that other group members are also annoyed; look for observable data that confirm or disconfirm this idea. If you conclude that your emotions are unrelated to what's happening in the group, then it helps to reflect on your reaction. (This is why working with a partner is important; it enables that person to take the lead for a while.) If you are working alone, recognize that you've become part of the problem. If you've already reacted, let the group know that. Owning your mistakes and publicly apologizing can also be a vital learning experience for the group.

Remind Yourself of Your Skills

One reason my facilitation and consulting students feel anxious is that they don't know what to say or do when group members get emotional. The mutual learning approach gives you a way of helping members deal with emotions. By using the mutual learning cycle and the eight behaviors, you can test your inferences about whether people are feeling a certain emotion and ask what has happened that led them to feel that way. Knowing that there are some standard interventions you can make when a group member expresses emotion can help a lot.

DECIDING HOW TO INTERVENE

There are a number of things to consider when you are deciding how to intervene.

Look for Gifts

A number of years ago, I took some courses in improvisational theater. In improv, you work with others to create a scene or play or song on the spot: None of the improv players knows what anyone will say or do before it happens. The conversation develops spontaneously, each improv player building on the other's comments to create a scene that is meaningful—and maybe even funny.

What I learned from my improv instructor Greg Hohn is that for improv to work, you need to accept the gift that you're given. The lines that your improv partners give you are the only lines you get to work with and respond to. You can build on them and play with them, but you have to work with the lines they give you. If you don't, the improv ends. By framing the lines that others give you as a gift, you can look for ways to accept and build on them.

The same is true in your facilitative role. The lines that group members say are the lines you have to work with. You can comment on them and ask the members about them, but you need to accept them as the basis for your interventions if your interventions are to be related to their conversation.

With the mutual learning approach, by listening carefully and curiously to what group members say, you receive the material for your next lines. If Lola says in a raised voice, "Tony, it's always like this. You're always putting yourself before the team!," you might respond, "Lola, you sound angry, yes?" If she agrees, you can continue: "Can you explain to Tony what he's done or not done that's leading you to be angry?"

Unfortunately, if you grow fearful, angry, or embarrassed and focus exclusively and extensively on your emotions, you stop attending to the group. Then you miss what people are saying and the gifts they are continuing to give you for intervention. A colleague and I were working with a group when she made what I thought was an inadvertent pejorative comment about a particular race, members of whom were in the group. I got embarrassed and put my head down, thereby missing the group members' reactions (which I could have used as information to intervene). A few minutes later, when I recovered from my embarrassment, I did intervene. I said to the group that when she made the remark, I felt embarrassed and as a result missed the members' reactions. I then asked them how they felt about the remark. The group, my colleague, and I discussed it; some group members said they had stopped paying attention after she made the comment, because it bothered them. After talking about it, the group, my colleague, and I were ready to return to the group's task.

Part of the difficulty is that when group members become emotional, the diagnostic and intervention gifts they give you are not nicely wrapped. They may come in loud, angry, or sullen packaging. But if you accept the gift, you may help the group unwrap some important issues that are hindering its effectiveness.

Move toward the Conflict

As conflict arises in a group and people get emotional, you may want to avoid it. You can try to switch the subject, squelch it, or defuse the situation, perhaps by calling a break. But moving away from conflict means you miss an opportunity to help the group.

I learned this lesson by facilitating for a nonprofit volunteer service organization. The organization was in trouble because the leadership was burned out. They had been providing almost all the services because they couldn't recruit other volunteer members to help. As a result, the leaders were planning to resign their positions en masse but couldn't find anyone to replace them. They believed that if they stepped down, the organization would die. They called a membership meeting to deal with this issue.

Unfortunately, my concern about the members' emotions and my inability to handle them led me to intervene in a way that steered the group away from the conflict rather than into it. The group didn't get to discuss the essence of the issue; the meeting ended without any agreement.

A principle of the mutual learning approach is to move toward conflict and differences. By publicly identifying the conflict in the group and engaging people in a conversation about it, you can help the group explore how people contribute to the conflict, how they are feeling about it, and how to manage it. The sooner you move toward the conflict, the more time the group has to discuss and resolve it.

Follow Through on Interventions

Interventions are not magic. Even if you move toward conflict and intervene, your initial intervention may not have the impact you intend. It's natural to have to make a series of interventions to help the group explore a particular issue.

Sometimes you may discontinue an intervention because you become frustrated as the group members remain silent or respond only indirectly to your questions. Sometimes you may drop an intervention because a group member responds angrily or tearfully.

Reframe Your Intervention. When I ask facilitators and consultants what leads them to not follow through on an emotionally difficult intervention, they usually explain that they inferred the member or entire group would be embarrassed and couldn't handle it. They also say they are uncomfortable when pursuing such an intervention. They recognize that by dropping the intervention, they are unilaterally protecting their clients and themselves.

Reframing how you think about intervening in conflict can make it easier for you to intervene. I often tell myself that the group is paying me to facilitate because they aren't able to pursue these difficult issues themselves. If I back off when my initial intervention isn't working, I may reinforce their belief that these issues are too difficult to handle. I may also lead them to infer that the mutual learning mindset and behaviors—on which my interventions are based—aren't effective in difficult situations. By pursuing interventions in a way that also maintains the group members' free and informed choice, I model what is possible and also give them optimism that they can address their difficult issues.

Make Meta-Interventions. If clients don't respond directly to your initial intervention or respond defensively, rather than repeating the same intervention, you can follow up with a meta-intervention. A *meta-intervention* is an intervention about a previous intervention. Meta-interventions enable the group and you to talk about interventions so you and the group can get to a root cause of a problem. In a meta-intervention, you explore with the group how it responded to your initial intervention and what led it to respond that way.

Consider, for example, a member who remains silent when you intervene to ask the member to identify her interests. You may respond with the general meta-intervention, "Jill, when I asked you what your interests were, you remained silent, yes? *[If yes]* Can you say what led you to be silent?"

Of course, making a meta-intervention can surface undiscussable issues that require deeper intervention. A meta-intervention may prompt members to discuss how they disagree with the goals of a program or how they question other members' performance. I don't become concerned if the group abandons my initial intervention to pursue the issue uncovered by the meta-intervention.

In fact, I consider this a success. Meta-intervention issues often help the group move beyond discussing symptoms, to explore underlying problems and causes.

INTERVENING ON EMOTIONS

To repeat an earlier point, the facilitator's role is to help the group identify, express, and discuss emotions in a way that increases group effectiveness. To do this, you can intervene in two ways: by helping members express their emotions effectively and by helping members learn to think differently—to change their mindset—so they can manage their emotions effectively themselves. The first approach is appropriate for both basic and developmental facilitation; the second is typically reserved for developmental facilitation.

HELPING PEOPLE EXPRESS EMOTIONS EFFECTIVELY

You help group members express their emotions effectively by having them use the mutual learning behaviors. In basic facilitation, you accomplish this by encouraging them to name their emotions, identifying comments that may upset other members, and rephrasing for members how they have expressed their emotions. The example in Exhibit 12.1 shows a basic facilitator intervention with a group of leaders who are discussing potential budget cuts. The conversation appears in the right column, and my analysis appears in the left column.

In developmental facilitation, you help members learn how to express their emotions consistently with the core values and behaviors, rather than relying on the facilitator to do it for them, as in basic facilitation. The intervention in Exhibit 12.2 continues essentially from where the earlier conversation ends, illustrating how you can move from a basic intervention to a developmental intervention.

HELPING PEOPLE REDUCE DEFENSIVE THINKING

The basic and developmental interventions in the following examples above help members express their emotions but don't help them change their underlying defensive behavior, because neither intervention addresses the root cause—their mindset. Instead, the facilitator helps members bypass the defensive behavior rather than "helping the group learn to [discuss these defensive behaviors] in order to get rid of them."[9]

Analysis of the Conversation	The Conversation
	DAN: I don't think Paco needs all his people because he's increased efficiencies significantly. I think we can cut some people in his area, meet the budget, and not reduce our productivity.
Facilitator observes Paco speaking in a loud voice, pointing to Dan with his finger, and the phrase, "I'm sick and tired" and infers emotion. Facilitator decides to intervene on the larger issues of Paco's emotions rather than the unexplained phrase, "you're like a little kid," which seems part of the larger issue.	PACO: *(to Dan in a loud voice)* I'm sick and tired of hearing this line from you. You talk as if every other department has to justify its existence except yours. Well, we've got real good reasons for our staffing numbers. *(waving his finger at Dan)* You know that, but you're more concerned about your own little kingdom instead of the bigger picture. You're like a little kid.
Facilitator describes the observable behavior, checks for agreement, and skips testing the observation because Paco just finished saying it. Facilitator shares his inference about what Paco is feeling and then tests it.	FACILITATOR: Paco, you raised your voice, waved your finger at Dan, and said you were "sick and tired of hearing this line." You sound really frustrated; what are you feeling?
Facilitator notes that Paco describes a type of anger: being ticked off. Paco has also identified this issue as a pattern, which he attributes to "Dan looking out for Dan."	PACO: I'll tell you what I'm feeling: ticked off. It's like this all the time. Dan is looking out for Dan.
Facilitator asks Paco to describe the thoughts that led him to be ticked off.	FACILITATOR: Okay. What I don't understand exactly is what Dan said that ticked you off. What were you thinking before you told Dan you were "sick and tired"? Can you say specifically?
Facilitator notes that Paco is attributing to Dan that Dan knows that what he is saying is not true and is just trying to protect people.	PACO: Dan knows the whole point of increasing efficiency wasn't to cut people in the department. It was to deploy people on more profitable services. There was never any intention of cutting people once we achieved the efficiencies. He's just trying to protect his own people—it's typical Dan.
Facilitator clarifies the source of Paco's anger and checks for agreement about the attribution.	FACILITATOR: So are you angry because you think Dan knows this but is trying to use that reason to cut your number of people?
	PACO: That's exactly what I'm saying.

Exhibit 12.1 Intervening on Emotion: Using Basic Facilitation

Analysis of the Conversation	The Conversation
Facilitator asks Paco whether he tested this inference and attribution about Dan.	FACILITATOR: Okay. Can you say what leads you to believe that Dan knows this? I'm asking because I'm wondering: Are you inferring it, or has Dan said this explicitly to you?
	PACO: I'm inferring it from a number of comments he made.
Facilitator asks Paco to test his inference with Dan.	FACILITATOR: Are you willing to share with Dan what data you used to make your inference and see if he sees it differently?
	PACO: Okay.

Exhibit 12.1   Intervening on Emotion: Using Basic Facilitation (*continued*)

Analysis of the Conversation	The Conversation
Facilitator clarifies the source of Paco's anger and checks for agreement about the attribution.	FACILITATOR: So are you angry because you think Dan knows this but is trying to use that reason to cut your number of people?
	PACO: That's exactly what I'm saying.
Facilitator describes the two issues, one content-related and the other emotion-related, and separates the two initially.	FACILITATOR: I think it can be useful to be angry in certain cases and then appropriately express your anger. I see two related issues here. One is whether Dan does know about the purpose of increasing efficiency and whether he was trying to protect his own people. The other issue is how you responded to Dan, given your thinking about the first issue. I'd like first to focus on how you responded because I think your reaction created some unintended consequences. Then I'd like to come back to the first issue. Any concerns about doing that?
	PACO: No, that's okay.
Facilitator identifies Paco's intent, to see if it will match the consequences he got.	FACILITATOR: When you got angry with Dan, what was your intent when you yelled that he was only concerned about his own little kingdom instead of the bigger picture and that he was acting like a little kid?
	PACO: I was so ticked off that I wanted to get his attention.

Exhibit 12.2   Intervening on Emotion: Using Developmental Facilitation

Analysis of the Conversation	The Conversation
	FACILITATOR: I think you definitely got Dan's attention. I think you may have also gotten some other consequences that you hadn't intended. Would you be willing to find out from Dan how he reacted to your comments?
	PACO: Okay, Dan, how did you react?
Facilitator chooses not to intervene on Dan's reaction, which includes an untested inference that Paco didn't want to hear what Dan had to say.	DAN: I got angry with you because you unfairly accused me, and I didn't think you wanted to hear what I had to say. At that point, I just shut down. I wasn't willing to hear what you had to say.
	FACILITATOR: Paco, can you let Dan know what you heard him say so that he's sure you got it as he meant it? What did you hear Dan say?
	PACO: Dan, what you're saying is that you got annoyed at me because you think I was accusing you unfairly and that I wasn't going to listen to your view of the situation. You basically turned me off at that point. Yes?
	DAN: You got it.
Facilitator states his willingness to share his thoughts and explains why he wants Paco to go first.	FACILITATOR: Paco, earlier I said that I thought you not only got Dan's attention but also got some other consequences you didn't intend. I'm willing to share my thoughts about what the consequences are, but I'm interested in seeing if you can identify any. What do you think?
	PACO: Well, I guess that in trying to get Dan's attention, I got it initially but then lost him completely because I ticked him off.
Facilitator agrees with Paco and then asks Paco to redesign his comment.	FACILITATOR: I agree with you completely. You got the opposite of the very thing you intended. Can you think what you could have said to Dan that would have let him know how you were feeling without contributing to his shutting you off?
	PACO: I'd say something like, "Dan, I'm angry with you. You said that my department could be cut without any loss of productivity. But when we talked

Exhibit 12.2   Intervening on Emotion: Using Developmental Facilitation (*continued*)

Analysis of the Conversation	The Conversation
	about increasing efficiency, you agreed that my department would use the increased efficiency to redeploy people to higher-margin services. Now you're saying something different than what you said before. Do you agree, Dan?" If Dan agreed, I'd say, "Well, that's what makes me angry."
Facilitator confirms Paco's statement and checks with the group for problems facilitator may not have seen.	FACILITATOR: I think that's consistent with mutual learning. Anyone see any problems with Paco's redesign?

Exhibit 12.2   Intervening on Emotion: Using Developmental Facilitation (*continued*)

By helping members identify and change their mindset, over time they think differently so that they perceive less of a threat and therefore don't experience the emotion so overwhelmingly or as a trigger to their defensive behavior. This kind of developmental intervention requires a skilled facilitator. Again, the conversation in Exhibit 12.3 begins by returning to an earlier part of the last example.

Analysis of the Conversation	The Conversation
Facilitator confirms Paco's statement and checks with the group for problems facilitator may not have seen.	FACILITATOR: I think that's consistent with the mutual learning approach. Anyone see any problems with Paco's redesign? *(members shake heads, say no)*
Facilitator returns to the first issue he identified.	FACILITATOR: Paco, I'd like to go back to the issue of whether Dan knows about the purpose of increasing efficiency and whether he was trying to protect his own people. Can we return to that?
	PACO: Okay.
Facilitator begins to determine whether Paco contributed to his emotional reaction by making untested inferences about what Dan knew.	FACILITATOR: I'm wondering whether you are inferring that Dan knows his two statements are different. Assuming you're correct that Dan knows this, I can understand how you would feel angry. How do you know that Dan knows the purpose of creating efficiencies wasn't to cut the number of people? Have you checked this out with Dan, or are you making an inference?
	PACO: Everybody knew it. We talked about it in a lot of meetings.

Exhibit 12.3   Using Developmental Facilitation to Identify Defensive Thinking

Analysis of the Conversation	The Conversation
Facilitator clarifies Paco's response in terms of the facilitator's question.	FACILITATOR: Are you saying that you checked out your inference directly with Dan, or are you saying something else?
	PACO: No, I didn't check it out. I just think you would have had to be totally out of the loop not to know it.
Facilitator shares observations and inferences and tests them with Paco.	FACILITATOR: Let me identify a pattern that I think led to your angry response and get your reaction. Dan suggests that with the new efficiencies, people in your department can be cut. You infer that Dan knows this wasn't the purpose of increasing efficiency, and you respond by getting angry with him. You attribute his actions to protecting his turf and then suggest that this is Dan's typical behavior. But you don't test your inference with Dan. Instead, you assume your inference is true and use your untested inference as the justification for your anger toward Dan. Have I accurately described what happened?
	PACO: Yeah, that pretty much captures it.
Facilitator identifies a pattern of behavior common to several group members. The facilitator then suggests the value of changing the dysfunctional pattern and asks the group to make a choice.	FACILITATOR: One thing we can spend some time on is talking about how you can reduce this kind of thinking. I raise this because you've had several occasions in which different members—Dan, Amy, and Paco—have experienced similar negative consequences from their thinking. Am I off? *[If members agree, then continue]* I think this would help your ability to deal with some of the difficult issues you still want to deal with, such as equitable workloads and coordination between departments. But the choice is yours. What are your thoughts about what I'm suggesting?

Exhibit 12.3   Using Developmental Facilitation to Identify Defensive Thinking (*continued*)

Dealing with Hot Buttons

A *hot button* is a characteristic or situation that has a particularly strong meaning for you and that leads you to respond defensively. For some people, a hot button might be perceiving they are not afforded the respect, deference, or attention they believe they deserve. Other people have a hot button pushed when they believe someone is questioning their ability, commitment, intelligence, or integrity. For still others, it's being manipulated or otherwise controlled. Because your own hot buttons lead you to misperceive others' remarks and actions, you often respond ineffectively even if others have acted effectively. We develop our hot buttons based on our experiences and our story about ourselves.

As a developmental facilitator, you can help group participants respond effectively by reducing the defensive thinking associated with their hot buttons. This involves first working with them to identify the trigger and then helping them reframe their thinking. Some people I have facilitated for find it difficult to respond effectively when a person—especially someone with less power or authority—raises his or her voice at them in anger. Granted, raising your voice or yelling is not a particularly skillful way of communicating, and those who do so are still accountable for their behavior, but people whose hot buttons are triggered by this behavior believe that a person yelling at them is showing disrespect for their official position or their personal dignity. They also believe that allowing a person to raise his voice gives him too much control.

In developmental facilitation, I help them respond effectively through reframing how they think about the person raising his voice. First, I ask them to reframe how they think about the other person's interests—perhaps to think of him not as being disrespectful but as having limited skills; the person yelling is not trying to make someone's life miserable but is trying to solve a problem without the ability to do so. In other words, the person is not interested in raising his voice for its own sake.

Next, I ask the participants to consider reframing how they think about their own role. Because they seek to manage conflict effectively, I ask them to think of themselves as being in the position of helping people who are less skilled at managing conflict.

HELPING THE GROUP EXPRESS POSITIVE EMOTIONS

Although many groups struggle with addressing such emotions as fear, anger, regret, and embarrassment, some groups also have difficulty handling positive emotions—happiness, joy, pride, satisfaction, and kindness. Emotions are neither positive nor negative in the sense of being good or bad; I use the term *positive emotion* to refer to those we typically associate with a positive experience. Helping group members learn to express their positive emotions is also important. In your facilitative role, you can help group members accomplish this in several ways.

Help the Group Celebrate Progress

One way to help people in a group express positive emotions is to help them to recognize and celebrate their achievements.[10] A group working through a difficult issue using new facilitative skills is in itself cause for recognizing its accomplishment. This includes members using their mutual learning mindset and skill set to deal with a challenging situation. This doesn't necessarily require a party to celebrate, but asking members to express their feelings about the achievement creates a group memory about their ability to work together effectively. Marking the accomplishment builds momentum that helps the group to move on to the next steps.

Find the Humor in Being Human

Serving in facilitative role doesn't mean being stoic or humorless. When group members say and do things that are genuinely funny, I laugh accordingly. I don't join in a group's humor if it's at the expense of a member or seems to be a defensive reaction to a genuine issue in the group, but I do bring my sense of humor to my work.

To me, part of being human is laughing at my own ineffectiveness. Yes, helping groups is serious business, but not so serious that I think we should lose sight of the comic absurdity of our ineffective behavior. Laughing with a group about how it creates the very unintended consequences it tries to avoid doesn't make the issue less serious; it just gives people more perspective. When we laugh at ourselves, we treat ourselves with compassion. Humor can be a powerful way to help people learn. **The key mutual learning principle is to laugh with others, not at others.**

Look for Missing Positive Emotions

Some groups have a group or organizational culture that doesn't value or believe in expressing positive emotions. A number of years ago, as a member of such a group, I heard the leader announce that one member had just received a prestigious award; the members agreed it was deserved and were delighted he had received it. Yet, when the leader made the announcement, no one applauded or cheered. In fact, no one said anything. My untested inference was that members felt awkward in openly expressing their positive feelings about another member.

If you observe that group members are not expressing positive emotions, you can share your observation and infer what meaning people make of this. Your intervention may lead to an important conversation about group values and norms.

WHEN PEOPLE GET ANGRY WITH YOU

Sometimes you're the subject of the group's emotions: They get angry with you. They may think you've acted ineffectively, or they may be redirecting their emotions toward you. As soon as you infer that a group member is feeling negatively toward you, it's critical to test your inference. If the inference is correct, then you're in what I call facilitator check. In the game of chess, if the other player has put your king in check, you can't make any other moves until you get your king out of check. In your facilitative role, you won't be able to work effectively until you resolve this issue with the group.

You might say, "From your frown and head shaking I'm thinking that you're frustrated with me; am I correct?" If the member agrees, you can start to identify the cause of the frustration: "I don't mean to do anything that will frustrate you, but I might be doing something I'm not aware of. Can you tell me what I said or did that led you to get frustrated with me?" After the group member describes your behavior, the members and you can jointly decide whether you have in fact behaved as the member described; if so, decide whether your behavior was inconsistent with the core values and ground rules.

If you've acted effectively, then you can help the group member explore what leads to his emotional reaction, as I described earlier in this chapter. If you've acted ineffectively, then you contributed to generating the member's emotional reaction. Acknowledge this, and commit to change your behavior in the future. In basic facilitation or consulting, you can simply identify what you will do differently in the future.

In the developmental form after you apologize, you can also ask the group member what led him not to say anything after seeing the group repeatedly go off task. By pursuing this, it's important to explain that you aren't trying to reduce your own accountability. Rather, you're helping the group become more independent by exploring why members don't intervene with the group when they believe it is necessary ("Sheryl, if you noticed that several times the group was off task and I didn't intervene, and you thought it would be helpful to intervene, I'm curious what led you not to intervene.").

LEARNING FROM YOUR EXPERIENCES

We aren't omniscient. If you haven't yet started in a facilitative role, expect at times to be stumped. If you're already working, you surely know the feeling. There are times when your intuition tells you that something is wrong, but you can't identify any group behavior to make a diagnosis. Or, having identified the problem, you may be uncertain about how to intervene. When this happens, consider asking the group for help: "I'm stumped. I think the group is having a problem, but I can't figure out what it is, and I also can't point to any behavior that leads me to conclude this. Does anyone else see something?" Although it's not helpful to the group if you intervene like this frequently, using it occasionally can use the group's skills to allow you to see things you are missing.

Even when you act ineffectively, you can create a learning opportunity for the group and yourself. By publicly acknowledging how you have acted ineffectively, you model accountability without defensiveness. I try to not act ineffectively, of course, but I have been surprised to find that some group members' most memorable learning has come from my publicly reflecting with the group on my ineffective behavior.

Through our work we come to know ourselves by reflecting on how we react to certain situations, understanding the source of our emotions, and learning how to work productively with our feelings. In doing so, we not only help ourselves but also increase our ability to help the groups we work with.

SUMMARY

In this chapter, I have explored how to deal with emotions that arise in our facilitative roles—for the group members and for you. Dealing productively with emotion is difficult because there are physiological reasons for emotion overriding rational thinking. Helping a group deal with emotion means showing group members how to use their emotions and thinking to inform each other, rather than avoid emotions or allow them to control the conversation; it also means helping group members express their emotions productively. Because you are susceptible to the same emotional reactions as the group members, you can do a number of things to manage your own emotions during your work.

When you intervene on group members' emotions, you can help them both express their emotions effectively and learn to reduce the defensive thinking that leads to ineffective emotional response. You can also help the group learn to express "positive" emotions as well. Finally, managing your own emotions includes responding effectively if a group member gets angry at you and being able to frame the situation as an opportunity for learning—for you and the group. Clearly, it's important to have an explicit agreement with the group about what kind of intervention you will make regarding emotion. In the next chapter, I will describe how to develop an explicit agreement with the group about how you will work together.

PART THREE

AGREEING TO WORK TOGETHER

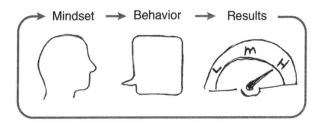

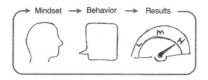

CHAPTER THIRTEEN

Contracting

Deciding Whether and How to Work with a Group

I n this chapter, I discuss the contracting stages that you and your clients go through to develop an agreement about whether and how you will work together to help the group accomplish its goals. For each of the stages, I discuss the issues that often arise and how to address them.

Before you agree to work with a group, you want to understand who is asking for help, what the group wants to accomplish, what might prevent it from achieving those objectives, and how the group sees you helping it. Likewise, the group often wants to know about your experience and how you can help it. **Through the *contracting* process, you and the client begin to develop a working relationship by exploring these questions, and you reach an agreement about whether and how to work together.**

During the contracting process, you and the client develop the foundation of your working relationship. **This contracting approach rests on the premise that only the primary client—the group you will be facilitating—has the relevant information to contract with you.** You and your client invest time in the contracting process, recognizing that ineffective contracting almost always leads to problems later.

WHY CONTRACT?

Contracting has several purposes. First, it ensures that the group and you understand and are committed to the conditions that govern your working relationship. This means clarifying expectations each of you have for each other: the objectives and boundaries of the work your role and the roles of group members and the formal group leader, how decisions will be made, how you will intervene with the group, any ground rules the group will use, issues of confidentiality, and when the work ends.

Second, because contracting is a microcosm of the larger facilitation, consulting, or coaching, it gives the group members and you an opportunity to observe each other work and to make a somewhat informed choice about whether you want to work with one another. Members can observe how you intervene with the group, and you can observe how they interact with each other and with you. These data help you anticipate some of the issues arising in the project and the kinds of interventions you may need to make.

Third, the contracting process enables the group and you to develop the trust necessary for you to serve in your facilitative role. This trust emerges from a variety of feelings. Group members may wonder whether you will treat them fairly, if you can help them create the future they want, and/or address the difficult conversations they haven't been able to manage effectively on their own. They may be excited about the possibility of improving their group and may feel vulnerable both for needing help in the first place and because you're asking questions about the group. Likewise, you may be excited to be working with a new group, eager to see how you can help it, and somewhat anxious about whether you will like the group and the group will like you. Trust develops as members find that you can help them discuss important topics in a way that doesn't place blame and that combines compassion and accountability, even while recognizing the ineffectiveness of the group's behaviors. As you learn about their situation and they learn about your approach, often your concerns about whether you can help them and whether they will find your approach useful dissipate.

I've learned that many of the problems I face during a project stem from my not having addressed an issue in contracting. **Ineffective contracting creates problems later in the work.**

FIVE STAGES OF CONTRACTING

We usually think of contracting as occurring between the time you initially speak with someone from the client organization seeking the help and the time

Stage	Major Tasks
1. Making initial contact with a primary group member	1. Identify and talk with a member of the primary client group and financial client. 2. Conduct initial diagnosis. 3. Discuss approach to facilitation. 4. Agree on whether to proceed to stage 2. If so . . .
2. Planning the facilitation	1. Set up a meeting for stage 2. 2. Before the meeting, send letter to planning group about purpose and agenda for planning meeting. 3. Before the meeting, identify financial client and arrange for her to share information with the primary client group and you. 4. Conduct diagnosis with full group or representatives of primary client group. 5. Agree on facilitation purpose, objectives, agenda, ground rules, and other elements. 6. Send tentative agreement to full client group.
3. Reaching agreement with the full primary client group	1. Identify any changes in conditions before actual facilitation occurs. 2. Agree on objectives, identify expectations, and address any concerns. 3. Agree on the agenda and time allocation. 4. Agree on the process, including ground rules. 5. Define roles.
4. Recontracting during facilitation	1. Continually check for facilitation challenges that may be caused by ineffective contracting or by changing circumstances. 2. Raise these issues with the full primary group and contract and/or recontract as necessary.
5. Completing and evaluating the facilitation	1. Evaluate the effectiveness of the facilitation, including the contracting process.

Exhibit 13.1 Contracting Stages and Major Tasks

the client group and you reach agreement about the goals of the facilitation and the conditions under which you and the group are to work together. That describes the predictable part of the contracting process. In addition, you'll likely need to contract and recontract throughout the facilitation process itself.

Exhibit 13.1 shows the five contracting stages. **Because the agreement defines how the group and you will work together, ultimately all members**

involved directly in the facilitation need to be part of the agreement. This ensures that all members are making an informed choice.

STAGE 1: MAKING INITIAL CONTACT WITH A PRIMARY CLIENT GROUP MEMBER

Stage 1 begins when someone contacts you to explore your facilitating a group he or she is associated with. You may be contacted by e-mail, text, or phone. The heart of this stage occurs either on a phone or video call, or an in-person meeting. In any case, the conversation may take from less than 15 minutes to more than an hour, depending on whether the person contacting you is a member of the group you will be facilitating; how complex the situation is; and on how much the client understands about facilitation in general, and your approach in particular.

Stage 1 has a number of purposes. First, it lets you determine whether the contact person is part of the group asking for help and, as a result, whether and how to continue the initial discussion. It also enables you to identify who the financial client is—the person responsible for paying for the services. Second, it enables you to make an initial diagnosis of the client's situation, to understand the extent to which the client contact can describe the results the group wants, and the degree to which the client has already identified ways to address its needs. Third, the conversation gives the potential client information about your approach. Fourth, you and the contact client use all of the information you have learned from each other to decide whether to move to stage 2 of contracting.

Recognizing Different Types of Clients

As you begin to contract, you'll encounter people who play different roles in the contracting process. It's important to recognize what role each of these people is playing to ensure that you're contracting with—and only with—the people who have the information and ability to contract with you. You may encounter as many as five different client roles.

The *primary client* is the group that has accepted responsibility for working on the issue—the group that you may eventually facilitate. **To ensure that the primary client group and you have relevant and valid information about the situation and that this group can make an informed choice about working with you, only the primary client group can agree to work with you.**

However, as Edgar Schein has noted, you encounter other kinds of clients who may or may not also be members of the primary client group (Figure 13.1).[1] The *contact client* makes the initial contact with you. The contact client may be a staff member or an administrative assistant who is not a member of the primary

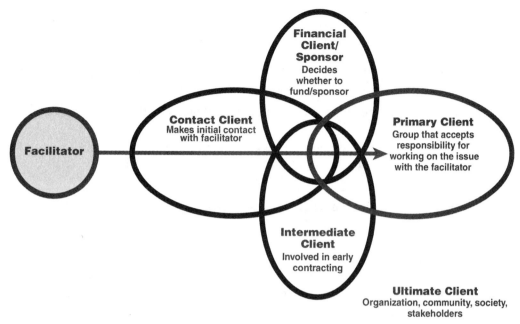

Figure 13.1   Five Types of Clients

client group but who has been asked to contact a facilitator or consultant on behalf of the primary client. An *intermediate client* serves as a link between the contact client and the primary client and is involved in the early part of contracting. You might get a call from an administrative assistant (contact client) who asks whether you're available to help her manager work with a group experiencing conflict. In conversation with the manager, it becomes clear that the manager is an intermediate client, not seeking help for himself but for a group of employees. HR managers frequently serve as intermediate clients, helping find a consultant for the leaders and teams they support. The *financial client/sponsor* is the person who decides whether to fund the facilitation and support it. This may be two different people.

Finally, the *ultimate clients* are "stakeholders whose interests should be protected even if they're not in direct contact with the consultant or manager."[2] The ultimate clients include the organization as a whole, the customers who use the services of the organization or buy its products, and the larger community or society. As Figure 13.1 shows, an individual may fall into more than one client category.

Working with the Contact Client

Because only the primary client group has the information necessary and the ability to contract with you, it's important to quickly determine whether the contact client is a member of the primary client group. You determine this by

1. Who is seeking the services?
2. Are you a member of this group?
3. Has the group committed to particular times for the work?
4. What has the group already planned for this work?
5. What does the group want to accomplish? What leads the group to want to accomplish this?
6. Is the group seeking to plan, address problems/challenges, or both? Can you describe the planning the group wants to do and/or some examples of the problems/challenges the group is experiencing?

Exhibit 13.2   Questions to Ask the Contact Client

asking what group would be using your services and whether the caller is a member of that group. After you've determined this, you can ask a series of questions and share relevant information. Exhibit 13.2 lists the questions to ask a contact client.

If you learn that the contact client isn't a member of the primary client group, you ask who the primary client group is, explain why you need to talk with a member of that group, and give the contact client sufficient general information about yourself to share with the primary client, who can decide whether to contact you.

Identifying the Primary Client Group

Determining who is the primary client isn't always easy. In one case, Ken, a county manager, called me to seek help for his public works director, Harris; some employees felt Harris had acted in a racist manner when he fired an African-American employee. Ken stated that Harris was interested in getting help and asked if I would come in, interview people, and give him (Ken) a report. I described my role and explained how giving him a report would be inconsistent with my role as facilitator. I then said that if Harris was interested in working with me, I would be happy to talk with him. I stated that if I did work with Harris, Ken was, of course, free to talk with Harris about the facilitation, but I wouldn't discuss the content of the facilitation with Ken. Because Ken had described Harris and his staff as having the problem, I defined my primary client as the group that included Harris and his employees.

In another case, Warren, an HR executive from a global bank, called to see if I could help Eduardo, a senior executive, and Helene, one of Eduardo's direct reports. The employees who reported to Helene and Eduardo considered Helene autocratic. Eduardo also believed he needed to improve his own relationship with Helene. In this case, Eduardo was a primary client because he had expressed responsibility for part of the problem—his relationship with Helene. Helene's employees were also primary clients because they were willing to discuss their ineffective relationship with their boss. However, Helene was only potentially a primary client, because she hadn't yet expressed an interest in working on the problem identified by her boss. The principle here is that **individuals are not primary clients until they've made a free and informed choice to ask for the facilitator's help**.

When There Is No Primary Client. In some cases, the contact client may represent a primary group that doesn't yet exist. The executive director of a health care foundation called to ask whether I was interested in facilitating a large commission to deal with health policy. The commission would comprise public and private leaders, and its report would be used to draft legislation. The foundation would appoint the commission, but no members had yet been appointed, nor had the commission chair been selected. Further, no member of the foundation, including the executive director, would be a member of the commission, so there was no primary client. I talked with the executive director about how I could work with the commission, but I stated that the commission members, when appointed, would need to decide whether they wanted to work with me.

This type of situation isn't unusual. Organizational planners, working on projects that may use a third-party facilitator, often try to identify a facilitator who can be available to the group immediately after it is formed.

After determining that the contact client isn't a primary client, you might say something like, "I'd be glad to talk with you in general about what I do as a facilitator. However, to figure out whether I can be of help to your organization, I would need to talk with the person who heads the group I'll be meeting with. This gives the person and me a chance to make sure that we clearly understand the situation. Do you see any problem in doing this?"

On the basis of the principle that **the primary client is responsible for seeking help**, I prefer that primary clients call me if they are still interested. This reduces the chance that I will call a primary client who isn't ready to pursue the conversation with me.

When the Contact Client Is a Primary Client Group Member. When the contact client is a member of the primary client group, consider yourself fortunate that you don't have to solve the can-you-find-the-primary-client puzzle. You use the initial conversation and the questions in Exhibit 13.3 to begin to understand the client's situation, identify factors that might affect the success of the facilitation, determine whether you have the skills and interest to facilitate, and discuss your approach to facilitation.

Opportunity-Oriented Issues

1. What are you trying to create? Does this exist in some form currently? If, so what does it look like?
2. What has led the group to create this now? How will creating this have an impact on people and on things that are happening in your group and organization?
3. What barriers do you or others anticipate facing as the group seeks to create this? What is in place in your group or organization that will help the group create this?

Identifying Problems

4. Describe to me the problems the group is having. What are some specific examples?
5. What do members in the group do (or not do) that you see as a problem? What are some specific examples?
6. How widespread are the problems? Do they occur all the time or only under certain conditions or with certain individuals?
7. When did the problems begin? What else was occurring at that time or shortly before the problems began?
8. In what ways do members contribute to the problems? In what ways do you contribute to the problems?

Effects of Problems on the Three Group Results

9. What are the consequences of these problems? How do the problems affect the group's ability to produce quality products or deliver quality services? Work together? Meet individual members' needs? What are some specific examples?

Potential Design Causes—Process, Structure, Organizational Context

10. What do you think are the causes of the problems? What have you seen or heard that leads you to think this?
11. What are the tasks around which the team is interdependent? How do they manage this interdependence? How do they solve problems and make decisions? Communicate and manage conflict? Coordinate its work with others in the organization? Do any of these seem related to the problems you described? If so, how?
12. Does the group have clear goals? Are members motivated by their tasks? Does the group have the right kind of members to do its work? What kinds of behaviors do members expect of each other? What are the core values and assumptions that members share about work? Do any of these seem related to the problems you have described? If so, how?
13. In what ways does the organization help or hinder the group? Does the larger organization have a clear mission and shared vision? Is the culture supportive of the team? How are group members rewarded? Does the group get enough information to do its work? Enough training and other resources? Appropriate physical space to work in? Do any of these seem related to the problems you described? How?
14. What's the history of the group? How has the membership and leadership changed?
15. How do you think other people in the group would identify the problems and their causes? Would others disagree?

Exhibit 13.3   Questions for Diagnosing the Primary Client Situation

Motivation and Resources for Change

16. What have you tried to do to improve the situation? What were the results?
17. Why do members want to work with a facilitator? How motivated is each member?
18. What are the group's strengths? How does the group act in ways that are effective?

Experience with Facilitators and Current Request for Help

19. Have you used other facilitators in the past, either for this situation or others? What role did the facilitators play? What were the results? What did the facilitators do that members found helpful or not helpful?
20. What has led you to contact someone now? What has happened or is about to happen in the group or organization?
21. What led you to call me? Who initiated it? How was it received by other group members?
22. How do you see me helping the group accomplish its objectives?
23. What criteria will you use to determine whether you want to hire me as the facilitator? What information do you need to determine this?
24. Who needs to approve the funds for the facilitation?

Measuring Success and Return on Investment

25. If you achieve your goals, how will you describe the value to the group? To the organization? What's the financial value of this?
26. How will you know when you have been successful?
27. How will you measure this?
28. What is the cost, if any, of not being successful?

Exhibit 13.3   Questions for Diagnosing the Primary Client Situation (*continued*)

Some primary clients aren't sure what kind of help they need. Others have already defined the problem or opportunity, have identified a specific process for you to facilitate, and want to know whether you can deliver the service they're requesting. In the latter case, you're more useful to the client if you explore with them how they reached their diagnosis and proposed process. This enables you to make your own judgment about the situation and talk with the clients about how your views may differ.

For example, a manager asked that I work with him and his board to develop funding priorities for the county. The manager said the board functioned by funding projects piecemeal, without a consensus on a larger set of goals. In our conversation, the manager also said that his relationship with the board was strained. The board had circumvented his hiring authority and excluded him from other important decisions. It became clear to me that the strained relationship between the manager and board would make it difficult for the group to set funding priorities. The manager agreed with me but was reluctant to discuss the relationship, fearing the situation would become worse. After discussing what could be done to reduce his concerns, he agreed to discuss the relationship with the board. Had I accepted the manager's definition of the problem, I would have worked with the board without understanding the full problem and thereby hindered the chance of their accomplishing the task.

So that clients don't misinterpret the reason for your questions, it's important to share your reasoning with them. After clients briefly describe their situation, you might say, "To figure out whether and how I can help you, I'd like to ask you some questions that improve my understanding of your situation and how you see it. Then I can share my thoughts with you and get your reaction. How does that sound as a next step?"

Conducting an Initial Diagnosis

Whether a group seeks help to solve problems or seize opportunities (for example, acquire another organization or expand its products or services), Exhibit 13.3 lists questions you can ask in the initial conversation with the primary client member. The questions help you identify the client's problem or opportunity, the impact on the group, and the potential causes of the issue or change. They also explore the client's motivation and resources for change, as well as experience the client has had with facilitators and how the current request for help came about. You don't need to ask all of these questions for each client; select them according to the client's situation. You may need to modify some questions according to the specific purpose of the facilitation.

The goal at this stage isn't to develop a complete diagnosis of the client's situation—that's impossible to achieve in one conversation—but to begin the diagnosis and determine whether facilitation is an appropriate method for helping the client. A skilled facilitator is flexible enough to begin diagnosing where the client begins the story, rather than requiring the client to respond in the facilitator's preset order of the questions. In fact, **a general principle underlying diagnosis and intervention is to begin with the client's interests and concerns.**

The questions about problems, effects on results, and potential causes, which are based on the Team Effectiveness Model I described in Chapter 6, enable you to quickly get an initial understanding of the team. The questions about problems don't correspond to a particular element of the model. Instead, they give clients a chance to begin describing the problem as they see it.

By learning how previous facilitators worked with the group and how the group found those facilitators helpful or not helpful, you can quickly identify what the group might expect from you. You can also start to explore whether you would be a better fit for the group than the previous facilitators they've used.

Understanding how the client came to contact you is also useful information. Knowing who referred the client to you is information about the client's expectations. Finding out whose idea it was to contact you, how the idea was received, and who was involved in deciding to make the contact can also offer information regarding support for you and for facilitation in general.

Describing Your Approach to Facilitation

At some point during the conversation, it's important to describe your approach to facilitation so that the client can make an informed choice about whether the client wants to continue exploring working with you. This includes describing exactly how you would help the group accomplish its goals, explaining why you would do it that way, how you see your role as facilitator, distinguishing between basic and developmental facilitation if it's relevant, and explaining how all this translates into working with the client given the client's situation. The challenge is to describe your approach so that the client gets a clear picture of what you would say and do and why you would do it—all without using facilitation jargon.

By describing your approach in the latter part of the conversation, you're able to refer to some of the issues the client raised with you, and you can refer to your own behavior in the conversation to describe how you would work with the group. You might say:

> I'd like to describe how I work as a facilitator and get your reaction. As a neutral party, I don't offer my opinion about the content of your discussions, but I will help the group have the most productive conversation it can have. I'll do a number of things to help that happen. For example, you mentioned that group members often dig in to their preferred solutions and as a result have a hard time making decisions. One thing I would do is help the group members step back from their solutions and identify the underlying needs they're trying to meet through their solution so they're better able to come up with solutions that work for the whole group.
>
> I would also help the group manage its time effectively and efficiently. That means that if I think members are going off the track that they said they wanted to be on, I would point it out, but they would decide how to spend their time. When I think members aren't agreeing on what important words mean, such as *strategy* or *authorization*, I'll help them reach a common understanding so there won't be misunderstandings. I'll help members explain the reasoning behind their comments so everyone can better understand what everyone's thinking. I was explaining my reasoning earlier when I explained why I was asking you the questions that I was asking. If I think people are making assumptions about the situation or about each other, I'll help them test out those assumptions so they'll know whether or not they are accurate. This will increase the team's ability to

make decisions based on solid information. I tested an inference with you a few minutes ago: I asked if you had asked Alan whether he thought you were micromanaging the group or whether you were just guessing that he felt that way.

In short, I'll help team members be transparent about what they're thinking and be curious about what others are thinking so the team can make informed decisions that ideally everyone can commit to. What are your thoughts about how I would work with your group?

If the group is seeking developmental facilitation, I offer a much more detailed explanation and have a conversation with the client group about whether it wants to learn this approach to build its own capacity.

Assessing Your Interest and Ability to Help

Assuming that facilitation is appropriate for the client's request, during the initial conversation you tell the primary client whether you have the ability to help and whether you're interested. Facilitators sometimes have types of work they prefer to do and types of work they choose not to do. Some facilitators choose not to work with a group that seeks to accomplish objectives at odds with their own strongly held values and beliefs. If you believe strongly that women have the right to control their reproductive lives, you may not be interested in facilitating a group that is seeking ways to make abortion illegal. Likewise, if you believe that life begins at conception and that the rights of that life take precedence over a woman's right to control her reproductive life, you may not be interested in facilitating a group that is seeking ways to increase women's access to abortion. Whatever your values and beliefs, it's important to be aware of how they may affect your interest in working with particular client groups and/or your ability to remain neutral.

Summarizing and Agreeing on Next Steps

After you have enough information to make an initial diagnosis, share it with the member and ask if she sees anything differently. Assuming the issues are appropriate for facilitation and you're interested and able to help, describe how you think you can be most effective with the group, and then ask for the client's reactions.

This is also the time to discuss any decisions or tentative decisions the client group has made that are likely to reduce its ability to achieve its stated objectives and to ask whether the client group is willing to reconsider those decisions. For example, you may note that the group has allocated insufficient time for the objectives it wants to accomplish. Or you may point out that excluding certain individuals is likely to reduce the group's ability to actively discuss the issues on which it seeks consensus. If any group decision is likely to reduce the group's effectiveness to the point where you're unwilling to facilitate unless the decision is changed, state that, share your reasoning, and ask the client if she is open to discussing this.

Finally, you and the client agree on the next steps. If the client is interested in pursuing your help, the next step is for the client to discuss your conversation with the full primary client group. If the group is interested, the contact client can arrange a conference call or meeting with either the primary client group representatives or the full group and you.

STAGE 2: PLANNING THE FACILITATION

The planning stage is similar to your stage 1 conversation with the primary client group member. The differences are that you're having the conversation with a group and you're actually planning the facilitation. Ideally, this planning meeting occurs in person, but videoconference calls or even phone conference calls can be used. The meeting usually lasts about two hours.

The purposes of this stage are to (1) continue to explore the client's request for help and the factors that affect facilitation, (2) tentatively plan the agenda, and (3) agree on conditions for the facilitation. In the planning session (or sessions, if you need more than one), the client group and you discuss the same kind of information that the primary client member and you discussed in your initial conversation. You also discuss and agree on the conditions of the facilitation and logistical issues: questions that are listed in Exhibit 13.4.

Before the planning meeting, you send a brief letter to the primary group members (through the initial primary group contact) asking that it be distributed to all members invited to attend the planning meeting. (Exhibit 13.5 presents a sample letter.) The letter explains the reason for the planning meeting, the objectives, and offers a proposed agenda for the planning meeting (not the facilitation itself). I usually include an electronic copy of two of my articles: "How to Hire a Team Facilitator," which describes what to look for when hiring a facilitator, and "Eight Behaviors for Smarter Teams," which describes the mutual learning behaviors I use as a facilitator and the behaviors I will ask the group if they want to use also.[3] Both articles are free to download on the Roger Schwarz & Associates website: www.schwarzassociates.com/resources/articles.

Who Should Be Involved in the Planning Meeting?

If feasible, it's best to have the full primary client group involved in the planning meeting. This enables you to watch (or listen to) how the full group works together, which is the group you'll be facilitating. It also increases the

1. Who is the primary client, and who will attend meetings?
2. What are the objectives of the meetings?
3. What is the agenda for the meetings or at least for the initial meeting?
4. Where and how long will the group meet?
5. What are the roles of the different parties?
    a. Facilitator?
    b. Formal leader?
    c. Members?
    d. Others available to provide information?
    e. Observers?
6. What ground rules will the group follow?
    a. What ground rules do participants commit to follow in the meetings?
    b. Is the group interested in using the mutual learning behaviors?
    c. Will the group make decisions? If so, what decision-making rule will be used for each decision?
    d. What will be the confidentiality agreement within the group?
    e. What will be the confidentiality agreement between the facilitator and the group?
7. How will the group assess its progress during the facilitation?
8. How will the facilitator receive feedback on his or her performance?
9. What are the facilitator's fees and other charges?
10. How long will the contract be in effect?
11. Under what conditions can the contract be changed?
12. How and when will the tentative contract be conveyed to all members of the group?

Exhibit 13.4   Questions for Developing an Effective Agreement

---

To:	Executive Leadership Team
Through:	Julius Marx, CEO
From:	Roger Schwarz, President
Re:	Planning Meeting for Executive Leadership Team Off-site
Date:	October 14, 2016

I am looking forward to meeting with you on November 4, 2016, from 9:00 AM to 11:00 AM to begin planning your executive leadership team off-site on December 5 and 6, 2016. Julius Marx called me last week and asked if I could facilitate the off-site planning meeting. Julius described the team's current situation and its needs, and I explained how I could help the team accomplish its off-site goals.

I've asked for the planning meeting for three purposes: (1) To give you enough information to decide as a team whether you want me to facilitate the off-site meeting, (2) to learn enough about your team for me to decide whether I can provide the

Exhibit 13.5   Sample Planning Meeting E-Mail

facilitation help you need, and (3) if we decide to work together, to identify the off-site objectives, a general agenda, how we will work together, and logistical issues. Below is my proposed agenda for the planning meeting; please see if there are any changes you want to make so that we can address them at the beginning of the meeting.

I have attached copies of two articles: "Hiring and Working with a Group Facilitator" and "Eight Behaviors for Smarter Teams." The first article briefly describes my approach to working with teams; the second article describes a set of behaviors that I use to help team members work together effectively. Please read the articles before the meeting so that we can explore any questions or concerns you have about how we would work together.

If you would like more information about Roger Schwarz & Associates, our approach to facilitation, or me, you may want to visit www.schwarzassociates.com.

Proposed Agenda for Executive Leadership Team Off-site Planning Meeting
November 4, 2016, 9:00–11:00 AM

1. Introductions
2. What changes should we make to the proposed agenda below?
3. Bringing everyone up to date: What conversations have occurred regarding the off-site? (Julius, followed by Roger)
4. How would you describe the purpose of the off-site?
   a. What leads you to want to hold an off-site now?
   b. What opportunities and problems are you facing now that may be relevant for the off-site?
   c. What outcomes do you need to accomplish to consider the off-site a success?
5. What questions do you have about my approach to facilitation?
   a. What led you to consider having me facilitate your off-site?
   b. Have you used other facilitators in the past? If so, what did they do that you found useful or not useful?
   c. How do you see me helping the group accomplish its objectives?
   d. Given our discussion, do you want me to facilitate your off-site?
   e. Do you need to get approval from anyone else to have me facilitate or to approve funds for the facilitation?
6. What will be the general agenda and schedule for the off-site?
   a. To accomplish your objectives of the off-site, what questions does the group need to answer during the meeting?
   b. What are the starting and ending times?
   c. Where will the off-site be held?

Exhibit 13.5   Sample Planning Meeting E-Mail (*continued*)

7. Who will attend the off-site?
   a. Who needs to attend the off-site for the group to have the relevant information and support necessary to achieve its objectives?
   b. What preparation is necessary in order for members to use their time efficiently and effectively in the meeting?
   c. Under what conditions will we agree to reschedule the off-site?
8. What will be the facilitator's, group leader's, and others' roles during the off-site?
   a. Does the group want to try to use the mutual learning behaviors during the off-site?
9. Is there anything we haven't discussed that we need to address at this point?
10. What next steps do we need to take?

Exhibit 13.5   Sample Planning Meeting E-Mail (*continued*)

chance that you'll hear and be able to resolve any differing views among team members about what the facilitation purpose, process, and your facilitative role should be.

In basic facilitation, if the entire group is unable to attend the planning meeting, then you can ask for a representative subset of the group to be selected. The key word here is *representative*, which I explain below. In developmental facilitation and in long-term basic facilitation (that is, basic facilitation lasting more than a few sessions), in which the group is making a significant commitment of time, it's important that all members of the client group be involved in the contracting process after the initial contact. In any case, until the whole group concurs, all agreements between the primary client group representatives and you are tentative.

Finding a Representative Subgroup. If the entire primary client group can't attend the planning meeting, then it's essential that the subgroup that attends is representative of the full group. By *representative*, I mean the subgroup includes people who together reflect the range and intensity of the differences in the full group that will be relevant to the facilitation. This increases the chance that you and the planning subgroup will have all the relevant information necessary to craft an agenda that the full group can support. If the subgroup isn't representative, those whose views are omitted may not attend the facilitation itself, let alone support decisions made during it.

The subgroup doesn't have to be representative of the full group in every way; only on those dimensions that are relevant to the facilitation. For example, a board of education and its superintendent once asked me to facilitate a meeting regarding the superintendent's performance after the board had voted (four to three) to reduce the superintendent's salary supplement. In this case, the client asked me to work with a subgroup comprising the superintendent and the board chair. However, it was critical to represent two other stakeholders for planning: the groups voting for and against reducing the salary. Because the chair had voted to reduce the salary, we added a member who had influenced others to vote against reducing the salary.

The Problem with the Formal Leader Delegating the Planning to Others. Problems sometimes occur when the formal leader of the group delegates the planning to others. The secretary of a state agency had delegated planning for a retreat of the top 60 leaders to a deputy secretary and a planning manager, both of whom were members of the primary client group. After my initial contact with the planning manager, I reluctantly agreed to plan the retreat with the planning manager and deputy director, with the condition that we would jointly meet with the secretary for the final planning session. In the first two planning meetings, the planning manager and deputy director emphasized that the secretary wanted the retreat to focus on long-term planning. However, in the final planning meeting, in which the deputy secretary, planning manager, and I presented the tentative plan to the secretary, the secretary emphasized the need to focus on building an effective team, given a recent reorganization. As a result, we had to redesign the retreat, which cost the organization more time and effort.

In retrospect, I contributed to the contracting problem. By planning with the deputy secretary and planning director, who were responsible for the retreat, I was trying to honor the division of labor in the organization. But by doing so, I failed to test whether their assumptions about the retreat were the same as the secretary's. We would have quickly discovered the different assumptions and been able to get agreement on them if all of us had met in the beginning of the planning process or if we had sent the secretary an e-mail testing our assumptions.

In some cases, the planning is delegated to an internal consultant who isn't part of the primary client group. An internal Organization Development consultant from a pharmaceutical firm asked me to work with one of the leadership teams he supported. He knew of my work and liked my approach to facilitation, but when I suggested that our next step would be to talk with either the head of the leadership team or the full team, he declined my request. He said that it was his job to contract on behalf of his client and her team. I responded that my interest was to ensure that his client and I—and ultimately the full team—had the relevant information necessary to figure out whether and how to work together and that the only way I knew of achieving that goal was for us to talk directly. I added that I would prefer for him to be part of that conversation. He insisted that he could represent his client and the team, and that I couldn't speak with them before we agreed on the work. I declined to work with him and the leadership he supported.

The principle here is that the planning stage process must allow the facilitator to directly understand and explore the formal leader's relevant information, interests, and assumptions that guide her need for the services she is requesting. Without this access, the facilitator will likely make uninformed choices that will create problems for the group and the facilitator.

Meeting Individually with Group Members and the Problem of Confidentiality. Sometimes clients ask you to meet individually with group members before you meet with the full group. You're likely to receive this type of request when the group is experiencing conflict and mistrust. Once I was asked to facilitate a meeting of the executive director and key individuals in a public health research organization. The executive director asked for my help in part because several incidents in the organization had led her to believe that people didn't trust her. Even before the planning meeting, the executive director told me that individuals would prefer to meet with me individually to discuss the retreat.

In another case, I was asked to facilitate resolution of a dispute between a developer and a town council that was being sued by the developer for not approving a subdivision plan. If the facilitation was successful, the developer would withdraw the lawsuit. The town council wanted to meet with me individually (in a session legally closed to the public) to assess my acceptability to them and to share their concerns with me. The attorney for the developers also wanted to talk with me privately to see whether I was acceptable to her client.

Many facilitators also prefer to meet with individuals before meeting with the full group. But if you meet with group members individually, you can quickly become entangled in and reinforce the group's ineffective dynamics. The facilitator and group members see the meetings as an opportunity for the facilitator to learn how different members think about the group and the challenges it's facing. The facilitator considers these meetings rich diagnostic interviews that can shape the agenda for the group and even for the interventions the facilitator may make. The facilitator reasons that group members will be more forthcoming in individual meetings, especially if they are promised confidentiality, than in the full group meeting—and the facilitator is correct. By the end of these interviews, the facilitator has become the central repository for members' hopes, dreams, and fears about the group. The facilitator may now know more about the group than the group does.

But when you offer confidentiality in this situation, you create a three-horned dilemma that leads you to act incongruently with the mutual learning core values of transparency, informed choice, and accountability. The first horn is this: If you honor the individual confidential conversations, you can't share with the group what individuals said and you certainly can't share who said it. That means if you use any of the information during the facilitation to make an intervention or suggest a process, you can't fully share your reasoning for it. This fails the transparency test. Because members know that you've met with them and others before the meeting, your lack of transparency makes it easy for group members to make high-level inferences about what others told you that led you to intervene the way you did. In short, you're now contributing to potential conflict and mistrust in the group.

For the second horn, even if you obtain permission to share information from the individual sessions, you're still reducing group members' accountability to each other by raising for them the issues that are theirs to raise. In short, you're carrying group members' water.

If you don't meet with members individually, you avoid these problems, but now face the third horn of the dilemma: your concern that you won't find out about important group issues or dynamics until you begin the actual facilitation, and some issues may not get raised at all by group members.

Managing the Three-Horned Dilemma of Confidentiality. There is a way to manage the dilemma of individual meetings. If members ask for individual meetings, it's likely they're facing conflict and mistrust and don't know how to raise these issues safely. The solution lies in jointly creating the conditions for members to say in the group what they want to but feel they cannot say.

You can ask to talk first with the members as a group. You can raise the dilemma that the group and you face, talk with members about their concerns regarding sharing information in the full planning session or facilitation, and ask what leads to these concerns. If members are willing to share some of their concerns, you can then ask, "What would need to happen for you to be willing to raise and address these concerns in the full group?" If group members—including the formal leader—agree to create these conditions (for example, no retaliation for raising an issue), they can then discuss issues that they previously chose not to discuss.

However, if members still don't want to continue planning in the full group, you might agree to talk to individuals or a subgroup if the planning group (1) agreed on how the information discussed in private meetings would be shared in the full group and (2) agreed that the responsibility for raising issues remained with group members. The purpose of these individual sessions would be for you to coach members on whether and how to raise these issues. You help them explore how they can raise the issues they want to discuss, including their concerns about doing so. You can also role-play with them to find the words to do this. You can make the same promise to all group members: "I can't raise your concern for you, but as soon as *you* raise your concern, I will do everything in my role to make the conversation as psychologically safe and productive as possible."

Ultimately, each member gets to make a free and informed choice about what to share and what not to. As facilitators, our role is to respect that choice, even if we would make a different one. **A nonobvious but powerful implication of combining informed choice, accountability, and the principle "go slow to go fast" is that we serve the group better when we ask each member to control what he or she shares and doesn't share with the group**. This may take more time, but it ensures that the group moves no faster than it chooses to move.

Deciding What Ground Rules to Use and How

Ground rules are the rules the group commits to follow when you're working with it. Because the mutual learning approach has a set of eight behaviors that can be used as ground rules, you and the group have three decisions to make.

Three Decisions. First, the members must decide whether they're willing to have you use the eight behaviors to intervene with them. This decision is really about whether they want to work with you at all because it's not possible to use the mutual learning approach without using the eight behaviors. If the group were to tell me that they didn't want me to use the eight behaviors (this has never happened), I would find out what the group's concerns were, and if I couldn't address their concerns, then I would decline the work.

The second decision for the group members to make is whether they want to practice the behaviors during their work with you. The group can revisit this choice if, after practicing and understanding them better, members have new concerns about using them.

In the course of making the first two decisions, the group and you make a third decision: whether to add or modify any ground rules. A group might add a ground rule about whether the information discussed in the meeting is confidential. It's important that any changes or additions be consistent with the underlying mutual learning core values and assumptions. Even if group members decide not to treat one of the eight behaviors as a ground rule, you can still intervene on that behavior if it's decreasing the group's effectiveness.

To help group members make a more informed choice about whether they want to use the eight behaviors, you can attach a copy of the "Eight Behaviors for Smarter Teams" article to the e-mail you send in advance of the planning meeting. You can ask them to read the article so that at the planning meeting you can discuss their questions and reactions. You can explain that the eight behaviors are an important part of your work and that you will recommend they also use the behaviors, if they're willing.

Why I Don't Ask Groups to Develop Their Own Ground Rules. On the belief that group members will support what they have developed, some facilitators ask groups to develop their ground rules for the meeting. This creates two potential problems: (1) Groups may develop ground rules that are inconsistent with effective group process or are too abstract to be useful, and (2) the facilitator isn't transparent about the behaviors he or she is using to diagnose and intervene.

I believe that groups often don't have the ability to identify behavioral ground rules that will help them improve their process. Asking them to generate these ground rules often yields nonbehavioral statements, such as "be respectful," that mean something different to each group member; suggestions like "praise in public, criticize in private," that are incongruent with the mutual learning approach; and procedural rules like "turn off mobile phones" that, while perhaps necessary, don't focus on how members will interact.

When groups hire us as facilitators, we represent ourselves as experts in group process. Therefore, it's our responsibility to offer a set of research-validated behaviors that contribute to effective group process. Groups don't have to develop their own ground rules to be committed to them; rather, they need to make a free and informed choice to use them.

Putting the Tentative Agreement in Writing

Assuming you have agreed to work together, by the end of the planning meeting or meetings, the planning group and you will have reached tentative agreement about the issues discussed in Exhibit 13.4 above. The next step is to send a memo stating your understanding of the agreements and asking them to contact you if their understanding differs from yours. Exhibit 13.6 provides a sample agreement for basic facilitation. If the planning group is a subgroup of an intact work group or team, I send the memo to all the members of the primary client group, even if they didn't attend the planning meeting. If the planning group is planning an event for a large group, I usually send the memo only to the planning group members. In any case, if I'm sending the memo to people who haven't previously received a copy of the article "Eight Behaviors for Smarter Teams," I attach it, explaining that I will use it to facilitate and, if the planning group has agreed, that the full group may also use it during the facilitation.

Putting the tentative agreement in writing enables you to make clear that the agreement isn't final until all group members have given their consent. It also enables all group members to read the agreement before the facilitation and raise any questions or concerns they might have.

Roger Schwarz & Associates

Get to the heart of it.®

Agreement between Summit Executive Leadership Team and Roger Schwarz, Roger Schwarz & Associates

This e-mail summarizes the agreement we reached during our planning meeting regarding the executive leadership team off-site.

Time and location

The off-site meeting will be held at the Coconut Grove Resort. On December 5, will meet from 9:00 AM to 5:00 PM On December 6, we will meet from 9:00 AM to 5:00 PM

Attendance and rescheduling

The senior executive leadership team will participate in the off-site meeting: Julius Marx, Margaret Dumont, Tina Fong, Geoffrey Spalding, Emmanuel Ravelli, Gloria Teasdale, and Rufus Firefly. To enable full discussion of all participants' views and to ensure adequate support for any decisions reached in the session, the participants agree to attend the full session, without interruption. We have agreed to reschedule the off-site meeting if any member is unable to attend.

Tentative objective and agenda

The objective of the off-site meeting is to improve the team's effectiveness by agreeing on its purpose, key tasks, and the structures and processes it will use. To accomplish this objective, the team will discuss and answer these five general questions: (1) What is the purpose of the executive leadership team?; (2) What are the tasks for which we are interdependent, jointly accountable to the team, and should make decisions as a team?; (3) What specific processes will we use for solving problems, making decisions and managing conflict?; (4) What specific behaviors should we expect of each other?; and (5) How will we plan for and manage our regular meetings? Based on our planning meeting, attached is a tentative agenda, including time estimates.

We will begin the off-site meeting by introducing all participants, reviewing the tentative agenda and making modifications if needed, reviewing the mutual learning behaviors you tentatively agreed to use as ground rules, and reviewing our roles. We will conclude the off-site meeting with a discussion of next steps and an evaluation of the off-site meeting, including my role. The objective and agenda remain tentative until the entire group of participants either confirms or modifies it.

Consultant roles and fees

I will serve as a facilitative consultant to the team, which includes two parts. I will help the team have the most productive conversation possible. This will include helping you (1) stay on topic, (2) see how your views are similar and different, (3) understand the assumptions underlying your discussion, and (4) identify solutions that ideally meet all of your interests. In addition, as we agreed, I will also share my expertise on leadership team effectiveness, when it's relevant to your discussion. You will decide whether and how to use my expertise as you make decisions about your team.

Roger Schwarz & Associates' fee for facilitation is $_____ for the two-day session, plus travel expenses.

Advance preparation

Please complete and return the attached questionnaire, providing your initial answers to questions you will be discussing at the retreat. Also, if you have not already done so, please read the attached article, "Eight Behaviors for Smarter Teams."

Notification of changes

Please contact me immediately if this e-mail is inconsistent with the agreements we have reached in our planning conversations. Julius will contact me in the event that any of you are unable to attend. If events or circumstances require modifying our agreement, we will jointly decide how to make the changes.

I look forward to working with you on December 5 and 6.

Sincerely,

Roger
Roger Schwarz
President and CEO
roger@schwarzassociates.com

Exhibit 13.6   Sample Basic Facilitation Tentative Agreement

STAGE 3: REACHING AGREEMENT WITH THE ENTIRE GROUP

Unless you've been planning with the entire primary client group, in the third contracting stage, you reach agreement with the entire group. This step usually occurs at the beginning of the meeting you're facilitating, when the entire group is present for the first time. But before you seek this agreement, there is an important first step.

Meeting Briefly with Planning Representatives

Before the facilitation begins, have a brief conversation with planning representatives to learn if anything has changed that might affect the contract or the facilitation and to address any remaining logistics. For developmental or long-term basic facilitation, the conversation is relevant each time the group is about to meet.

In a developmental facilitation with a group of school administrators and faculty who were trying to resolve a difficult conflict, I asked someone before a meeting if anything was new. I was informed that the executive director—a focal point of the conflict—had announced his resignation, effective at the end of the school year. Given this, I began the session by asking the group how his resignation affected our work together and whether we should change our contract. Similarly, in working with a global transportation company, I learned on CNN at 6:00 AM that my client had just filed for Chapter 11 bankruptcy. Before our meeting was scheduled to begin at 8:00 AM, I asked the VP whether his group would even be available to meet, given the news, and, if so, how we should proceed.

If the client and you haven't already agreed on the details of starting the first meeting, this is the time to do it. This includes agreeing on who will start the meeting, introduce you as the facilitator, introduce other participants, describe the events that led up to the meeting, and the like.

Reaching Agreement with the Full Group

In short-term basic facilitation, this conversation occurs in the beginning of the meeting, after all the clients and you have introduced yourselves, and a planning group representative and you have described the planning process that has led to the current meeting. You review each key element of the tentative agreement and ask whether anyone has any questions or concerns: (1) meeting purpose and objectives, (2) the agenda and time allocation, (3) the process for each agenda item, (4) ground rules, and (5) roles (including your role, the formal leader, and others).

This is a moment of truth. If the planning subgroup and you have addressed the entire group's interests, the full group will quickly agree to the tentative agreement. But if the planning subgroup hasn't adequately represented the range of the full group's interests, you now face recontracting with the full group before the group can begin its work. I have found myself in this situation (actually, I helped create it), and it's not fun, especially if the group is large or has serious concerns about the agreement reached in the subgroup. I know of only one way to avoid this situation: Make sure that you plan with a representative subgroup.

Agreeing on the Ground Rules

If the entire group attended the planning meeting, you can quickly remind it of how you will use the eight mutual learning behaviors to intervene and whether it agreed to use them as the ground rules for the meeting.

If the entire client group didn't attend the planning meeting and the facilitation is a basic one, ask whether participants have read the article you sent them, and if so, what questions or concerns they have about using the ground rules. After responding to their questions and concerns, briefly describe the eight behaviors, including how you would use them and how they might use them. Then ask if people want to use the behaviors during the facilitation.

In my years of facilitating with the mutual learning behaviors, few group members have ever expressed concern about using them. (This may be partly because clients who hire me often know of my work and the behaviors.) If members express concern, you use the mutual learning approach to get curious, understand the members' concerns, identify any incorrect assumptions they may be making about the eight behaviors or what people will expect of them, and jointly design a solution that meets the group's interests.

When I work with a group to resolve a difficult conflict among members, I contract to spend more time discussing the behaviors. A city council that had recently expanded in size and included several factions that were in conflict wanted to resolve things. The council members agreed to spend several hours learning how to use the mutual learning behaviors and then begin the facilitation to resolve the conflicts. During the facilitation, council members used the behaviors, and afterwards they reported that those several hours enabled them to work more productively during the facilitation.

Addressing Members' Concerns

Psychologically, this is a critical time in the facilitation for members who haven't been involved in planning the facilitation. Having seen the tentative agreement in writing, they may wonder whether the objectives and agenda can be changed, whether they can influence the process, and if their interests will be addressed. They may also wonder whether you, as the facilitator, will help them meet their interests.

Sometimes members are eager to get to the content of the facilitation and want to shorten or eliminate this beginning-of-meeting contracting with the full group. They may feel frustrated spending time on what they consider unnecessary issues that everyone agrees on, or they may be worried that if you ask about people's concerns with the tentative agreement, members will raise all kinds of objections and the group will never get to the content of the facilitation.

You can respond to these concerns by pointing out that if the full group has no concerns about the tentative agreement, then the conversation will be very brief. If, however, there are concerns and the group doesn't identify or address them, they're likely to surface either during the meeting or, worse, after the meeting, as members voice their lack of commitment to the process. Spending the extra time in the beginning of the meeting reduces the chance that the group will need to invest even more time later. As the systems thinking phrase advises, "Go slow to go fast."

STAGE 4: CONDUCTING THE FACILITATION

Stage 4 is the facilitation itself, not a contracting stage by itself. I have included it as a contracting stage because in almost every facilitation I have conducted, the group and I have modified some element of the agreement.

There are a number of questions that often arise during facilitations that lead to modifying some element of the agreement. These include, "Should we start on time if not everyone is present?"; "Should we end early if certain people need to leave early?"; "Should we have the meeting or keep the same topics if certain members are unable to attend?"; "Should we change the order of the agenda?"; "How should we modify the agenda given that we won't have enough time to complete all the topics?"

In addition, if you're facilitating a group for more than one day, you're likely to conduct a plus/delta at the end of each day to learn what worked well and what to do differently for the next session. In a plus/delta, you ask the group two questions: (1) What did we do that worked well today? and (2) What should we do differently next time? These deltas can naturally lead to recontracting.

In general, during this stage of contracting, it's helpful to look for any signs that there may be some element of the agreement that is not working as well as it could for the group.

STAGE 5: COMPLETING AND EVALUATING THE FACILITATION

In stage 5, you and the client complete and evaluate the facilitation.

Completing the Facilitation

Deciding when a basic facilitation contract has been completed is relatively easy and can usually be determined before the actual facilitation begins. A basic facilitation contract, especially a short-term one, is normally designed around a specific date or set of dates on which you will work with the client. After you have worked with the client on these dates, the contract work has been completed. If you have contracted to help the group until it reaches decisions on some specified issues, the work is complete when the group has made the decisions.

Deciding when a developmental facilitation contract has been completed is more difficult and can rarely be identified before the facilitation begins. The client typically doesn't know enough in advance to specify the level of mutual learning mindset and skill set it wants to achieve. The group can make an informed choice only by practicing mutual learning and assessing its progress. Consequently, as a developmental facilitator, you want to periodically help the group consider how much further it wants to improve its mutual learning mindset and skill set.

At times, the group or you may want to terminate a contract before the other party believes the agreed-upon work has been completed. The client may shift priorities or become dissatisfied with your ability to help, or you may infer that the client isn't sufficiently committed to the facilitation. When you are contracting with a developmental client, ask to meet with the client group one more time if either party decides to prematurely terminate the contract. This meeting helps the client and you understand the reason for terminating the contract and provides each of you feedback about your behavior.

Evaluating the Facilitation

There are two separate but related foci for the evaluation: the actual facilitation and the underlying contract. Evaluating the actual facilitation involves exploring how the group members and you have acted to either enhance or reduce the group's effectiveness. Evaluating the contract involves assessing the extent to which the terms of the contract (which members should be involved, how frequently the group meets with the facilitator, and so on) met the client's and your needs.

As I mentioned in stage 4, evaluating the facilitation or contract can occur at any time during a facilitation. Still, for long-term facilitation, it's useful to set times for evaluating the contract regularly so the client and you can decide how well it is serving the client's needs and make any necessary changes.

To evaluate the facilitation, I contract with the client to spend time at the end of each meeting to conduct a plus/delta.

SUMMARY

In this chapter, I have described the process that a client and you use to agree on whether and how you will work together. The five contracting stages are (1) making initial contact with a primary client group member, (2) planning the facilitation, (3) reaching agreement with the full primary client group, (4) recontracting during facilitation, and (5) completing and evaluating the facilitation.

Many problems that occur during facilitation are caused by ineffective contracting. The contracting process establishes an effective relationship between the client and you and greatly increases the chance that the facilitation will be effective.

In the next chapter, we will explore whether and how to work with a partner, so you can better help the group you are working with.

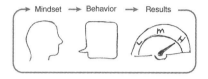

Mindset → Behavior → Results

CHAPTER FOURTEEN

Working with a Partner

T his chapter describes how you and a partner can work together to help a
group. The chapter has three parts. In the first part, I describe the
advantages and disadvantages of partnering and when it's beneficial. In
the second part, I describe how you and a partner can divide and coordinate
your work. The last part discusses how you and your partner can reflect on your
work to improve it.

Facilitating, coaching, or consulting to a group is mentally challenging work.
You need to simultaneously pay attention to content and process, verbal and
nonverbal behavior, those who are speaking and those who aren't, and what is
currently happening in the group compared to what has happened in the past
and what will likely happen in the future. While considering all this, you also
have to think about whether to intervene, what interventions to make and how,
when to intervene, who to make your interventions with, and the effects of the
intervention on the group once you make them. Then you intervene. Quite
often, you have to do all this in less time than it took you to read this paragraph.

Because of the high demands of the work, you may sometimes work together
with the same group. In partnering, both people are usually with the group at all
times.

DECIDING WHETHER TO PARTNER

When partners work well together, both they and the group benefit; when they
don't, everyone suffers. In this section, which is drawn largely from the work of

J. William Pfeiffer and John Jones, I describe tensions that partners need to manage.[1] They arise from differences between the partners and from the simple fact of having two helpers. The underlying principle in choosing to partner is that together the partners can intervene in a greater range of situations and with greater skill than either one can manage alone. **For partnering to be effective, the partners' approaches need to be congruent. Where they have differences, they must be able to use their differences to help the group rather than hinder it.**

Do You Have Congruent or Conflicting Mindsets?

Perhaps the most important factor in deciding whether to partner is whether you and your partner have congruent mindsets. If your core values and assumptions about your work differ, you may make fundamentally different interventions with a group and will have a difficult time coordinating your work to help the group.

I discovered this in an early cofacilitation, when a colleague and I worked with a city council and the city manager. At one point early in the meeting, there was some disagreement among group members about which issues to address. My colleague called a break and told me that he wanted to see how the manager wanted to proceed, explaining that it was the manager's choice. I saw the situation differently and explained that I considered the group as a whole to have the relevant information; I felt the choice was to be made by the group. My explanation raised more concerns for my cofacilitator, and in the minute that we had to resolve our differences, we reached a compromise to talk with the manager and then raise the issue in the full group. Yet, the solution compromised core values and assumptions for each of us. This turned out to be the first of many differences my cofacilitator and I had during the facilitation, most of which resulted from our contrasting mindsets; we turned our attention away from helping the group and toward working on our own conflict.

If you're working from a mutual learning mindset and your partner isn't, a lot of conflicts can occur. To take a simple example, your partner may enforce a predetermined time frame for discussing agenda items, while you seek to jointly control the process and ask group members if they want to alter the schedule as they proceed. If your partner assumes that how he sees things is correct, he'll consider it unnecessary to test his inferences and may act on relatively high-level inferences without publicly testing them. If your partner values minimizing expression of negative feelings, she may craft interventions designed to bypass group member emotions, whereas you're likely to move toward those feelings, believing that it gets to the root of the issue. In a study of coleaders of therapy groups—a role relationship similar to cofacilitator's—difference in orientation (values and beliefs) was the reason most cited for not wanting to work together again.[2]

There are times when you may want to work with a partner because you have differing mindsets; the contrast can help both of you learn. Still, it's important to determine whether the differences between you and your potential partner's core values and assumptions are great enough that your learning will come at the expense of helping the group.

Do You Have Complementary or Competing Foci and Styles?

Even if you and your partner have a shared mindset, you may focus on different things in a group. One of you may focus more on helping individual members improve their communication skills; the other may focus more on improving group structure and process. When individual-level and group-level partners work together, they might compensate for each other's blind spots and misplaced interventions, rather than reinforce them, which occurs when cofacilitators have the same orientation.

Partners also have differing styles—the particular way in which they conduct themselves in applying their mindset and focus. Style varies along many dimensions, including the degree of seriousness versus humor, inclination toward confrontation, and the pace of intervention.

Here too, different styles can help the group so long as you and your partner are not incompatible. The two of you can use the difference in pacing or sense of humor as the situation calls for it. However, largely divergent styles may lead group members to feel disjointed by having to continually adjust to two opposed styles.[3]

Will You Be Overwhelmed or Will the Group Be Overwhelmed?

As a individual working alone, you may sometimes leave a session overwhelmed, feeling that much more was occurring in the group than you could even make sense of, let alone intervene on. In addition, you may wonder whether your perception of the situation was realistic or distorted, even if you tested your inferences with the group. This often happens when there is a high level of overt activity or energy in the group; things are occurring at several levels simultaneously and at a fast pace; a high-conflict situation is one example. But you can also be overwhelmed by a level of activity that isn't observably high, if every interaction seems laden with interpersonal issues in the group. Partnering reduces the chance of being overwhelmed and gives you an opportunity to use your partner for reality checks. Partnering is also useful when a group is large or the plan is to work part of the time in subgroups.

The extra capacity to intervene that you and your partner bring to the group can become a liability if it leads to excessive intervention. As facilitators, we have a need to feel useful, and we usually fulfill that need by intervening. However, at times one partner may have little opportunity for intervening because the partner is already making the necessary intervention. If partners attempt to meet their own needs rather than their clients', they may intervene unnecessarily and slow the group's progress. The problem can be reduced or prevented so long as you and your partner place the group's needs first and divide the labor so that you both have ample opportunity to intervene. Finally, you can reframe the meaning of being useful to include refraining from unnecessary intervention.

Will Your Partnership Generate Learning and Support or Competition and Control?

Partnering enables you to develop your professional skills by learning from and with a person who has a different approach, technique, or style. During breaks and after the work, you can discuss various interventions and why each of you made them. In this way, you can use specific data to reflect on and learn about your partnering.

There is a saying, "How you do anything is how you do everything." In other words, in different situations, in different parts of our life, fundamentally we operate from the same mindset that generates the same behaviors and results. If you've read this far into the book, that shouldn't surprise you. How you facilitate, consult, or coach is probably based on the same mindset that drives your everyday behavior—and the same is true for your partner.

That means that whatever personal issues have a negative impact in your "nonfacilitative" life will also show up in your facilitative role if the situation triggers those issues. This includes challenges you have dealing with authority, ambiguity, control, commitment, status, and intimacy. If you have problems with authority, for example, you may inappropriately confront (or avoid) the formal leader of a group. If you have problems with control, you may frequently interrupt while your partner is intervening.

Partnering can bring out these issues, but it can also help you learn from them if you and your partner are willing and able to help each other. If the two of you are willing to share these personal challenges with each other, you can help each other become aware of how these issues affect your work and explore how you might change your behavior as well as the values and assumptions that generate it. For example, through cofacilitating and coteaching facilitation, I have learned how my own seemingly well-intended interventions actually reduce my cofacilitator or coteacher's ability to establish a relationship with the group. Similarly, one of my colleagues has learned how she designs interventions in a way that reduces group members' ability to disagree with her. In helping each other in this way, we are really serving as mutual developmental facilitators.

Of course, the issues that are your food for learning are the same ones that can undermine your ability to partner and learn from the practice. Your unilateral control mindset, mixed with your personal issues, can lead you to view a partnership as competition with your partner instead of as an opportunity for colearning. When this occurs, the group loses as well.

Are Both of You Internal or External, or Not?

An internal is employed in the same organization as the groups he helps. An external works for herself or another organization. If you're an internal you may seek an external partner to help with a large or difficult assignment; if you're an external you may seek an internal partner to build capacity in the organization and to better understand the organization's culture.

Internals and externals each have advantages, which I describe in Chapter 15. This includes access to the client, understanding the organizational culture, and being able to challenge clients.

Here, too, the differences can be a benefit or liability to you and your partner and the group. When there is disagreement, your external partner may think you don't focus enough on process issues, are too deferential to authority, or are inhibited by the culture of your organization. Conversely, you may think your external partner is too idealistic and challenging and doesn't appreciate the culture of the organization and the need for the group to get its work done.

Are the Benefits Worth the Investment?

In addition to the energy that every facilitator, consultant, or coach expends working with a group, partners expend energy coordinating their work with each other. First, you have to spend time talking with your partner to determine whether you're compatible enough to work together. Second, if you decide to partner, you need to plan how to manage your differences. Third, you need to divide the labor between yourselves and develop a way to coordinate your division of labor.

For example, before a session, you and your partner can plan how to divide up the opening remarks and how to hand off the lead role to one another during the session. Less predictable aspects of coordination can be partially planned but must also be partially coordinated at the time of the intervention. As a simple illustration, if you agree to write on a flipchart or whiteboard while your partner intervenes, you both need a way to ensure that what (and when) you write is congruent with your partner's intervention. A much more difficult and frequent problem is to coordinate the interventions each of you makes so that together you help the group make progress rather than take the group in opposing directions. This kind of coordination is difficult because it usually needs to be done in the moment and continuously.

Aside from expending energy dividing and coordinating your labor, partnering can burn up psychological energy. You or your partner may worry that the other will make a significant mistake. Finally, you may expend psychological energy struggling with a tension inherent in collaboration: Each of you must temporarily yield some identity to the collaboration so that together you can become something neither alone can be.[4]

Questions for Deciding Whether to Partner

A good way for you and your potential partner to find out about each other's similarities and differences is to discuss the issues directly. You can use the questions and statements in Figure 14.1 to guide your conversation so you can both decide whether you can work effectively, and to reach agreement about how to work together. Keep in mind that to obtain useful information, you need to discuss these questions at the level of directly observable behavior, describing what each of you would think and say in specific instances.

Approach and Style

1. The major values, assumptions, and principles that guide my work are . . .
2. The major values, assumptions, and principles that others in my facilitative role hold and that I strongly disagree with are . . .
3. When contracting with this type of group, I usually . . .
4. When starting a meeting with this type of group, I usually . . .
5. At the end of a meeting with this type of group, I usually . . .
6. When someone talks too much, I usually . . .
7. When the group is silent, I usually . . .
8. When an individual is silent for a long time, I usually . . .
9. When someone gets upset, I usually . . .
10. When someone comes late, I usually . . .
11. When someone leaves early, I usually . . .
12. When group members are excessively polite and do not confront each other, I usually . . .
13. When there is conflict in the group, I usually . . .
14. When the group verbally attacks one member, I usually . . .
15. When a group member takes a cheap shot at me or implies I am ineffective, I usually . . .
16. When members focus on positions, I usually . . .
17. When members seem to be going off track, I usually . . .
18. When someone takes a cheap shot, I usually . . .
19. My favorite interventions for this type of group are . . .

Exhibit 14.1   Statements for Deciding Whether to Work as Partners

20. Interventions that this type of group usually needs but that I often don't make are . . .
21. In working with this type of group, the things I find most satisfying are . . .
22. The things I find most frustrating in working with this type of group are . . .
23. The things that make me most uncomfortable in working with this type of group are . . .
24. In terms of combining accountability and compassion in my interventions, I am [low, medium, high] on compassion and [low, medium, high] on accountability. For example, . . .
25. My typical "intervention rhythm" is [fast, slow, other]. For example, . . .

Experience and Background

1. Discuss your experience in your facilitative role. What types of groups have you worked with? What were the content and process issues in the groups?
2. Discuss your best facilitative and cofacilitative experiences. What was it that made them so successful?
3. Discuss your worst facilitative and cofacilitative experiences. What was it that made them so negative?
4. Describe some of your facilitative behaviors that a cofacilitator might consider idiosyncratic.
5. Describe issues that have arisen between you and other partners.
6. Describe the areas in which you are trying to improve your facilitative practice. How would you like me to help you improve?
7. What issues do you have that might hinder the ability of you and me to work with each other or with the client?
8. Given what you know about me, what concerns do you have about working with me?

Partner Coordination

1. Who will sit where in the group meetings?
2. Who will start the session? Who will finish it?
3. Will both of us need to be present at all times? How will breakout sessions be handled?
4. How will we handle the role of recorder?
5. How will we divide labor (for example, primary-secondary, task-relationship, intervener-recorder)?
6. What kinds of interventions and behaviors are inside and outside the zone of deference for each other?
7. Where, when, and how will we deal with challenges that arise between the two of us?
8. What kind of differences between the two of us are you willing and not willing to show in front of the group?
9. How closely should we expect each other to adhere to the designated roles we have jointly agreed on?
10. What is nonnegotiable for each of us as cofacilitator? What leads those issues to be nonnegotiable?

Exhibit 14.1 Statements for Deciding Whether to Work as Partners (*continued*)

DIVIDING AND COORDINATING THE LABOR

If you have decided to partner, you still need to decide how you and your partner divide the work and coordinate your roles during the facilitative work. Below I discuss six ways to divide up the work and the coordination challenges that arise from them.

Intervener-Recorder

In the intervener-recorder arrangement, one partner intervenes while the other takes notes on a computer (projected for the view of the group), whiteboard, flipchart, or some other technology. This division of labor is useful if the group is generating many ideas—as in brainstorming—and doesn't want to be slowed down by the partner's writing each idea before asking for the next one. Still, either the intervener or the recorder has to check that the written statements represent what the members have said.

Coordinating the two roles also requires that you and your partner and members agree on when a member's idea is to be written on the flipchart. This can be as direct as saying, "Let's write down all the potential causes of the delays." The issue is simple, but it can create problems if not addressed. Writing a member's idea on the flipchart symbolizes that the idea is valuable. A member whose contributions aren't written down and doesn't know why may feel discounted and begin to distrust the intervener and recorder. So if the recorder decides not to write down an idea, a brief explanation is appropriate. For example, the recorder might say, "Dan, I was asking for causes, and your comment looks like a solution. Do you see it differently? [If not] Can you think of any causes?" In this way, the recorder temporarily becomes the intervener.

Primary-Secondary

In the primary-secondary arrangement, one partner takes the primary role for all interventions, while the other plays backup, intervening only when necessary. This works well if the group process is easy enough for one partner to manage or if the partners are concerned about intervening too much. It also gives the secondary partner a chance to rest.

The coordination challenge here is that the secondary may intervene on some behavior that the primary intentionally avoids. For example, as the primary partner, you may avoid clarifying an off-track disagreement among members and instead try to get the group on track. If the secondary partner jumps in and clarifies the disagreement, the clarification would continue to take the group off track. This challenge occurs because the secondary partner is actively looking for opportunities that the primary partner missed. To reduce this problem, you and your partner can discuss each other's intervention orientation well enough so that you have a shared understanding about the conditions under which you would choose not to intervene.

Online-Offline

In the online-offline division of labor, one partner intervenes (online), while the other silently works on some task associated with the work. The task could be how to describe a complex group pattern, how to spend the remaining time if the group has fallen behind schedule, or simply setting up an activity. This arrangement is useful when you and your partner need to solve a problem that is difficult to attend to while observing and intervening and that is either not appropriate to raise with the group or not a good use of the group's time.

Task-Relationship

In this arrangement, both partners actively observe and intervene, but one focuses on what is referred to as task process while the other concentrates on relationship (or interpersonal) process.[5] If, for example, a group is setting performance goals, the task-process partner focuses on the content by helping the group keep on track, think logically about what goals are needed, and establish clear goals. In contrast, the relationship-process partner pays more attention to the group's social and emotional interactions by silently asking herself, *What do members' words, style, and nature of discussion say about how they are feeling about the task, each other, and the two of us?*[6] You can think of the task-relationship division of labor as paying attention to effects that the group behavior is having on its performance and working relationship results, respectively.

Task-relationship is often a natural way for partners to divide the labor. Research shows that some people are predominantly task-oriented and others relationship-oriented.[7] Task and relationship orientations are relative. Whether you are more task- or relationship-oriented depends how task- or relationship-oriented your partner is. This approach often lets partners take advantage of their strengths. It works well when the group generates many task and relationship issues simultaneously.

Because a group, especially in basic facilitation, generally views task intervention as more appropriate than relationship intervention, the relationship partner often needs to clearly show how the relationship issue affects the group's ability to perform effectively.

Intervention-Reaction

In the fifth division of labor, one partner concentrates on intervening with one or a few members, while the other pays attention to the rest of the group. The division is useful should one member be the subject of much intervention and other members are reacting strongly to the member's comments (or to the intervention). The coordination challenge here involves knowing whether, and when, to shift the focus of the intervention from one member to the others' reactions. Should the second partner immediately point out the reactions or wait until the first partner completes the intervention?

No Explicit Division of Labor

Having no *explicit* division of labor doesn't mean there is *no* division of labor. It means that you and your partner pay attention to what appears to need attention, without first talking with the other. Using this approach, you can instantly switch roles to adjust to the group's needs and the needs of the partner. You can also respond quickly and potentially make the best use of your partner skills.

As the least structured way to divide the labor, it is also the most difficult to coordinate. You and your partner risk intervening on the same issues while ignoring others, failing to capture members' ideas on the flipchart, and both going offline at the same time, thus temporarily abandoning the group. The approach works if you and your partner have worked together long enough and in enough situations to anticipate each other's moves and adjust automatically, just as improv actors respond to each other's lines. I have this relationship with a couple of my colleagues. We are so in sync and so familiar with each other's facilitation that often all we need to do to coordinate our interventions is to give each other a knowing glance.

I have described six different ways of dividing the labor between you and your partner. It's not necessarily desirable to use only one division of labor throughout an entire session or work. If you and your partner are working effectively together, you can shift among these divisions of labor to meet the changing needs of the group.

ALLOCATING ROLES WITHIN YOUR DIVISION OF LABOR

After selecting how you and your partner will divide your labor (intervener-recorder, task-relationship, and so on), together you can decide who will play which role. In making this decision, here are a number of factors to consider.

Skill with Potential Interventions

Here you choose your roles so that whoever is more skilled at interventions has primary responsibility for intervening. Even if it's not possible to predict the kinds of interventions you will have to make, you may quickly be able to identify a pattern in the kinds of interventions that you and your cofacilitator are making in a given session. Knowing this pattern, you and your partner can decide who is better suited to take the lead on these kinds of interventions.

Knowledge of Content Problems

Partners vary in their knowledge about the content problems their clients face. For example, I used to cofacilitate with a colleague who knows a lot about finance. When we cofacilitated a group that was discussing financial issues, he usually took the first role in the intervener-recorder, task-relationship, inter-vention-reaction, or primary-secondary divisions of labor. He could keep up when the discussion became so technical that I would have to slow the group's pace by frequently asking for definition of terms. (Here I am assuming that members agree on the definitions and would be clarifying them only for me.) Still, if a partner's knowledge about and interest in an issue tempts the partner to stray into the content of the discussion, the less knowledgeable partner may choose the active intervention role.

Internal-External Differences

Similarly, the internal partner can often intervene easily in a highly technical discussion. By contrast, if you and your partner want to confront the group— especially about members' core values and beliefs—without raising the issue of the internal partner's credibility or seeming disloyal, the external partner may actively intervene. But in a developmental group, having the internal partner confront the group about its assumptions is powerful precisely because it can raise the issue of credibility and disloyalty. Done well, you and your partner can use members' reactions to the internal partner to discuss why members who chal-lenge the assumption of the organization are seen as disloyal.

Pace

You and your partner can switch roles for each to take on the less active role when one gets tired. You can also take advantage of your different paces by matching the needs of the group. For example, the faster-paced partner can actively intervene when the group is behind schedule and nearing the end of the session. The slower-paced partner can actively intervene when members are struggling to understand each other.

Training and Development

At times, a partner may choose to play a role to help the group develop particular skills. Obviously, the person who is best suited to teach this topic is likely to take on that role.

DEVELOPING HEALTHY BOUNDARIES BETWEEN YOU AND YOUR PARTNER

In a good relationship, you and your partner agree on when and how to modify each other's interventions, correct one another, reinforce the other's interventions, and help when one gets tangled in a conflict with the group. You do this in a way that integrates your skills while preserving your individual identity. It's a matter of setting boundaries.[8] If you and your partner routinely interrupt and modify one another's interventions, both of you lose your individual identity, in addition to confusing the group. Conversely, if you never respond to each other, you don't get the full benefit of collaboration. You can discuss and agree on several issues before working with a group.

Agree on the Zone of Deference

An important part of intervening is knowing when not to. Organizational theorist Chester Barnard used the phrase "zone of indifference" to refer to the range within which employees obey orders without considering the merits of the order.[9] I use the phrase *zone of deference* to describe the area in which one cofacilitator lets the other's interventions stand, although the former would intervene differently. Without an agreed-on zone of deference, you and your partner may constantly correct each other's interventions, confusing the group in your attempt to make things clear. Or, to avoid being seen as nitpicking or overbearing, the two of you may fail to modify any of each other's interventions, which deprives the group of the benefits of partnering.

There are a number of questions you can ask yourself to decide whether your partner's intervention is in or out of the zone of deference. If your answer to any of the following questions is "yes," then it's in the group's best interest for you to intervene on your partner's intervention—or for your partner to do the same for you.

Will the Client Suffer Harm? The most elementary responsibility you and your partner have is to do nothing that harms the group. An intervention that causes harm might be deceiving or demeaning a member, breaking a promise, or disobeying the law. Making an intervention that is beyond your skills can also harm the group.[10] If you infer your partner is doing one of these things, you have an obligation to intervene.

Is the Intervention Incongruent with the Mutual Learning Mindset or Behaviors? Interventions that are incongruent with the mutual learning core values and assumptions or behaviors can reduce the group's effectiveness and your credibility as cofacilitators, consultants, or coaches. Although minor incongruences may fall in the zone of deference, others are important to intervene on.

Does the Intervention Change the Facilitative Role? Leaving your facilitative role is inconsistent with your client agreement, unless the group and you and your partner explicitly agree that one of you will temporarily leave the role. Leaving the facilitator role includes acting as a group member, a group decision maker, a content expert, or intermediary between the group and others.

Will the Intervention Prevent or Hinder the Group from Accomplishing Its Goals? Interventions that prevent or hinder the group from accomplishing its goals include taking the group off track; using methods or tools that are more elaborate than is necessary; or employing exercises that, although interesting, neither contribute to the task nor meet the group's needs for effective working relationships.

Agree on When You Will Support Each Other's Interventions

In contrast to the zone of deference, in which one partner makes an intervention that the other partner might not, supporting an intervention occurs when you or your partner emphasizes the other's intervention. Here conflicts can occur when the partner who makes the initial intervention expects support, while the other, believing the first doesn't need it, fails to provide it. In the reverse situation, a partner offers support when the initial partner thinks it is unnecessary. Again, to avoid this discrepancy in expectations, you and your partner can discuss when and how to support each other's interventions and how each one can ask for support.

Don't Rescue Each Other

Sometimes you or your partner may get into conflict with the client group. For example, your partner might intervene in a way that divides the group and causes part of the group to express concern about his role. Or a group may draw him into its own conflict, without him recognizing it.

What should you do when he is in conflict with the group? A natural reaction is to intervene and protect or rescue him from the conflict with the group. This saves your partner and relieves your concern about becoming a victim of his conflict with the group.[11] Unfortunately, this discounts your partner and can reinforce the group's belief that he is ineffective. Group members may reason that if he can't extricate himself from the conflict without your help, the group's negative assessment of his ability to deal with conflict must be accurate.

A more effective response—one that avoids reinforcing the group's negative views—is to wait for your partner to ask for help. Waiting increases the chance that he will manage the conflict with the group and may simultaneously enhance the group's image of him. Allowing him to choose when to receive help increases the partner's free choice and reduces his image as helpless.

In some cases, a conflict between one partner and the group becomes known to the other partner first. Suppose a leader in a senior executive retreat approaches you during a break and says, "Listen, your cofacilitator Tina is a nice person, but she's stirring up issues the group doesn't need to deal with, and people are getting upset with her. Don't tell her I said anything, but just steer the conversation back when she starts challenging the group, okay?" To avoid rescuing Tina, colluding with the client, or acting as an intermediary, you can explain that unless Tina talks directly with those who are concerned, she will not have the relevant information to make an informed choice about whether or how to change her behavior. This is true whether or not you believe Tina is acting ineffectively. Ideally, the conversation with Tina occurs with the entire group, because it involves all members. Once the conversation is raised with the entire group, Tina can ask you for help.

Openly Coordinate with Your Partner

Because intervention is based on diagnosis, to coordinate your work, you and your partner need some way to discuss with each other what is happening in the group. Aside from telepathy, I know of only two ways for partners to coordinate their work in front of the group: They can either talk openly or try to hide their discussion by using some secret language.

It turns out that facilitators openly coordinating in front of their client group has a long history that began with an event that helped found the field of facilitation.

Kurt Lewin and the T-Group. The genesis of the training group (T-group), which is a source of many group facilitation techniques, reveals the advantages and risks of the open approach.[12] The principles of the T-group were developed in the summer of 1946 by social psychologist Kurt Lewin and his colleagues. Lewin, then a professor at the Massachusetts Institute of Technology, was asked to help the Connecticut State Commission, which was troubled by the staff's inability to help communities overcome bias and discrimination. Following his motto of "no action without research; no research without action," Lewin proposed a two-week workshop that would simultaneously train three groups of commission staff members and provide research data on what produced the changes.[13] A psychologist led each of the three groups, and a researcher observed each one.

Every evening, the researchers met with the group leaders to discuss and record on tape their process observations of the groups and the leaders. One day, a few workshop participants asked to attend the evening meetings. Most researchers and group leaders feared that it would be harmful for the partic-ipants to hear discussion of their behavior. But Lewin, an advocate of feedback, saw no reason the researchers and leaders should withhold data from the participants and believed the feedback could be helpful.

The evening sessions had an energizing effect on everyone involved. When leaders and researchers analyzed an event in a group, the actual participants interrupted with their interpretation. Members found that when they participated nondefensively, they learned important things about their behavior, how others reacted to them, and how groups in general behave. Together, the researchers, leaders, and participants had found a powerful method of learning. By watching leaders discuss their work, group members learned how a group acts and how leaders can create change. By participating in the discussion, members clarified leaders' diagnoses and helped the leaders select appropriate interventions.

Openly Coordinating in Front of the Group. Lewin's findings suggest that when developmental cofacilitators openly coordinate their work in front of the group and encourage members to participate, the group members and cofacilitators increase their learning. A goal of developmental facilitation is for group members to facilitate their own process. You and your partner take the first step in the shift by enabling group members to observe and question the "backstage" part of your cofacilitative work.

There are risks in open coordination. If the group is frustrated with you or your partner, members may use your openness to suggest that you or your partner aren't competent. In some situations, partner openness doesn't help the members achieve their goal. If you and your partner spend an inordinate amount of time intervening with each other, the group may consider it a waste of time. Another problematic situation occurs when partners disagree with each other without using effective behavior.[14] In the first few meetings, the lack of group cohesiveness can lead to divisiveness if partners disagree with each other, even by doing so appropriately.[15] But partners have to be careful not to discount members' ability. It's easy to justify not being open with members by claiming they aren't ready to handle it or would consider it a waste of time.

In basic facilitation, even if cofacilitator openness doesn't help the group directly achieve its primary goal, it can enhance trust. Members are more likely to trust partners when they coordinate their work openly rather than use ambiguous gestures such as a nod, frown, or hand motion. Like whispering or note passing, a secret signal may lead members to question whether you and your partner are withholding relevant information from them.

Yet there are times when signals are useful, not because you and your partner want to hide what you are saying, but because openly coordinating would simply be a distraction. How to solve the problem?

One approach, based on the behavior, "share all relevant information," is to tell members about the coordinating actions they might observe (such as nodding or a hand signal) and to point out that the purpose is to avoid distracting the group, not to keep secrets from them. As assurance, you can promise to share your private discussion whenever a member asks. Finally, members can agree to tell you and your partner if the secret coordination becomes distracting. The approach maintains or enhances trust. **The underlying principle is that partners coordinate their work in a manner consistent with the core values and the client's goals.**

DEBRIEFING WITH YOUR PARTNER

After each session, it's helpful for you and your partner to conduct your own debriefing. I can remember many more details of the conversation if my partner and I have this conversation immediately after the session.

In addition to discussing what's happened in the group, you can discuss how you worked together well and where you need to improve. One approach is to analyze the critical incidents of a session, comparing how you had agreed to handle them given your partner agreement with how you actually handled them. After one facilitation session, I asked my cofacilitator whether I was adding to his interventions too frequently. I said I was concerned that he might see my additions as intrusive. He saw them as appropriate and consistent with our agreement, and he wanted me to continue them. On another occasion with another facilitator, I asked the same question and found that my interventions were causing my cofacilitator to lose her focus.

You and your partner can also discuss your behaviors, feelings, and thoughts toward one another, identifying the causes and dealing with them so they don't contribute negatively to the group's dynamics. Issues such as status, control, competence, and support are all important to discuss. The principle is that your partner effectiveness depends partly on your ability to constructively talk about and manage the issues that affect your working relationship.

In developmental facilitation, you and your partner may also share some of your own debriefing with group members. This helps you understand how the participants responded to you and your partner's behavior and it also models for the group how you can share what you've learned to work more effectively with the group.

SUMMARY

In this chapter, we explored how you and your partner can work together to better serve the group and to improve your own skills. I began by considering the potential advantages and disadvantages of partnering. In deciding whether to use it, the underlying principle is that together partners should be able to diagnose and intervene in a greater range of situations and with greater skill than one facilitator, consultant, or coach can manage alone. Partners can work together effectively to the extent that their core values and assumptions are congruent.

I have also described how you and your partner can divide and coordinate your labor and, after selecting a division of labor, factors that you can consider in deciding who will fill which role. The final section of the chapter addressed how you and your partner maintain healthy boundaries and how you can coordinate their work in front of the group. Finally, we discussed how you can use debriefings to improve your partner effectiveness.

In the next chapter, I will describe how you can use your facilitative skills to help your own organization.

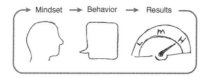

Mindset → Behavior → Results

CHAPTER FIFTEEN

Serving in a Facilitative Role in Your Own Organization

This chapter examines the issues you face when serving in a facilitative role in your own organization. I describe the advantages and disadvantages of the internal role, how the internal's facilitative role develops, strategies for shaping the role, and how to improve your internal role when you're not actively working in that role. If you're not an internal facilitator, consultant, coach, or trainer, you may want to skip this chapter.

If you're an internal facilitator, consultant, or coach and have read this far, you may be thinking, *The mutual learning approach could really improve my organization, but how do I apply it as an internal person? I don't have the freedom or power of an external facilitator, consultant, or coach, and I can't say what an external person can say—the risks are greater than I can take.*

There is essentially no difference between what constitutes effective behavior for internal facilitators, consultants, and coaches, and external ones. The mutual learning values and assumptions guide the behavior of internals and externals alike. These are the same core values and assumptions that generate effective behavior for all members of an organization. Although internals and externals start with some different challenges, they both use the same behavior.

ADVANTAGES AND DISADVANTAGES OF THE INTERNAL FACILITATIVE ROLE

When I talk with internal facilitators and consultants about their roles, they often tell me about the limitations they face. Many of these limitations are real.

But if you're an internal you probably also enjoy some advantages compared with your external colleagues. Drawing heavily on the work of Fritz Steele, in this first section I place the internal role in perspective by considering a few of the structural differences between internal and external facilitators and consultants and the advantages and disadvantages they create.[1]

Accessibility

An internal has a different kind of access to the organization than an external does, and the same goes for the organization's access to the internal.

Access and Information about the Organization. As an internal facilitator or consultant, you know a lot about your organization's history, structure, dynamics, and people. Sometimes you know a lot about the potential client group. All this information helps you quickly understand the client group's situation and encourage the group to analyze its decisions in the context of the culture of the organization. However, familiarity with the group's situation can lead you to presume your information, assumptions, and inferences are valid, even if you haven't tested them. To the extent that you're part of the culture, it's more difficult to see the assumptions embedded in it.

Access and Continuity of Work. Because you're in an internal facilitative role, it's usually easier for a group to get access to you than to an external person. It can be as simple as texting you, sending you an e-mail, giving you a call, or stopping by your office. You can more easily become involved in a project from beginning to end and see the long-term results of the project. Typically, a group views an internal as being more available for ongoing support than an external counterpart.

However, this relatively easy access can create conflict. The group may expect you to be available to help on a moment's notice and without adequate contracting. You may be expected to devote more time than you can allot to a particular group. This can be especially difficult if your manager expects you to devote less time to facilitation or consulting. Because you're available for ongoing support, it's difficult to determine when a project has ended and whether the terms of the project agreement have been fulfilled.

It may also be difficult for you to work with or maintain credibility with certain levels of the organization. More than the external facilitator or consultant, an internal one is identified with a particular level in the organization's hierarchy. Consequently, a group significantly above your organizational level may wonder whether you are up to its facilitative task, and one significantly below your organizational level may wonder whether you are there to meet the needs of senior leaders instead of the group's needs.

The Insider Image

There are several potential advantages to being considered an insider. The group may consider you "one of us." The members are likely to value your insider knowledge of the organization and of them. For these reasons, the group may be comfortable with you from the beginning of a project. If you have modeled your facilitative skills in your other roles, the group may consider you credible, especially if members have observed you directly in those roles. If you are part of an internal staff group that provides facilitation, consulting, or coaching services, this reputation may allow client groups to feel some confidence in you, even if they have not worked with you personally.

At the same time, being "one of us" is a liability if the client sees you as either too close to the problem to be neutral or blind to the client's assumptions and unable to challenge the client's thinking.

Internals tell me they have a difficult time establishing credibility compared with external counterparts, whom they bring in to help with a specific situation. This can be especially true when you raise issues that challenge the culture of the group or organization. One of the most subtle but powerful expectations of group members is that people act consistently with the culture of the organization. Although members may not agree with certain aspects of the culture, at some level they value the culture because it is predictable and meets some of their needs. Consequently, if you identify how group members contribute to the dysfunctional aspects of the culture, people may see you as inappropriately challenging the culture.

Job Security

As an internal, you have the relative security of a regular paycheck and many potential clients available without much marketing effort. In theory, however, the increased security that comes from working for a single organization also brings increased risk whenever that security is threatened. If a significant project experiences major problems, an external may lose a client, but you may lose your job or your influence. Consequently, as an internal, you may be more concerned about your financial security if your interventions involve confronting a group or leader, even if they are consistent with the mutual learning approach.

In practice, I have never met any skilled internal facilitators or consultants who were fired or forced to resign simply because they raised difficult issues with the client (if you are out there, let me know). However, I have worked with internals who decided to leave the organization because they felt they could not help it create significant change.

HOW YOUR INTERNAL FACILITATIVE ROLE IS SHAPED

Many of the challenges that you face as an internal stem from how the role has developed in your organization. Fortunately, you can shape your role to address these problems. To understand how, we first need to understand how your role develops.

You and Others Create Your Role

Like any organizational role, your internal role develops through an iterative process in which you and those who work with you share expectations about and attempt to influence how you will do your work. These people include your manager direct reports and peers, your primary client groups, and those that the primary client groups report to. Because each of these people depends on you in some way, each has some stake in and expectation of how you should fill your internal facilitative role.

These individuals may attempt to influence you, either directly or indirectly. Your manager may tell you directly that you can't work with certain groups in the organization. Or she may simply imply through actions that you should evaluate client-group members for purposes of a merit increase. Similarly, someone may tell you directly, "Don't turn down any assignment from a client group high in the organizational hierarchy." Or the expectation can be vague: "We want you to be available when we need you."

Of course, you also have expectations about how you should fulfill your internal role, and you convey that to people, directly or indirectly. You may tell client groups that you can't mediate between the group and the manager but that you can help the client group figure out how to raise a difficult issue with the manager. Or you may tell your own manager that the rules of confidentiality in the group prevent you from sharing with him specific comments that members make in their meetings.

Your role develops as the people you work with communicate their expectations to you, and vice versa, about what kind of work you will do and how you will do it. The more similar the expectations are, the less role conflict between you and these people. One reason you may face role conflict is that when you're working with a large number of people, it's likely that some of their expectations for you are incompatible.

To make matters more complex, the expectations that develop for your role are influenced by organizational, interpersonal, and individual factors. This includes the nature of your interpersonal relationships with others and your personality and personal style, such as how you use humor or how formal you are.

Your Other Roles Influence Your Facilitative Role

Finally, your internal facilitative role may be complicated by the fact that you fill at least one other role in the organization. Serving as an internal may be part of your larger role as an HR manager, Lean or Six Sigma manager, or your regular managerial or nonmanagerial position. Any organizational member can also serve in an internal facilitative role, regardless of his or her other organizational roles.

Role conflict can occur when the people you're working with expect you to take on elements of your "nonfacilitative" role. For example, if your non-facilitative position is higher in the organizational hierarchy than your clients' position, the group members may expect you to convey their message to people above them in the hierarchy. Your manager may expect you to evaluate the group members' performance as part of the performance appraisal process. If you are the HR director, the client group may expect you to make decisions on HR matters. If you are the finance director, the client group may expect you to pass judgment on finance matters.

Role conflict arises because the people you are facilitating usually don't think of you as performing two different roles: your regular role in the organization and your facilitator role. They simply think of you as someone who performs a variety of tasks and who can and should be able to perform all of those tasks or behaviors at any time. The challenge is to help the people you work with learn to think in terms of the different roles you serve in and to explain that while serving as facilitator, it may create problems if you engage in behaviors that are associated with your other role or roles.

SHAPING YOUR FACILITATIVE ROLE

You can change your internal facilitative role to make it more effective. People develop expectations of your facilitative role on the basis of their values, assumptions, and interests. By exploring these with others and explaining your own values, assumptions, and interests, you can shape your role. In this section, I describe strategies for improving your role, some of which are from the work of Fritz Steele.[2]

The strategies in Exhibit 15.1 seek to increase your effectiveness as an internal. This means that your primary task is to define your role consistently with the core values and assumptions of mutual learning. This creates a paradox; in the short run, you may have more opportunity to help groups if you agree to act inconsistently with the core values and assumptions. Yet, by doing so, you become less able to model effective behavior and help groups. The strategies below deal with this paradox by helping you improve your role without acting inconsistently with the mutual learning approach.

- Decide which facilitative role is appropriate.
- Discuss potential role conflicts before they arise.
- Seek agreement to switch facilitative roles.
- Discuss problems in your past relationships with client groups.
- Be willing to give up your facilitative role.
- Use the contracting process.
- Honor the core values, assumptions, and principles of mutual learning; tailor the methods.

Exhibit 15.1   Strategies for Shaping Your Internal Facilitative Role

Decide Which Facilitative Role Is Appropriate

An easy way to get into difficulty is to serve as a facilitator when that role is inappropriate. Unlike a facilitative consultant, trainer, or leader, a facilitator is content neutral. Content neutral is a relative term; you may wonder as an internal facilitator if you can ever be totally neutral about issues within the organization. However, there are two working criteria for judging neutrality: (1) You believe that personal views about the content of the facilitation do not significantly affect your facilitation, and (2) the client group believes that your personal views about the substance of the facilitation do not significantly affect your facilitation.

Unless you have little interaction with the group you are working with, serving as a facilitative consultant or even a facilitative leader may be more appropriate than acting in the facilitator role. In these two roles, you can offer essentially the same help as a facilitator and at the same time share the views and expertise that the group understands you have.

Discuss Potential Role Conflicts before They Arise

It's easier to discuss expectations of your internal facilitative role with groups before a conflict actually arises than after a conflict has occurred. For example, it's easier to discuss whether you should serve as an intermediary between a client group and its manager before the manager asks you to do so. This requires anticipating the role conflict that is likely to arise. The challenge is to reach agreement with all constituents so that everyone's expectations are compatible. This conversation is best held during the contracting process.

If you also hold nonfacilitator roles in the organization, you may experience pressure to use information you receive in the facilitator role to act in a nonfacilitator role. Consider a situation in which you are an organization development manager who also serves as a facilitator. You are facilitating an organizational task force that reports to your manager. Your manager tells you that she is concerned the task force is not making progress quickly enough. In an effort to address your manager's concern, you act as a mediator and convey the message directly to the group. Or you attempt to speed the group's progress by making content suggestions. Both of these actions are outside the facilitator role.

To remain consistent with the role, you can explain to your manager your interest in having her convey the message directly to the task force. If you're concerned that your manager thinks you are not doing your job effectively, you can test this with her. In doing so, you may learn that she either has an unrealistic expectation for the facilitation process or is unclear about your facilitator role.

Another source of role conflict is being pressured to obtain information in your facilitative role that is relevant to a nonfacilitative role. What should you do if you learn something in your facilitative role that you would act on if you had obtained it in a nonfacilitative role? Consider the example of my colleague who is an internal facilitator and HR director for his organization. While facilitating a quality improvement group, a discussion began about departmental policy on overtime. The facilitator quickly realized that if the members' comments were accurate, the departmental policy was in violation of the organizational policy. Had he heard the discussion when he was acting in his HR role, he would have contacted the department head to discuss the apparent violation. If you were in this situation, should you take different action because you obtained the information in your facilitator role and in the context of a confidentiality agreement?

The situation poses a dilemma because part of the client's trust in you as a facilitator stems from the fact that, theoretically, you have no influence over what happens to the members outside the facilitated group. But if you act on the information in your nonfacilitator role, you've exerted influence. In this example, your influence would benefit the group members, but in another situation, it may disadvantage them. If you don't act on the information and neither does the group, you may be in the position of knowing that some HR policies are being violated but not able to act on that knowledge. On the other hand, if you act on the information in your nonfacilitator role, group members may in the future withhold relevant information, concerned that you will act on it in your other role.

One approach to the dilemma lies in the core value of informed choice. In an organization that acts consistently with this value, members would consider it appropriate for you to act on the information in the nonfacilitator role. This suggests that a client group that espouses the core values would act accordingly.

However you decide to deal with this kind of dilemma, clearly contracting with members about how you treat such knowledge gives them relevant information with which they can then decide whether to share or withhold certain information in their discussion. Anticipating a conflicting issue means contracting about it before it arises.

Seek Agreement to Switch Facilitative Roles

If you serve as a facilitator as part of or in addition to your regular organizational role, at times you may have subject-matter information that, if you shared it, would take you out of your facilitator role. Before you leave the facilitator role, it's important to have agreement from the group.

Consider a group that is discussing how to establish self-managing work teams in its department: Team members are deciding how to plan, divide, and coordinate the work among them. To fully implement the change, the group may need to modify the means by which the performance of team members is assessed. If you're the facilitator for this group and also serve as HR director, you may know how the group can change its performance appraisal system. In this situation, if you have the agreement of the group, it's appropriate to temporarily leave your facilitator role and in your HR director role describe the process by which the client group can modify its performance appraisal system.

You could do this by saying, "You've raised an issue of HR policy that I have relevant information about as the HR director, and I think you might find it useful. I'd like to share this information. Does anyone have any concerns about my temporarily stepping out of the facilitator role to share this information?" After sharing the information, you clearly identify when you return to the facilitator role by simply saying, "I'm back in the facilitator role."

Discuss Problems in Your Past Client Relationships

If you've been using a unilateral control approach, your current and potential client groups may see you as unilaterally controlling and may not fully trust you. To determine if that's the case, you can begin by testing your inference about whether anything has occurred in the working relationship that prompts them to mistrust you, explaining your reason for asking.

Also, if you're aware of times when you acted inconsistently with the mutual learning approach, you can share the relevant information, explain why you now consider your behavior ineffective, and tell them how you would act differently now. Volunteering the information shows the group that you're aware of your own ineffective behavior and are capable of changing. Sharing the information also demonstrates that you can discuss your own behavior without getting defensive. This makes it easier for potential clients to raise concerns that they might have considered undiscussable with you. Through these discussions, potential clients begin to increase their trust in you.

Be Willing to Give Up Your Facilitative Role. If you're willing to give up your facilitative role when you can't fill it congruently with the mutual learning core values and assumptions, then it will be easier to take the risks necessary to openly confront role conflict, even with people who have more power and authority than you. Ironically, your willingness to step aside may increase the chance that you will end up not having to do so.

Still, in some cases, you may find that it's not possible to fill your facilitative role without repeatedly acting inconsistently with the mutual learning approach. For some people, giving up the internal facilitative role may also mean having to leave a job and an organization. Financially, this is the most serious consequence an internal faces. Yet continuing to serve in an internal facilitative role while acting inconsistently with the mutual learning approach leads back to the problem that opened this section. By acting that way, you grow ever less able to help groups.

Use the Contracting Process

Using the contracting process is a direct way of shaping your facilitative role and mitigating the potential problems I have discussed. As an internal, you may want to (or be pressured to) cut short the contracting process. You might assume that you're familiar enough with the members of a client group or that the client group seems to agree on what it needs to accomplish. Or you may feel pressured by a client group saying it doesn't have time for the planning meeting. Unfortunately, cutting short the contracting process almost always creates problems later in the process; the client doesn't adequately understand your role, or you and the client are unaware that you disagree on some aspect of the facilitation or consulting process.

When talking with internal clients about the need for planning a meeting time, you can explain that it will increase the group's ability to use the facilitation or consulting time effectively and efficiently. If the client insists that the planning meeting time is unnecessary because the group agrees on the objectives and other issues, you can ask why she considers it unnecessary and explain that if the client's assumptions are correct, then the meeting will certainly be brief. Still, if the client doesn't agree to the planning meeting, you have to decide whether the risk of carrying out a (presumably not very effective) facilitation or consultation is greater than the risk of not agreeing to do it at all.

Honor the Mutual Learning Approach, Tailor the Techniques

The mindset, behaviors, and principles of the mutual learning approach are its core. The methods and techniques are a way of operationalizing the mindset, behaviors, and principles. As an internal, you may find that some of the methods or techniques in this book don't seem to fit and that your organization will not change to adapt to them.

The methods and techniques that I describe throughout this book are not the only ones consistent with mutual learning; they are ones that I have used with good results. Using the mutual learning approach entails adapting and discovering techniques and methods that fit your organization and that are still congruent with the mindset, behaviors, and principles.

Contract with Your Manager First

One of the most important people to contract—and contract first—with is your manager. If your manager understands your internal facilitative role and the importance of your contracting directly with the groups you work with, you reduce potential misunderstandings between the group, your manager, and you. Here are a series of questions that you and your manager can discuss and reach agreements on.

How Will Groups Request My Facilitative Services? If the client initially contacts you rather than your manager, you're more likely to accurately represent your own facilitative approach and not inappropriately commit yourself. Your manager and you can also agree on how a request that comes directly to her will be handled. For example, your manager may generally describe your role to those requesting services and ask the potential client to contact you to discuss the specific situation.

Under What Conditions May I Decline or Accept a Request for Service? There are many appropriate reasons for declining a group's request for help. You may not have the skills or time to help the group, or you may not be able to be neutral on a facilitation topic. Or the group may want you to act in a way that is incongruent with the mutual learning approach. The group may have insufficient motivation or time to accomplish its objectives, or other factors within or outside the group may significantly reduce the likelihood of success.

If you can't decline a request under these or other legitimate conditions, at least tell the group that you will work with it, but explain the factors that you believe could hinder the group in accomplishing its objectives.

Who Will Decide Whether I Can Work with a Group? Ideally, you would decide whether to work with the group because you have the relevant information as the person filling the facilitative role. If not, you and your manager can jointly make the decision.

In some cases, your manager may want you to decline a request that, from your perspective, meets all the necessary conditions for acceptability. Your manager may consider the group relatively unimportant to the organization and not worth the investment. Alternatively, he may want you to accept a request that fails to meet the necessary conditions, in response to pressure to give the group a quick fix.

What Are My Limits for Contracting and Terminating a Contract with a Group? You and your manager need to agree on your limits, if any, for contracting and terminating an agreement. For example, does she need to approve requests that require more than a certain number of hours of commitment? Or does she need to approve requests for a certain level or area of the organization? Can you contract for a high-risk developmental request without approval? In some cases, you may need to terminate a contract with the client. What conversation, if any, do you need to have with your manager before terminating work with a group?

What Group Information Will I Need to Share with You or Others in the Organization? In considering confidentiality, there are several sets of interests to consider: the client group, yours, your manager, and the larger organization. If there are certain types of information you learn during your facilitative work that you will be required to share with your manager, it's important to know this before working with a group. This enables you to share that information with the group so that it can make an informed choice about working with you.

Will I Be Required to Evaluate My Client Group Members' Performance? You face a role conflict when someone other than the client—such as your manager—wants you to share your evaluation of a group member. Group members trust you as a facilitator (and usually in other facilitative roles) partly because you won't exercise any power in the organization that will affect them. Evaluating members means exercising that power (if you have it), and it changes the dynamic with the group. This is true even if you evaluate the group member positively.

The need to evaluate the process can be especially strong if members of a facilitated group spend a significant amount of their working time in the group. For example, I worked with a federal agency and its national union to establish a cooperative effort program. A small union-management committee worked almost full-time to administer the program. Managers often wanted the local internal facilitator to evaluate committee members' contributions. In fact, the managers believed the members were performing well and were looking for more detailed evaluation data to support giving them bonuses.

How Will My Performance in a Facilitative Role Be Evaluated? It's difficult for people to evaluate your performance in a facilitative role without observing you directly. The assumption underlying group facilitation is that effective group process contributes to high-quality, acceptable group decisions. But because the group maintains the choice over its actions, the group's performance is not determined by your performance. You can perform effectively, yet the group may not achieve any of its objectives. Alternatively, you can perform poorly, and the group can still accomplish its objectives.

An effective way to evaluate someone in a facilitative role is to observe his performance or review recordings of the facilitation, consulting, or coaching. (This requires agreement from the group about confidentiality regarding the recordings or group observations.) Both methods use valid information in the form of directly observable data. Recordings also enable you and your manager to review the data, which eliminates problems with recall and is of value in using the evaluation developmentally. If your facilitative role is only a small part of your responsibilities, evaluation may not be as important for purposes of reward.

What Arrangements Will We Make for My Other Work While I Am Serving in My Facilitative Role? If you serve part-time in facilitative roles, you can reduce role conflict by agreeing on how your "nonfacilitative" responsibilities will be handled while you're serving in your facilitative role. For example, you may delegate those responsibilities if possible, or you and your manager may agree that you will be responsible only for priority nonfacilitative work.

What Agreements Do We Need If I Work with a Group That You Are a Member Of? At some point, you may receive a request to work with a group that includes your manager. If you treat her differently from other group members, it reduces your credibility and effectiveness. Even if you and your manager agree that you will not treat her differently, when you are contracting with the full client group, it's important to raise this issue and ask the group to decide if it wants to work with you in your facilitative role.

What Will Each of Us Do to Ensure That Others Understand and Honor Our Agreement? If your manager understands your facilitative approach, he can help potential clients understand how you work. It's useful to discuss how your manager is willing to do this. Similarly, you have a role in helping key organization members understand your facilitative role. Together, you and your manager can decide what initiatives to take to accomplish this objective.

What Will We Do If Either of Us Believes the Other Has Acted Inconsistently with Our Agreement? Finally, it's useful for you and your manager to have an agreement about how you will proceed if one of you believes the other has acted inconsistently with your agreement. Agreeing to such a process at the time of contracting makes it easier to raise the issue if a conflict does arise.

CHANGING YOUR FACILITATIVE ROLE FROM THE OUTSIDE IN

How you act outside your facilitative role can improve your effectiveness within it. Here are some ways to improve your facilitative role even when you're not actively serving in that role.

Educate Others about Your Facilitative Role

Role conflict often occurs simply because people who work with a facilitator don't know what a facilitator is or does. In fact, many people equate facilitators with mediators or arbitrators. You can avoid or reduce these conflicts by creating opportunities to educate others about the facilitator's role—or any other facilitative role. Once someone understands your facilitative role, he may no longer consider you remiss upon hearing that you allowed a client group to make a "poor" decision. Educating others also generates future clients, as employees understand how a facilitator or coach can help them. But education is a process, not an event; it means constantly finding ways to help others understand the role and its benefits.

Become an Informal Change Agent

By becoming an informal change agent, you can attempt to influence the contextual factors that make it difficult to effectively fulfill your facilitative role. In some cases, the organizational factors that hinder you from fulfilling your facilitative role are the same ones that contribute to a client group's problems and lead it to ask you for help.

As the Team Effectiveness Model indicates, one contextual factor is organizational culture. Culture has a strong and pervasive influence on the behavior of members; it's very difficult to change. However, beginning to influence a group or organizational culture can lead to significant change—in your facilitative role as well. Of course, it's essential to use the mutual learning core values and assumptions in your role of informal change agent.

Model the Way

Gandhi has been attributed with the quote, "Be the change you want to see in the world." It turns out he didn't say exactly that, but he did say, "If we could change ourselves, the tendencies in the world would also change. As a man changes his own nature, so does the attitude of the world change toward him. . . . We need not wait to see what others do."[3] At the heart of being a change agent is modeling the way. As an internal, you ask others in your organization to follow the mutual learning core values, assumptions, and behaviors—to suspend their normal behavior and to take a risk with new behavior, expecting that these risks generate more effective behavior that leads to higher-quality decisions, greater learning, and better relationships.

If you've modeled this mindset and behavior in your own nonfacilitative roles, then clients see you as credible, especially if they have observed your behavior directly. If you haven't, clients may reasonably ask how you can advocate that they use the mutual learning approach when you haven't.

Modeling the way is essential. People look to a facilitator to see what is possible. Group members know how to act in accordance with the status quo. What isn't clear to them is how they can change their thinking and behavior to help create the kind of work relationships they say they want and need. When you model this behavior in your nonfacilitator role(s), you become a facilitative leader, creating the kind of relationship that others seek.

If you're concerned that modeling the mutual learning approach as a facilitative leader is a risk, your feeling is natural. Many of my clients and colleagues who are internal facilitators are initially worried that if they use the approach—particularly with people who have more power than them—those people will see their behavior as inappropriate or challenging. The risk may exist. However, in general, my clients and colleagues have found that they can reduce the risk by being explicit about their intentions, stating their concerns about how others might interpret their behavior, and asking whether others do see their behavior as ineffective. It's easy to overlook the risks of *not* using the facilitative skills—the risks of not testing an inference, withholding relevant information, and not asking genuine questions. Using the mutual learning approach doesn't require that you get rid of your concerns, or even make believe they don't exist; it requires only that you move forward with your concerns, making them part of the conversation when it's relevant.

SUMMARY

As an internal facilitator, consultant, coach, or trainer, you face various issues as you work with groups in your own organization. The issues are the advantages and disadvantages of your internal facilitative role, how the role develops, strategies for shaping it, and ways to improve your role when not actively serving in that role.

Although the expectations that organizational members have for you as an internal often differ from those of your external counterparts, a basic principle underlies this chapter: There is essentially no difference between what constitutes effective behavior for you as an internal and for externals. The mutual learning mindset and behaviors guide the behavior of both. This is the same mindset and behaviors that also generate effective behavior for all members of an organization. By modeling the mutual learning approach as a facilitative leader, you increase your credibility with groups and help your organization see what is possible using this approach.

In the next chapter, we will explore how to work with groups when everyone is not in the same room.

PART FOUR

WORKING WITH TECHNOLOGY

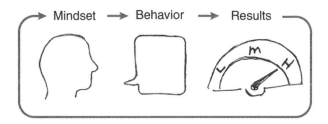

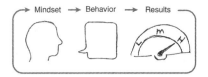

Mindset → Behavior → Results

CHAPTER SIXTEEN

Using Virtual Meetings

I n this chapter, I describe when to use virtual meetings, how to decide among different virtual meeting technologies, identify the special challenges of facilitating virtual meetings, and explain how to effectively address the challenges.

By *virtual meetings* (also referred to as online, electronic, distributed, or remote meetings), I'm referring to *synchronous meetings*—ones in which all members are online at the same specified time, but not all in the same physical room or in the same time zone. You can use virtual meetings with groups or teams that don't typically meet virtually or with groups or teams that consider themselves to be virtual, rarely if ever meeting face-to-face. This chapter doesn't address *asynchronous* meetings, in which members may not be online at the same time; nor does it address using computer technology as part of face-to-face meetings. Finally, the chapter does not address how to create effective virtual teams, which rely heavily on asynchronous meetings.[1] All of these topics are important but beyond the scope of this chapter.

Finally, virtual meeting technology is constantly changing, but this chapter—even if you're reading it on a virtual page—is not. Researchers at the University of Arizona, pioneers of virtual facilitation technology, have facilitated virtual meetings since the mid-1980s, and the field is still developing. Use this chapter to consider the issues involved in using virtual meetings, including congruence with mutual learning. Then go online or consult with others to learn about the most recent versions and functions of virtual meeting technology.

CHOOSING WHICH TYPE OF VIRTUAL MEETING TECHNOLOGY TO USE—IF ANY

You can hold a virtual meeting using different kinds of technology. The technology you and the group use—and whether you decide to use any technology—determines the opportunities and challenges you face.

Types of Virtual Meeting Technologies

There are several broad categories of virtual meeting technologies. Here is a list identifying the functions each provides:

- Audioconferencing: Participants are able to hear (but not see) each other through a common audio connection.

- Videoconferencing: Participants are able to hear and see each other through a common video connection.

- Screen sharing: Participants are able to see the facilitator's (or consultant's) or other team member's computer screen and can share control of the screen with each other.

- Web conferencing: This technology combines audio and/or video conferencing with text chatting, screen sharing, and sometimes other simple tools, such as sharing a presenter's whiteboard, or simple voting tools. Examples include GoToMeeting and WebEx.

- Electronic meeting system (EMS): EMSs (also known as Group Support Systems, or GSS) are specifically designed to help groups be effective and efficient using technology—whether all members are in the same physical room face-to-face (colocated) or in different locations (differently located)—and improve group problem solving and decision making by providing electronic tools for structuring group process. This includes brainstorming, discussion, analysis and voting, tracking actions, reviewing document and briefing, and documenting the meeting. In general, EMSs are designed to address issues that reduce the effectiveness of groups by increasing process gains and reduce process losses. Specifically, two common problems are poorly structured and inefficient meeting process, and over- or undervaluing group members' contributions based on factors other than the quality of their contributions (for example, formal authority, gender, race).[2] The first problem is addressed by creating a structure by using specific tools or activities for group tasks. The second problem is addressed by using anonymity so that members cannot be individually identified. EMSs do have the option to identify individuals or subgroups.

- Combined technologies: Some meeting technologies combine two or more of the above technologies. For example, EMS technologies can be used with GoToMeeting or Skype for Business to combine structured meeting processes with audio and/or videoconferencing. Also EMSs can be used on smart phones with audio and video capability as well as the structured process.

In the rest of the chapter, I focus mostly on the choice between using an EMS or working face-to-face.

Deciding Which Technology to Use

When you and the group decide which technology to use, you are trying to find the best fit among several sometimes conflicting criteria: (1) technology that is most effective for the group's task, (2) technology that is available to participants, and (3) technology that participants can use effectively. Here are questions to answer:

What technology is available to participants? No matter how useful the technology is, it's useless if participants can't access it. For example, participants may not have a webcam for web conferencing or may be located in an area without Internet access. Even if participants have access to the group's technology, they may not be able to use it reliably because they don't have a fast enough Internet connection or have out-of-date hardware or operating system software. To avoid spending time considering technologies that your group can't use, it helps to know the user requirements for the technology and quickly learn whether your group and you meet them.

How large is the group? As the number of participants increases, so does the need for technology that can be used to efficiently accept input from all the participants and organize and make sense of it so that the group can act on it. This often means shifting away from video and using web conferencing or EMSs. The number of people who can videoconference and see each other (assuming each person uses a separate webcam) is significantly less than the number who can audioconference or use an EMS. In audioconferencing, videoconferencing, and even face-to-face meetings, it's also difficult for a group of more than about 15 people to hear from everyone on the same topic before people become disengaged. Facilitators often address the problems of limited time and potential disengagement by creating breakout groups, in which each group addresses the same or related topics at the same time. The breakout groups briefly summarize their work to the large group, which seeks to converge on the various group ideas. One of EMS's defining features is providing simultaneous (often called parallel) input to manage these tasks efficiently, even in large groups.

What process tools does the meeting require?   My father, who was an engineer by training, used to tell me, "Use the right tool for the job." If your process requires people to view a video or document, web conferencing can be an appropriate choice. But if participants need to simultaneously work on a document or generate data that become input for this decision-making process, EMS technology is a better fit. EMS tools structure various elements of the problem-solving and decision-making process, such as brainstorming, organizing and refining ideas, prioritizing, converging on options, and building consensus.

What level of skill is required for participants and you to use the technology effectively?   For any meeting technology to be effective, group members need the skill to use it. Although the skill required to use any virtual technology has reduced as these technologies have been refined, as the technology moves from face-to-face, audioconferencing, videoconferencing, to EMSs, the level of skill required to use the technology increases. Asking the group members whether they have used the proposed technology before or performed similar functions on a computer or smartphone, and if so, how comfortable they were using it will help you and the group decide if the technology will ultimately contribute to or detract from the meeting process.

Anonymity and Incongruence between EMS Technology and Mutual Learning

EMS providers tout user anonymity as a key feature of their software. They explain that when users anonymously enter their comments or votes, it increases the dysfunctional dynamics in which some members' comments are given more attention and credence while others are ignored. In short, it levels the playing field, leading to more creative, higher-quality decisions.

Unless you've skipped the chapters before this one, you know that mutual learning considers anonymity inconsistent with accountability. Although it may be true that anonymous comments reduce irrelevant disparities in how participant's comments are evaluated, they do so by preventing participants from using member's names to create context for the comments. Anonymity comes with a price. In addition, anonymity is a solution that does not address the cause of the problem; it simply bypasses it, leaving it to surface another day in another setting. In contrast, mutual learning is designed to address the undiscussable issues in groups and teams that undermine their effectiveness.

During the early development of EMSs, I collaborated with some of the designers of EMS software and shared my concerns about designing EMSs that did not allow users to identify themselves by name. At least one system's designer designed the software so that the group could choose to identify everyone individually. Some EMSs may not allow individual users to identify themselves but do allow individuals to be identified according to the team they belong to. In this case, you may be able to assign each member a unique team name—his or her own individual name.

THE CHALLENGES THAT VIRTUAL MEETINGS CREATE

Where the group meets, how members are able to communicate with each other and what skills and processes they need to accomplish their task all affect how you need to design the meeting. The technology that makes virtual meetings possible also creates a different meeting "space" that changes how people communicate with each other, and that requires additional skills to accomplish their tasks.

Let's look at how virtual meetings create challenges that the group and you will need to address.[3]

It's more difficult to follow what is happening in a virtual meeting. Participants in different locations can't see everything going on in the meeting because there is not a physical meeting room that members can observe. If you're in a face-to-face meeting, you can quickly scan the entire room and the people in it, glance down at the agenda of the person sitting next to you, and use other cues to figure what the group is focused on. There are fewer natural cues in virtual meetings to tell you what agenda item the group is discussing. This requires facilitators to be much more explicit about where the group is in the process at any given time.

It's more difficult to get feedback on comments and questions. While this is true of face-to-face meetings—people are not good at making statements and combining questions—the problem is exacerbated in virtual meetings. Technology often makes it difficult to hear what someone has said or identify who said it and to ensure that the group responds to a member's comment or question. With EMSs, it's very difficult for participants to ask the group to respond to your input or to point out that the group has been ignoring your comments, although the facilitator can intervene on behalf of participants. Finally, if the group is using older meeting technology that includes half-duplex technology or certain types of speakerphones, people using different microphones cannot be heard at the same time.

It's easier to get distracted and to multitask. During face-to-face meetings, participants often are on their smartphones conducting other business or nonbusiness activities, even when there are group norms about not using these devices. Group members can easily convey their displeasure verbally and nonverbally. In virtual meetings, it's more difficult for members to get the full attention of all group members and to name behavior that is inconsistent with group norms.

It's easier to disengage. Even when people aren't distracted, they can become disengaged. If the effort needed to attend to the content and process of the meeting and to participate is too great, it's easy to disengage. And this assumes that the meeting process is effective, which it may not be.

You can forget who is in the meeting. When a majority of people are meeting in one room and the minority are meeting in one or more other rooms, it's common for the majority to forget that the others are present. This is made worse when the remote members are not connected by video.

There is less accountability to others. One of the key features of EMSs is that group members' input is anonymous (at least by default with some software), which has the unintended consequence of reducing accountability, one of the mutual learning core values.

It's easier to create information overload. When people use meeting technology tools, they can quickly create large amounts of information. Meeting technology tools are like Post-It notes on steroids; group members can simultaneously create a large amount of information that becomes challenging to organize and also poses more difficulties to developing a common understanding.[4]

It's more difficult to effectively build a team or repair it. Developing trust within a team is critical for its development, and building trust is particularly challenging for virtual teams.[5] When teams effectively address challenging issues, they observe and test their inferences about each other's verbal and nonverbal behaviors. Virtual teams create greater risk for team members because it's difficult to see many of these behaviors and respond to them. This makes it particularly difficult to address issues of trust, defensiveness, and other typical undiscussable issues. In general, experts on virtual teams advise against using virtual meetings to launch a team. Trying to rebuild trust in a virtual team can be even more difficult.[6]

EMS technology makes it more difficult to immediately intervene on participant contributions that are incongruent with mutual learning. Because

EMS technology enables participants to simultaneously enter their thoughts and respond to each other's comments, facilitators are unable to read all the data in real time as they would in a single group conversation.[7] This increases the chance that participants' comments will be incongruent with mutual learning behaviors and lead to negative consequences of unilateral control. This problem is exacerbated when participants' comments are anonymous.

Technology can be unpredictable. Although technology is becoming increasingly more stable, members may not be able to get an adequate connection or may lose their connection, software can freeze and may need to be rebooted, and the entire system can crash. I've experienced all of these problems, as have most facilitators who conduct virtual facilitation. Having a backup plan is essential.

DESIGNING AND FACILITATING VIRTUAL MEETINGS TO MEET THESE CHALLENGES

As a facilitator, consultant, or coach, your task is to jointly plan and design the meeting, and to use your facilitative role during the meeting so it addresses the challenges I described above. The solutions to some virtual meeting challenges are the same for face-to-face meetings. I won't repeat them here. Instead, in this section, I revisit some previous chapters and describe additional or different actions you can take for virtual meetings.

The Facilitative Role

Virtual meetings requires an expanded facilitative role and additional competencies that stem from the expanded role. That said, **most online facilitative competencies are the same as regular facilitative competencies**, but there are a few additions.

My colleague Mark Adkins and I identified 12 facilitative functions that were common to EMS and non-EMS meetings and only three facilitative functions that were specific to EMS meetings. These were:

1. **Appropriately selecting and preparing technology.**
2. **Creating comfort with and promoting understanding of technology and technology outputs.**
3. **Understanding the technology and its capabilities.**[8] A research study in the International Association of Facilitators journal *Group Facilitation* reached similar results, adding the online facilitative competency of being able to communicate with presence online.[9]

To be clear, there are facilitative functions and competencies specific to virtual meetings, but they are required in addition to the much larger set of functions and competencies that apply to all facilitative roles. In other words, a lot of what makes you effective online in your facilitative role is what makes you effective offline in your facilitative role.

Working with a Partner

Given the extra demands of virtual meetings, working with a partner is very helpful for you and the group. If you do work with a cofacilitator, you will need to decide how to divide and coordinate your roles. In virtual meetings, it's common for one partner to serve as the group process partner and another to serve as the technical partner.

As the *group process partner*, you're performing the tasks of a face-to-face facilitator that we've explored throughout the book. This includes ensuring that group members' contributions are congruent with the task and the group's ground rules; helping the group distill, make meaning of, and make decisions based on the group input; and jointly modifying the agenda so it continues to meet the group's needs. As the *technical partner*, you focus on the meeting technology, including setting up the technology before the session with the appropriate tools, initiating these tools for the various group tasks during the session, helping group members use the technology, monitoring problems with technology, and responding to participants' problems using the technology.[10] If you plan to work with a partner, this becomes part of the contracting conversation with the group.

Contracting

Most of the contracting questions you would ask in face-to-face work are relevant for virtual meetings, except for questions about where the meeting will be held. Instead there are other questions to ask about the virtual meeting technology the group will use:

- What technology, if any, does the organization currently use for virtual meetings? What are the versions of browser and applications it uses?
- What virtual technology is appropriate given the group's goals, the proposed agenda and process, the number of participants, and the participants' location, access to hardware, and Internet connections?
- Will each participant be using the full technology or only a portion of it (for example, calling in to a video-based online technology)?[11]
- What will be the backup plan in the event of various technology failures?
- Will you use facilitative partners for the meeting? If so, what roles will each of them serve in?

Designing the Meeting

Designing the virtual meeting begins during the first stage of contracting, continues with the second stage during the planning meeting, and continues after the planning meeting as you and your partner design the details of the meeting process. Remember that if you're planning a virtual meeting, the planning meeting in stage two is more likely to be virtual.

Here are six recommendations for designing virtual meetings so they address the virtual meeting challenges I described above:[12]

1. **Identify each participant's interests in the meeting and design the meeting to incorporate those interests.** Researchers found that when participants could not articulate their interest in the meeting, they did not show up at virtual meetings. Unlike face-to-face meetings, which seem to generate high accountability for attendance, it is easier to not show up at a virtual meeting if you believe it won't meet your needs. Ideally, this means that the planning meeting should include all participants. If all participants' interests are addressed in the design stage, you reduce the chance that people will disengage during the meeting.

2. **Assume everything will take longer until people learn the technology.** There is a learning curve for any technology that is new to participants, even processes that face-to-face groups use. After you use a particular technology with a number of groups, you will be better able to estimate the time required. Until then, talk with colleagues who have used the technology in similar circumstances to get a realistic estimate of the time required.

3. **Design agenda processes so they explicitly identify the technology tools you will use in each step of the process and the estimated time for each step.** EMS technology uses a number of specific tools for guiding the group through problem solving and decision making. By identifying these tools and estimated times, you help participants better understand the course of the meeting and reduce disengagement that stems from disorientation.

4. **Distribute photos and short bios of people who will be at the meeting.** Unless you're working with an intact team that meets regularly, providing photos and short bios reminds people who is in the room and enables them to connect faces with names and voices. In EMSs, you can upload these before the session and ask people to review them.

5. **Use video whenever it's feasible.** Communication research consistently finds that the information available to make sense of situations declines as people move from face-to-face communication, to video, to audio, and ultimately to textual communication. Being able to

see others on video enables you and participants to make inferences about others—and then test them. It also enables people to determine if someone is still present and engaged. However, it's often difficult to get video technology to work well, especially as the group size increases. So facilitators often start the meeting with video for introductions and then drop it, continuing with EMS or audio alone.[13]

6. **Have a technology fallback plan.** The meeting design should include a backup plan for possible technical failures, ranging from individual participants being unable to connect or use some function, to the system needing to be rebooted, to system failures that cannot be resolved. Having on-call technical support available is also important.

During the Meeting

Your facilitative role includes maximizing the advantages of the technology you use with the group while reducing the challenges associated with it. Some of the challenges of virtual meetings can be addressed through design while others need to be addressed during the meeting stage or in both stages. Here are eight recommendations for your facilitative role during virtual meetings so they address the challenges I describe above:[14]

1. **Use back channels for handling technology issues and nonagenda issues.** At the beginning of the meeting, clearly describe how participants should seek help for technology and nonagenda issues. By using a separate process, such as a dedicated text chat box, the technical partner can quickly identify participants' requests, and they will not distract the participants engaged in the task.

2. **If you have to choose between focusing the video camera on shared information or on the presenter or other attendees, focus it on the shared information.** The shared information is more useful for participants to engage in the conversation than seeing the presenter or others. Participants will still be able to hear the presenter while seeing the shared information.

3. **During the meeting, use the agenda regularly to show participants where they are in the process.** When using an EMS, if participants don't follow the transition from one task to another, they can't participate in the current task. Clearly identifying and announcing these transitions is central to any effective meeting.

4. **Address people by name and ask people to state their name when they speak.** Unless everyone is on video, this increases the chance that everyone will remember who is in the room. It also enables people to connect a person's previous comments with that person's current

comments and to make more sense of the conversation by understanding who is responding to whose comments.

5. **Check frequently to see how members are doing.** In virtual meetings, you have less or no ability to scan the room and see whether any group members are disengaged, frustrated, or puzzled. However, in your facilitative role, you can conduct quick polls to identify how the group is doing.

6. **Intervene when the group does not respond to comments.** With an EMS, it is easy for you to not intervene because of the speed at which participants can enter a large number of comments. This makes it more important to watch for cases in which individuals are asking questions and not receiving answers from the group.

7. **Intervene when group members are not using the mutual learning behaviors.** Of course, this is a central part of your facilitative role. Yet, here, too, it can be difficult to intervene on behaviors inconsistent with mutual learning because of the speed at which participants can enter a large number of comments.

8. **Have people describe the nonverbal behaviors among people in the location.** If you aren't using video or can't see everyone, ask others to describe the nonverbal behaviors they are seeing in the location. I'll often say something like, "I can't see people's reactions in the room; can you describe their facial expressions?" People will often respond by saying, "Joe and I are smiling, and Bernie is shaking his head."

Virtual meetings offer groups the ability to accomplish work when they aren't physically in the same place. Although face-to-face interactions provide participants information and an experience not currently available through virtual meeting technology, the technology is constantly improving. EMSs provide helpful structure for many group tasks. Research has shown that when using an EMS, structuring verbal and electronic communication improved the quality of the output, reduced time to completion, and increased satisfaction with the planning process.[15]

SUMMARY

In this chapter, I described several types of virtual meeting technologies that you can use with groups that are not able to meet face-to-face: audioconferencing, videoconferencing, screen sharing, web conferencing, and electronic meeting systems (EMS). I described the functions of each technology and how to decide which technology to use. I described the challenges that virtual meeting technologies presents and how you can address these challenges through contracting, design, and during the meeting.

NOTES

CHAPTER 1. THE SKILLED FACILITATOR APPROACH

1. Argyris, C. (1982). *Reasoning, learning, and action: Individual and organizational.* San Francisco, CA: Jossey-Bass; Argyris, C. (1985). *Strategy, change, and defensive routines.* Boston, MA: Pitman; C. Argyris, C. (1990). *Overcoming organizational defenses: Facilitating organizational learning.* Boston, MA: Allyn & Bacon; Argyris, C., Putnam, R., & Smith, D. M. (1985). *Action science: Concepts, methods, and skills for research and intervention.* San Francisco, CA: Jossey-Bass; Argyris, C., & Schön, D. A. (1974). *Theory in practice: Increasing professional effectiveness.* San Francisco, CA: Jossey-Bass; Argyris, C., & Schön, D. A. (1978). *Organizational learning: A theory of action perspective.* Reading, MA: Addison-Wesley.

CHAPTER 2. THE FACILITATOR AND OTHER FACILITATIVE ROLES

1. Silsbee, D. (2010). *The mindful coach: Seven roles for facilitating leader development* (2nd ed.). San Francisco, CA: Jossey-Bass.

2. Clutterbuck, D. Coaching the team. In D. B. Drake, D. Brennan, & K. Gørtz (Eds.), *The philosophy and practice of coaching: Insights and issues for a new era* (pp. 219–238). San Francisco, CA: Jossey-Bass.

3. Hackman, J. R., and Wageman, R. (2005). A Theory of Team Coaching. *The Academy of Management Review* 30(2), 269–287, p. 269.

4. Clutterbuck, D. (2008). *Coaching the team at work.* Boston: Nicholas Brealey International (p. 77).

5. Hawkins, P. (2011). *Leadership team coaching.* Philadelphia, PA: Kegan Paul (p. 80).

6. Moore, C. W. (2014). *The mediation process: Practical strategies for resolving conflict* (4th ed., pp. 8–9). San Francisco, CA: Jossey-Bass.

7. Bush, R.A.B., & Folger, J. P. (2004). *The promise of mediation: The transformative approach to conflict* (2nd ed.). San Francisco, CA: Jossey-Bass.

CHAPTER 3. HOW YOU THINK IS HOW YOU FACILITATE

1. Argyris, C., & Schön, D. A. (1996). *Organizational learning II: Theory, method, and practice.* Reading, MA: Addison-Wesley.

2. For a review of some of this research, see Kahneman, D. (2011). *Thinking: Fast and slow.* New York, NY: Farrar, Straus and Giroux.

3. Chris Argyris and Donald Schön identified this important and problematic gap in their research as the difference between our espoused theory and our theory-in-use.

4. I have developed the unilateral control model based on the work of Argyris and Schön [see Argyris, C., & Schön, D. A. (1974). *Theory in practice: Increasing professional effectiveness.* San Francisco: Jossey-Bass Publishers], who developed an initial model and called it Model I, and Robert Putnam, Diana McLain Smith, and Phil McArthur, who adapted Model I and referred to it as the unilateral control model. Robert Putnam, Phil McArthur, and Diana McLain Smith founded Action Design, an organizational and management development firm that has built on the work of Argyris and Schön. Putnam and McLain Smith are coauthors, with Chris Argyris, of *Action Science*, published by Jossey-Bass.

5. The give-up-control model was developed by Argyris [Argyris, C. (1979). Reflecting on laboratory education from a theory of action perspective. *Journal of Applied Behavioral Science, 15*(3), 296–310], who called it Opposite Model I. Robert Putnam, Diana McLain Smith, and Phil McArthur at Action Design (Workshop materials. www.actiondesign, 1997) adapted it and refer to it as the give-up-control model.

6. Argyris, C., Putnam, R., & Smith, D. M. (1985). *Action science: Concepts, methods, and skills for research and intervention.* San Francisco, CA: Jossey-Bass.

CHAPTER 4. FACILITATING WITH THE MUTUAL LEARNING APPROACH

1. Camerer, C., Loewenstein, G., & Weber, M. (1989). The curse of knowledge in economic settings: An experimental analysis. *Journal of Political Economy.* http://doi.org/10.1086/261651

2. Norman, S. M., B. J. Avolio, & Luthans, F. 2010. The impact of positivity and transparency on trust in leaders and their perceived effectiveness. *Leadership Quarterly, 21,* 350–364.

3. Kay, B., & Christophel, D. M. (1995). The relationships among manager communication openness, nonverbal immediacy, and subordinate motivation. *Communication Research Reports, 12,* 200–205.

4. Burke, R. J., & Wilcox, D. S. (1969). Effects of different patterns and degrees of openness in superior-subordinate communication on subordinate job satisfaction. *Academy of Management Journal, 12,* 319–326. Korsgaard, M. A., Brodt, S. E., & Whitener, E. M. (2002). Trust in the face of conflict: The role of managerial trustworthy behavior and organizational context. *Journal of Applied Psychology, 87,* 312–319.

5. Wanberg, C. R., & Banas, J. T. (2000). Predictors and outcomes of openness to changes in a reorganizing workplace. *Journal of Applied Psychology, 85,* 132–142.

6. Mesmer-Magnus, J. R., & Dechurch, L. A. (2009). Information sharing and team performance: A meta-analysis. *Journal of Applied Psychology, 94,* 535–546.

7. Jassawalla, A. R., Sashittal, H. C., & Malshe, A. (2010). Effects of transparency and at-stakeness on students' perceptions of their ability to work collaboratively in effective classroom teams: A partial test of the Jassawalla and Sashittal model. *Decision Sciences Journal of Innovative Education, 8,* 35–53.

8. Edmondson, A. C. (2003). Speaking up in the operating room: How team leaders promote learning in interdisciplinary action teams. *Journal of Management Studies, 40,* 1419–1452.

9. Moye, N. A., & Langfred, C. W. (2004). Information sharing and group conflict: Going beyond decision making to understand the effects of information sharing on group performance. *International Journal of Conflict Management, 15,* 381–410.

10. Tschan, F., Semmer, N. K., Gurtner, A., Bizzari, L., Spychiger, M., Breuer, M., & Marsch, S. U. (2009). Explicit reasoning, confirmation bias, and illusory transactive memory: A simulation study of group medical decision making. *Small Group Research, 40,* 271–300.

11. Ibid., p. 137.

12. Paul Ekman, quoted in ibid., p. 139.

13. Ibid., pp. 35–50.

14. Ibid., p. 138.

15. Homan, A. C., Hollenbeck, J. R., Humphrey, S. E., Van Knippenberg, D., Ilgen, D. R., & Van Kleef, G. A. (2008). Facing differences with an open mind: Openness to experience, salience of intragroup differences, and performance of diverse work groups. *Academy of Management Journal, 51,* 1204–1222.

16. Ibid., p. 137.

17. Fairfield, K. D., & Allred, K. G. (2007). Skillful inquiry as a means to success in mixed-motive negotiation. *Journal of Applied Social Psychology, 37,* 1837–1855.

18. Kashdan, T. B., & Steger, M. F. (2007). Curiosity and pathways to well-being and meaning in life: Traits, states, and everyday behaviors. *Motivation and Emotion, 31,* 159–173.

19. Cacioppo, J. T., Petty, R. E., Feinstein, J. A., & Jarvis, W. B. G. (1996). Dispositional differences in cognitive motivation: The life and times of individuals varying in need for cognition. *Psychological Bulletin, 119,* 197–253.

20. Kashdan, T. (2009). *Curious?: Discover the missing ingredient to a fulfilling life* (pp. 35–50). New York, NY: Collins Living.

21. Losada, M. (1999). The complex dynamics of high-performance teams. *Mathematical and Computer Modelling, 30,* 179–92.

22. Wood, J. A., Jr., & Winston, B. E. (2005). Toward a new understanding of leader accountability: Defining a critical construct. *Journal of Leadership & Organizational Studies, 11,* 84–94.

23. I have not been able to find the source of the quote. Please let me know if you know it.

24. Scott-Ladd, B., Travaglione, A., & Marshall, V. (2006). Causal inferences between participation in decision making, task attributes, work effort, rewards, job satisfaction, and commitment. *Leadership & Organization Development Journal, 27,* 399–414.

25. Black, J. S., & Gregersen, H. B. (1997). Participative decision making: An integration of multiple dimensions. *Human Relations*, 50, 859–878.

26. Kashdan, T. (2009). *Curious?: Discover the missing ingredient to a fulfilling life.* New York, NY: Collins Living.

27. Carmeli, A., Sheaffer, Z., & Halevi, M. Y. (2009). Does participatory decision-making in top management teams enhance decision effectiveness and firm performance? *Personnel Review, 38,* 696–714.

28. Black, J. S., & Gregersen, H. B. (1997). Particpative decision making: An integration of multiple dimensions. *Human Relations, 50,* 859–878.

29. Carmeli, A. (2008). Top management team behavioral integration and the performance of service organizations. *Group & Organization Management, 33,* 712–735.

30. Scott-Ladd, B., Travaglione, A., & Marshall, V. (2006). Causal inferences between participation in decision making, task attributes, work effort, rewards, job satisfaction, and commitment. *Leadership & Organization Development Journal, 27,* 399–414.

31. Davis, W. D., Mero, N., & Goodman, J. M. (2007). The interactive effects of goal orientation and accountability on task performance. *Human Performance, 20,* 1–21.

32. Ford, J. K., & Weldon, E. (1981). Forewarning and accountability: Effects on memory-based interpersonal judgments. *Personality and Social Psychology Bulletin, 7,* 264–268.

33. Ashton, R. H. (1992). Effects of justification and a mechanical aid on judgment performance. *Personality and Social Psychology Bulletin, 52,* 292–306.

34. Rozelle, R. M., & Baxter, J. C. (1981). Influence of role pressures on the perceiver: Judgments of videotape interviews varying judge accountability and responsibility. *Journal of Applied Psychology, 66,* 437–441.

35. Tetlock, P. E. (1985). Accountability: A social check on the fundamental attribution error. *Social Psychology Quarterly, 48,* 227–236.

36. Condon, P., & Desteno, D. (2011). Compassion for one reduces punishment for another. *Journal of Experimental Social Psychology, 47,* 698–701.

37. Rudolph, U., Roesch, S. C., Greitemeyer, T., & Weiner, B. (2004). A meta-analytic review of help giving and aggression from an attributional perspective: Contributions to a general theory of motivation. *Cognition & Emotion, 18,* 815–848.

38. Allred, K. G., Mallozzi, J. S., Matsui, F., & Raia, C. P. (1997). The influence of anger and compassion on negotiation performance. *Organizational Behavior & Human Decision Processes, 70,* 175–187.

39. Grant, A. M., Dutton, J. E., & Rosso, B. D. (2008). Giving commitment: Employee support programs and the prosocial sensemaking process. *Academy of Management Journal, 51,* 898–918.

40. Berke, D. (1995). *The gentle smile: Practicing oneness in daily life.* New York, NY: Crossroad.

41. Scholten, L., Van Knippenberg, D., Nijstad, B. A., & De Dreu, C. K. W. (2007). Motivated information processing and group decision-making: Effects of process accountability on information processing and decision quality. *Journal of Experimental Social Psychology, 43,* 539–552.

CHAPTER 5. EIGHT BEHAVIORS FOR MUTUAL LEARNING

1. In general, the behaviors are derived from Argyris and Argyris and Schön [Argyris, C. (1982). *Reasoning, learning, and action: Individual and organizational.* San Francisco: Jossey-Bass. Argyris, C., & Schön, D. A. (1974). *Theory in practice: Increasing professional effectiveness.* San Francisco, CA: Jossey-Bass]. Behavior 5 is from Fisher and Ury [Fisher, R. L., & Ury, W. (1991). *Getting to yes: Negotiating without giving in.* New York, NY: Penguin Books], which was based on the work of Mary Parker Follett in the early 1900s [Follett, M. P., & Graham, P. (1995). *Mary Parker Follett—Prophet of management.* Boston: Harvard Business School Press].

2. In fact, in previous versions of this book, I referred to similar lists of these behaviors as ground rules for effective groups. I have changed the term to *behaviors* because even when groups choose not to use them as ground rules, they are still behaviors for mutual learning.

3. This behavior was originally described by Chris Argyris and Donald Schön as combining advocacy and inquiry. Argyris, C., & Schön, D. A. (1974). *Theory in practice: Increasing professional effectiveness.* San Francisco, CA: Jossey-Bass.

4. Fisher, R. L., & Ury, W. (1991). *Getting to yes: Negotiating without giving in.* New York, NY: Penguin Books.

CHAPTER 6. DESIGNING AND DEVELOPING EFFECTIVE GROUPS

1. Hackman, J. Richard (2002). *Leading teams: Setting the stage for great performances.* Boston, MA: Harvard Business School Publishing.

2. Wageman, R. (1999). The meaning of interdependence. In M. Turner (Ed.), *Groups at work: Advances in theory and research.* Hillsdale, NJ: Erlbaum.

3. Hackman, J. Richard (2002). *Leading teams: Setting the stage for great performances.* Boston, MA: Harvard Business School Publishing.

4. Ibid.

5. Cheng, J. L. C. (1983). Interdependence and coordination in organizations: A role-system analysis. *Academy of Management Journal, 26*(1), 156.

6. Thompson, J. (1967). *Organizations in action.* New York, NY: McGraw-Hill. Thompson was describing three types of interdependence that occurred between units of organizations: pooled, sequential, and reciprocal. However, I believe these same relationships hold within teams.

7. My discussion of interdependence draws heavily on the research and writing of Ruth Wageman, who has greatly contributed to explaining how interdependence is designed and why it matters. Wageman, R. (1999). The meaning of interdependence. In M. Turner (Ed.), *Groups at work: Advances in theory and research.* Hillsdale, NJ: Erlbaum.

8. Box, G. E. P., & Draper, N. R. (1987). *Empirical model building and response surfaces.* New York, NY: Wiley.

9. Tuckman, Bruce W. (1965). Developmental sequence in small groups. *Psychological Bulletin, 63,* 384–399.

10. Sutton, R. I., & Staw, B. M. (1995). What theory is not. *Administrative Science Quarterly, 40*(3), 371–384.

11. This section is adapted from the chapter "Designing for Mutual Learning" in *Smart Leaders, Smarter Teams.*

12. The sections on team structure, process, and context are adapted from the chapter "Designing for Mutual Learning" in *Smart Leaders, Smarter Teams.*

13. Allport, F. H. (1967). A theory of enestruence (event-structure theory): Report of progress. *American Psychologist, 22*(1), 1–24.

14. Locke, E. A., & Latham, G. P. (2002). Building a practically useful theory of goal setting and task motivation: A 35-year odyssey. *American Psychologist, 57*(9), 705–717.

15. Hackman, J. Richard (1987). The design of work teams. In J. Lorsch (Ed.), *Handbook of organizational behavior* (pp. 315–342). Upper Saddle River, NJ: Prentice-Hall (p. 324).

16. Bell, S. T. (2007). Deep-level composition variables as predictors of team performance: A meta-analysis. *Journal of Applied Psychology, 92*(3), 595.

17. Wageman, R., & Gordon, F. M. (2005). As the twig is bent: How group values shape emergent task interdependence in groups. *Organization Science, 16*(6), 687–700.

18. Wageman, R. (2001). The meaning of interdependence. In M. Turner (Ed.), *Groups at work: Theory and research* (pp. 197–217). Mahwah, NJ: Erlbaum.

19. Lowry, T. (1910). *Personal reminiscences of Abraham Lincoln.* London, England, privately printed.

20. Kozlowski, S. W. J., & Bell, B. S. (2003). Work groups and teams in organizations. In W. C. Borman & D. R. Ilgen (Eds.), *Handbook of psychology: Industrial and organizational psychology* (pp. 333–375). Hoboken, NJ: Wiley.

21. Burke, C. S., Stagl, K. C., Klein, C., Goodwin, G. F., Salas, E., & Halpin, S. M. (2006). What type of leadership behaviors are functional in teams? A meta-analysis. *Leadership Quarterly, 17*(3), 288–307.

22. Argyris, C., & Schön, D. A. (1978). *Organizational learning: A theory of action perspective.* Reading, MA: Addison-Wesley.

23. Schein, E. H. (1985). *Organizational culture and leadership.* San Francisco, CA: Jossey-Bass.

24. Argyris, C. (1990). *Overcoming organizational defenses: Facilitating organizational learning.* Boston, MA: Allyn & Bacon.

25. Thomas, K., & Kilmann, R. (1974). *Thomas-Kilmann conflict mode instrument.* Tuxedo, NY: XICOM.

26. Amason, A. C. (1996). Distinguishing the effects of functional and dysfunctional conflict on strategic decision making: Resolving a paradox for top management teams. *Academy of Management Journal, 39*(1), 123–148.

27. Crawford, J. L., Haaland, G. A. (1972). Predecisional information-seeking and subsequent conformity in the social influence process. *Journal of Personality and Social Psychology, 23*(1), 12–119.

28. Jehn, K. A., Northcraft, G. B., & Neale, M. A. (1999). Why differences make a difference: A field study of diversity, conflict, and performance in work groups. *Administrative Science Quart*erly, *44,* 741–763.

29. Sundstrom, E., de Meuse, K. P., & Futrell, D. (1990). Work teams: Applications and effectiveness. *American Psychologist, 45*(2), 120–133.

30. This assumes that team members have direct contact with each other.

31. Rosenbaum, M. E., Moore, D. L., Cotton, J. L., Cook, M. S., Hieser, R. A., Shovar, M. N., & Gray, M. J. (1980). Group productivity and process: Pure and mixed reward structures and task interdependence. *Journal of Personality and Social Psychology, 39*(4), 626–642; Wageman, R., & Baker, G. (1997). Incentives and cooperation: The joint effects of task and reward interdependence on group performance. *Journal of Organizational Behavior (1986–1998), 18*(2), 139.

32. Wageman, R. (2001). The meaning of interdependence. In M. Turner (Ed.), *Groups at work: Theory and research* (pp. 197–217). Mahwah, NJ: Erlbaum.

33. Kerr, S. (1975). On the folly of rewarding A, while hoping for B. *Academy of Management Journal, 18,* 769–783.

34. Carlson, P. (2005). Do surveys provide valid information for organizational change? In R. Schwarz, A. Davidson, P. Carlson, & S. McKinney (Eds.), *The skilled facilitator fieldbook: Tips, tools, and tested methods for consultants, facilitators, managers, trainers, and coaches* (pp. 409–412). San Francisco, CA: Jossey-Bass.

35. Wageman, R., & Gordon, F. M. (2005). As the twig is bent: How group values shape emergent task interdependence in groups. *Organization Science, 16*(6), 687–700.

CHAPTER 7. DIAGNOSING AND INTERVENING WITH GROUPS

1. Retrieved March 2, 2016, from http://www.oxforddictionaries.com/us/definition/american_english/diagnosis.

2. Retrieved March 2, 2016, from http://www.oxforddictionaries.com/us/definition/american_english/intervene.

3. Schein, E. H. (1987). *Process consultation: Lessons for managers and consultants,* Vol. 2. Reading, MA: Addison-Wesley.

CHAPTER 8. HOW TO DIAGNOSE GROUPS

1. Bandler, R., & Grinder, J. (1982). *Reframing: Neuro-linguistic programming and the transformation of meaning.* Moab, UT: Real People Press; Bateson, G. (1972). *Steps to an ecology of mind.* San Francisco, CA: Chandler.

2. Hirokawa, R. Y. (1988). Group communication and decision-making performance: A continued test of the functional perspective. *Human Communication Research, 14*(4), 487–515; Senge, P. (1990). *The fifth discipline: The art and practice of the learning organization.* New York, NY: Doubleday; Watzlawick, P., Beavin, J. J., & Jackson, D. D. (1967). *Pragmatics of human communication: A study of interactional patterns, pathologies, and paradoxes.* New York, NY: Norton.

3. Haselton, M. G., Nettle, D., & Andrews, P. W. (2005). The evolution of cognitive bias. In D. M. Buss (Ed.), *The handbook of evolutionary psychology* (pp. 724–746). Hoboken, NJ: Wiley.

4. Kahneman, D. (2011). *Thinking, fast and slow.* New York, NY: Farrar, Straus and Giroux.

5. Wilke, A., & Mata, R. (2012). Cognitive bias. In V. S. Ramachandran (Ed.), *The encyclopedia of human behavior* (Vol. 1, pp. 531–535). New York, NY: Academic Press.

6. This quote has been attributed to a variety of sources, including Anaïs Nin, Immanuel Kant, and the Babylonian version of the Talmud. Retrieved March 19, 2016 from: http://quoteinvestigator.com/2014/03/09/as-we-are.

7. Kaplan, A. (1964). *The conduct of inquiry: Methodology for behavioral science.* New York, NY: Thomas Y. Crowell.

CHAPTER 9. HOW TO INTERVENE WITH GROUPS

1. Nisbett, R. E., & Ross, L. (1980). *Human inference: Strategies and shortcomings of social judgment.* Upper Saddle River, NJ: Prentice-Hall.

2. Merton, R. K. (1968). *Social theory and social structure.* New York, NY: Simon & Schuster.

3. See, for example, Snyder, M., & Swann, W. B., Jr. (1978). Behavioral confirmation in social interaction: From social perception to social reality. *Journal of Experimental Social Psychology, 162,* 148–162.

4. See, for example, Schein, E. H. (1987). *Process consultation: Lessons for managers and consultants* (Vol. 2). Reading, MA: Addison Wesley.

5. Schein, E. H. (1987). *Process consultation: Lessons for managers and consultants* (Vol. 2). Reading, MA: Addison Wesley, p. 158.

CHAPTER 10. DIAGNOSING AND INTERVENING ON THE MUTUAL LEARNING BEHAVIORS

1. Ground rules. (2015, December 16). Retrieved March 25, 2016, from https://en.wikipedia.org/w/index.php?title=Ground_rules&oldid=695552129.

CHAPTER 11. USING MUTUAL LEARNING TO IMPROVE OTHER PROCESSES AND TECHNIQUES

1. Schuman, S. M. (moderator). (2001, March 1). *Ice breakers, introductions, energizers, and other experiential exercises.* The Electronic Discussion on Group Facilitation. Retrieved from http://www.albany.edu/cpr/gf/resources/Icebreakers-and-Introductions.htm.

2. Edmondson, A. (1999). Psychological safety and learning behavior in work teams. *Administrative Science Quarterly, 44*(2), 350–383.

3. Cardon, N., & Bribiescas, F. (2015). Respect for people: The forgotten principle in Lean manufacturing implementation. *European Scientific Journal, 11*(13), 45–61.

4. Emiliani, B. (2015, February 16). *Defining "respect for people."* Retrieved April 19, 2016, from http://www.bobemiliani.com/defining-respect-for-people.

5. Ulhassan, W., Westerlund, H., Thor, J., Sandahl, C., & Schwarz, U. V. T. (2014). Does Lean implementation interact with group functioning? *Journal of Health Organization and Management, 28*(2), 196–213. http://doi.org/10.1108/JHOM-03-2013-0065.

6. Emiliani, M. L. (1998). Lean behaviors. *Management Decision, 36*(9), 615–631.

7. Lacksonen, T., Rathinam, B., Pakdil, F., & Gülel, D. (2010). Cultural issues in implementing Lean production. *Proceedings of the 2010 Industrial Engineering Research Conference, 2010,* 1–6.

8. Womack, J. T., Jones, D. T., & Roos, D. (1990). *The machine that changed the world.* New York, NY: Scribner.

9. Ibid.

CHAPTER 12. DIAGNOSING AND INTERVENING ON EMOTIONS—THE GROUP'S AND YOURS

1. Unfortunately, there is no common definition of *emotions* in the affective sciences. Mulligan, K., & Scherer, K. R. (2012). Toward a working definition of emotion. *Emotion Review, 4*(4), 345–357.

2. Goleman, D. (1995). *Emotional intelligence.* New York, NY: Bantam Books; Goleman, D. (1998). *Working with emotional intelligence.* New York, NY: Bantam Books.

3. Salovey, P., & Mayer, J. (1990). Emotional intelligence. *Imagination, Cognition and Personality, 9,* 185–211.

4. Goleman, D. (1995). *Emotional intelligence.* New York, NY: Bantam Books.

5. Barrett, L. F. (2015, July 31). What emotions are (and aren't). *New York Times.* Retrieved from http://www.nytimes.com/2015/08/02/opinion/sunday/what-emotions-are-and-arent.html?smprod=nytcore-iphone&smid=nytcore-iphone-share; Lindquist, K. A., Wager, T. D., Bliss-Moreau, E., Kober, H., & Barrett, L. F. (2012). What are emotions and how are they created in the brain? *Behavioral and Brain Sciences, 35*(3), 172–202; Wilson-Mendenhall, C. D., Barrett, L. F., & Barsalou, L. W. (2013). Neural evidence that human emotions share core affective properties. *Psychological Science, 24*(6), 947–56; Pessoa, L., & Adolphs, R. (2011). Emotion processing and the amygdala: From a "low road" to "many roads" of evaluating biological significance. *NIH Public Access, 11*(11), 773–783; Pessoa, L. (2015). Precis on the cognitive-emotional brain. *The Behavioral and Brain Sciences, 38,* e71.

6. McConnell, J. V. (1985). *Understanding human behavior* (5th ed.). Austin, TX: Holt, Rinehart, and Winston.

7. Argyris, C. (1990). *Overcoming organizational defenses: Facilitating organizational learning.* Boston, MA: Allyn & Bacon.

8. Smith, K. K., & Zane, N. (2004). Organizational reflections: Parallel processes at work in a dual consultation. *Journal of Applied Behavioral Science, 40*(1), 31–48; Sullivan, C. C. (2002). Finding the thou in the I: Countertransference and parallel process analysis in organizational research and consultation. *The Journal of Applied Behavioral Science, 38*(3), 375–392.

9. Argyris, C. (1990). *Overcoming organizational defenses: Facilitating organizational learning.* Boston, MA: Allyn & Bacon, p. 102.

10. Cuellar, G. (1986). *Creative and survival behaviors: Assessing a creative behavior model.* Unpublished doctoral dissertation, University of Massachusetts.

CHAPTER 13. CONTRACTING

1. Schein, E. H. (1987). *Process consultation: Lessons for managers and consultants,* Vol. 2. Reading, MA: Addison-Wesley.

2. Ibid., p. 125.

3. Schwarz, R. (2012). *How to hire a team facilitator.* Chapel Hill, NC: Roger Schwarz & Associates; Schwarz, R. (2013). *Eight behaviors for smarter teams.* Chapel Hill, NC: Roger Schwarz & Associates.

CHAPTER 14. WORKING WITH A PARTNER

1. Pfeiffer, J. W., & Jones, J. E. (1975). Cofacilitating. *The 1975 annual handbook for group facilitators* (pp. 219–223). Iowa City, IA: University Associates.

2. Paulson, I., Burroughs, J. C., & Gelb, C. B. (1976). Cotherapy: What is the crux of the relationship? *International Journal of Group Psychotherapy*, *26*(2), 213–224.

3. Paulson, I., Burroughs, J. C., & Gelb, C. B. (1976). Cotherapy: What is the crux of the relationship? *International Journal of Group Psychotherapy*, *26*(2), 213–224.

4. Smith, K. K., & Berg, D. N. (1987). *Paradoxes of group life: Understanding conflict, paralysis, and movement in group dynamics.* Jossey-Bass management series. San Francisco, CA: Jossey-Bass.

5. Schein, E. H. (1987). *Process consultation: Lessons for managers and consultants,* Vol. 2. Reading, MA: Addison-Wesley.

6. Yalom, I. D. (1985). *The theory and practice of group psychotherapy.* New York, NY: Basic Books.

7. Bales, cited in Yalom, 1985; Blake, R. R. (1964). *The managerial grid: Key orientations for achieving production through people.* Houston, TX: Gulf.

8. Alderfer, C. P. (1976). Group processes in organizations. In M. D. Dunnette (Ed.), *Handbook of industrial and organizational psychology.* Chicago, IL: Rand McNally.

9. Barnard, C. I. (1938). *The functions of the executive.* Cambridge, MA: Harvard University Press.

10. Gellermann, W., Frankel, M. S., & Ladenson, R. F. (1990). *Values and ethics in organization and human systems development.* San Francisco, CA: Jossey-Bass.

11. Steiner, C. M. (1974). *Scripts people live: Transactional analysis of life scripts.* New York, NY: Bantam Books.

12. Benne, K. D. (1964). History of the T group in the laboratory setting. In L. P. Bradford, J. R. Gibb, & K. D. Benne (Eds.), *T-group theory and laboratory method.* New York, NY: Wiley; Marrow, A. J. (1969). *The practical theorist: The life and work of Kurt Lewin.* New York, NY: Teachers College Press.

13. Marrow, A. J. (1969). *The practical theorist: The life and work of Kurt Lewin.* New York, NY: Teachers College Press, p. 193.

14. Dies, R. R. (1979). Openness in the Coleader relationship: Its effect on group process and outcome. *Small Group Behavior, 10*(4), 523–546.

15. Yalom, I. D. (1985). *The theory and practice of group psychotherapy.* New York, NY: Basic Books.

CHAPTER 15. SERVING IN A FACILITATIVE ROLE IN YOUR OWN ORGANIZATION

1. Steele, F. (1982). *The role of the internal consultant.* Boston, MA: CBI.

2. Ibid.

3. Quote available online, accessed September 24, 2012: www.gandhitopia.org/forum/topics/a-gandhi-quote?xg_source=activity.

CHAPTER 16. USING VIRTUAL MEETINGS

1. Berry, G. R. (2011). Enhancing effectiveness on virtual teams: Understanding why traditional team skills are insufficient. *Journal of Business Communication, 48*(2), 186–206.

2. Yao, J., Wang, J., Xing, R., & Lu, J. (2010, May 20–21). Group support systems: Tools for HR decision making. In S. Strohmeier & A. Diederichsen (Eds.), *Evidence-based e-HRM? On the way to rigorous and relevant research, Proceedings of the Third European Academic Workshop on Electronic Human Resource Management,* Vol. 570 (pp. 400–409). Bamberg, Germany. Retrieved from http://ceur-ws.org/Vol-570/paper023.pdf.

3. Mittleman, D. D., Briggs, R. O., & Nunamaker, J.F.J. (2000). Best practices in facilitating virtual meetings: Some notes from initial experiences. *Group Facilitation: A Research & Application Journal, 2*(2), 6–15.

4. Kolfschoten, G. L., & Brazier, F.M.T. (2013). Cognitive load in collaboration: Convergence. *Group Decision and Negotiation, 22*(5), 975–996.

5. Dubé, L., & Robey, D. (2009). Surviving the paradoxes of virtual teamwork. *Information Systems Journal, 19*(1), 3–30.

6. Hertel, G., Geister, S., & Konradt, U. (2005). Managing virtual teams: A review of current empirical research. *Human Resource Management Review, 15*(1), 69–95.

7. Adkins, M., Younger, R., & Schwarz, R. (2003). Information technology augmentation of the Skilled Facilitator approach. In *Proceedings of the 36th Hawaii International Conference on System Sciences (HICSS'03)* (pp. 1–10).

8. Adkins, M., & Schwarz, R. (2002). Embedded facilitation requirements using the Skilled Facilitator approach: With and across time and space. *Proceedings of the Annual Hawaii International Conference on System Sciences*, 560–567.

9. Thorpe, S. J. (2016). Online facilitator competencies for group facilitators. *Group Facilitation: A Research & Application Journal, 13*, 79–91, p. 83.

10. Adla, A., Zarate, P., & Soubie, J. L. (2011). A proposal of a toolkit for GDSS facilitators. *Group Decision and Negotiation, 20*(1), 57–77.

11. Bradley, L., & Beyerlein, M. (2005). Facilitation of the future: How virtual meetings are changing the work of the facilitator. In S. Schuman (Ed.), *The IAF handbook of group facilitation* (pp. 295–311). San Francisco, CA: Jossey-Bass.

12. Mittleman, D. D., Briggs, R. O., & Nunamaker, J. F. J. (2000). Best practices in facilitating virtual meetings: Some notes from initial experiences. *Group Facilitation: A Research & Application Journal, 2*(2), 6–15.

13. Mark Adkins, personal communication, June 1, 2016.

14. Mittleman, D. D., Briggs, R. O., & Nunamaker, J. F. J. (2000). Best practices in facilitating virtual meetings: Some notes from initial experiences. *Group Facilitation: A Research & Application Journal, 2*(2), 6–15.

15. Adkins, M., Burgoon, M., & Nunamaker, J. F. (2003). Using group support systems for strategic planning with the United States Air Force. *Decision Support Systems, 34*(2002), 315–337.

ACKNOWLEDGMENTS

Many people helped me write this book, and I want to thank them. Carrie Hays, Gail Young, Terrie Hutaff, and Betsy Monier-Williams, my colleagues at Roger Schwarz & Associates, read chapters and gave me helpful feedback. So did former Roger Schwarz & Associates consultant Peg Carlson, Larry Dressler, and Mark Adkins. Ruth Wageman helped me think more comprehensively and clearly about interdependence in teams. In addition, each of these colleagues has shaped my thinking about facilitation and groups.

For more than 20 years, Anne Davidson and I have worked together helping Roger Schwarz & Associates clients get better results. We've spent countless hours discussing how best to think about, write about, practice, and help others use mutual learning. In addition to reading chapters for the book and giving me feedback, Anne has helped me think differently about many aspects of facilitation, consulting, coaching, and training. You can't see it, but her influence is on most pages of this book.

I am grateful to have clients who think rigorously about my work and challenge me to answer the difficult questions they pose. This includes clients whom I have worked with in their organizations and clients who have attended open enrollment workshops. They have helped me see when the Skilled Facilitator approach doesn't fully take into account the realities of their work situation, and they have encouraged me to think through how I can improve the Skilled Facilitator approach to do so.

Dale Schwarz, an art therapist and coach—and most important to me, my sister—has continually encouraged me to put more of myself into the book—and just plain encouraged me in my work and life in general. She helped me think through the chapter on emotions and the role of compassion. She is a wonderful role model for integrating thoughts and feelings. Dale and Anne Davidson are the coauthors of the book *Facilitative Coaching*, which shows coaches how to apply mutual learning in their work.

There are two people whose work has shaped mine and is reflected throughout this book. Chris Argyris gave me a wonderful gift: a framework for thinking about consulting, facilitation, and human and organizational behavior in general. In the early 1980s, I was one of Chris's graduate students at Harvard. He taught me his approach to improving life and learning in organizations; he inspired me to live my life and practice my profession congruent with the same set of core values I ask my clients to apply; and he stimulated me to continue developing my own thinking about organizations. Richard Hackman's work on teams provided the basis for my thinking about what makes teams effective. He helped me see how interdependence and team design are powerful factors in creating more effective teams. Both Chris and Richard died in 2013. In my work, I seek to integrate, build on, and honor theirs.

At Jossey-Bass, I worked with a skilled team who brought the book into the form you're now reading: Jeanenne Ray, Lauren Freestone, Pete Gaughan, Heather Brosius, Shannon Vargo, and Ellen Dendy. David Kerr of David Kerr Design created the clear and engaging graphic art for the models and the cover art.

Mike Mitchell, who manages operations for Roger Schwarz & Associates, helped to lighten my load so that I could make time for writing this edition.

Finally, I want to thank my wife, Kathleen Rounds, and my adult children, Noah and Hannah. For more than 30 years, Kathleen has helped me become the better person I want to be. Noah and Hannah have watched me carefully and have pointed out when I was not acting congruently with the values I espoused. Through our conversations, they have helped me become a better father. I am blessed to have the three of them in my life.

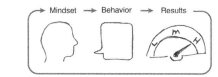

ABOUT THE AUTHOR

R oger Schwarz is an organizational psychologist and president and CEO of Roger Schwarz & Associates Inc., a consulting firm that helps leaders and their teams, organizations, and those who support them use facilitative skills to create fundamental change. For more than 35 years, he has consulted, taught, facilitated, coached, and spoken with groups on the subjects of facilitation, teams, and leadership. His clients include corporations; federal, state, and local governments; educational institutions; and nonprofit organizations. He is also the author of *Smart Leaders, Smarter Teams* and coauthor with Anne Davidson, Peg Carlson, and Sue McKinney of *The Skilled Facilitator Fieldbook.* His writing also appears in *Harvard Business Review* online.

Roger was formerly associate professor of public management and government and assistant director at the Institute of Government, the University of North Carolina at Chapel Hill. In 1996, he left his tenured position to found Roger Schwarz & Associates.

Roger earned his PhD and AM in organizational psychology from the University of Michigan, his MEd. degree from Harvard University Graduate School of Education, and his BS degree in psychology from Tufts University. He lives and works in Chapel Hill, North Carolina.

You can learn more about Roger Schwarz & Associates, including speaking, consulting, training, and coaching services, as well as open-enrollment workshops, at www.schwarzassociates.com or by calling 919–932–3343.

ABOUT ROGER SCHWARZ & ASSOCIATES' WORK WITH CLIENTS

Roger Schwarz & Associates provides a rigorous and compassionate method for leaders and their teams—and those who support them—to get stronger performance, more productive working relationships, and increased individual well-being. Through diagnosis, consulting, training, facilitation, coaching, and measurements, we have helped the Boeing Company, Chevron, American Airlines, Consumer Financial Protection Bureau, U.S. Food and Drug Administration, Federal Aviation Administration, U.S. Department of Interior, the World Bank, the American Red Cross, and many other organizations address their toughest challenges to create significantly better results.

We work with two kinds of clients: (1) the facilitators, consultants, coaches, and trainers who help leaders and their teams; and (2) the leaders and the teams themselves. Often, we work with both groups at the same time, working with internal consultants, facilitators, and coaches, as we jointly help their leaders and teams get better results.

To continue benefiting from the mutual learning approach:

- Schedule a one-day overview to introduce the mutual learning approach to your team or organization.
- Attend an open-enrollment workshop or bring a workshop to your organization.
- Engage a facilitator, consultant, or coach to work with your team on your real work.
- Subscribe to our free, online idealetter *Mindset. Behavior. Results.* to read the latest practical ideas on mutual learning.

To learn more about these and other ways Roger Schwarz & Associates can help you, your team, and your organization become more effective, visit www.schwarzassociates.com or contact us at 919–932–3343.

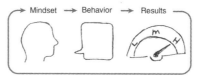

THE SKILLED FACILITATOR INTENSIVE WORKSHOP

I f you've found *The Skilled Facilitator* helpful and want to develop your mutual learning mindset and skill set to help groups get better results, consider attending a Skilled Facilitator Intensive workshop. Roger Schwarz & Associates offers open-enrollment workshops and delivers workshops at your organization.

In this five-day workshop, you will engage in intensive, instructor-guided practice based on your real work facilitative challenges. You will:

- Review the core values, assumptions, and principles of the Skilled Facilitator approach with practical examples of how to apply them.

- Practice applying mutual learning strategies and techniques to create more productive meetings, groups, and teams.

- Get detailed, real-time instructor feedback as you practice the mutual learning approach using your real facilitative challenges.

Throughout the workshop, you will get answers to three questions: What do I do? How do I do it? Why do I do it that way? You will learn:

- How the roles of facilitator, leader, consultant, coach, and trainer are similar and different, and when it is appropriate to serve in each of these roles.

- How to identify and deal with situations in which groups ask you to act inconsistently with your role.
- Strategies and techniques to address the specific challenges you face when facilitating, consulting, training, or coaching groups.
- How your mindset may lead you to create the very situations you are trying to avoid: mistrust, defensive behavior, poor problem solving, and limited group learning.
- How to shift from a unilateral control mindset to a mutual learning mindset.
- How to use the five core values of the Mutual Learning approach—transparency, curiosity, accountability, informed choice, and compassion—to guide your work with groups.
- How to diagnose and intervene with groups using the Team Effectiveness Model.
- How to intervene in a group to improve its process, including what to say, how to say it, when to say it, who to say it to, and why.
- How to contract for a solid working relationship and avoid many problems that reduce your ability to help the group.

To learn more about The Skilled Facilitator Intensive workshop, visit www.schwarzassociates.com or call us at 919–932–3343.

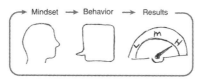

INDEX

Note: Page references in *italics* refer to exhibits and figures.

A

accessibility, to organization by internal facilitators, 318

accountability
    defined, 69–70
    power of informed choice compassion and, 72
    as a Core Value, 61, *62–64, 65* (*See also* Five Core Values and, 70–71
    in virtual meetings, 340

accuracy, word choice and, 209

Action Design, 61

active voice, 210–211

adjourning stage of teams (Tuckman), 128

Adkins, Mark, 341

ambiguity, 189–190

anger, dealing with, 267

anonymity, of electronic meeting systems, 338–339

Argyris, Chris, 12, 61, 104

Aristotle, 96, 252

assessment, of facilitator's interest and ability to help, 282

assumptions
    about shared information, 75–76

Team Effectiveness Model (TEM) and, 129–131, *130, 131,* 132–133, *133*
    of unilateral control mindset, *43,* 45–46
    See also Test Assumptions and Inferences (Behavior 6)

attending
    constant need to attend to group for diagnosing behavior, 189
    for inferring emotion, 172–173
    need for, 5–6
    See also inferences

attribution
    attributing motives, 173–174
    fundamental attribution error, 190
    testing assumptions and inferences, 103–104
    testing meaning, 200–201
    testing observations, *198,* 198–199

audioconferencing, 336

authority, in teams, 124

autonomy, 137

awareness
    compassion and, 61, *62–64, 65,* 71–75 (*See also* Five Core Values)
    emotional intelligence and, 250